MORTALITY IN MID 19TH CENTURY BRITAIN

MORTALITY IN MID 19TH CENTURY BRITAIN

W. FARR

Vital statistics or the statistics of health,
sickness, diseases and death
(1837)

H. RATCLIFFE

Observations on the rate of mortality and sickness
existing amongst friendly societies
(1850)

With an introduction

by

RICHARD WALL

1974

GREGG INTERNATIONAL

ISBN 0 576 53291 6

Printed in offset by Franz Wolf, Heppenheim/Bergstrasse
Western Germany

INTRODUCTION

It was once said of William Farr that he was too well known to need an introduction although very few have ever been able to claim familiarity with the detail of his work. There is something about the mass of tables he produced which precluded argument and which has left him with the last word on every subject. Despite his humble and somewhat obscure origins (he was the son of an agricultural labourer) he was able to pursue a career in the General Register Office which gave him the opportunity of controlling the 'products' of civil registration, the statistics of births, marriages and deaths.[1] There can be little doubt that it was Farr's use of this material, the emphasis on mortality, particularly in relation to occupation, and on cause of death, which earned the English system its international reputation.[2] However, the paper of Farr's which we have decided to reproduce is an early one which he contributed to J. R. McCulloch's *A statistical account of the British Empire*, a bulky but impressive compendium on climate, agriculture, manufacture and Parliament as well as vital statistics. At the time Farr was still a general practitioner supplementing his income by medical journalism and with his future career anything but determined. There was, of course, no army of 2,000-odd Registrars on whose services he could draw. Despite this Humphreys still wrote in 1885[3] that 'there is no other treatise on this subject (thoroughly and soundly treated in all its branches) that could be more profitably studied by students of vital statistics. This article may be said to be the foundation of a new science . . .'. And Major Greenwood, fifty years later, went even further by saying that it 'ranks not much below Graunt's *Observations* as an original contribution to medical-statistical science'.[4] Greenwood saw it as closing the epoch which had opened with Graunt but this was perhaps due less to the merits of the article itself than to the fact that the institution of civil registration brought with it not only records, improved in both quantity and quality, but also the professional demographer. The days of the gifted 'part-timer', the city tradesman, Graunt, the provincial doctor, Thomas Short, were over.

To judge Farr's article in the light of what he produced later in vastly different circumstances is perhaps a little unfair, even though it cannot be denied, for instance, that his classification of causes of death in the Fourth Annual Report of the Registrar General is both more comprehensive and easier to follow than his earlier attempts at a statistical nosology.[5] Another weakness is the lack of conspicuous originality which Greenwood himself noted.[6] By drawing so heavily on the work of his predecessors and contemporaries, Farr not only repeated some of their mistakes but had to base his observations on their sources, Rickman's parish register returns and the London Bills of Mortality, two sources which have never enjoyed unqualified approval and which have come under increasing attack since Farr's time.[7] If Professor Krause is correct in arguing that parochial registration virtually collapsed between the 1790s and 1820 then the statistics for both town and country will be utterly misleading — including Farr's own analysis of mortality levels, since it would be a considerable surprise if Anglican negligence and a revived dissent were to be evenly distributed throughout the country. In Farr's favour is the fact that his calculations were based on the burial statistics of 1813-1830, eight years of bad and ten of improved registration, again according to Professor Krause.[8] It might also be thought that Farr's principal finding, that the counties having the greatest proportion of inhabitants congregating in towns were the most unhealthy, would be strengthened and not weakened if Rickman had included in every year the returns of the non-Anglican burial grounds, the largest of which were located in the cities. Yet comparison with early civil registration data is not reassuring. In 1841 deaths among children aged 0-4 were a third higher than in 1821, and this at a time when the adult mortality had fallen by 11%.[9] Nor were the apparent levels of 1821 to be achieved again before the twentieth century.[10] If the under-recording of child burials was anything like as high as these figures suggest then it would clearly be wisest to set the 1821 data to one side, although their elders would appear to be rather better recorded unless the fall in mortality was considerably above the 11% mark. This difference, providing it can be assumed genuine, might point to the burial of the unbaptised and not to nonconformity *per se* or the establishment of non-Anglican burial grounds as the chief cause of error in the Rickman returns.

However, as was hinted above, Farr's regional analysis of mortality is not to be dismissed so lightly. Any attempt to use the level of mortality in 1841 as a base is fraught with danger since it is not to be expected that counties undergoing intensive industrialisation will retain an advantage they have had over a neighbour twenty years earlier. Such an argument assumes in any case perfect registration in every county in 1841, which is unlikely. Yet in many respects the returns do make 'sense'; for example in both years mortality was exceptionally high in the counties of Middlesex, Lancashire and Nottinghamshire. It is interesting also that in 1841 as in 1821 Cornwall turns out particularly healthy for both children and adults, for this was one of the areas where Krause, relating infant burials to baptisms, felt registration was most defective in the early nineteenth century.[11] There is also some agreement as to the counties in which adult and child mortality levels were markedly dissimilar at both dates; for example, in Bedfordshire, Westmorland and Wiltshire adult mortality was relatively high in relation to the number of child deaths, while the reverse was true of two other counties, Norfolk and Cumberland.[12] Nevertheless, it would be unwise to stress the measure of agreement for it is not difficult to find counties experiencing high mortality on one occasion and low on another[13] with Northumberland furnishing the supreme example: one of the healthiest counties in 1821, it had become one of the worst by 1841 if the records are to be believed.

Before leaving this subject one further analysis might be attempted and that is to measure the mortality of children aged less than five years in relation to the proportion which this group formed of the total population. There are two reasons for thinking that mortality might vary according to the number of children in the population. The first is that a high dependency ratio could lead to an overstraining of a family's resources; the second, that large concentrations of children would hasten the spread of infectious disease through the community. The data, however, scarcely bear this out for although there are counties, both in 1821 and in 1841, with high mortality paralleled by a high proportion of children in the population (Lancashire, Cambridgeshire), and low mortality with a low proportion of children (Herefordshire), it is possible to find others which break the pattern: Cornwall and

Bedfordshire, for instance, with among the largest proportion of the population within the 0-4 group, experienced relatively low mortality; Middlesex, with comparatively few children, quite high levels. In 1821 (but not 1841) Middlesex is joined by Surrey, Nottinghamshire, Warwickshire and Worcestershire; in 1841 (but not 1821) by Monmouthshire and the East Riding of Yorkshire.[14] The variability is clearly great and the only safe conclusion would appear to be that there are rather more important factors determining the level of child mortality than the proportion of children in the community.

If Farr's analysis of mortality in his own century, the nineteenth, has to be put on one side, must his work on the Bills of Mortality suffer the same fate? On first view the situation is hardly promising, for on the crucial question of the meaning to be attached to particular diseases in the Bills he is clearly at odds with the latest authority on the subject. In *Numbering the People*, Professor Glass has criticised William Heberden Junior for insisting that 'griping in the guts' was dysentery when, as Creighton was later to show, it was to be equated with infantile diarrhoea. Farr, however, is of the same opinion as Heberden.[15] Glass further identifies a disease known as the 'rising of the lights' as a pulmonary infection, while Farr has it as a disease of women in childbed, with its name apparently derived from the hysteria which tended to accompany this event.[16] Of course Glass is not necessarily right and Farr wrong. The latter's explanation of 'rising of the lights' was taken from Sydenham, whom Creighton for one was prepared to credit with having seen diseases he had never seen.[17] On dysentery, however, the gap between their respective positions is not as wide as first appeared for Farr was later to emphasise the links between diarrhoea and dysentery.[18] The point is an important one in another respect. Farr linked the incidence of diarrhoea to an 'insufficient supply of varied food' and it has recently been established that infantile diarrhoea is very closely related to deficiencies in the diet of children while they are being weaned.[19] The London Bills, therefore, seem to provide an opportunity for measuring the importance of malnutrition as far back as the middle of the seventeenth century when information on all causes of death was first included. It is right, however, not to underestimate the difficulties: of classification, of disease names whose meaning varied with the generation recording them, of imperfect diagnosis (Farr for instance commented on the absence from the otherwise excellent Carlisle Bills of deaths ascribed to diseases of the heart).[20] There is the further point, too, that it is difficult to consider malnutrition separately from other diseases such as the infectious diseases of childhood, tuberculosis and intestinal worms, many of which throve on the environment created by general undernourishment. W. Harding le Riche and Jean Milner in their recent book also add a timely warning that malnutrition can in certain cases be due to simple physical causes such as dental cavities, lack of teeth or neoplasm of the intestinal tract.[21]

There can be little surprise therefore that the Bills do not readily yield the required information. There is independent evidence, certainly, of the importance of infantile diarrhoea as a major killer of the late seventeenth century,[22] but if one searches the Bills for a disease which declined as the number of child deaths fell in relation to adult deaths,[23] then the most likely candidates are convulsions and teething, two 'diseases' whose names scarcely suggest that they will provide much of an explanation for the fall in mortality. Nor is the timing quite right.[24] Both diseases may seem to encompass a whole variety of infantile complaints which the medical practitioner of the eighteenth century was unable to diagnose. Creighton, however, was convinced from a careful appraisal of its incidence that the major category of 'convulsions' was little more than a successor of 'griping in the guts', in due course to be replaced in its turn by the 'infantile diarrhoea' of the civil registration era.[25] He was less sure about the reasons for its prominence, suspecting for the seventeenth century the closely packed urban environment and for his own time the extensive employment of married women in factories, which affected the health of the child in two different ways, first retarding its growth in the womb, later encouraging the use of the feeding-bottle, not harmful in its own right but disastrous if the bottle was dirty. Nutrition was not stressed although there was evidence to indicate its importance.[26] It is less clear though whether he was wrong in thinking of infantile diarrhoea as a distinctively urban disease, and the relationship of malnutrition to mortality was certainly not the straightforward and direct one of the extreme Malthusianist. Deaths from starvation, as Farr was to make clear elsewhere, were almost unknown in nineteenth-century England and its importance had been over-stressed.[27]

This of course is not to exhaust the interest of the Bills. It has yet to be satisfactorily explained, for instance, why miscarriages and deaths in childbed were so much rarer in the eighteenth than in the seventeenth century. Also calling for further investigation is the contemporaneous decline in mortality from smallpox and fever *after 1780* which would suggest that inoculation was not the all-important reason, as some have imagined, for the lower mortality levels of the end of the century. It is only fair to add that on most of these points it is difficult to be sure.[28] Farr's analysis, though considerably more extensive than Glass's recent survey,[29] did not cover every decade and further work on the Bills themselves and on the contemporary medical records may suggest important modifications to many of the arguments that have been advanced. Here, anyway, we must leave this subject and turn to a part of Farr's treatise which we have yet to discuss, the section on morbidity, the measurement of the propensity of particular populations to sickness as opposed to death.

Greenwood considered this the most original part of Farr's contribution, qualifying this only with the remark that Farr had omitted to say how he had reached one of his more startling conclusions, that two persons were sick for every one who died.[30] In fact, a glance at the second work which we have decided to reprint in this volume shows how little support there is for such a conclusion.[31] There are problems too with inadequate data and Farr was quite prepared to sprinkle a table with a liberal supply of question marks when he was unsure of his ground. Nevertheless, there is some fascinating information to be gleaned. At the height of cholera and influenza epidemics between 40 and 50 of the East India Company's labourers were said to have attended daily the Company's surgery for coughs and bowel complaints.[32] Even at the lower figure this yields an average of six calls on medical assistance for minor complaints per year for each person in their service. In the naval dockyards where the standard of health was in any case below the national average[33] the gravity of what would now be termed industrial injuries is particularly revealing. In the Portsmouth dockyard in 1830, for example, lay-offs because of accidents were likely to last longer than absences through sickness for caulkers, metal workers, carpenters, sawyers, shipwrights and workmen in the woodmill and millwright's shop, who together constituted the major part of the workforce.[34]

In general, however, it has to be said that Farr succeeded only in making it clear how little the figures could actually reveal. The attempt by Chadwick to relate the number of deaths and amount of sickness to the quality of prisoners' diet, with the suggestion that the poorest diet risked little increase in either, was a failure[35] because supplementary information on the age, social background and condition of the prisoners and the state of the prison itself was not available. There can be no doubt as to the major problem, though, which was that it was impossible to come anywhere near a standard definition of sickness. For instance, care was taken to register even the minor ailments of soldiers,[36] and were the figures to be injudiciously compared with those for the general population, it would imply that the Empire was policed by an army of invalids. Even within the confines of the same establishment it is often difficult to be certain of the validity of a particular comparison. In the Lancashire and Glasgow cotton factories, for example, it was clearly unusual for either men or women to remain in factory employment beyond the age of 30[37] and the sickness experience of the few that did is unlikely to have been typical of the population at large. Even if there was no improvement in the health of the younger generation of employees there is certainly no guarantee that this would be the amount of sickness they would experience as they matured. It has also to be borne in mind that certain sections of the population were less likely to declare themselves as 'sick' than others. The man with family responsibilities, for instance, would certainly try to ignore a minor ailment and continue working and thence the fewer recorded attacks of illness amongst the males aged 30-50 working for the East India Company in London compared with younger and older men in the same employment.[38] It would follow that women would leave work and seek medical advice more frequently than men and this is exactly what Farr found,[39] except in Glasgow where it is possible that the wages of the women, although lagging as far behind those of the men as elsewhere, were considered vital for the family budget. A further and even more fundamental point is that all the statistics we have been considering relate to the population that was either still in work or intended to resume it. If an employee became sick and failed to return or was placed on the pension list in his old age, the sickness he experienced after that was no longer recorded, and since not just new members of friendly societies but even labourers entering the service of the East India Company were subject to medical examination,[40] the unfit being rejected, it will be seen how far short we are of knowing the level of sickness amongst the 'general population'.

All this must be borne in mind as we consider Henry Ratcliffe's data on sickness and mortality drawn from the experience of the members of one of the largest of the friendly societies with a typically ponderous title, The Independent Order of Odd Fellows, Manchester Unity. Two editions of this work were published, and we have chosen to reprint the earlier. This was a decision that was taken with some reluctance, for the increase in membership which the Society experienced in the interval between the two surveys must have reduced the risk of an irregular pattern to the returns due to small numbers in certain categories, when, for instance, the population was broken down by occupation and age. There are, however, important drawbacks to the 1862 edition which make it less suitable, even less 'honest' than its predecessor, particularly important being the omission of the number of members in each occupational group and the absence of any comment on the very uneven distribution of these groups throughout the country.[41] On the other hand there can be no doubt that the analysis of mortality is much improved by 1862[42] and we shall in this introduction have to draw on this edition from time to time.

Both editions, it must be admitted, have an unprepossessing appearance with their interminable columns of figures and a text which often does little more than repeat details contained in the tables. Ratcliffe was concerned with the value of various forms of life assurance, with annuities and sickness benefits, concerned that the premiums reserved by the Society should be sufficient to meet all their commitments. In order to be sure of this, however, he had to calculate exactly the chances of sickness and death from the age of 18, measure their variability in country, town and city, and by occupation, and this is where the demographer's interest is aroused. It is a simple procedure to place the occupations in a rank order according to the levels of mortality and sickness they experienced at various ages. In 1850, or rather 1846-48, life expectancy was highest for rural labourers and carpenters, lowest for clerks and printers, while miners and potters suffered most from sickness, clerks and butchers the least.[43] It would seem fairly logical that occupations which experienced most sickness would be those in which mortality was heaviest but as the wayward behaviour of the clerks makes clear this was by no means always the case. Admittedly there are occupations with both a high sickness and a high mortality rate (miners, stonemasons and watermen) and others where both were low (wheelwrights and shoemakers) but there are rather more occupations where the two diverge quite markedly, including the well-represented groups of urban and rural labourers who made frequent calls on the sick fund while experiencing relatively low mortality.[44] For the majority of occupations there was no correlation between their mortality and sickness experiences in either 1846-48 or 1856-60.[45]

It might also be thought that those occupations with the highest mortality and sickness rates would place most value on continued membership of the society, that is they would be less likely to secede than members following other occupations. A few figures suffice to show the importance of this practice. In 1844 7% of the entire membership left as a result of secession or expulsion (3% of those entitled to draw benefits) and although this proportion later declined, secessions still outnumbered deaths in 1856-60 for those aged between 18 and 41.[46] For our present purpose, it is unfortunate that it is impossible to measure the number of secessions by occupation. The loss of members between successive age groups can be calculated easily, but it includes those who had died as well as those who made a less serious exit from the society's annals. However, the fact that there is no positive or negative correlation[47] with the level of either sickness or mortality reflects less the crudity of the measure than the presence of other factors keeping a member in the society. What these factors might be is difficult to say but there is certainly an industrial air about these groups who had a comparatively large proportion of members over 50. It is also significant, no doubt, that the hatters, dyers, town labourers, mill operatives, miners, potters, spinners, weavers and woolcombers were to be found only in certain areas, whereas almost without exception those occupations who lost most members were said by Ratcliffe to be 'well distributed'.[48]

Two further lines of enquiry must also be touched upon briefly. The first concerns the possible comparison of the 1846-48 data with the later returns. There are in fact considerable differences. While mortality fell there were if anything rather more claims for sickness in the later period than in the earlier.[49] There are also considerable differences in the ranking of the various occupations according to the levels of sickness and mortality experienced in each period.[50] All this is perhaps not surprising in view of the changes that had occurred within the society since 1848 with the older members coming to form a much more important section of the society. In 1856-58 those aged between 56 and 60 were in the city and town districts about 25 per cent of those aged 26 to 30, which may not seem a significant proportion until it is set alongside the 1846-48 figures of 5.3 per cent (town) and 3.7 per cent. (city). There was similar although less marked improvement in rural areas. Comparison with the numbers in the relevant age group 10 years earlier (i.e., comparing those aged 21-5 in 1846-48 with those 31-5 in 1856-60) shows that in urban areas at any rate the society was not only retaining the loyalty of former members but had succeeded in attracting new ones.[51] The stimulus for these changes may possibly have come partly from the society stressing benefits such as deferred annuities which could only be enjoyed if membership was continued until the age of 70. At the same time it must reflect also greater faith in the society, a growing willingness on the part of members to pay for benefits which were likely to be a long time in the coming. To tide a working man over a short illness may have been the prime task of the society. Increasingly, however, it seems to have been valued as a support in old age.

The second enquiry is prompted by an observation of Ratcliffe's in 1862 that the trade of a person had a greater influence on mortality and the amount of sickness than the locality in which he resided.[52] His argument was based on the difference between areas (city, town and country) being less than those between certain occupations, which of course, completely ignores the fact that many of these groups will be concentrated in particular localities. His cautious statement[53] of 1850, that 'whether locality or employment be most destructive to human life, appears a question not yet solved', would have been more appropriate in the circumstances. The data on the variation in sickness and mortality by locality are not comprehensive, available for 23 'places' in addition to the broad regions mentioned above, and the correlation between the rates of mortality and sickness is not particularly good although certainly far stronger than was suggested in the occupational survey.[54]

It will have been noticed that we have tended to brush aside the issue of defective and incomplete data. This is a particularly intractable problem but some idea of its significance can be gained from an examination of the level of mortality and sickness at particular ages. Not that it is to be expected that the rural labourer of 60 will fill exactly the same position *vis à vis* other workers as he did at 20. Nevertheless, when we find that potters rank fourth as regards sickness at age 40, twenty-fifth at age 50 and fourth again at 60, when the average rank was fifteenth, then clearly there is reason to suspect that there were insufficient members in these particular age groups to yield a reliable result.[55] Additional difficulties arise when comparisons are attempted with data drawn from the records of other friendly societies, since they could not be expected to draw support from exactly the same occupations or areas as the Manchester Unity. Neison's rural area data, for instance, came from a population a third of which was composed of agricultural labourers as opposed to the 20 per cent in the Unity, and there can be little reason for surprise that Neison found more sickness but less mortality than Ratcliffe.[56] Nor should it be forgotten that the demographic situation to some extent dictated the whole range of events under consideration. Premiums were not the same in city, town and country because the chances of death or illness were very different in the respective areas.[57] In the country, for instance, on the whole people lived longer and this meant lower annual premiums for assurance on death as the contributions would be spread out over a longer period. Yet as in old age more frequent calls had to be made on the sick fund because of inability to follow employment, the cost of sickness benefits was relatively high, and the same applied to deferred annuities. In the cities, on the other hand, so few could expect to live to enjoy the latter benefits (from the age of 70) that these could be purchased comparatively cheaply. The sort of benefit one went for, of course, was not solely or even principally dependent on the amount of the premium but with wages low and any long-term form of insurance looking like something of a luxury, it must have had some effect in dissuading people from entering the society, or persuading them to select one sort of benefit rather than another. And to the extent that this varied from area to area, members, as they aged, would secede in greater or lesser numbers leaving only a minority, larger at some times than others but always dangerously unrepresentative of the whole, to have its sickness and mortality entered in the records of the society.

This is not to deny the general thoroughness of Ratcliffe's *Observations on the rate of mortality and sickness*. Only one calculation is open to serious question and that is the assurance payable on the death of a member's wife which was based on assumptions that Ratcliffe knew to be false, of the man and his wife being of the same age and experiencing exactly the same mortality.[58] There can be no disputing the fact, however, that Ratcliffe's study has not the breadth of Farr's piece on vital statistics. With this article, with its denunciations of the prevailing system of the collection and presentation of statistics ('the omission of the ages in 1831 is discreditable to the persons who directed the last census'),[59] he launched himself into the career which was to see him replace those whom he had attacked. If one man, John Rickman, dominated the collection of vital registration and census data in the early nineteenth century, Farr's influence is scarcely less powerful in the middle period and the improvement was immeasurable. Yet Farr hoped for more: publish the facts, discover the causes of high mortality, act,[60] and Manchester could enjoy the health of Cornwall. It was not to be nearly so easy.

Richard Wall
Cambridge Group for the History of Population and Social Structure
April 1974.

Notes

[1]   There are short biographies of Farr by F. A. C. Hare, *William Farr* (1884), and by Noel A. Humphreys as an introduction to a selection of Farr's writings which was published at the expense of the Sanitary Institute of Great Britain in 1885 under the title of *Vital Statistics*. It is almost impossible to write on the demography of nineteenth-century Britain without mentioning Farr: there are many references in the various publications of David Glass, most recently in *Numbering the People* (1973) p. 130. Included (pp. 168-9) is Farr's own account of his duties as Statistical Superintendent in the General Register Office. Yet for a portrait of the man and his work it would be difficult to better the chapter on Farr in Major Greenwood's, *The Medical Dictator* (1936).

[2]   Humphreys (1885) p. XIX, however, argues that the administrative acumen of the second Registrar General (Major Graham) should be taken into account in any assessment of the department's record. Farr, of course, never became Registrar General, resigning when the appointment was refused him on the retirement of Major Graham. For all that his age was by then against him, and his administrative ability in question, the overtly political nature of the first two appointments scarcely augured well for the statistician-demographer.

3   Humphreys (1885) p. XII.

4   Greenwood, *Medical Statistics from Graunt to Farr* (1948) p. 69.

5   Compare his 'Letter to the Registrar General on the registration and classification of the causes of death' in the *Fourth Annual Report of the Registrar General* (1842) pp. 142ff, particularly the alphabetical list of diseases together with synonyms and cross references to the nosology on pp. 166ff, with his necessarily much briefer remarks on p. 590 of his article 'Vital statistics, or the statistics of health, sickness, diseases and death' in J. R. McCulloch, *A statistical account of the British Empire* (1837) which is reprinted below.

6   Greenwood (1948) p. 69.

7   Professor Krause has led the attack on the accuracy of Anglican registers in general and Rickman's national estimates in particular. See 'The changing adequacy of English registration, 1690-1837' in D. Glass and D. E. C. Eversley (eds), *Population in History* (1965) p. 390. For a pessimistic view of the usefulness of the Bills see W. Ogle, 'An enquiry into the trustworthiness of the Old Bills of Mortality', *Journal of the Royal Statistical Society*, LV (1892) pp. 437-60.

8   This at least would appear to be the sense of Krause (1965) p. 390 fn. 46.

9   Based on the male population 0-4 and the female population 30-59, in 1821, see Table III, p. 570 of Farr's article which appears below with comparable data from 1841 derived from the *Fifth Annual Report of the Registrar General* (1843) and the *Census of Great Britain 1841 Population Age Abstract*. The figures in the text represent the average (median) experience of 42 counties plus Wales at the two dates.

10   Compare for example annual death rates of males aged 0-4, 1856-1905, in the *Sixty-eighth Annual Report of the Registrar General 1905* (1907), Table 13, p. 14.

11   Krause (1965) p. 391.

12   Measured by ranking each county in 1821 and 1841 according to the level of mortality experienced by the 0-4 group (male) and the 30-59 group (female). Mortality was arbitrarily considered high if the county was on each occasion ranked between 1 and 10, and low if it was ranked between 34 and 43. Even more arbitrarily the pattern of mortality was considered 'dissimilar' if there was a difference in rank of more than 10 positions.

13   The correlation between adult mortality in 1821 and 1841 is weaker than that for child mortality despite the fact that there was far less significant change in the absolute level of mortality. The difference is slight (average variation in rank 10.6 for the adults and 7.3 for the children), but it does suggest that the under-registration of child burials in 1821 may have been fairly general rather than confined to certain urbanising or dissenter-prone counties.

14   The presence of the East Riding in this category is perhaps to be explained by the inclusion within it of the city of York.

15   D. Glass, *Numbering the people* (1973) p. 133 fn. 11. Farr (1837), p. 590.

16   Glass (1973) p. 203 fn. 46. Farr (1837) p. 592.

17   Charles Creighton, *A history of epidemics in Britain,* 2nd edition (1965), Vol. 2, p. 4.

18   'It is exceedingly difficult in practice to draw a strict line of demarcation between diarrhoea and dysentery, the one frequently passes into the other, so that it may be laid down, as a proposition from which few persons acquainted with statistical returns would dissent, that diarrhoea should be placed in close juxtaposition with cholera, dysentery and the dothinenteric form of typhus.' See William Farr, 'Note in reply to some observations in a "Report for a sub-committee of the Royal College

of Physicians in Edinburgh" ' in the *Fourth Annual Report of the Registrar General* (1842), p. 213.

[19] Ibid. Compare W. Harding le Riche and Jean Milner, *Epidemiology as medical ecology* (1971), p. 387.

[20] Farr (1837), p. 593.

[21] Harding le Riche and Milner (1971), p. 374.

[22] Doctor Walter Harris cited by Creighton (1965), Vol. 2, p. 750.

[23] In making this claim Farr was following Edmonds who based his calculations on the proportion of deaths under 5 to recorded births, and there are problems (ignored here) not only of the completeness of registration but of shifting in the age structure, and then there is the changing relationship between those parts of the metropolis lying within and without the area covered by the Bills, the popularity of sending infants to be nursed, and often to die, in the country, and so on. Farr did not succeed in avoiding all these problems with calculations based on the proportion of deaths in various classes and their proportion to an estimated total population, but there is the added danger with Edmonds' work that it is vulnerable to any change in the regularity with which births as well as deaths were registered.

[24] Edmonds' data suggest a fairly steady fall in child mortality between 1750 and 1810. Farr unfortunately arranged his material in different periods but the major diseases of childhood were scarcely less virulent in the 1770s than they had been in the 1740s, the major fall being reserved for the years after 1780. See also J. Brownlee, 'The health of London in the eighteenth century', *Journal Royal Society of Medicine*, 18.3 (1925), p. 74.

[25] The relevant section is in Creighton (1965), Vol. 2, pp. 747-68. See also Brownlee (1925), pp. 79, 81, who noted a change in the seasonal incidence of diarrhoea after 1760 for which he thought a climatic explanation most likely.

[26] Sir William Fordyce whose observations on the health of the poor in London are quoted by Creighton (1965), Vol. 2, p. 756.

[27] See his correspondence with Chadwick reprinted in Glass (1973), pp. 146-67, particularly his criticism of Malthus on p. 165.

[28] Brownlee's comments are also relevant. He saw a decline in childbed mortality only after 1740 with a further decline after 1770. On smallpox he argued that there was no more than ordinary epidemic variation decade to decade in the eighteenth century. Brownlee (1925), p. 74.

[29] Compare Glass (1973), Table 5, pp. 190-1 with Farr (1837), Table XVII, p. 591.

[30] Greenwood (1948), p. 69.

[31] See for example the proportion sick and dying, in country, town and city districts. Henry Ratcliffe, *Observations on the rate of mortality and sickness* (1850), Table IV, pp. 15-19.

[32] Farr (1837), p. 579.

[33] Farr (1837), p. 582.

[34] This analysis was based on a reworking of Table IX in Farr (1837), p. 575. Only those occupations represented by more than 20 men were selected.

[35] Farr (1837), pp. 582-3.

[36] See Farr (1837), p. 584.

[37] Farr (1837), Tables XV, XVI, pp. 579-80.

[38] Farr (1837), p. 584.

[39] Lancashire women apparently suffered from more frequent illnesses but were away from work for shorter periods. Compare the Tables in Farr (1837), pp. 579,

584. In Glasgow, on the other hand, the difference was far less marked, a point which Farr picked up (p. 583).

[40] Hernia and varicose veins were the chief reasons for exclusion. Farr (1837), p. 579. Friendly societies excluded (amongst others) those suffering from syphilitic diseases and from injuries received as a result of drunkenness or brawls.

[41] In 1850, for instance, it is clear that butchers were well distributed but that half of the hatters were to be found in the two counties of Lancashire and Middlesex, 70% of the dyers in the manufacturing areas of Lancashire and Yorkshire, and 83% of the wool combers in Yorkshire. See Ratcliffe (1850), pp. 44, 46, 60.

[42] Only in 1862 do we know for each occupation the proportion dying at various ages as opposed to the average life expectancy, which measures not only the twenty-year-old's chances of dying within (say) the next five years but at all superior ages.

[43] Based on life expectancy and amount of sickness at age 30. Ratcliffe (1850), pp. 38, 40.

[44] Rural labourers had the lowest mortality but were ranked 7th (out of 23) as regards sickness in 1862 and labourers in town and city 15th and third, respectively. Based on Ratcliffe (1862), pp. 40-1.

[45] The average variation in rank was over 8 in both periods compared with a possible maximum of 12.5.

[46] Ratcliffe (1862), pp. 93-4.

[47] A negative correlation with the levels of sickness would have suggested that illness affected a person's ability to keep up his payments to the society so that he lost its support when it was most needed. It is correct to point out, though, that if his contributions ceased immediately on his falling sick and leaving employment then it is likely that the sickness would remain unrecorded.

[48] Ratcliffe (1850), pp. 42-60.

[49] Compare the mortality and sickness rates at ages 20-60 in the three areas (city, town and country) in Ratcliffe (1862), pp. 27-8, 36-7.

[50] It will be noted that the average variation in rank (5.8 for mortality, 4.4 for sickness) is considerably less than that found when testing for a correlation *between* the rates of mortality and sickness at either date.

[51] In rural areas on the other hand the society seems to have lost ground with the younger age groups (35 and under).

[52] Ratcliffe (1862), p. 28.

[53] Ratcliffe (1850), p. 131.

[54] Based on Ratcliffe (1850), Tables LXXXI, LXXXIII, pp. 133, 135. The average variation in rank was 4.1 compared with a maximum of 11.5. See above fn. 45 for mortality and sickness in relation to occupation.

[55] Based on Ratcliffe (1862) Table XVI, p. 41 and see his own observations on this, p. 70. It is interesting that the number of suspect values (a rank more than ten places from the average) is greatest at the two extremes (ages 20 and 60) when the number of members could be expected to be particularly low. Unfortunately there is no information on the number of members by occupation in 1862 but if we take the 12 occupations with more than 300 members in 1846-8 only 4 have any extreme values as regards sickness and only 2 as regards mortality. A check on the mortality and sickness of the above occupations in 1850 showed, however, that the correlation between them was even weaker than for the whole group of 26 occupations.

[56] This point is also made by Ratcliffe (1850), p. 36. See also pp. 11, 25. The low mortality but large amount of sickness of rural labourers as evidenced by Ratcliffe's data has already received attention, see above fn. 44.

[57] The information on premiums is in Ratcliffe (1850), p. 151.

[58] See Ratcliffe (1862), p. 102.

[59] Farr (1837), p. 571.

[60] His precise recommendations on the training of medical men are set out in Farr (1837), p. 600. For his pronouncements on how the health of insalubrious areas might be improved see pp. 568, 572.

CHAPTER IV. — Vital Statistics; or, the Statistics of Health, Sickness, Diseases, and Death.

To exhibit the sanatory state of the British population as accurately as existing materials permit, we shall severally examine the mortality, the sickness, the endemics, the prevailing forms of disease, and the various ways in which, at all ages, its successive generations perish.

Man's existence may terminate at any instant between 0 and 100 years: it may be a constant process of disease, or remain uninterrupted by a day's sickness. On opening a watch, or any piece of mechanism, and observing the state of its springs, chains, or wheels, it is not difficult to foresee how long its movements will continue; but no one, contemplating a solitary individual of the human species, and ignorant of the secret sources of his life, as well as of the many conjunctures of external circumstances in which he may be placed, can foretel the period when some mortal derangement will occur in his organisation, what diseases he will encounter, how long he will suffer, or the hour when his sufferings and his existence will end. The same uncertainty is extended in the popular thought to families, nations, and mankind, considered in collective masses; but observation proves that generations succeed each other, develope their energies, are afflicted with sickness, and waste in the procession of their life, according to fixed laws; that the mortality and sickness of a people are constant in the same circumstances, or only revolve through a prescribed cycle, varying as the causes favourable or unfavourable to health preponderate.

The physiological changes in the human body intimate that it was formed to continue in healthy action 70 or 80 years: yet owing to hereditary weakness, or a vicious tendency, and the imperfect adaptation of parts of the external world to its organisation, a certain number of every generation fall sick, and of these a certain number die at all ages: in such a ratio, however, that from birth to the age of puberty the sickness and mortality decline; while from puberty they increase slowly, but in a geometrical progression, up to the 50th or 60th year, and then more rapidly to the end. In comparing, therefore, the sanatory state of different nations, it is not enough to know the absolute mortality or sickness to which they are subject; as experience has proved that these may be nearly the same, yet, from their bearing differently on the periods of childhood, manhood, or old age, have a very different effect on the national strength and resources.

From observations to which we shall again have occasion to recur, it appears that in manhood, when 1 person in 100 dies annually, 2 are constantly sick; and although this exact relation is, perhaps, not preserved in infancy and old age, or where the rate of mortality deviates much from the standard, it may be safely assumed as a near approximation to the truth. Admitting, then, that the annual mortality is 2·13 per cent. after the corrected returns, and that the population of England and Wales is 14,000,000, the total number constantly disabled by sickness will at least amount to 600,000 persons; and if the same proportions be extended to Scotland and Ireland, to 1,130,000. This reduces the efficient population of the empire 1-23d part; and the productive power, so far as it depends on human labour, 1-17th part, if the maintenance and attendance of the sick cost half the produce of their labour in health *: but an example will show that it would be erroneous to suppose that two populations, in which the same absolute proportion of sick existed, suffered consequently to an equal extent. A third of the registered deaths occur below 5 years of age, yet the mortality in England has latterly (1813–30) not been more than 49·7 per 1,000: in Sweden it was (1755–75) 90·1 per 1,000; and it is probable that at the same period the mortality of infants in England was not

---

* In the English provincial hospitals the maintenance and the drugs administered to each patient cost 1s. 5d. daily; in Paris 1s. 5½d.; in London considerably more. — (*British Medical Almanac*, p. 118.)

a great deal lower than in Sweden: so that, if sickness have diminished at the same rate, the proportion of infants constantly ill is not half so great as it was a century ago.　But children being entirely helpless, and in no way contributing to the nation's actual strength, a diminution of sickness among them, however desirable, adds little immediately to national power and happiness, compared with an improvement in the health of adults, between the ages of 15 and 70 years, such as has been observed in London since the 16th century, when the destructive epidemics ceased.

The magnitude of the subject, and the fact that more than a million of the inhabitants of the United Kingdom are disabled by disease and suffering, is of less importance than the consideration that their condition may be ameliorated to an immeasurable extent.　In one class of English counties the mortality of males below 5 years of age is still 81·9 per 1,000, in others 41·9; and between the ages of 15 and 60 it varies from 11·0 to 19·0; implying a difference of 16 per 1,000 in the sickness: so that, if the health of the entire 13½ millions now between the ages of 15 and 60, in these islands, were as good as that enjoyed by the inhabitants of some counties, the numbers constantly sick would not be so numerous by 554,000 as if the standard of health were reduced to that obtaining in the more insalubrious districts.　In the one case, the mean number sick would be 773,300; in the other, 1,336,000.　Whether it be possible or not to raise the standard of health to the height enjoyed in the former counties, or to one still higher, the importance of the subject recommends it to a careful experimental investigation; because, when the character and causes of our diseases are known, some provision may be made for their alleviation: the extent of the injuries they inflict on the public will be determined; and the standard of salubrity, indicating an increase or diminution of physical strength, will afford the best index of the prosperity of the nation, and of the extent to which it is affected by atmospherical, political, or economical influences. Without an accurate acquaintaintance with their sanatory state, and the agents by which it is influenced, how can the Poor Law Commissioners deal advantageously with the mass of paupers placed at their disposal?

Mortality. — The general question of population has already been examined, and requires no further notice; but the deaths at different ages are so closely connected with health and with the great apparent changes in the diseases of this country, that we shall here present a comparative view of the rate of mortality that prevailed in England, Carlisle, Belgium, and Sweden, from an article by Mr. Edmonds, in the *British Medical Almanac* for 1836.

I. Table showing, in each of Thirteen Intervals of Age, the Number of Deaths which occur annually for every 1,000 Persons, living at the same Age, in England, Sweden, and Belgium.

Between Ages.	England and Wales.					Carlisle.	Belgium.	Sweden.	
	Females, 7 Years, 1818-24.			18 Years, 1813-30.		9 Years, 1779-87.	1829, both Sexes.	21 Years, 1755-75, both Sexes.	20 Years, 1776-95, both Sexes.
	Living in 1821.	Dying in 7 Years.	Annual Deaths per 1,000.	Males.	Females.				
0 and 5	774,689	239,482	45·6	53·5	46.0	82·3	65·8	90·1	85·0
5 — 10	682,457	30,173	6·5	7·2	6·7	10·2	8·7	14·2	13·6
10 — 15	569,366	20,244	5·3	5·0	5·2	5·0	5·4	6·6	6·2
15 — 20	535,569	27,391	7·6	7·2	7·6	6·8	6·6	7·6	7·0
20 — 30	901,338	61,701	10·1	10·1	10·4	7·5	9·1	9·2	8·9
30 — 40	649,507	53,417	12·1	11·4	12·4	10·6	10·0	12·2	11·6
40 — 50	500,977	50,214	14·8	14·9	14·9	14·3	13·6	17·4	16·1
50 — 60.	352,160	49,671	20·8	23·4	21·6	18·3	21·7	26·4	23·9
60 — 70	249,184	67,918	40·2	45·3	41·2	41·2	38·5	48·1	49·3
70 — 80	124,648	80,138	94·9	101·2	96·9	83·0	99·9	102·3	104·1
80 — 90	36,315	52,318	212·7	227·1	214·6	175·6	178·8	207·8	197·4
90 — 100	3,280	8,169	367·8	370·1	371·9	284·4	304·7	394·1	351·3
Above 100	129	512	586·1	611·1	560·6				
Ages specified -	5,379,619	741,348	20·3	21·7	20·7	25·0	22·7	28·9	26·8
Ages omitted -	765,090	27,157							
Total enumerated	6,144,709	768,505							
Estimated omission -		106,780							

Here it appears that the mortality of the whole English population, between the ages of 20 and 40, was higher than in Belgium and Sweden, while the mortality in early life was much lower; and if the Carlisle observations ever approximatively represented the mortality of England, the waste of life in the 5 years of infancy has almost diminished one half during the last 100 years. Other observations support this probability. The method pursued in obtaining the following results is unexceptionable, and demonstrates that for the last century the mortality of children in London has constantly been on the decline.

II. Table showing the Births and the Deaths under 5 Years of Age, according to the "London Bills of Mortality" for 100 Years, in 5 Periods of 20 Years each; also showing the Number dying under 5 Years out of 100 born. *

	1730-49.	1750-69.	1770-89.	1790-1809.	1810-29.
Total births · · · · ·	315,456	307,395	349,477	386,393	477,910
Total deaths under 5 years · ·	235,087	193,694	180,058	·159,571	151,794
Dying per cent. under 5 years ·	74·5	63·0	51·5	41·3	31·8

In the 20 years, 1730–49, out of 100 born, 74·5 died under the age of 5 years. During the 20 years, 1810–29, only 31·8 died out of the same number. This table is from a paper of Mr. Edmonds, to whose admirable investigations of the English population returns we shall have frequently to refer.

If half the children formerly cut off at an early age in England be now reared, and form part of the adult population; while the annual deaths between 20 and 30, instead of being 7·6, or 9·1, or 8·9 per 1,000, as in Carlisle, Belgium, and Sweden, are 10·1; it will appear that a vast number of weakly children are every year introduced into the English population, and that, unless proper means are taken to fortify the constitution in manhood, the relative vigour will not increase in the same ratio as the population.

Contrary to the Swedish observations, the mortality of females between the ages of 10 and 40 is higher than that of males: it is only in childhood, and after the 50th year, that the mortality of females is lower than that of males. This will correct some very exaggerated notions of the duration of female life, founded on tables of annuitants, by Mr. Finlaison, in which the disturbing influences of selection, and of the age at which the annuitants entered, was not properly taken into account.

The extent to which at 5 intervals of age the mortality, and consequently the intensity of disease, differs in the English counties, is exhibited in the subsequent table (III.), calculated by Mr. Edmonds, on the ascertained ages of the living in 1821, and the deaths during the 18 years, 1813–30. The counties are arranged chiefly according to the rate of mortality among females between the ages of 15 and 60 years. Mr. Edmonds conceived that the mortality of males at the same interval of age would not serve as a good index of the healthfulness of a locality, unless we could abstract the detrimental effect of their occupations, leading to fatal accidents or to loss of health. In many counties, also, the amount of the military and maritime population (which was not enumerated) diminishes considerably the value of the apparent mortality of the male sex. † (See Table III. next page).

We leave to the reader to investigate the causes which increase or diminish mortality in the several counties, and to compare their geological, botanical, meteorological, and economical states, with this table. It will be observed, that the healthiness of each class of counties decreases from Cornwall and Devon, the healthiest in England, to Cambridge, Kent. Surrey, and Middlesex, where the mortality is greatest. A slight diminution of the mortality, varying from ·05 to ·09, is required, between the ages of 15 to 60, in some of the counties where the maritime and military population was not enumerated, although its deaths are recorded in the parish registers. This correction has been made in Table IV.

* On the Diminution in the Mortality of Infants in England, by T. R. Edmonds, Esq. — *Lancet*, vol. i. 1835–36.

† *Lancet*, vol. i. 1835–36. No. 12

III. Table showing for each County of England the Annual Deaths which occur for every Hundred Living in each of Five Gradations of Age, the Counties being classified according to the Mortality of Females between the Ages of Fifteen and Sixty Years.

Wales and the Forty-two Counties.	Males (without correction).						Females.						Living 1821.	Proportion engaged in Agriculture, 1821.
	0-5	5-15	15-30	30-60	Above 60.	All Ages.	0-5	5-15	15-30	30-60	Above 60.	All Ages.		
1. Cornwall	3·59	·50	·79	1·41	7·63	1·82	3·12	·52	·67	1·10	7·18	1·67	133	38 per cent.
Devon	4·55	·53	·82	1·43	7·56	2·04	3·96	·54	·71	1·23	7·12	1·85	231	41 —
2. Wales	3·84	·53	·90	1·38	7·50	1·90	3·38	·52	·75	1·25	7·08	1·79	367	51 —
Monmouth	4·23	·49	·76	1·25	7·12	1·79	3·51	·49	·77	1·32	6·82	1·80	35	43 —
Dorset	3·93	·47	·81	1·25	7·02	1·86	3·32	·51	·85	1·35	7·12	1·81	76	43 —
Somerset	4·34	·56	·80	1·41	7·37	1·97	3·80	·57	·83	1·34	7·09	1·87	185	43 —
Wilts	3·66	·49	·79	1·31	7·21	1·83	3·25	·53	·87	1·40	7·40	1·84	114	52 —
3. Gloucester	4·24	·55	·83	1·48	6·80	1·91	3·55	·49	·83	1·35	6·50	1·76	175	32 —
Hereford	3·88	·46	·78	1·28	7·66	1·90	3·13	·51	·95	1·36	7·27	1·88	52	62 —
Northumberland	3·97	·59	·88	1·38	6·73	1·90	3·35	·54	·74	1·32	6·55	1·72	104	27 —
Cumberland	4·74	·61	·87	1·42	7·68	2·06	4·46	·61	·81	1·35	7·32	1·98	81	36 —
Westmoreland	3·87	·67	·87	1·30	7·54	1·97	3·49	·58	·93	1·47	7·85	2·03	26	49 —
North York	3·79	·53	·87	1·24	7·30	1·91	3·17	·55	·96	1·34	7·04	1·88	93	43 —
4. Rutland	4·37	·44	·68	1·31	7·59	1·98	3·84	·55	·93	1·38	7·32	2·01	9	61 —
Norfolk	5·20	·54	·84	1·24	7·21	2·08	4·40	·55	·88	1·31	7·02	1·97	177	49 —
Suffolk	3·73	·45	·81	1·19	6·86	1·78	3·24	·49	·95	1·37	6·83	1·80	138	56 —
Hertford	4·48	·54	·80	1·45	8·22	2·00	4·03	·54	·92	1·42	7·62	1·91	66	52 —
Durham	5·34	·84	1·15	1·51	7·97	2·38	4·49	·72	·91	1·54	7·53	2·14	109	21 —
5. East York	5·48	·63	·94	1·38	7·59	2·17	4·66	·60	·89	1·41	7·17	1·98	98	38 —
West York	5·18	·62	·88	1·41	7·58	2·09	4·57	·56	·93	1·48	7·32	1·98	402	20 —
Leicester	5·21	·52	·81	1·33	7·26	2·04	4·38	·51	·91	1·41	7·30	1·95	88	35 —
Lincoln	5·13	·56	·78	1·44	7·39	2·07	4·39	·58	·97	1·45	7·25	1·98	141	59 —
Salop	4·56	·61	·98	1·52	7·45	2·08	3·91	·57	1·02	1·42	7·37	1·98	101	44 —
Derby	4·38	·56	·92	1·29	7·38	1·94	3·72	·54	1·07	1·50	7·63	1·91	107	31 —
Northampton	4·64	·55	·81	1·32	7·37	2·05	3·97	·63	1·10	1·52	7·49	2·08	83	53 —
Huntingdon	4·72	·57	·84	1·55	7·65	2·09	4·21	·63	1·00	1·52	7·22	2·02	25	62 —
Essex	4·41	·56	·92	1·54	7·88	2·05	3·95	·61	1·06	1·53	7·29	1·97	145	56 —
6. Bedford	4·17	·58	·78	1·34	7·51	1·92	3·49	·65	1·14	1·58	7·40	1·95	43	62 —
Bucks	4·72	·53	·81	1·34	7·65	2·05	3·98	·63	1·10	1·54	7·96	2·08	69	58 —
Oxford	4·97	·50	·78	1·36	7·82	2·05	4·14	·53	·99	1·47	7·82	2·04	68	55 —
Berks	4·72	·53	·90	1·51	7·99	2·12	4·16	·55	1·05	1·53	7·69	2·08	66	53 —
Southampton	4·43	·55	·99	1·53	7·88	2·10	3·77	·53	·96	1·52	7·68	1·91	145	42 —
Sussex	3·93	·51	·91	1·35	7·16	1·87	3·21	·50	1·08	1·45	7·00	1·79	116	50 —
Lancaster	6·56	·71	1·04	1·64	7·66	2·40	5·78	·65	1·02	1·73	7·59	2·24	540	11 —
Chester	5·57	·71	1·07	1·63	8·20	2·32	4·78	·68	1·11	1·76	8·22	2·22	137	35 —
Nottingham	6·38	·61	·90	1·41	7·18	2·27	5·37	·62	1·06	1·57	7·04	2·16	95	35 —
Stafford	5·96	·68	1·06	1·60	7·80	2·34	5·43	·62	1·07	1·58	7·41	2·20	169	27 —
7. Warwick	6·12	·63	·90	1·63	6·16	2·26	5·29	·64	·93	1·53	6·03	2·08	141	28 —
Worcester	5·81	·65	·93	1·47	7·32	2·26	5·21	·62	1·04	1·51	7·21	2·15	94	38 —
Cambridge	5·96	·71	·90	1·63	7·85	2·34	5·08	·71	1·03	1·62	7·85	2·23	62	61 —
Kent	5·60	·66	1·41	2·04	7·82	2·54	4·75	·61	1·02	1·63	7·69	2·11	216	36 —
8. Surrey	7·75	·71	1·05	2·12	9·81	2·81	6·40	·69	·92	1·77	8·78	2·41	209	17 —
Middlesex	8·34	·84	1·06	2·46	11·02	3·03	6·77	·78	·83	1·96	10·36	2·53	611	4 —
England and Wales	5·30	·61	·94	1·59	7·77	2·21	4·56	·60	·93	1·52	7·53	2·05	6,145	34 per cent.

The numbers representing the mortality in thirty-nine counties, have been obtained by increasing the registered deaths one ninth part. In the case of Wales, Monmouth, Middlesex, and Surrey, the increase has been one fourth part. The relative weight of each observation is indicated by the additional column representing in thousands the amount of the female population of each county.

IV. Table showing, in each of Six Gradations of Age, the Mortality per cent. of each Sex in each of Eight Classes of English Counties.

Class.	Males (corrected).*							Females.						
	0-5	5-10	10-15	15-30	30-60	Above 60	All Ages	0-5	5-10	10-15	15-30	30-60	Above 60	All Ages
1	4·19	·63	·38	·75	1·36 (1·10)	7·58	1·90	3·65	·63	·41	·70	1·18	7·14	1·78
2	3·87	·60	·44	·83	1·31	7·46	1·83	3·39	·59	·43	·75	1·26	7·06	1·79
3	4·14	·63	·44	·76	1·32	7·15	1·86	3·58	·59	·47	·83	1·35	6·96	1·83
4	4·36	·58	·44	·80	1·23	7·30	1·92	3·76	·55	·52	·92	1·35	7·12	1·90
5	5·24	·72	·52	·86	1·38	7·47	2·09	4·52	·64	·52	·92	1·47	7·33	2·00
6	4·45	·62	·47	·87	1·40	7·62	1·99	3·81	·58	·55	1·05	1·50	7·51	1·96
7	6·11	·78	·56	1·03	1·64	7·64	2·34	5·33	·71	·56	1·03	1·65	7·48	2·18
8	8·19	1·05	·53	·95	2·27 (1·90)	10·72	2·88	6·68	·95	·53	·85	1·91	9·95	2·50
Totals	5·30	·72	·49	·88	1·53 (1·33)	7·77	2·15	4·56	·66	52	·93	1·52	7·53	2·05
Table of "Mean Mortality," when period of "Infancy" terminates at seven years								4·47	·77	·65	·86	1·66	7·62	2·09

* The apparent mortality of the male sex between 15 and 30, between 30 and 60, and at all ages, has been diminished by 06 in the total, and in classes 1, 2, and 3; it has been diminished by 03 in classes 4, 5, 6, and 7; and by ·10 in the eighth class.

Except Cambridge, it will be found that, generally, the counties having the greatest proportion of inhabitants congregated in towns are the most unhealthy. Above 60 the mortality in these counties would have been higher, had the ages of the inhabitants of Birmingham, Bristol, Newcastle upon Tyne, Manchester, Leeds, and some other large towns, not been omitted, in some unaccountable manner, in the specification made in 1821. Through this omission, and the uncertainty in the parish registry, it is impossible to ascertain the present mortality prevailing in many of our large towns. The population returns furnish materials for determining the mortality in only the 6 towns subjoined : the absolute mortality in which is stated on the assumption that the registered deaths are to be increased 20 per cent. in order to obtain the true number of deaths; while, in the whole of England and Wales, the estimated increase was 13·92 per cent. Fortunately the invaluable observations collected in Glasgow by the " Committee on Churchyards," comprehending an accurate return of the deaths during 15 years (1821–35), and two enumerations of the living, and their ages, come here to our assistance : they have furnished Mr. Edmonds the materials for determining very accurately the mortality in Glasgow during the three last quinquennial periods. The public spirit of the Glasgow town council, and the enlightened exertions of Dr. Cleland, in obtaining a second voluntary enumeration of the living, and their ages, in 1831, are as honourable to them, as the omission of the ages in 1831 is discreditable to the persons who directed the last census in England and Scotland.

V. Table of the Annual Mortality per Cent. at every Age in Glasgow during the 15 Years, 1821–35, compared with the Mortality prevailing during 18 Years, 1813–30, in 6 large English Towns, viz. York, Norwich, Plymouth, Hull, Portsmouth, Liverpool, — and in London.*

Between Ages.	1813-30, Six Towns of England.	1821-35, Glasgow.	1813-30, London.	Between Ages.	1813-30, Six Towns of England.	1821-35, Glasgow.	1813-30, London.
0— 5	8·63	8·10	8·27	60—70	5·83	6·04	7·34
5—10	1·03	1·24	1·08	70—80	12·10	13·57	15·23
10—20	0·73	0·76	0·60	80—90	24·62	23·81	29·91
20—30	1·39	1·17	1·07	Above 90	42·72	42·55	33·55
30—40	1·56	1·57	1·52				
40—50	1·96	2·31	2·29	All Ages	2·95	2·83	2·84
50—60	3·00	3·50	3·61				

By comparing the mortality prevailing in all these towns with that of England, it will be seen how much the chances of dying are increased among the mass of people dwelling in cities.

To show what variation has taken place in Glasgow during the last 15 years, the following table was constructed.

VI. Table showing for each of Three Quinquennial Periods the average Annual Deaths which occurred in each Interval of Age, out of 100 living at the same Interval; also showing the Annual Mortality for the 4 last Years, exclusive of the Year of Cholera.

Between Ages.	Males.			Females.			Third Period exclusive of Year of Cholera.	
	1821-25.	1826-30.	1831-35.	1821-25.	1826-30.	1831-35.	Males.	Females.
0— 5	8·08	7·47	9·78	7·66	7·10	8·52	9·51	8·29
5—10	1·31	1·14	1·31	1·26	1·11	1·31	1·26	1·24
10—20	·74	·82	·95	·71	·61	·72	·93	·67
20—30	1·23	1·39	1·51	·88	·84	1·12	1·46	·92
30—40	1·35	1·56	2·14	1·24	1·32	1·85	1·77	1·48
40—50	1·82	2·31	3·19	1·65	2·06	2·87	2·60	2·41
50—60	2·84	3·71	4·11	2·68	3·36	4·30	3·29	3·51
60—70	5·72	6·38	6·97	4·67	5·74	6·72	6·00	5·50
70—80	12·70	15·45	17·90	10·48	11·88	13·02	15·54	11·02
80—90	21·27	29·07	30·53	16·72	21·97	23·50	28·34	22·72
Above 90	56·29	54·60	37·36	31·04	31·52	44·48	36·69	42·76
All Ages	2·78	2·91	3·59	2·37	2·40	2·93	3·31	2·62
30—60	1·84	2·27	2·89	1·69	1·98	2·66	2·35	2·12
Above 60	8·81	10·23	10·95	7·32	8·70	9·77	9·60	8·57

* Lancet, 1835–36, No. 12. The materials from which these tables have been deduced were communicated to Mr. Edmonds by Henry Paul, Esq., the present convener of the Committee on Churchyards in Glasgow ; and have been published in the Lancet.

This table deserves most serious attention; it places beyond all doubt the remarkable fact that, " between the ages of 30 and 60, the mortality of each sex increased 20 per cent. every 5 years. This is the case after deducting 10 per cent. from the actual average of the 5 years, 1831-35, as the effect of the cholera visitation in 1832. The mortality in 1832, between the ages of 30 and 60, really raised the average 20 per cent." By comparing the two last columns of the table with the third and sixth, it becomes evident that cholera increased the mortality principally between the ages of 20 and 70.

Through the ignorance, not yet wholly dispelled, of the conditions of animal existence prevailing when large towns were built, the social and intellectual advantages which they offered were in part neutralised, and in some instances overbalanced, by their baleful influence upon the health and physical strength of the inhabitants. It is probable that the population of several cities in Europe was only maintained by immigration ; and when large towns were designated by Dr Price " the graves of mankind," experience and calculation sanctioned the appellation. Besides certain vices and the misery of the poor in cities, the privation of atmospheric air in narrow streets or close rooms, and the accumulation of carbonic acid preventing the escape of that gas from the lungs, as well as the collection of putrid effluvia, and the imperfect drainage of excretions and refuse animal or vegetable matter, are the main sources of insalubrity where masses of men are collected. A city on a well selected site, constructed with a view to the supply of atmospheric air, and the removal of all refuse matter, whether gaseous, liquid, or solid, may, undoubtedly, be made little less healthy than the country. The increasing mortality in Glasgow is, no doubt, in part due to the accession of Irish population, who amounted, in 1831, to 35,554, or to more than a sixth of the inhabitants. The poor Irish, we strongly suspect, are keeping up, if they be not introducing, the fevers of their wretched country in the heart of the British cities: this is confirmed in the case of Glasgow by the ages at which the mortality is augmented, and by a Report of the Glasgow Infirmary before us, from which it appears that, in the year 1835, out of 3,260 patients treated, 1,258 had fevers, and of these 125 died.

No materials exist for determining the relative mortality at different ages in Scotland and Ireland; the proportions specified, in the enumeration of ages above 60, furnish, however, a certain approximation to the truth. The number living above 60, for every 100 living between 30 and 60 years was in,

England and Wales	(Females)	-	27·5
Scotland	- (Females)	-	28·0
Ireland	- (Males and Females)		15·7
Belgium	- (Males and Females)		30·3 *

The proportion of old people in Ireland is little more than half the proportion living in Belgium: Scotland, in this respect, differs little from England.

The people of this country have extended their power into all the quarters and climates of the globe; the mortality of the military will show at what expense of life and health. The constitution of a race of men is fitted to the locality and the atmosphere in which they are born ; and they must possess a redundant vitality to acquire and retain possessions in a climate different from their own, and destructive of a body not moulded by its influences into the correspondent temperament. By the subjoined table of the mortality of the British army it will be seen that the soldier, in the prime of his physical powers, is rendered more liable to death every step he takes from his native climate, till at last the man of 28 years is subject, in the West Indies, to the same mortality as the man of 80 remaining in Britain. By a judicious choice of stations, some very obvious hygienic precautions, and a temperate regimen, little doubt can be entertained that the European mortality may be diminished a half in the tropical colonies. The mortality of the troops is double that of the officers. Is not this mainly due to the crowding the men in barracks?

---

* On the Law of Mortality in each English County, by T. R. Edmonds, Esq. — Lancet, 1835-36, vol. i. p. 415.

VII. Table of the Mortality of the British Army, showing the mean Number of Annual Deaths out of 100 living at each Station mentioned.*

Time and Place of Observation.	English Army.	Extent of Observations.		Annual Rate of Mortality per Cent.		
		Average Force.	Years.	Maximum.	Mean.	Minimum.
*The United Kingdom -	British army -	46,460	10	- - -	1·5	
*Ireland, 1797-1828 -	Ditto -	36,921	32	2·0	1·5	1·1
Mediterranean.						
*Malta, 1824-31 - -	The garrison -	2,296	8	2·8	1·5	1·0
*Gibraltar - -	Ditto -	3,267	17	13·4	2·0	0·7
*Ionian Islands -	The troops -	3,467	13	3·6	2·6	1·4
East Indies.						
*Fort St. George Presidency -	(1)European troops	11,820	4	7·1	4·8	3·2
*Madras, 1827-30 -	Native troops -	69,550	4	1·6	1·4	1·0
*Bengal, 1826-32 - -	2)European troops	8,700	7	9·7	5·7	3·8
West Indies.						
*Windward Islands -	1796-1805, ditto -	13,610	10	27·7	18·3	8·0
*Leeward Islands -	1810-28, ditto -	5,768	19	23·4	11·3	4·7
*Jamaica, Honduras, 1810-28 -	Ditto -	2,528	19	47·2	15·5	7·8
*Jamaica, Honduras, Windward and Leeward Islands - -	Colonial troops, (Blacks) -	2,733	19	8·4	5·5	1·8

The mortality of the native troops in the Madras presidency was only 1·4 per cent. ; that of the European troops was quadrupled in Bengal. At home 1·5, in Bengal 5·7 per cent. of the European troops died. The climate of the East Indies is, therefore, congenial to the Hindoos, and only extraordinarily fatal to foreigners. The same holds of other countries, not poisoned by vegetable or animal effluvia, when their extremes of heat and cold, moisture and dryness, are not excessive.

The mean mortality of the French infantry at home is higher than that stated above for the English army.†

FRENCH INFANTRY.

	Extent of Observations.		Annual Rate of Mortality per Cent.		
	Force.	Years.	Maximum.	Mean.	Minimum.
Troops of the line -	106,700	6	- -	2·00	
Garde royale - -	13,924	6	- -	1·47	
The whole army - -	120,604	6	2·38	1·91	1·55

Sickness. — A bill embodying a plan for enabling the labouring poor to provide support for themselves in sickness and old age, by small weekly savings from their wages, was introduced by Mr. Dowdeswell, and approved by the House of Commons, in 1773 ; but it met with the same fate as another bill framed by the Commons in 1789, and founded on tables computed, at the request of a committee, by Dr. Price. The Lords rejected both bills ; and thus deprived the labouring poor of the guidance of a legislative act in the formation of friendly societies for half a century.‡ The tables of sickness, computed for the first bill, were published by Baron Maseres in the second volume of his *Treatise on the Doctrine of Life Annuities :* Dr. Price's tables, which have since been in general use, were published in the edition of his work on annuities by Mr. Morgan. These tables were founded partly on observation and partly on an ingenious hypothesis: no extensive observations were ever made to determine the average time of incapacitation from labour, produced by sickness, till the subject was taken up and investigated by the Highland Society (1824). Since then two committees of the House of Commons have sat on benefit societies, and the subject has obtained more attention.§

---

* *Edinburgh Medical Journal.* Mr. Marshall has the merit of having first investigated with success the statistics of the British army. Lieutenant Tulloch has published several valuable papers on the subject in the *United Service Journal.* Both these esteemed writers publish the materials from which their results are deduced.

† *Benoiston de Chateauneuf, Annales d'Hygiène,* t. x.

‡ A bill for the registration of births and deaths in England and Wales has been passed during the present session, and a Registrar General appointed to superintend its execution.

§ Notwithstanding the writings of Dr. Price, and the publication of the Highland Society (1824), an actuary, Mr. Finlaison, affirmed, before the first committee, that " there is a constant and given mortality operating upon life, but no such law exists as to sickness." Evidence before Select Committee on Benefit Societies, 1825. He of course retracted this opinion.

Sickness, in practical statistics, is employed in a general sense. If we consider man as a material body, acting intelligently, any thing in the condition of the body itself, which interrupts or impedes that action, is sickness. Any disturbance in the functions of the body, or alteration in the organs by which they are executed — from the skin to the brain and spinal marrow — from the time the food enters the mouth, till it exhales from the skin and lungs in vapour and gas — is a disease: and the sum of sick-time, produced by all diseases, constitutes the sickness of which statisticians speak. It is of various kinds. In acute or severe diseases, such as fever, inflammation of an important part, or malignant ulcer, a man is often able to think and move, just as he can digest a small quantity of food; but not with any energy, or at least with the energy required by an ordinary occupation. Any attempt at exertion aggravates and prolongs the sickness. This, we believe, is called *bedfast* sickness by the friendly societies. In other chronic diseases, slow inflammations of internal organs, reduced dislocations, rheumatisms, ulcerations, the patient can attend partially to his business: he is in possession of half his faculties; whether he can make them in any way available, depends on circumstances. This is walking sickness. The infirm, the crippled, the maimed, may either be entirely helpless and bedridden, or capable of some of the duties of life: their sickness differs from the bedfast, and from the walking, in being beyond the pale of recovery. The Highland Society calculated that of ten weeks' sickness, among persons of all ages under 70, two may be assumed as bedfast sickness, five as walking, and three as permanent. *

The following table of sickness, from the *British Medical Almanac*, presents a comparative view of the mean proportion of sickness incidental to members of English and Scotch benefit societies, according to (1.) the observations of the Highland Society; (2.) returns obtained by the Society for promoting Useful Knowledge; (3.) and a table of Mr. Edmonds's, agreeing very nearly with Dr. Price's, in universal use.

VIII. Table showing the Proportion of Sick out of 100 living at each Interval of Age in Friendly Societies.

Between Ages.	Sick Time in 100 of Life Time.			Between Ages.	Sick Time in 100 of Life Time.		
	Scotch Benefit Societies.	English Benefit Societies.	Theoretical Table by Mr.Edmonds.		Scotch Benefit Societies.	English Benefit Societies.	Theoretical Table by Mr.Edmonds.
20 to 30	1·14	1·54	1·72	70 to 80	⎫	32·50	—
30 — 40	1·32	1·83	2·30	80 — 90	⎬ 31·70	40·00	—
40 — 50	1·97	2·56	3·10	90 — 93	⎭	67·00	—
50 — 60	3·60	4·32	4·51				
60 — 70	10·80	11·26	9·36	All ages	2·45	2·76	—

These observations show that, in the different circumstances, 1·32, 1·83, and 2·30 men in 100, between the ages of 30 and 40, were constantly ill: the sick-time increasing regularly with age. It is easy to deduce from this table the days of sickness of each individual.

The Scotch and English observations represent, so far as limited numbers can, the sickness to which men, who are healthy at the time of entering benefit societies, are subsequently liable: the general proportion of sickness is higher. Tables of sickness for the entire population would be formed by taking 100,000 persons, of given ages, indiscriminately, and observing them for one, two, three, &c., years: they would, consequently, comprehend 4,000 or 5,000 individuals sick when the observation commenced, expressly excluded, by the rules of benefit societies, as well as those suffering from syphilitic diseases, and accidents incurred through drunkenness or brawls. In the parish of Methven, Perthshire, it was ascertained that 35 out of 743, or 4·7 per cent. of the male population above 15, would, from bodily or mental infirmity, not have been admitted as members of the friendly societies. † Medical men are well aware that labourers often go about their work with diseases of the heart, tubercles in the lungs, and disorders of considerable severity: Dr. Forbes ascertained, by personal examination of 120 Cornish miners, in actual employment, that only 63 had good health; of the remaining half, 26 had

---

* *Report of Friendly Societies*, by a committee of the Highland Society, p. 108.
† Ibid. p. 280.

difficulty of breathing, 14 pain of chest, 10 pain of stomach and bowels, 5 lumbago, pain of shoulder, palpitation, scrofula, or fits.* Out of 115 ch ' lren below 18 years of age, Dr. Bisset Hawkins states, that 84 had good health ; 25 middling health ; 6 bad health.† Of the miners at work only 53, of the factory children only 7:°, per cent. enjoyed good health.

How much sickness exists among the actual labourers of this country, independently of those definitively incapacitated by disease. and who are either discharged on this account or set aside as inefficient? For resolving this question. there are valuable materials in the *Supplementary Report* of the Factory Commissioners, of which we shall avail ourselves; regretting, at the same time, that, from several omissions, and the returns not being procured in proper forms, the information they afford is not so complete as it might easily have been rendered.

The first returns deserving notice relate to the workmen employed in his Majesty's dock yards, at Woolwich, Sheerness, Chatham, Portsmouth, Devonport, and Pembroke. That from Portsmouth, made by Mr. Pennell, is the most complete, as it distinguishes the cases, and the duration of diseases, from the consequences of injuries incurred in the yards. It has likewise the advantage of exhibiting the liability to accidents and sickness among different classes of workmen.

IX. An Account of the Number of Workmen employed in Portsmouth Dock Yard, and of the Cases of Absence from Work, on account of Sickness, during the last 3 Years. Prepared agreeably to Mem. of 9th of May, 1833.

Description of Workmen.	1830. Average Number borne	Number of Cases Sick.	Hurt.	Days Sick.	Days Hurt.	1831. Average Number borne	Number of Cases Sick.	Hurt.	Days Sick.	Days Hurt.	1832. Average Number borne	Number of Cases Sick.	Hurt.	Days Sick.	Days Hurt.
Blockmakers	5	3	2	10	13	5	5	1	31	18	4	2	-	61	
Boys, house and oakum	29	8	3	238	37	26	7	3	40	31	20	5	1	48	23
Braziers and tinmen	3	-	1	-	16	3	-	-	-	-	3	1	-	6	
Bricklayers and labourers	29	5	4	158	43	26	5	5	255	46	24	3	5	178	38
Caulkers	90	30	16	384	236	88	52	12	512	106	84	27	23	331	360
Cooper	1	-	-	-	-	1	-	-	-	-	1	-	-	-	
House carpenters	16	3	-	41	-	16	7	2	104	25	16	6	-	195	
Joiners	81	23	6	355	83	80	20	16	157	190	74	20	12	247	164
Labourers, storehouse	19	2		28	95	17	4	-	22	-	17	6	-	18	
Yard and house carpenters employed as labourers	209	50	11	900	279	198	57	21	729	483	182	44	10	852	225
Locksmiths	2	-	-	-	-	2	1	-	11	-	2				
Masons	11	2	2	13	22	11	2	-	3	-	10	1	1	6	44
Messengers	7	3	-	20	-	7	-	-	-	-	7				
Painters and glaziers	29	11	7	198	73	26	14	5	356	94	22	7	1	156	11
Plumbers	6	6	-	42	-	6	5	-	39	-	6	2	-	9	
Pitch heater	1	-	-	-	-	1	1	-	-	-	1				
Riggers and labourers	74	11	11	74	137	71	22	11	162	177	69	16	11	223	162
Sail makers	46	15	1	189	10	45	22	2	284	10	41	20	3	530	42
Sawyers	99	27	31	233	553	96	31	13	357	228	93	23	9	214	124
Scavelmen	64	16	7	292	96	63	14	7	233	115	54	13	4	133	65
Shipwrights	827	318	196	3,702	3,079	800	410	179	4,729	2,463	746	198		3,170	3,007
Smiths	153	70	25	900	275	151	117	27	656	296	150	66	26	682	351
Rope makers	111	35	-	589	-	107	44	7	381	80	100	36	4	707	85
Warders	35	17	9	336	111	28	9	1	35	29	26	11	2	257	11
Wheelwrights	3	-	1	-	13	3	-	-	-	-	3				
Workmen at wood mills	25	9	1	114	32	24	6	-	268	-	21	2	2	168	36
at metal	52	24	15	162	195	51	26	10	214	99	46	27	7	319	96
millwright's shop	52	9	7	210	486	50	7	3	26	130	45	12	10	107	242

X. Table presenting a condensed View of the above Facts.

Years.	Average Number of Men.	Number of Cases. Diseases.	Hurts.	Days of Sickness from spontaneous Disease.	Days of Sickness from Injuries.	Total Days of Sickness.
1830	2,079	697	357	9,188	5,884	15,072
1831	2,002	888	325	9,605	4,620	14,225
1832	1,867	665	329	8,617	5,086	13,703
3 years	5,939	2,250	1,011	27,410	15,590	43,000

This table furnishes, as the mean of the three years, the following interesting results. In the year, 1 man in 6 is seriously hurt ; 2 in 5 fall ill. Each man, on

* *Medical Topography of Penwith, Cornwall,* by J. Forbes, M. D. ; Trans. of the Medical Association, vol. iv. p. 187.

† *Supplement to Factories Inquiry.*

an average, has an attack of illness, either spontaneous or caused by external injury, every 2 years; and, at an average, each disease lasts 14 days. In a tabular form the results will be more distinctly perceptible.

XI. Annual Proportion of Attacks and Accidents occurring to 100 Men in the Portsmouth Dock Yard: and the mean Duration of each Case.

	Number per Cent.	Duration of each Case, in Days.	
Spontaneous attacks - - - - -	37·8	12·2	
Injuries - - - - -	16·0	15·6	
Both - -	53·8	13·2 mean duration of all cases.	

So far as the returns from the other dock yards can be understood, and admit of comparison, they confirm these results; and between Woolwich and Portsmouth, where hurts and sickness are distinguished, there is a remarkable coincidence in the time lost by sickness, although that from injuries is very different.

XII. Table showing the Time lost by Sickness, whether induced by Accident or otherwise, among the Labourers in Portsmouth and Woolwich Dock Yards.

	Mean Number of Workmen.	Days lost by Sickness.	Days lost by Accidents.	Constantly sick, per Cent.	Constantly suffering from Accidents, per Cent.	Constantly ill from both Causes, per Cent.
Portsmouth -	5,939	27,410	15,590	1·26	0·73	1·99
Woolwich -	2,243	10,593	8,594	1·29	1·05	2.34

It may be safely assumed that, of the 21,000 labourers employed in the dock yards, 2 per cent., or more than 420, are constantly kept at home, by diseases of one kind or another; and that diseases arising in the body itself, independent of external mechanical injury, constitute almost two thirds of the entire sickness. No details or explanations accompany the original returns; they do not appear to have been demanded: but it may be presumed that the sickness only of the men who recovered, and returned to the dock yards, is intended in the tables, and this, with the selection on entering, excludes the greater proportion of sickness prevailing in a population, although it expresses that experienced by the actually working class. The sickness of the working labourers in the East India Company's service was, we shall show, 1·65 per cent.; and this is little more than a fourth part of the entire sick-time experienced by the whole number employed, including those pensioned. This proportion would make the sick-time of the dock yard labourers 7·8 per cent. of the life-time.

A return of the state of health among the men employed by the East India Company in London deserves especial attention, as no observations so accurate or extensive have before been published, relative to the sickness and mortality among labourers in large cities. This return was obtained "in the form of a large volume, containing a list of 2,461 labourers, employed in the month of April, 1823, with a statement of the number of days' illness experienced by these labourers, one by one, year by year, for the 10 succeeding years; also the date of every death, and the date when any labourer ceased to be employed, by being superannuated and pensioned, dismissed, or by voluntarily leaving the service of the Company." *

Every labourer put upon the sick list is allowed 1s. 6d. a day, Sundays included; he is also seen every day by the surgeon, and, therefore, remains no longer absent than the case requires.

During the 10 years, 496 died, 248 were pensioned, and 208 left the service or were dismissed. The reporter, Dr. Mitchell, has calculated a table of the duration of sickness per annum for every age, from 16 to 81, which we subjoin: —

Age.	Average Duration of Sickness per Annum for every Man employed.	Average Duration of Sickness for every Man sick.	Age.	Average Duration of Sickness per Annum for every Man employed.	Average Duration of Sickness for every Man sick.
	Days.	Days.		Days.	Days.
Under 21	4·02	13·96	51 to 61	7·00	28·60
21 to 31	4·94	18·70	61 — 71	10·08	29·07
31 — 41	5·06	22·63	71 — 81	11·63	31·77
41 — 51	5·31	23·21			

* *Factories Inquiry; Supplementary Report*, by Dr. Mitchell, vol. i. p. 48.

Dr. Mitchell has unfortunately withheld the *data* from which these results were derived. He has not stated the total days' sickness, and attacks at each age, nor arranged the observations so as to exhibit the complete years of life. But the report contains tables showing the number of the men at every year of age, from 16 to 78, in the beginning of April, 1823; the ages at which the 248 pensioners were put upon the list; and the ages at which the 496 men died whilst classed as workmen, as well as the ages at which 161 of the pensioners died. It appears that the deaths of the pensioners were obtained in a separate return, extending from April, 1823, to January, 1834, nine months over the ten years in which the other deaths happened. From these facts we first deduced the number living at each decennial period of life, on the supposition that the 2,461 individuals alive in 1823 had remained in the service ten years; and thence subtracted the years of life lost by deaths and dismissals. Dr. Mitchell having omitted to state when or at what age the 208 men left the service, it has been assumed that the younger men left in rather greater proportion than the aged, but that all remained in the service five full years; which is the same as supposing the dismissals were equally distributed over the ten years. A similar correction was made for the deaths: 1-14th was deducted from the deaths of pensioners for the nine excessive months in which they were observed.

XIII. Table showing the Number of Labourers in the East India Company's Service, April, 1823; and, from Ten Years' Observations, the Number living complete Years between 16 and 90 years of age; the Deaths among the Workmen and Pensioners; the resulting Mortality compared with the Mortality among Males in London and Stockholm.

Ages.	Labourers.			Deaths		Annual Deaths per Cent. among the				Annual Mortality, per Cent.	
	On the Books April, 1823.	Living in One Year.	Living during One complete Year.	of Work-men.	of Pen-sioners.	Workmen.		Pen-sioners.	Entire Class of Labour-ers.	London, 1813–30. Males.	Stock-holm, 1755–63. Males.
						Entire Number.	Attacked.				
16—20	31	48	38	16	1	·78	2·9	} 6·4 {	0·82	1·22	2·63
20—30	437	2,301	2,066	86	2	1·46	6·5		1·48	1·69	3·54
30—40	779	6,677	5,939	136	8	2·38	10·4	} 17·7 {	2·43	2·54	4·67
40—50	599	6,749	5,764	147	40	3·52	14·2		4·27	4·04	6·46
50—60	451	5,365	4,255	95	75	5·88	15·7	} 16·5 {	9·24	8·12	10·10
60—70	137	2,739	1,819	16	30	6·66	11·7		10·71	15·97	15·87
70—80	27	675	426·5		5			23·2	13·90	30·91	31·94
80—90	- -	56	35·5							33·84	37·50
	2,461	24,610	20,343	496	161	2·50	10·6	16·5	3·13	.	

These observations are equivalent to observations on 20,343 men during one complete year, and between the ages of 30 and 70 are sufficiently extensive to furnish a near approximation to the mortality in four decennial periods: earlier or later they are of little separate value. The annual rate of mortality was 3·13 per cent.; and, notwithstanding the selection, it agrees, between 40 and 60, very nearly with the general mortality of males in London (1813–30).

The mortality under 40 is not so high among the labourers, because the greater part of them are selected healthy men, received into the service between the age of 20 and 35; after 50 it is higher than the general mortality in London. These men were well supplied with food and clothing; their work without being hard insured regular muscular exercise; in sickness they had rest and proper medical attendance; yet between 40 and 50 the mortality was 67 per cent., between 50 and 60 as much as 82 per cent. higher than the mortality at the same ages in all England. Such facts as these annihilate the supposition that the increased mortality in cities is due to want of food, and greater misery; nor, although these men drank freely, can we admit that their moral habits differed so greatly from those of country labourers as to account for their greater mortality.

Of the 2,461 labourers, 10 per cent. were pensioned in the course of ten years; 8 per cent. were discharged, or quitted the service; 1 man in 81 working a year was pensioned; 1 in 4 had an attack of sickness; 1 in 60 was constantly on the sick list; 1 in 21 (4·79 per cent.) of the labourers was a pensioner; and 1 in 6 of the pensioners died annually. The mean duration of life, after being pensioned, would therefore be six years; five years and a half less than the mean duration of life among the general class of men in cities at the same ages.* This and the evidence of the medical attendant Mr. Lewis Leese prove clearly that the greater part of the pension time comes under any comprehensive definition of sickness : the pensioners were declared by a special report of the surgeon, permanently disqualified for labour ; and that not by age alone. for the majority were pensioned between the ages of 50 and 70, but by the mechanical injury of a limb, some infirmity, or a slow but fatal disease. Half the pension time may therefore be safely viewed as sick time.

XIV. Showing the Number of the East India Company's Labourers at several Periods of Age working a complete Year ; the Number attacked by Sickness ; the Days of Sickness experienced ; the Pensioned ; the Pensioners on the List One complete Year. Also the Proportion that annually fall sick or are pensioned out of 100 working ; the Proportion sick of the Class still on the working List ; the average Number of Labourers on the Pension List ; the Proportion of the Living disabled, and either on the Sick or Pension List.

	Labourers employed a complete Year.	Attacks of Sickness.	Days of Sickness.†	Pensioned.	On the Pension List One complete Year.	Out of 100 Men working One Year.		Sick in 100 Workmen.*	Of 100 living.	
						Cases of Sickness.	Pensioned.		On the Pension List.	Sick and on the Pension List.
16—20	138	10·9	152	-	- -	28·5	-	1·10	- -	1·10
20—30	2065	546·5	10,203	4	5·5	26·4	·20	1·36	·27	1·62
30—40	5907·5	1320·5	29,891	13	41	22·4	·22	1·38	·69	2·06
40—50	5703·5	1305·5	30,286	13	72	22·9	·23	1·46	1·25	2·69
50—60	4169·	1020·4	29,183	76	193	24·5	1·82	1·91	4·70	6·58
60—70	1615·5	560	16,284	105	433·5	34·7	6·50	2·76	23·85	26·50
70—80	1316·5	116	3,681	35	201·	36·6	11·06	3·20	46·49	48·78
80—90	23·	1 ?	35 ?	2	21·5	- -	8·70	?	69·65	- -
	19,838	4880·8	119,715	248	973·5	24·6	1·23	1·65	4·79	6·44
						1—4	1—81	1—60	1—21	1—15·5

The proportion attacked by sickness out of 100 men, at each age, working one year, differed inconsiderably between 20 and 60 ; the number pensioned between 20 and 50 was also the same (·0022) ; from 6 to 11 per cent. of the workmen were placed on the pension list between the ages of 60 and 90 ; of the actually working class the sick time increased with age from 1·1 to 3·2 per cent. ; the pensioners at the ages 60–70 formed 24, at 70–80 more than 46 per cent. of the living. The total sick time (including pension time) increased up to 50, in geometrical progression, at the rate of nearly 1-3rd every ten years ; and if half the pension time after 60 be counted as sickness, it rather more than doubled in the subsequent decennial periods. The rate of sickness, including all the pension time under 50 years of age, is much higher than that found by the Highland Society : it lies between the rate assumed by Dr. Price and the observations on the English benefit societies. (See tab. VIII.). There were two years of incapacitation for labour to each death. The deaths were to the sick and pension time as 3·13 to 6·44.

Friendly societies, and companies who, like the East India Company, may deem it prudent to make their men subscribe to a sick and pension fund, will find these tables very valuable. They also throw great light on the state of health prevailing in the metropolis : the mortality and other considerations show that these men, labouring in warehouses in the heart of the city, yet well provided for, occupy, as regards health, a middle point between the worst classes and the inhabitants of the cleaner and less crowded districts. ‡

---

* The expectation of life at the mean age when the 248 men were pensioned was 11·4 years, according to the city table of Mr. Edmonds.

† Obtained by multiplying the mean number working by the days of sickness experienced by one person : this sickness is a fraction higher than that given by Dr. Mitchell, as the days opposite 21—31, &c., in his table were applied to the numbers 20—30, &c., in this. He has improperly compared the 9th instead of the last column with the sickness of the Highland Societies, which comprehended every kind of incapacitation for labour.

‡ In addition to the statements in the report, we have ascertained from Mr. Lewis Leese, the intelligent surgeon who with his father and another surgeon

The comparative health of children in factories could be satisfactorily determined only by an enumeration of the living and sick in the manufacturing and other towns. The following tables by Dr. Mitchell are, however, not uninteresting. In reading them it must be borne in mind that the fourth column does not represent, as stated, the " average duration of sickness per annum for every person employed ; " for the operatives were generally examined at the end of the year, and from their statement of the sickness they had experienced in the preceding year, reported by their employers, this sick time was deduced : a method which would exclude the sickness of all who had died, or been prevented by chronic diseases from resuming their labour. The " number employed " applies solely to the wages ; only a certain proportion of them, not mentioned by Dr. Mitchell, furnished the average rate of sickness. Tables of sickness are given for 8 places ; but the extent of observation in the other places was so small, as to render the results quite irregular, and of no separate value. Through the omission of the number of observations, and of the other data, it is impossible to combine the facts together, so as to obtain a general result.*

XV. Lancashire.

	Males.				Females.			
Age.	Number employed.	Average weekly Wages.	Average Duration of Sickness per Annum for every Person employed.	Average Duration of Sickness per Annum for every Person Sick.	Number employed.	Average weekly Wages.	Average Duration of Sickness per Annum for every Person employed.	Average Duration of Sickness per Annum for every Person Sick.
			Days and Decimal Parts.	Days and Decimal Parts.			Days and Decimal Parts.	Days and Decimal Parts.
		s. d.				s. d.		
Below 11	246	2 3½	2·46	13·04	155	2 4¾	8·03	
11—16	1,169	4 1¾	3·81	14·58	1,123	4 3	4·25	11·98
16—21	736	10 2½	4·42	16·43	1,240	7 3½	5·56	12·63
21—26	612	17 2¼	4·91	18·27	780	8 5	6·85	16·42
26—31	355	20 4½	6·88	22·14	295	8 7¾	8·62	18·51
31—36	215	22 8½	3·85	12·19	100	8 9½	9·29	21·77
36—41	168	21 7¼	4·13	13·75	81	9 8¼	6·16	19·19
41—46	98	20 3¼	5·09	14·25	38	9 3½	14·67	14·41
46—51	88	16 7¼	7·18	30·31	23	8 10	20·34	26·43
51—56	41	16 4	3·47	13·10	4	8 4½	15·75	21·00
56—61	28	13 6½	12·68	11·5	3	6 4	15·75	21·00
61—66	8	13 7	- -	- -	1	6 0		
66—71	4	10 10	- -	- -	1	6 0		
71—76	1	18 0						
76—81	1	8 8						
Totals -	3,770				3,844			

---

attended the East India Company's labourers, that they were selected chiefly between the ages of 25 and 35, when they became ineligible, or only obtained admission by special favour. To keep up a body of 1,984 men, and compensate for the dying, the pensioned, and the discharged, 94 recruits were required every year ; and from a book kept by Mr. Leese, who saw about three-fifths of the whole, it appears that he examined during fifteen years, 1808–1822, 69 annually, about 7·5 per cent. of whom were rejected, chiefly for hernia and varicose veins. For various reasons the Company only took sound healthy men into their service. The diseases in the report were all of a severe nature : when influenza and cholera prevailed, 40 or 50 attended daily at the surgery for coughs and bowel complaints ; but, as in other slight cases, they continued at work, were *favoured* by the *commodore*, and were not entered on the sick list. Venereal complaints were also excluded, as well as accidents from drinking, &c., when their cause was discovered. The old men gave up more readily than men between the ages of 30 and 50. Consumption and pulmonary complaints were very prevalent, so was fever formerly. Consumptive patients remained on the sick list. Some of the men were Irish ; the majority came from the country ; the *alongshore* men were very liable to phthisis.

* Dr. Mitchell is by no means singular in not publishing official observations in their simple form : we need not urge the importance of furnishing the data, whatever they are, of calculations in statistical documents. The *data* are the essential part of a statistical report : the *results* without these are of no weight.

XVI. GLASGOW.

	Males.				Females.			
Age.	Number employed.	Average weekly Wages.	Average Duration of Sickness per Annum for every Person employed.	Average Duration of Sickness per Annum for every Person Sick.	Number employed.	Average weekly Wages.	Average Duration of Sickness per Annum for every Person employed.	Average Duration of Sickness per Annum for every Person Sick.
		s. d.				s. d.		
Below 11	283	1 11¾	1·01	3·61	256	1 10½	2·63	14·90
11—16	1,519	4 7	4·80	12·35	2,162	3 8½	6·18	13·81
16—21	881	9 7	5·52	17·14	2,452	6 2	6·38	15·54
21—26	541	18 6	9·11	20·12	1,252	7 2¼	8·16	18·96
26—31	358	19 11¼	7·05	16·05	674	7 1	7·38	19·81
31—36	331	20 9	7·65	16·93	255	7 4½	6·05	13·05
36—41	279	19 8½	8·50	22·58	218	6 7¾	4·16	16·00
41—46	159	19 6	5·12	16·41	92	6 6	11·94	20·36
46—51	117	19 2	4·84	20·57	41	6 10	11·7½	40·60
51—56	69	17 9¾	4·90	16·41	18	6 1½	16·50	25·85
56—61	45	16 1¼	3·27	8·84	16	6 0	15·0	30·2
61—66	17	17 7	·	·	7	5 5		
66—71	15	15 9¼	·	·	2	4 0		
71—77	11	10 11						
77—81	5	9 6						
81—86								
86—91	1	8 0						
Totals -	4,631				7,445			

The mortality of the English army is higher than the mortality of the general population; and the sickness, including every class of disease, is more than twice as great as that recorded in the preceding tables, at the ages 20–35, which correspond nearly with the ages of the troops. The mean proportion sick per cent. in Ireland (1797–1828), observed on an average force of 36,921 men, amounted to 5·1 [*]; but a certain proportion of the sickness in the army is from syphilis, and this is not included in the other observations.

From 24 monthly Musters, Mr. Finlaison deduced the following Rates of Sickness in the Two Years 1823-4. [†]

	The total Rank and File present or accounted for in 24 monthly Musters.	Sick at the Time the Musters took place.	Sick per Cent.
Cavalry	94,293	3,791	4·02
Foot guards	92,889	3,961	4·26
Infantry	126,513	6,297	4·98
Totals and mean	313,695	14,049	4·48

The sick time in Madras, 1808–9, was 12·4 per cent. of the lifetime. Annesley considered 10 per cent. in that climate healthy; and this appears to be near the mean proportion of European troops constantly sick in the East Indies. In places where the mortality is high, the rate of sickness fluctuates very much from year to year; and, exclusive of losses in battle, the mortality and sickness are tripled or quadrupled in a campaign. This kind of knowledge is still imperfect, although indispensable to those who would employ masses of men with effect in different circumstances.

The army pensioners — the out-pensioners of Chelsea Hospital — besides officers on half-pay, amounted, in 1835–6, to 80,749. They received 1,377,662l. in the year. For the last 10 years they have been equal in numbers to the efficient force of the army; and it is stated that their lives are as long as the lives of men who have never entered the service. A return should be called for of the ages of the pensioners, the ages at which they were pensioned, and the deaths at each age. The greatest ignorance and mismanagement have hitherto prevailed in every department of the pension list.

[*] H. Marshall. *Edinburgh Medical and Surgical Journal.*
[†] Evidence before Select Committee on Friendly Societies, 1825.

MORBILITY; ATTACKS OF SICKNESS.

The sickness to which mankind is liable does not occur at any one time or age, but in an interspersed manner over the lifetime of each person. The constant quantity of sickness is kept up by a succession of diseases attacking the body at intervals and in paroxysms, which, however irregular they appear, in a limited sphere of observation, are really definite in number, and separated by stated spaces As a certain order is preserved in the performances of the healthy functions, so their derangements, in similar circumstances, also observe an order and regularity or succession. To accuse the human frame of perpetual malady is as ridiculous as to attribute, with some theological writers, unintermitting wickedness to the human heart; but if every alteration of the multiplied parts of the human body, every transient trouble of its infinite movements, every indigestion in man, and every fit of hysteria in woman, were reckoned, few days of human life would remain entirely clear; and, if the same scrutiny were extended to the state of the brain, the world may very civilly be sent to Anticyra — *naviget Anticyram.* In determining the amount of sickness, and the attacks of disease, the slighter affections are therefore passed over; as, whatever difference there may be in the representation and expression, it is probable they bear a tolerably constant relation, in the same class of society, to the severer cases recognised, directly diminishing production by arresting labour. The first of the following observations only embraced attacks of an intensity sufficient to prostrate the bodily strength: they relate also to the labouring classes.

	Years of Life.	Attacks of Sickness.	Annual Attacks per Cent.	Mean Duration of each Case.
				Days.
East India Company's labourers, London, 1823-32	19,838	4,880	24·6	24·5
Children between the ages of 5-20 in the Sick Society of Bennet Street School, Manchester, 1830-2 *	2,716	609	22·4	31·2
Artizans and apprentices, Wurzburgh, Germany, mean age 15-35, 1786-1834 †	58,195	13,268	22·8	
Labourers in the British Dockyards.				
Plymouth, 1829-31 ‡ sick?	6,186	2,145	34·7	12·2
Portsmouth, 1830-32, sick		2,250	37·8	12·2
—— hurt		1,001	16·0	15·6
—— sick and hurt	5,939	3,251	53·8	13·2
Sheerness, 1830-32, sick	1,422	622	43·7	
Chatham, 1830-32, only the sick?	3,941	1,939	49·2	11·7
Pembroke, 1830-32, only the sick?	1,338	701	52·4	

	Average Numbers living.	Annual Attacks.	Annual Attacks per Cent.	Mean Duration of Attacks in Days.
Lancashire, working in cotton factories. §				
Males, ages 11-31			27·8	16·43
Females, ages 11-31			41·7	12·63
Glasgow, working in cotton factories.				
Males, ages 11-31			40·3	17·14
Females, ages 11-31			41·3	15·54
Deanston cotton works, 2 years, 1831-2 ‖				
Males	231	46	20·0	
Females	439	196	44·8	
Liverpool Friendly Society, 2 years, 1829-30*	2,307	1,319	57·2	
Self-supporting Dispensary, Burton-upon-Trent, 1835 ¶	2,207	1,131	51·3	

* *Factories' Inquiry Report,* by Dr. B. Hawkins, Supplement, p. i. p. 276.

† *Hecker's Medical Journal,* 1836.

‡ Returns made by E. Jessep, W. Pennell, J. Ward, D. Rowland, W. P. Smith, R. Laws, and R. Tobin, Esquires, pursuant to an order of Admiralty. *Supp. Report, Factories' Inquiry,* p. 54–58.

§ *Dr. Mitchell's Report. Data* not given. Deduced from the *Lancashire and Glasgow Factory Tables,* p.   .

‖ *Factories' Inquiry, Supp. Report,* p. i. p. 80–82. Appendix to evidence taken by Mr. Stuart, a return very judiciously drawn up by the manager, Mr. Smith.

¶ *Dr. Bigsby on Dispensaries.* The Burton-upon-Trent Self-supporting Dispensary included men, women, and children.

Observations of 60 Gaols in England and Wales during 5 Years, 1830-4.	Committed.	Prisoners in the Gaol at the Time of the Returns.	Cases of Sickness.	Deaths.	Annual Cases of Sickness on an average Population of 100.	Annual Deaths out of 100 Prisoners.	Deaths in 100 Cases of Sickness.
20 gaols where the dietary is low	164,714	15,173	6,127	243	40·4	1·60	3·97
20 gaols where the dietary is intermediate	63,440	12,598	11,550	188	93·15	1·52	1·63
20 gaols where the dietary is highest	39,717	7,932	8,937	137	112·7	1·73	1·53
	267,871	35,503	26,614	568	75·0	1·60	2.13
Détenus de la Maison Centrale de Nimes, one year, 1835 *		1,219	1,272	107	101·3	8·77	8·41

		Average Force.	Annual Attacks.	Annual Attacks per cent.
BRITISH TROOPS.				
Corfu, 6 years, 1816-21		1,974	2,350	112
Bengal, 7 yeass, 1826-32		8,700	14,933	173
Fort St. George, Madras Presidency, 4 years, 1827-30		11,820	21,178	179
NATIVE TROOPS.				
Fort St. George, Madras Presidency, 4 years, 1827-30		74,851	39,449	54

The attacks of disease vary in frequency to a great extent in unhealthy and salubrious situations: but the experience of the East India Company's labourers, of the children belonging to the Bennet Street School, which has the best regulated sick society of any in Manchester, and of the artisans of the Trades Club in Wurzburgh, all receiving pay during sickness, and only falling on the funds in cases of some duration and severity, tends to show that 100 of the efficient male population of this country are not liable to more than 25 severe attacks of disease in the year. Each man is liable to a protracted disease, disabling him from work, every four years: this forms one great section of the sickness of the country ; but it does not include syphilis, accidents from fighting and drunkenness, or the many ailments which make men apply for medical advice, while they carry on their occupation, comprising, perhaps, as many more cases of a slighter character, which raise to 50 per cent. the proportion of the population attacked annually. In the Portsmouth dockyard 37·8 per cent. of the men fall ill, 16 per cent. meet with accidents, in the year : besides accidents, the attacks of sickness in Sheerness amounted to 43·7 per cent. The reported attacks of sickness in Sheerness are exclusive of accidents ; and if, as is probable, the same exclusion was made in the other returns, the spontaneous cases amounted to nearly 50 per cent. in Chatham and Pembroke. By excluding the slighter cases, the attacks of sickness may be reduced near the level of the preceding series: in the healthiest dockyard, Plymouth for example, out of 2,147 cases, 635 did not exceed three days' duration ; and, by subtracting these, the proportion attacked in 100 will be reduced from 34·7 to 24·4. Accidents, although excepted here, ought not to be excluded, because they occur as common inevitable causes of disease among all classes of the people, and raise the sickness to a considerable, although varying, extent ; in Portsmouth, the increase of cases from this cause was 42 per cent. Except Plymouth, the dockyards appear to fall somewhat below the national standard of health ; more than 50 in 100 of the men are attacked by sickness of one sort or other annually. In Sheerness, out of 1,422 cases of sickness, 263 were agues, 142 rheumatisms, 68 cholics and cholera. The Report of the Liverpool Society, by the surgeon, Mr. Parr, shows that 57·2 per cent. of the members receive medical advice in the year. Mr. Parr makes a useful distinction between the patients attended at their own houses and those seen at his surgery : the first, not quite comprehending all disabled for work, were 17·8 per cent., nearly a third of all the patients treated. Among 100 members, 8·6 met with accidents

---

* *Annales d'Hygiène*, p. 462. Avril, 1836. There were in this Maison Centrale 24 prisoners between 13 and 16 years of age. The rest were, no doubt, much older than the English prisoners ; which will partly account for the high rate of mortality. The days of sickness amounted to 24.313 ; or 22·3 days each case. During this year cholera was in Nimes. In the 60 English prisons the mean number of annual deaths in the four years 1830, 1831, 1833, 1834, was 101 ; in 1832, the year cholera prevailed, 162 died.

in the year. The return from the Deanston cotton works, in Scotland, after deducting cases of less than three days' duration, makes the annual attacks of sickness among males 20, among females 44·8 per cent. This difference between males and females deserves attention ; it is produced by rheumatisms, diarrhœas, and even wounds, but more particularly by catarrh and headach. The female cases approach the nearest to the total attacks ; as the wages of women are lower, and they give over working abroad on slighter occasions than males. Almost an equal difference is visible in the Lancashire cotton works ; in Glasgow the difference is trifling. Females leave off work, and apply for medical advice, more frequently than males ; but as their mortality between 15 and 40 is but a little higher, the same must hold respecting severe illnesses. The cases observed in factories, only reported on the recollection of the workmen, would very likely include nearly all the serious diseases, and a varying proportion of the slighter distempers which detained them from work. The attacks of sickness among paupers, — the feeble, crippled, maimed, idiotic, crazy, miserable, dirty, dissolute, vicious, unfortunate,—rejected as refuse from all the foregoing classes, are more numerous than the attacks to which select labourers are liable ; and medical men, in undertaking to attend paupers, should bear this in recollection. For the facts relating to English prisoners we are indebted to a highly interesting paper of Mr. Chadwick, in which, by collating the dietaries of 60 prisons in England and Wales, he has rendered it probable that the lowest prison *diet* does not increase sickness. An accurate return of the average population of the prisons, the ages of the prisoners, the diseases and deaths, the amount of labour performed, and information concerning the ventilation of the cells, will, in a few years, settle this question : the average population in this table was assumed to be furnished by the numbers remaining at 5 times in each of the 60 prisons.

We are unacquainted with any data from which the absolute morbility of the British population can be deduced, any more than the mean duration of each case, and the mortality of the sick, with which it is intimately connected. Several interesting observations on distinct classes, and on the morbility, and duration of sickness at different ages, however, exist. At the age of 20 — 50 the duration of each attack among the East India Company's labourers was 22·2 days, and with the pension time 36 days : 7·8 in 100 cases died, or 7·4 exclusive of pensioners. The duration of these cases approaches very near the term of treatment in 14 Paris hospitals, where patients are admitted indiscriminately, and continue till they recover or die ; in 1819—1825, the mean number, 3,947 patients, remained 35 days. In the hospitals of this country, where adults and more chronic cases are received, but at the same time are often sent out before death occurs, the patients continue longer under treatment ; in the county hospitals (31) of Ireland, 38·3 days ; of England, 39·4 days ; of the metropolis 42 days.* Where slighter and ephemeral cases are counted, and organic diseases are excluded, the duration of cases among adults does not, according to the returns from the dockyards, exceed 12 days. In Corfu, 1816–1821, the mean duration of all the diseases (14,098) was 16·1 days.

It is of great importance for medical men to know the average number of deaths in all the cases that come under their care, in order to judge of the remedial influence of medical appliances. The hospitals furnish some, although inadequate information on this head. The sanability of the sick appears to decrease in the large cities ; partly, it may be, because more serious accidents are admitted.

Hospitals.	In-Patients treated in 1 Year.	Mean Number of In-Patients.	Deaths.	Deaths out of 100 Patients.	Deaths in 36·5 Days out of 100 Patients.
Salop, 4 years (1830—33) - -	955	92	34	3·7	3·6
Winchester, 1 year (1833—34) -	798	83	31	3·8	3·7
Salisbury, 1 year (1833—4) - -	894	88	27	3·1	3·1
Chester, 2 years (1833—5) - -	489	45	20	4·2	4·5
Manchester, 1 year (1831—2)† - -	1,784	128	128	7·2	10·0
Liverpool, 1 year (1831)‡ -	1,960	220	109	5·6	5·0
Bristol, 1 year (1828—9) -	1,483	195	160	9·5	8·2
London, 7 hospitals - -	18,740	2,191	1,605	9·0	7·6

* *British Medical Almanac* for 1836.

† Deaths rather higher in 1833–4. In the 80 years, 1752—1832, only 4·93 per cent. of the patients died.

‡ *Factories' Inquiry, Sup.*, p. 306. The other facts are from the *British Medical Almanac.*

These observations are in conformity with what is seen in other hospitals: the deaths among the patients in the London hospitals agree very nearly, when the time is the same (36 days), with the deaths among the London labourers (7·5 : 7·8), and the ratio of their ages is not very different. The deaths in 100 attacks were, among the Bennet Street Scholars 4·24; the Wurzburgh artisans, 3·33; the British troops in Corfu, 2·3; in Fort St. George, 2·7; in Bengal, 3·3; the native troops, Fort St. George, 2·6; while the deaths out of 100 living in these places were respectively 0·95, 0·76, 2·74, 4·8, 5·7, 1·4. The higher absolute mortality produced by external causes is due in part to the increased number of attacks, and in part to the greater fatality of the cases. * In like manner the sick time is augmented principally by the attacks, and but slightly by the cases lasting longer.

Men placed in the same circumstances appear equally liable to an attack of sickness between 11 and 60 years of age; 100 of the London labourers, in each of the decennial periods, 20–30, 30-40, 40-50, 50-60, had nearly 23·5 attacks of sickness annually; the highest number was 26·4, the lowest 22·4. A closer agreem   ld not, considering the extent of observation, and all accessory circumstances, .   . pected. A greater number of cases appear under 30, and as age advances; because, as Mr. Leese, when questioned, informed us, old and young men were placed on the sick list for slighter ailments than men between 30 and 50; and this is confirmed by the fatality of the cases at these early and late ages not being proportionally great. The proportion of attacks (Table 14. col. 7.) was deduced from the men on the working list; it should have been calculated from all the men living †, including pensioners, and this would have raised the proportion of attacks after 40; for the proposition is, that 100 men aged 30 will suffer in the same circumstances as many attacks of disease as 100 men aged 50 or 60; and the 100 men embrace the sick, pensioned, or disabled, which become more numerous as age advances. Collected for another purpose, the Factories' Returns of sickness, notwithstanding the irregularity resulting necessarily from limited observations and defects which pervade equally the whole series, exhibit between 11–31 but inconsiderable oscillations in the number of attacks, whether among males or females. Out of eight series of tables we select those founded on the greatest number of facts. ‡

Attacks of Illness in each Quinquennial Period of Age, indicated by the Interval between each Attack.

Ages.	Lancashire.		Glasgow.	
	Males.	Females.	Males.	Females.
11—16	3·8 years	2·8 years	2·6 years	2·2 years
16—21	3·7 —	2·3 —	3·1 —	2·4 —
21—26	3·7 —	2·4 —	2·2 —	2·3 —
26—31	3·2 —	2·1 —	2·3 —	2·4 —

The mean duration of each case increases as age advances. So if we take in the pension time under 60, inasmuch as the greater part of it legitimately appertains to the antecedent attack, the mean duration of each case among the East India Company's labourers was in the four decennial periods 20–60 respectively 22·5, 33·9, 47·7, 98·8 days. In all the Factory Returns, the duration of the cases increases in like manner, although, for obvious reasons, not so fast,

The mortality among the attacked augments with age at the same rate as the mortality among the entire number living. Out of 100 attacked in each of the three decennial periods (Table II.), 20-50, the deaths were respectively 2·9, 6·5, 10·4; the deaths out of 100 labourers, whether sick or healthy, were, in the same periods, 0·82, 1·48, 2·43. The rate of increase was nearly the same.

The sick time increases with age in a geometrical progression (see Tables VIII. IX. &c.). If, therefore, the number of attacks at each age be the same, the duration of

---

* It must always be recollected that the army observations comprise every case treated; half of which probably would not throw a man on a sick pension fund; so to compare them with the latter, the deaths should be divided by about half the cases. To obtain a rough approximation, therefore, multiply the above army deaths in 100 cases by 2.

† The difference below 50 is trifling; the observation was imperfect, and could only have been calculated on the living by hypothesis.

‡ Deduced from Tables 13, 14.

each attack will increase in the same ratio; and conversely if the duration of the cases and the sick time augment at the same rate, the number of attacks at every age will be equal. Any two of the elements being given, the third may always be deduced from them. Again, if the mortality of the attacked increase at the same rate as the mortality of the entire population, the proportion attacked at every age will be the same. Among the London labourers the mortality between 30-40, 40-50, was 1·48, 2·43 in 100 living; the mortality among 100 attacked was 6·5, 10·4. Now 1·48 is to 2·43 very nearly as 6·5 is to 10·4; and it results from this that the attacks, whatever their absolute number may be, whether 22 or 52, were the same in both periods. The deaths below apply equally to the attacks and to the living: they apply, however high the absolute number of attacks be raised, provided it be raised to the same degree in both periods; but cease to apply if the number of attacks in each period be different.

Ages.	Mean Number living.	Annual Attacks.	Annual Deaths.
30—40	100	22	1·48
40—50	100	22	2·43

We pass over several important applications of these facts to practical medicine, and to practical statistics, where, as in trigonometry, two of the elements of calculation can frequently be measured when the third is inattainable; expressing a hope, however, that they may be made available in the next census to throw much light on the sanatory state of different classes of the population.

Mr. Edmonds first showed, from tables published by Dr. Southwood Smith, that the mortality of the fever patients in the London Fever Hospital between 15—60 increased every year at a rate measured by a constant (1·03) discovered by him, and applied to the construction of tables of mortality; he also first announced, that if the mortality of all patients increased in the same ratio, the number attacked at each age between 15 and 60 must be the same; and moreover, that as the amount of sick time increases as the mortality, the duration of each case will increase in the same ratio.*

External circumstances have the greatest influence in augmenting the attacks of diseases; age and the internal state of the body determine their mortality and duration. When the people of this country are placed amidst destructive agencies, these, like balls in battle, carry them off, by attacking a greater number; they also add to the fatality of the attack; but after a man is seized, age and vital tenacity, exclusively of medicine, are the great modifiers on which his life and sufferings depend. In epidemics the attacks generally become much more fatal at the same time that they are more numerous.

DISEASES.

" *Mille mali species, mille salutis erunt.*"

The diseases which constitute the sickness, disable, and carry off the people of this country, in the midst of their life, form the next section of this investigation. Man's body is compounded of many parts, performing many offices, so diversified in nature that there is, perhaps, no extensive train of phenomena in the universe that does not find its counterpart in his organization; crowned with other and higher faculties of sense and intellect, far removed from any thing observed in inorganic matter. This complexity and completeness of the human body almost justified the ancient opinion " that man was microcosmus, — an abstract or model of the world." For, dust and ashes as it is, who can survey the ruins of the human frame, the bare skeleton to

---

* *Lancet*, vol. i. 1835-6, p. 855. The rate of sick time rises among the London labourers at the rate indicated by the above constant (1 343 in 10 years); so consequently does the duration of the cases up to 50; when another constant takes its place, and the sickness is doubled (2·15 decennial constant from the age of 50) every ten years. The mortality of the cases, and of the living, increases in a more rapid progression even than in the general population of London; this is due probably to the selection at 20—35.

which it is at last reduced, and in clothing it with muscle and tendon, artery and vein, delicate and incessant chemical action, forces adjusted for circulating fluids, and producing motion, sight, and all sense,—affection, passion, thought,—the history of all it may have done and suffered,—without feeling that a world wrecked in space — a planet in all its aberrations — offers a less interesting spectacle than the phenomena manifested by the human body in its progress to death !

With whatever precision the inquiries in which we have hitherto been engaged may measure the magnitude of the national loss by sickness, in seeking remedies a careful examination of the derangements and distempers to which the variable composition of man's body has made it accessible is required; for disease and death come not in one form or garb, nor can they be arrested in one way : " this subject of man's body," Lord Bacon truly observes, " is of all other things in nature most susceptible of remedy, but then that remedy is most susceptible of error."

The first and most important statistical division of diseases is into epidemics, which attack and often destroy in a short time great numbers of people; endemics, such as marsh fevers, confined to particular localities; and sporadic affections, occurring in an isolated manner, under the ordinary atmospherical influences. The epidemics of this country we have not space to examine here ; so we pass at once to the endemics.

ENDEMICS.

The medical topography of England is yet imperfect; but the Provincial Medical Association is now diligently prosecuting this important part of medical inquiry, to which their attention was specially directed in an able paper by Dr. Conolly. The last volumes of the Transactions contain some good topographical articles; that of Dr. Forbes on the Land's End, to which we shall again have occasion to refer, is distinguished for the comprehensiveness, candour, and good sense with which it is drawn up. From the volumes of the association before us, and other sources of information, it does not appear that at present any special endemic prevails in England. Agues are frequent in the marshy districts of the low eastern coast, in Lincoln, in Essex, in Kent, and in Cambridgeshire. The mortality of the latter county, in which the agricultural is 61 per cent. of the total population, rises very high; the marshy isle of Ely making it one of the most unhealthy counties in England. The mortality does not fall particularly on infancy, as M. Villermé inferred, from the error committed by Mr. Rickman, in calculating, against every principle of statistics, tables of mortality, for each county, from the deaths only, The mortality at several intervals of age, calculated from the numbers living and the deaths in the marshy and other counties, may be compared in the table, p. 570.

Wen, *Derbyshire neck*, or bronchocele, exists all over England to a greater or less extent. It is not frequent, except in some of the close valleys, surrounded by hills : from its having been common in Derbyshire, the *Derbyshire* neck designates the peculiar disease in this country. Besides the thyroid gland, this affection involves the brain and the organs of sense : in the Valais, and on both sides the Alps, bands of idiotic Cretins are seen, who almost form a distinct variety in our race. The disease has rarely been carried to this extent in England; moreover, in iodine, medical men have now an almost unfailing remedy for the early stages of bronchocele, as well as for scrofula.

COMMON DISEASES.

Sporadic diseases are the great class of isolated disorders, attacking not by sudden outbreaks, but regularly and constantly a certain proportion of the living. Inflammation of the lungs, consumption, apoplexy, cataract, are examples. No definite line separates them from epidemics and endemics. To discover their relative frequency, and the share each particular malady has in the sum of constant sickness, it is not enough to resort to the bills of mortality ; for these only record fatal diseases, taking no notice of the slighter affections, which partially or entirely render a man unequal to his duties : besides, the proportion of deaths from two kinds of disease is rarely, if ever, the same as the relative frequency of their attacks. The deaths induced by consumption, by inflammation of the lungs, and by measles, furnish no direct index of the numbers attacked by these maladies.

Again, in estimating the prevalence of diseases, two things must be distinctly considered; the relative frequency of their attacks, and the relative proportion of sick time they produce. The first may be determined at once, by a comparison of the number of attacks with the numbers living; the second, by enumerating several times the living and the actually sick of each disease, and thence deducing the mean proportion suffering constantly. Time here is taken into account: and the sick time, if the attacks of two diseases be equal, will vary as their duration varies, and whatever the number of attacks may be, multiplying them by the mean duration of each disease will give the sick time.

In Paris the mean duration of fatal cases of cholera was 2 days 13 hours and 8 minutes; 18,400 cases occurred which ended in death; probably an equal number recovered after being ill a week: the entire sick time induced by cholera was, therefore, about 158,118 days, which, divided by the population (774,338) gives less than 5 hours' sickness for each person. The cholera sickness amounted through the year to no more than ·00056 constantly sick. This distinction is of vast importance; for the constantly sick, contributing nothing to their own subsistence, and requiring the care of others, bear with a heavy weight on the community, and when the diseases are chronic only prolonged pains and gloomy prospects brood over the sufferers. For this reason, where the conditions of existence are unfavourable, and a great proportion of the people are weak, sickly, and doomed to untimely death, a sudden epidemic cuts short their agonies, and purifies the race: it is an amputation of members already gangrened, and falling off by inches; at the same time, however, it carries off a great number of the healthy. If those who had cholera in Paris had been seized by consumption, they would have endured 73,600 years of sickness instead of 158,118 days: the living in the epidemics of the middle ages could not have watched the sick if their diseases had been protracted. In this sense only, epidemics can be looked upon as merciful visitations of Providence, for moderating evils self-inflicted on mankind. The comparative prevalence of diseases, of which medical men speak in their writings, seems to involve a compound notion, including the attacks and their duration. As there are few statistical data for determining the relative prevalence of each form of disease, we have only some general remarks to offer.

Insanity has been said to be on the increase in this country. Dr. Powell, secretary to the commissioners for licensing madhouses, showed that the number of lunatics confined in private asylums in England augmented in eight quinquennial periods (1775–1814) from 1,783 to 3,647; and thence deduced the above inference. Willan, Bateman, and Burrows held an opposite opinion. Notwithstanding the returns made to the House of Commons, the data necessary to determine the prevalence of insanity are yet imperfect. Sir A. Halliday, who has collected much information on the subject, states, as the last results of his inquiries, the following facts : —

	Lunatics.	Idiots.	Total Insane.	Proportion of the Population.
England	6,806	5,741	12,547	1 in 1,000
Naval Asylum, Haslar, and the Military Asylum, Chatham	. .	. .	277	
Wales	153	763	896	1 — 800
Scotland	. .	. .	5,659	1 — 574
			19,372	

For deficiencies in the returns, he thinks the total number insane in South Britain should be raised to 16,500. Of the insane enumerated in England, 11,000 are paupers, maintained principally at the expense of parishes. The insane are more numerous in agricultural than in manufacturing districts; they are also more numerous in Scotland than in England.

	Population.	Insane.	Proportion.
12 agricultural counties - . . -	2,012,979	2,526	1 to 820
12 manufacturing or mining counties . . -	4,493,194	3,910	1 — 1,200

Do these returns prove that the tendency to insanity is greatest in agricultural districts? We do not think they do. It is doubtful whether the greater proportion of idiots, indicated by the returns, proves that proportionally more idiots are *born* in the country, in Wales, or in Scotland, than in London. The number of idiots living at any one time depends on the duration of their life, as well as on the proportion born: if the Welsh idiots live twice as long as the idiots born in London, twice as many would enter into Sir A. Halliday's enumeration, although the tendency to idiocy was the same in either place. In Wales, and remote villages, the idiot lodges in a cottage, and, supported by the parish, is the qualified butt, and of course the favourite, of the neighbourhood: in towns, he would have more difficulty to survive the nursing in a workhouse. An idiot, Jack of Pool, in Montgomeryshire, lately died, aged 109: he lived near the residence of old Parr, and was clothed by a neighbouring lord, who secured his vote at every election. If we exclude congenital idiots, and only calculate the proportions insane, it is likely that the tendency to madness would be found greater in towns than in the country, — in England than in Wales and Scotland. If lunatics in this and other countries be now better treated than formerly, — and this is incontestibly the case, — their life is necessarily prolonged; and the proportion to the population is increased, although the tendency to insanity may be diminished. The horrible dens in which lunatics were formerly lodged must have greatly diminished their numbers. The number of lunatics, members of the Society of Friends, in the Retreat, near York, has been of late years 64; the mean annual admissions 1812—33 were 15·2 *; and the Quakers in England do not exceed 23,000: consequently out of 10,000 of that body 7 become insane every year, and 28 are constantly in the asylum. But as it appears, from the report of Mr. Tuke, that more than 6 months elapse after the attack before the patient enters the asylum, while 14 per cent. quit the Retreat unrelieved, at least 6 more lunatics out of the asylum must be added to the 28 confined; which will make the insane amongst the Quakers 3·4 per 1000. Is not this a nearer approximation to the insane among the richer classes in England than the calculation of Sir A. Halliday, founded on imperfect parliamentary returns? The Swedish returns of the insane are the only ones obtained in a proper form; they may be recommended to the attention of those called to procure another return for the House of Commons.

Consumption is a disease in which the lungs are principally affected: it begins with a change in the constitution, followed by the deposit of a cheese-like matter, forming tubercles in the lungs, and other parts, ending in ulceration: when this tuberculous matter is deposited in the glands of the neck, and in the bones and joints, it constitutes scrofula; in the glands of the abdomen, mesenteric disease; neither of which affections differs from consumption in its essential anatomical cause. Foreign writers appear to think this disease more prevalent in England than on the Continent; a prejudice probably derived from statistical reports ill understood. Dr. Young and Dr. Woolcombe calculated, from bills of mortality, that in England and Ireland consumption causes one fourth part of the deaths. Dr. Clark believes that, after deducting the deaths in early infancy, a third part of the mortality in this country arises from tuberculous diseases. It is the opinion of this eminent physician, whose opportunities of observation have been very extensive, that consumption and scrofula are stationary among the labouring classes of the country. "But," he adds, "whether tuberculous diseases have diminished or not during the last century among the labouring part of our population, I am of opinion that they have increased in the middle and upper ranks." † The number of children reared has doubled within the last century, and the mortality between 20 and 30 appears on the increase; so that, unless the hygienic precautions, very ably enforced by Dr. Clark, be followed, it is not improbable that an increase of weakly bodies and of consumption may be observed.

Stone. — Mr. Smith of Bristol, and Dr. Yellowly, have bestowed great pains in forming a statistical account of calculous diseases. According to the estimate of Dr. Yellowly, 111 persons are cut every year in England and Wales for stone in the bladder: of these 15½ cases occur among the inhabitants of Norfolk and Suffolk,

---

* *A Treatise on Insanity*, by J. C. Prichard, p. 145. A few of the lunatics admitted at the Retreat were apparently not Quakers; but these would not compensate for cases of a mild character never sent to the asylum. See also, pp. 198—201., and pp. 328—351.

† *A Treatise on Pulmonary Consumption*, by J. Clark, M.D. F.R.S., p. 10.

and 31 in London. This will be seen, and the proportion to the population, in the following table. *

TABLE.

Place.	Number of Stone Cases.	Cases per Annum.	Comparative Frequency.
Norfolk, including Norwich	575	10·26	1 in 34,000
Norfolk, excluding Norwich	447	7·98	1 — 38,100
Suffolk		5·26	1 — 44,000
London		31·	1 — 38,000
Adjacent counties		16·	1 — 76,000
England and Wales		111·	1 — 108,000
England and Wales, excluding Norfolk and Suffolk		95·5	1 — 118,000
Bristol and Liberties	173	2·1	1 — 41,000
Bristol county district	181	2·2	1 — 340,000
Scotland		8·	1 — 250,000
Dundee	26	·86	1 — 41,300

The *venereal disease* has diminished in intensity, if not in the frequency of its onsets ; it is now, certainly, never communicated by the breath, as it is reported to have been in the fifteenth century. A mild treatment suffices to effect the cure of its common forms, and mercury is no longer employed to an enormous and noxious extent. Syphilis was at first confounded with leprosy ; and its virulent eruptions on the skin, aggravated, like other skin diseases, by the filth and vitiated health of the people at the time it became exceedingly prevalent, have subsided into milder forms. The skin diseases, designated leprosy in the middle ages, for the reception (not the cure) of which so many hospitals were erected, survive in the itch, and a few, but not very malignant, eruptions. An able writer in the *British and Foreign Medical Review* † says, " Herpes zoster (shingles) is seldom, in truth, here thought of any importance, although the details of many continental authors abound with descriptions which plainly connect it with formidable constitutional disease. The same, and perhaps a greater degree of violence of character, will be found to prevail in cases of herpes in unhealthy localities, where the people are miserably fed and hardly worked. We see in the descriptions of Alibert, and the author before us, as well as in many others, accounts of almost all diseases of the skin so widely different from any which are observed in the British Islands, that we doubt and occasionally deny their identity." The common acne of the chin, on a part covered with hair, becomes a frightful disease in France. Among the better classes of society in England, if we except lepra, impetigo is more frequently seen than any other skin disease. Scald head and itch are the most frequent among the dirty children of paupers.

FATAL DISEASES, AND THE CAUSES OF DEATH.

Violent death takes place in a thousand forms : but it may generally be referred to obstructed respiration, as in hanging, drowning, suffocation ; to loss of blood, as in severe wounds, hæmorrhage, rupture of vessels ; to destruction of structure, and a shock, as in falls, blows on the head or spinal marrow, contusions, gunshot wounds; and to devitalisation, if the word may be used, by prussic acid, mental emotion, lightning. Death in its most common form is the effect of disease in the brain and spinal marrow, the blood, the lungs, the heart and blood-vessels, the bowels. Fever, inflammation, and various morbid products, infect the whole system, and prove fatal sometimes by the mechanical injury they do, but more frequently by an alteration of the chemical, physical, and vital processes. Persons die of inflammation in the stomach before its structure is disorganised : fever is at times fatal without producing any essential lesion of a vital part : cholera, plague, and other epidemics, extinguish existence as rapidly as poison.

In presenting a tabular view of fatal diseases, it is desirable on many accounts to arrange them in groups, related as regards their locality, and their essential forms or phenomena. To examine them in these two points of view, we have classified the

---

* Remarks on the Tendency to Calculous Disorders, by J. Yellowly, M.D. The subject is difficult ; but it has been skilfully handled by Mr. Smith and Dr. Yellowly, and every effort was made to obtain the numbers occurring in each particular locality. — (*Trans. of Royal Society*, 1829, p. 1. 55.)

† No. 3., Review of M. Rayer on Diseases of the Skin, p. 149.

several observations (1.) according to the organs or systems of organs implicated; and (2.) according to the special nature of the disease. But with the London bills of mortality a different arrangement was necessary: without following any classification, we have placed infantile diseases, eruptive fevers, plague and fevers, diseases of the bowels, and diseases most resembling each other in their essential phenomena, in the same group. This was necessary, as the nomenclature necessarily varied in the course of two centuries, and the same disease passed under another title. The names of diseases, although derived generally from some very striking feature in the case, are not unfrequently vague and obsolete, so that it is only by a careful study of the contemporary writers that any hope of interpreting them can be entertained.

Col. A. in the annexed table is deduced from 65,706 observations made in the 7 years, 1629-1635, the first published: col. B. from 426,253 diseases recorded in the 20 years, 1660-1679, a period made the subject of Sydenham's immortal works: col. C. from 732,873 deaths occurring in the 30 years, 1728-1757: cols. D. and E. are in great part from Mr. Milne's work on Annuities: col. F. presents the results of the five last bills (1831-5), and the actual fatal diseases of London, so far as they are exhibited by the present system of registration. It is calculated on 118,895, the total deaths, exclusive of the still-born.

XVII. Table of the fatal Diseases of London for the last Two Centuries; showing, in 1,000 Deaths, the Proportion by each particular Disease.* (See next page.)

Some of the terms in this table require explanation. The moldshot head, or horseshoe head, was a chronic form of water on the brain (hydrocephalus); but under the name of dropsy or sometimes inflammation on the brain, the acute stage of this disease, before deformity supervenes, is now registered. It is really inflammation of the brain in scrofulous children. Livergrown was applied to the swelling of the abdomen, the liver, and spleen, occurring in children after intermittents.† Rickets, a form of scrofula, is now exceedingly rare. Sydenham acutely remarks, that the true rickets rarely happen, except in those years when autumnal intermittents prevail‡: livergrown and rickets, apparently confounded at first, disappeared from the bills with the reign of intermittent fevers. Croup and hooping cough are increasing rapidly, if they were not formerly mixed up with convulsions, which took the place of chrisomes, in expressing the undefined diseases of infancy. The common diseases of childhood are irritation of the mucous membranes, inflammation, and scrofula. § Tubercles are rare in the first year; between the ninth and tenth year of age, M. Papavoine found tubercles in 70 per cent. of the children that died in the Hôpital des Enfans Malades in Paris. They were, doubtless, equally frequent in London.

Scarlet fever was at first confounded with measles; it was joined, in 1731, with fever, and only made a separate item in 1831. Griping, twisting of the guts, bloody flux, and plague in the guts, were the homely Saxon synonyms of dysentery. *Surfeit*, with respect to its symptoms, resembled *cholera morbus*, which, raging epidemically in August, was attributed by the vulgar to eating too much fruit. Stopping of the stomach is the iliac or cœliac passion, "which," says Sydenham, "deserves to be enumerated among the symptoms consequent upon fevers." Its great frequency (1629-79) was probably owing to contraction of the bowel after fever and dysentery. No commentator on the bills of mortality has been able to explain the great mortality attributed to *rising of the lights*; Sydenham, however, solves the question, in

---

* Column C. was calculated by Mr. Corbyn Morris; it includes, as well as col. B., the still-born: to compare these columns, therefore, strictly, with cols. A., D., E., F., from which the still born were excluded, the items of col. B. must be raised 1-36th, of col. C. 1-42d. Col. E. is from Mr. Milne's work on annuities; who, it will be perceived did not calculate the minor items.

† *Sydenham's Works*, vol. i. p. 102-10.

‡ Ibid. vol. i. p. 104.

§ *Traité des Maladies des Enfans.* Par C. Billard.

	A. 7 Years, 1629–35.	B. 20 Years, 1660–79.	C. 30 Years, 1728–57.	D. 10 Years, 1771–80.	E. 10 Years, 1801–10.	F. 5 Years, 1831–35.
Abortives and stillborn	-	26·8	23·0	-	-	-
Chrisomes	247·7	36·1	-	-	-	-
Overlaid	1·1	2·8	-	·2	'	-
Convulsions	22·2	77·8	277·0	271·0	-	92·6
Worms	2·7	1·5	0·5	·3	-	·2
Teething	49·7	54·0	50·0	36·0	-	14·1
Inflammation of the brain						5·7
Mold-shot head, dropsy on the brain	-	0·4	4·0	1·0	-	33·2
Rickets	1·0	17·6	2·0	·1	-	-
Livergrown	8·5	0·9	0·2	·05		
Canker, thrush	3·3	3·4	4·3	3·8	-	4·4
Croup						5·8
Chin-cough	*	1·2	5·2	17·3	-	39·5
The above infantile diseases	336·2	195·7	343·2	329·75	270·3	195·3
Smallpox	37·8	50·9	80·0	100·3	69·5	26·9
Measles	3·3	5·8	7·0	9·5	32·1	27·0
Swine-pox, chicken-pox, rash	·6	·1	1·01	·1		
St. Anthony's fire, or erysipelas	-	0·06	0·1	·1	-	2·9
Fever, scarlet						16·7
Fever	127·1	95·9	148·3	124·1	89·9	33·8
intermittent						·8
spotted	9·0	11·1				
Plague	25·0	161·7				
Griping of the guts, colic, twisting, wind	2·2	102·5	9·0	2·3		0·4
Bloody flux, flux	42·5	6·7	1·4	1·0	·3	
Cholera morbus or surfeit	12·6	18·5	0·1	0·5		42·3
Vomiting and looseness, diarrhœa	0·3	1·6	0·6	·3		1·4
Stopping of the stomach	·3	12·6	5·0	·6		
Constipation						1·0
Rupture	·6	1·3	0·7	·5	-	1·2
Quinsey, sore throat	·8	1·5	0·7	1·0	-	1·5
Cough and cold	5·1			0·2		
Pleurisy	2·8	0·7	2·0	1·0	1·3	12·1
Influenza						1·2
Inflammation			2·0	6·2	34·5	96·0
of bowels, stomach						15·2
Indigestion						0·3
Disease of the heart						5·4
Asthma and tissick			21·0	17·1	30·3	42·4
Consumption	201·1	153·4	170·0	224·3	243·5	177·2
King's evil	2·7	2·4	1·0	1·0	-	0·9
Fistula	2·6	2·1	0·5	·2	-	0·1
Stricture						0·7
French pox	1·5	3·0	3·0	3·1	-	0·2
Cancer			2·0	3·4	-	4·4
Sores, ulcers	2·4	2·6	1·0	·8		
Mortification	-	v. fistula	9·0	9·9	-	10·6
Abcess, imposthume	17·3	5·0	1·0	·2	-	6·6
Tumour				·1		1·2
Scald head, itch, leprosy	†	†	0·4	·2		
Scurvy	0·4	2·6	0·1	·2		
Gravel, stone, strangury	5·0	3·0	1·0	1·9	-	0·9
Gout, sciatica	·3	0·6	2·0	3·1	4·5	3·1
Rheumatism						1·7
Jaundice	6·5	3·7	5·0	5·8	-	2·1
Liver disease			·-			12·8
Diabetes			0·06	·05		0·3
Dropsy	29·7	42·6	41·0	45·1	44·5	37·6
on the chest						4·0
Bleeding piles	0·4	0·1	·2	·4	-	2·0
Apoplexy	2·5	3·7	9·0	11·1	16·6	18·5
suddenly	6·7					
Palsy, lethargy	2·8	2·0	2·3	3·7	6·5	8·6
Spleen and vapours	-	·3	0·05			
Green sickness			·002			
Rising of the lights and mother	8·3	9·1	0·5	·02		
Grief	1·7	·6	0·4	·2		
Fright	·03	·1				
Falling sickness	·6	·06	·01	-	-	1·5
Jawfallen	1·1	·02	-	-	-	·2
Spasm						2·9
Blasted, planet-struck	·8	·1				
Calenture, megrims	·4	·2				
Headach			0·03	·05		
Lunacy	·5	·4	3·0	2·7	-	7·6
Hydrophobia				·03	-	·2
Various	·4	·8	-	·02		
Old age, bedridden	74·1	47·4	78·0	64·7	81·8	111·5
Unknown causes	-	-				27·4
Found dead	1·9	·4	-	·3	-	·3
Visitation of God	-	-	-	•	-	1·8
Starved	-	·04	-	·2	-	·01
Killed by drinking to excess	-	-	-	·3	-	·4
Suicide	·7	·7	-	1·6	1·93	2·2
Drowned	3·8	3·3	-	5·8	6·65	5·0
Smothered	·6	·1	-	·3	-	0·04
Burned	·6	·4	-	·6		
Poisoned	·03	·1	-	·06		0·3
Killed	5·4	2·8	-	3·1		
Accidents	-	-	-	·3	-	7·4
Murdered	·3	·6	-	·3	-	·17
Executed	1·6	·8	-	1·1	-	·16
Total of the above casualties	14·9	9·2	16·0	14·0	17·2	17·78
Childbed and miscarriage	16·1	12·2	8·0	9·4	10·9	13·4

* Perhaps cough and cold should come in this place.
† Under " Various."

treating of this distemper under hysteria, which, as it simulates, was confounded in females with almost every other disease. Diseases of childbed, often accompanied with hysterical symptoms, were evidently reported under this title. *

The preceding table, founded on the deaths, only indicates the relative mortality produced by different classes of disease. The following table expresses the liability of the living to death by all the great classes of diseases during 6 periods of the last two centuries. The first and most difficult step here was to determine the absolute rate of mortality in the 6 periods. The population in the liberties of London, enumerated in 1631, was 130,178; the deaths in the liberties during the 8 years, 1628-35, were 54,299, of which 1-24th were still-born : excluding these, the annual mortality was 5 per cent. This represents the mortality of years free from pestilence, but not the absolute mortality of the period, which, for the 24 years, 1620-43, was 7 per cent. Column A. shows, therefore, the fatality of diseases in years intercurrent between epidemic years. Column B. is an approximation to the mortality and diseases of London in the middle ages, although it includes 14 years subsequent to the great fire, and to the last epidemic. † The mortality of London in the 17th century did not differ very sensibly, before the French revolution, from the mortality in the current years, 1629-35 : the mean expectation of life at birth, 1728-37, was calculated by Mr. Simpson to be 19 2 years; while in the 10 years, 1771-80, it was 19·6 by Dr. Price's 16th table. Nearly 5·2 and 5·1 deaths happened annually out of 100 persons living. The mortality of London in 1801-10 had considerably diminished, and was estimated by Mr. Milne to be 1-34·19 annually — 2·92 per cent. ‡ The annual deaths in the 18 years, 1813-30, are stated by Mr. Edmonds at 2·82 per cent. ; and as the deaths reported in the bills, 1831-5, were 1-8th more than the deaths in the 5 years preceding, the mortality has been assumed to be 3·2 per cent. in this period, including an epidemic year.

III. Table showing the mean annual Number of Deaths in London produced by 20 Classes of Disease out of 100,000 living.

By	A. 1629—35.	B. 1660—79.	C. 1728—57.	D. 1771—80.	E. 1801—10.	F. 1831—5.
Chrisomes, overlaid, convulsions, worms, teething, mold-shot head, dropsy on the head, inflammation of brain, rickets, livergrown, canker, thrush, croup, hooping cough	1,681	1,591	1,827	1,682	789	625
Smallpox	189	417	426	502	204	83
Measles	16	47	37	48	94	86
Scarlet fever	-	-	-	-	-	53
Fever	636	785	785	621	264	111
spotted	45	90				
Plague	125	1,223				
Dysentery	221	894	50	17	1	1
Surfeit or cholera	63	148	1	-	-	135
Inflammation	-	-	10	31	101	307
Pleurisy	14	6	10	5	4	39
Asthma and tissick	-	-	112	85	89	136
Consumption	1,021	1,255	905	1,121	716	567
King's evil, scrofula	14	19	5	5		3
Dropsy	146	349	218	225	131	133
Apoplexy and suddenly	47	30	48	55	49	59
Palsy and lethargy	14	17	12	18	19	28
Old age, bedridden	370	388	415	324	241	357
Casualties	65	76	85	70	40	57
Childbed and miscarriages	80	100	43	47	32	43
Unknown causes	-	-	-	-	-	88
Other diseases	253	565	211	144	146	289
Deaths in 100,000 living	5,000	8,000	5,200	5,000	2,920	3,200

* *Sydenham's Works*, vol. ii. pp. 103-114.

† The enumeration of 1631 was published by Graunt in the Appendix to his observations under the title " Anno 1631, ann. 7 Caroli I. The Number of Men, Women, and Children, in the several Wards of London, and Liberties, taken in August, 1631, by special Command from the Right Honourable the Lords of His Majesty's Privy Council." The results agree remarkably with the later enumerations, three of which, 1801, 1811, and 1821, make the population of the liberties of London (97 parishes within and 16 parishes without the walls) 130,100, including a correction for seamen and strangers. Without correction, the population, in 1831, was 123,683. The enumeration of 1631 has, therefore, been made the basis

‡ *Treatise on Annuities, &c.*, by Mr. Milne, vol. ii. p. 428.

REMARKS.

1. The diseases of London in the 16th century still prevail in unhealthy climates: not only the diseases and the manner of death have changed in this metropolis, but the frequency and fatality of the principal diseases have diminished.

2. The reported cases of fever, plague, cholera, and dysentery, constituted 4-10ths (·396) of the diseases: they destroyed annually, on an average, 31 per 1,000 of the inhabitants; five times as many as are now carried off by consumption.

3. *Fever, plague,* and *dysentery,* were most fatal to adults; but they of course carried off a considerable number of children. Convulsions, and other diseases of infancy, did not decline till the 18th century. The diseases of adults first diminished in violence; and as the state of the city and medical knowledge improved, the diseases of infants decreased.

4. *Smallpox* attained its maximum mortality after inoculation was introduced. The annual deaths of smallpox registered 1760-79, were 2,323; in the next 20 years, 1780-99, they declined to 1,740: this disease, therefore, began to grow less fatal before vaccination was discovered; indicating, together with the diminution of fever, the general improvement of health then taking place. In 1771-80, not less than 5 in 1,000 died annually of smallpox; in 1801-10 the mortality sank to 2; and in 1831-5 to 0·83.

5. *Measles* became gradually more general in the 18th century; but in 1801-1810, after vaccination was introduced, twice as many died of measles as had died of this exanthem in 1771-80. If scarlet fever and measles, however, have somewhat increased in frequency, the mortality of the three diseases, smallpox, measles, scarlet fever, is only half as great (·0022) as the mortality formerly occasioned by smallpox alone (·005).

6. *Fever,* exclusively of the plague, has progressively subsided: since 1771, *fever has declined nearly in the same ratio as smallpox.* In the 3 latter periods of the table the deaths from fever decreased as 621 : 264 : 114; from smallpox as 502 : 204 : 83.

7. *Cholera morbus* was as fatal in 1660-79 as in 1831-5: in 1831-5 out of 1,000, but 1·35 are stated to have died of cholera; in 1660-79, the deaths from this disease were 1·48. *

8. Other *inflammations* besides inflammation of the lungs unquestionably prevailed in London before 1704, when the word found its way into the bills; but its present comparative frequency is not entirely due to a change of nomenclature. Fevers were the reigning diseases, and an impure atmosphere communicated their character to the inflammations; which are still relatively less frequent where fever and dysentery prevail. In Corfu, 1815-21, out of 325 deaths among our troops, 12 were attributed to inflammations, besides 10 to hepatitis; while 223 were ascribed

---

of these calculations; as it is not probable the population, in the same space, ever exceeded 130,178. The deaths in the 97 + 16 parishes during 31 years, 1616-46, amounted to 279,964; which diminished $\frac{1}{27}$ for the still-born, and divided by the population (130,178) of the intermediate year, give 6·68 as the annual rate of mortality. The fire disturbed the observations in 1666, so that it was more difficult to obtain an approximation to the mortality in the 20 years, 1660-79: but the enumerated deaths in the 10 years, 1670-79, were 94,644; in the 5 years, 1660-4, 483,000; in 1665, the epidemic year, 56,558; whence 237,349 were deduced as the total deaths in the 20 years. Reduced $\frac{1}{27}$ for the still-born, the annual rate of mortality was 8·85 per cent.; but, to avoid the risk of exaggeration, the rate of this period, including the plague year, 1665, has been stated in the table at 8 per cent.

* *Sydenham's Works,* vol. i. pp. 218. 433. "Cholera comes almost as constant at the close of summer, and towards the beginning of autumn, as swallows in the beginning of spring, and cuckows towards midsummer." He closes an accurate description by remarking, that it "often destroyed the patient in 24 hours." Dr. Craigie has demonstrated the antiquity and identity of cholera all over the world: before the last eruption, it had been epidemic in India. He cites a remarkable case from Morton. *Edinburgh Journal,* 1853.

to fever, plague, and dysentery. Sydenham classes pleurisy, bastard pneumonia, rheumatism, erysipelas, and quinsey, together, under the title " intercurrent fevers:" after distinguishing the idiopathic from the symptomatic disease, he says, " I conceive pleurisy to be only a fever occasioned by a peculiar *inflammation of the blood*, whereby nature throws off the peccant matter upon the pleura, and sometimes upon the lungs, whence a pneumonia arises." Fever, then, involved in its vortex the comparatively rare inflammations; inflammation (a vague term) now happening more frequently in a pure form, and proved by *post mortem* examinations to prevail very extensively, has apparently 'recovered, not only its rightful possessions, but several of the unappropriated, unknown diseases, particularly of children.

9. *Consumption* was exceedingly fatal when fevers and dysentery reigned: it is now very fatal among the British troops in the West Indies. Its relative frequency increased down to 1810; in other words, fever and dysentery decreased more rapidly than consumption. The actual proportion of persons destroyed by this disease, as well as other forms of scrofula (rickets, and evil) has, except in the anomalous period of 1771–80, progressively declined among the mass of the population in London. If asthma and tissick be added, the declension will be little less apparent.

10. *Dropsy* has latterly been proved to depend frequently on diseases of the heart and of the kidneys: its connection with agues and dysentery, and with diseases of the liver and spleen, is confirmed by the table.

FATAL DISEASES AT DIFFERENT AGES.

THE diseases proving fatal in childhood, manhood, and old age, are not the same: for this reason, to determine the peculiar diseases — the nature of the dangers — we have to encounter at different periods of life, becomes a most important problem. Very few statistical observations exist, in which the deaths from each disease, at different ages, are enumerated. The observations of Dr. Heysham, at Carlisle, when he collected the facts on which the Carlisle table is formed; the diseases of which 4,095 persons, assured in the Equitable Office, died; the bills of mortality of the Anglo-American population in Philadelphia, — are, we believe, the only data of the kind yet published, either in Europe or America. *

Mr. Milne, in whose valuable work the Carlisle observations were published, justly remarks, that " the tables of Dr. Heysham had the advantage of being constructed by a skilful physician, capable of discriminating accurately between the different diseases; who either visited the patients himself, or had the means of procuring accurate reports from his medical friends." The arrangement of Cullen, which Dr. Heysham followed, is so artificial, as to render it very ill suited to statistical purposes, where it is desirous to bring facts together not only allied in one fugitive point, but in their fixed anatomical or general characters. The arrangement adopted in the following tables is twofold : fatal diseases are (1) arranged according to the organs they involved, (2) and according to their pathological nature. The arrangement, we admit, is imperfect; but some arrangement was necessary, and this brings together many interesting features.

* According to the late act providing for the registration of births and deaths, the causes of death are to be recorded. This is one of the most important clauses of that measure, and, in a few years, will enable us to determine of what diseases the different classes of the English people die, at all ages, and in all circumstances.

I. Table which shows the Number of Deaths by each Disease, that took place in each of the undermentioned Intervals of Age, at Carlisle, during 8 Years, commencing with 1779, and ending 1787, excepting 1780.

Diseases arranged according to their Seat.	Ages.												
	0-5.	5-10.	10-15.	15-20.	20-30.	30-40.	40-50.	50-60.	60-70.	70-80.	80-90.	90 &c.	Total.
BRAIN.													
Dropsy of	2	2	1	.	.	.	.	.	.	.	.	.	5
Apoplexy	.	.	.	1	.	2	5	9	11	4	.	.	32
Palsy	.	.	.	.	.	.	1	5	4	3	1	.	14
Convulsions	10	.	.	.	.	.	.	.	.	.	.	.	10
Epilepsy	.	.	.	1	1	1	.	1	.	.	.	.	4
Insanity	.	.	.	.	.	1	.	.	.	1	.	.	2
	12	2	1	2	1	4	6	15	15	8	1		67
LUNGS.													
Pleurisy	3	2	1	1	.	1	2	2	5	2	.	.	19
Consumption	34	15	10	15	45	34	31	15	15	.	.	.	214
Asthma	1	.	.	.	.	.	2	9	11	4	.	.	27
Chin-cough	18	1	.	.	.	.	.	.	.	.	.	.	19
Influenza	.	.	.	.	.	.	.	.	1	.	.	.	1
	56	18	11	16	45	35	35	26	32	6			280
BLOOD.													
(1.) *Intestines.*													
Fever, inflammatory	3	.	.	.	1	.	.	1	.	.	.	.	5
— nervous	2	3	1	4	3	9	15	13	7	2	.	.	59
— putrid	5	4	1	2	8	5	8	4	5	1	.	.	43
— jail	4	2	1	2	.	2	3	.	.	.	.	.	14
— intermittent	.	.	.	.	.	.	.	1	.	.	.	.	1
— infantile remittent	19	8	.	.	.	.	.	.	.	.	.	.	27
(2.) *Skin.*													
Scarlet fever	{34	4	2	1	1	.	.	.	.	.	.	.	42
Sore throat 3													
Measles	28	2	1	.	.	.	.	.	.	.	.	.	31
Smallpox	225	8	2	.	3	.	.	.	.	.	.	.	238
Aphthæ	63	2	.	.	.	.	.	.	.	.	.	.	65
Miliary fever	.	.	.	.	1	.	.	.	.	.	.	.	1
	383	33	8	9	17	16	26	19	12	3			526
HEART.													
Fainting	.	1	.	1	.	1	2	1	.	1	.	.	6
ORGANS OF DIGESTION.													
Mouth.													
Teething	3	.	.	.	.	.	.	.	.	.	.	.	3
Stomach.													
Indigestion	.	.	?.	.	.	1	6	5	8	1	.	.	21
Inflammation	.	.	.	1	.	.	.	1	.	.	.	.	2
Tumour 1													
Intestines.													
Diarrhœa	7	1	1	1	.	1	2	2	1	2	.	.	18
Costiveness	1	.	.	.	1	.	.	.	.	.	.	.	2
Colic 1													
Rupture	.	.	.	1	.	.	1	.	.	.	.	.	1
Liver.													
Jaundice	3	.	.	.	1	.	5	2	.	2	.	.	13
Abscess	.	.	.	.	.	.	1	.	.	.	.	.	1
	14	1	1	3	2	2	14	10	9	5	.	.	61
URINARY ORGANS.													
Diabetes	.	.	.	.	.	1	.	.	.	.	.	.	1
Stone and gravel	.	.	.	.	1	.	1	.	6	1	.	.	9
Suppression of urine	.	.	.	.	.	.	.	.	1	.	.	.	1
					1	1	1		7	1			11
ORGANS OF GENERATION.													
Venereal disease	.	.	.	.	.	1	.	1	.	.	.	.	2
Uterus.													
Amenorrhœa	.	.	.	.	.	1	.	.	.	.	.	.	1
Menorrhagia lochialis	.	.	.	.	.	.	3	.	.	.	.	.	3
Difficult delivery	.	.	.	.	4	4	1	.	.	.	.	.	9
					5	5	5						15
SUMMARY.													
Organs of generation	.	.	.	.	5	5	5	.	.	.	.	.	15
Urinary organs	.	.	.	.	1	1	1	.	7	1	.	.	11
Organs of digestion	14	1	1	3	2	2	14	10	9	5	.	.	61
Heart	.	1	.	.	1	2	1	.	1	.	.	.	6
Blood	383	33	8	9	17	16	26	19	12	3	.	.	526
Lungs	56	18	11	16	45	35	35	26	32	6	.	.	280
Brain and spinal marrow	12	2	1	2	1	4	6	15	15	8	1	.	67
* Diseases of different organs	466	52	21	30	72	65	88	70	76	23	1	.	966
* Of uncertain seat	243	20	9	8	7	16	20	24	76	111	88	27	619
Total	709	74	30	38	79	81	108	94	152	134	89	27	1,615

* Mortifications 3, rheumatism 6, gout 4, weakness of infancy 204, decay of age 226, dropsy 49, scrofula 3, cancer 5, unknown diseases 115, accidents 29, green sickness 1, discharge of blood 1, ulcer 3=649. All these diseases, exept the two last, are classified in Table II.

II. Fatal Diseases observed in Carlisle, from 1779 to 1787, and registered by
Dr. Heysham; arranged in Groups according to their Nature.

Diseases.	Ages.								
	0-5.	5-10.	10-20.	0-20.	20-40.	40-60.	60-80.	80-105.	Total.
Living -	1,096	967	1,481	3,544	2,348·5	1,540	669	74	8,177
INFLAMMATIONS.									
Pleurisy and pneumonia	3	2	2	7	1	4	7	-	19
Inflammation of stomach -	-	-	1	1	-	-	-	-	1
Diarrhœa -	7	1	2	10	1	4	3	-	18
Abscess of the liver -	-	-	-	-	-	1	-	-	1
Ulcer 3, and Mortification -}	-	-	-	-	-	2	3	1	6
Rheumatism -	-	-	-	-	-	1	5	-	6
Gout -	-	-	-	-	-	3	1	-	4
FEVERS.									
Inflammatory (synocha) -	3	-	-	3	1	1	-	-	5
Typhus {nervous 59, putrid 43, jail 14} -	11	9	11	31	27	43	15	-	116
Infantile remittent, Intermittent 1 -}	19	8	-	27	-	1	-	-	28
Scarlet fever, Sore throat 3 -}	34	4	3	41	1	-	-	-	42
Measles	28	2	1	31	-	-	-	-	31
Smallpox -	225	8	2	235	3	-	-	-	238
Miliary fever	-	-	-	-	1	-	-	-	1
Aphthæ (thrush) -	63	2	-	65	-	-	-	-	65
SEROUS EFFUSIONS.									
Anasarca and ascites	1	1	5	7	8	12	19	3	49
Hydrocephalus -	2	2	1	5	-	-	-	-	5
Consumption and Scrofula 3 -}	34	17	25	76	79	47	15	-	217
Cancer -, Tumour of the stomach 1 (scirrhus) -}	-	-	-	-	-	2	4	-	6
Stone and gravel -	-	-	-	-	1	1	7	-	9
FRAGILITY OF BLOODVESSELS.									
Apoplexy -	-	-	1	1	2	14	15	0	32
Palsy -	-	-	-	-	-	6	7	1	14
WANT OF VITAL POWER.									
Weakness of infancy -	204	-	-	204	-	-	-	-	204
Decay of age -	-	-	-	-	-	-	116	110	216
EXTERNAL VIOLENCE.									
Accidents -	7	5	6	18	7	3	1	-	29
Unknown diseases' -	32	11	5	48	10	18	38	1	115
SUMMARY.									
Inflammations -	10	3	5	18	2	11	13	1	45
Dropsies	3	3	6	12	8	12	19	3	54
Fevers -	33	17	11	61	28	45	15	-	149
Exanthemata	350	16	6	372	5	-	-	-	377
Consumption and scrofula -	34	17	25	76	79	47	15	-	217
Cancer -	-	-	-	-	-	2	4	-	6
Stone and gravel -	-	-	-	-	1	1	7	-	9
Gout and rheumatism -	-	-	-	-	-	4	6	-	10
Apoplexy, palsy -	-	-	1	1	2	20	22	1	46
Feeble vitality	204	-	-	204	-	-	116	110	430
Unknown diseases	32	11	5	48	10	18	38	1	115
Accidents	7	5	6	18	7	3	1	-	29
Classified diseases -	673	72	65	810	142	163	256	116	1,487
Diseases not classified * -	36	2	3	41	18	39	30	-	128
Total -	709	74	68	851	160	202	286	116	1,615

* Convulsions 10, epilepsy 4, insanity 2, asthma 27, chin-cough 19, influenza 1, fainting 6, teething 3, indigestion 12,
colic 1, costiveness 1, rupture 1, jaundice 13, venereal disease 2, amenorrhœa 1, difficult delivery 9, menorrhagia
lochialis 3, diabetes 1, suppression of urine 1. These will all be found in Table I. Green sickness 1, age 15-20; and
discharge of blood 1, age 40-50 ; are in neither.

The assurance offices obtain from the medical attendant a certificate of the dis-
order of which every person assured has died : the Tables III. and V. have been
arranged from a recent publication of the Equitable Society, detailing the diseases
fatal to 4,095 individuals during the 32 years, 1801–1832.

III. Table of 4,095 fatal Diseases happening among Persons assured by the Equitable Society, arranged according to the Parts affected.

Diseases.	Ages.								Total.
	10-20.	20-30.	30-40.	40-50.	50-60.	60-70.	70-80.	80,&c.	
I. Brain and Spinal Marrow.									
Inflammation of the brain	1	4	15	16	13	12	2	1	64
Water on brain	-	-	1	3	4	1	-	-	9
Convulsion fits	-	-	-	4	1	3	-	-	9
Epilepsy	-	1	2	8	2	2	4	-	19
Suicide	-	1	2	6	15	5	-	-	29
Apoplexy	1	4	25	56	129	169	86	16	486
Palsy	-	1	5	15	47	84	74	9	235
	2	11	50	108	211	276	166	26	850
II. Respiratory Organs.									
Quinsey	-	-	-	1	1	1	-	-	3
Inflammation of the lungs	0	2	12	12	41	56	45	17	185
chest	1	1	11	8	11	21	12	-	59
Pleuritis	-	-	-	1	1	2	-	-	4
Dropsy of the chest	-	1	3	23	52	59	42	3	183
Consumption	4	23	63	83	81	66	18	1	339
Asthma	-	-	-	2	20	26	22	4	74
	5	27	79	130	207	231	139	29	847
III. Organs of Circulation.									
Aneurism	-	-	1	2	-	-	1	-	4
Angina pectoris	-	-	8	16	45	47	26	3	145
Rupture of a blood-vessel	1	-	12	19	19	22	9	-	82
	1	-	21	37	64	69	36	3	231
IV. Organs of Digestion.									
Inflammation of bowels	2	2	14	20	26	44	16	2	126
Disease of stomach and digestive organs	-	2	9	12	28	31	22	2	106
liver	-	2	8	37	54	49	23	2	175
Dysentery	-	-	1	3	5	11	11	3	34
	2	6	32	72	113	135	72	9	441
BLOOD. **V. Skin and Intestinal Tube.**									
Cholera	-	-	2	5	5	9	5	1	27
Fevers	-	14	47	88	97	99	48	8	401
Smallpox	-	-	-	-	-	-	-	1	1
Erysipelas	-	1	2	7	6	7	3	-	26
	-	15	51	100	108	115	56	10	455
VI. Genital and Urinary Organs.									
Diabetes	-	-	-	3	2	1	1	1	8
Stone	-	-	-	-	1	2	7	2	12
Disease of the bladder and urinary passages	-	-	3	9	25	44	41	6	128
Childbirth	-	-	2	2	-	-	-	-	4
	-	-	5	14	28	47	49	9	152
VII. Of uncertain Seat.									
Gout	-	-	2	6	8	14	7	1	38
Mortification	-	-	2	2	12	14	12	6	46
Cancer	-	-	2	5	14	15	4	3	43
Atrophy	-	-	4	7	11	15	6	-	43
Decay (natural) and old age	-	-	-	-	10	128	241	187	566
Dropsy	1	-	10	39	67	83	50	7	257
	1	-	18	59	122	269	320	204	993
Disorders not properly defined	-	-	9	11	20	27	12	-	79
VIII. External Violence.									
Murdered	-	-	-	1	1	-	1	-	3
Slain in war	1	1	1	1	-	-	-	-	4
Accidents	-	7	-	11	9	4	5	4	40
	1	8	1	13	10	4	6	4	47

IV. Table showing the annual Proportion of Deaths in 10,000 living, at all Ages, produced by Diseases of different Organs, in Carlisle.

Organs affected.	0-20.	20-40.	40-60.	60-80.	80-105.	0-105.	20-105.
Brain	6	3	17	43	17	10	14
Heart	0·3	2	1	2	-	1	1
Lungs	36	45	48	72	-	43	48
Organs of digestion	7	2	19	26	-	9	11
generation	-	6	4	-	-	2	4
Urinary organs	-	1	1	15	-	3	3
Blood { Skin	134	16	-	-	-	45 }	25
Blood { Intestines	22	3	35	28	-	36 }	
Diseases of uncertain seat	101	13	34	353	1,922	101	100
All diseases	306·3	91	159	539	1,939	250	206

V. Table of 4,095 fatal Diseases happening among Persons assured by the Equitable Society, arranged according to their Nature.

Diseases.	10-20.	20-30.	30-40.	40-50.	50-60.	60-70.	70-80.	80.	At all Ages.
Inflammations.									
Inflammation of the bowels	2	2	14	20	26	44	16	2	126
lungs		2	12	12	41	56	45	17	185
brain	1	4	15	16	13	12	2	1	64
lungs and chest	1	1	1	8	11	21	12	4	59
Pleurisy				1	1	2	-	-	4
Mortification				2	12	14	12	6	46
Quinsey				1	1	1	-	-	3
	4	9	42	60	105	150	87	30	487
Fevers.									
Fevers, general		5	30	55	61	70	34	7	262
bilious		1	5	10	10	8	2	1	37
nervous		3	3	13	9	9	5	-	42
inflammatory		3	2	6	10	5	6	-	32
putrid		2	7	4	7	7	1	-	28
Cholera		-	2	5	5	9	5	1	27
Dysentery		-	1	3	5	11	11	3	34
Smallpox		-	-	-	-	-	-	1	1
Erysipelas		1	2	7	6	7	3	-	26
	-	13	47	105	114	133	73	14	499
Serous Effusions.									
Dropsy	1	-	10	39	67	83	50	7	257
on the chest		1	3	23	52	59	42	3	183
Water on the brain		-	1	3	4	1	-	-	9
	1	1	14	65	123	143	92	10	449
Consumption	4	23	63	83	81	66	18	1	339
Cancer	-	-	2	5	14	15	4	3	43
Stone	-	-	-	-	1	2	7	2	12
Gout	-	-	2	6	8	14	7	1	38
Fragility of the Vascular System.									
Aneurism	-	-	1	2	-	-	1	-	4
Rupture of a bloodvessel	1	-	12	19	19	22	9	-	82
Apoplexy	1	4	25	56	129	169	86	16	486
Palsy	-	1	5	15	47	84	74	9	235
	2	5	43	92	195	275	170	25	807

VI. Equitable Society. — Deaths out of 10,000 constantly living, at Four Periods of Life; distributed in Groups of fatal Diseases, (I.) according to the Nature, (II.) and Seat.

No. of Observations.		20—40.	40—60.	60—80.	80—110.	20—110.
	I. *Diseases grouped according to their nature.*					
27	Exanthemata (smallpox 1, erysipelas 26)	1	1·4	3	7	1
401	Fevers	17	21	39	53	20
61	Cholera and dysentery	1	2	10	26	3
47	Mechanical injuries	2	3	3	26	2
487	Inflammations	14	18	63	198	25
449	Dropsies	4	21	62	66	22
339	Consumption	24	18	22	7	17
12	Stone	-	0·1	2	14	1
38	Gout	0·5	1·5	6	7	2
43	Cancer	0·5	2	5	21	2
807	Fragility of the vascular system, aneurism 4, rupture of blood-vessel 82, apoplexy, palsy	13	32	118	165	41
43	Atrophy	1	2	6	-	2
566	Feeble vitality (decay, natural, and old age)	-	1	98	1,230	28
79	Diseases not properly defined	2	4	10	-	4
696*	Diseases not classed	11	32	92	119	36
4,095		91	159	539	1,939	206
	II. *Diseases grouped according to their Seat.*					
850	Brain	17	36	117	170	43
847	Organs of respiration	29	38	98	191	43
231	circulation	6	11	28	20	11·5
407	digestion	10	20	49	40	21
4	generation (childbirth)	0·5	0·2	-	-	0·2
148	Urinary organs	1	4	25	59	7
489	Blood { Skin / Intestines	1 / 18	1·4 / 23	3 / 49	7 / 79	1 / 23
79	Not properly defined	2	3	10	-	4
993†	Of uncertain seat	5	20	157	1,346	50
47	External violence	2	3	3	26	2·5
4,095		91·5	159·6	539	1,939	206·2

* Convulsion fits 8, epilepsy 19, suicide 29, asthma 74, angina pectoris 145, disease of the stomach and digestive organs 106, disease of liver 175, diabetes 8, bladder and disease of 128, childbirth 4 = 696. All these diseases are included in the section following.
† Gout 38, mortification 46, cancer 43, atrophy 43, decay natural 566, dropsy 257.

VII. Table showing the annual Deaths by 10 Classes of Disease, out of 10,000 living at each Age, deduced from Dr. Heysham's Observations.

Diseases.	0-20.	20-40.	40-60.	60-80.	80-105.	All Ages.	20-105.
Eruptive fevers*	134	16	-	-	-	45	1
Fevers	22	3	35	28	-	36	24
Accidents	7	4	2	2	-	4	3
Inflammations	7	1	9	25	17	7	7
Dropsies	4·5	5	9	36	50	8	11
Consumption	27	45	37	28	-	34	38
Cancer	-	-	2	7	-	1	2
Stone and gravel	-	6	1	13	-	1	2
Gout	-	-	3	11	-	2	3
Apoplexy and palsy	0·3	1	16	41	17	7	12
Feeble vitality	73	-	-	219	1,838	67	61
Diseases unknown	17	6	14	72	17	18	18
Diseases not classed	15	10	31	57	-	20	24
	307·3	91	159	539	1,939	250	206

* Of the 134 deaths by eruptive fevers between the ages 0-20, 20-40, the deaths by smallpox were 84 and 1.

REMARKS.

1. Tables IV., VI., and VII. have been deduced from the four other tables: the absolute mortality was derived, in the same manner as the Carlisle table, from two enumerations of the living at different ages, and the deaths registered during 9 years (1779—1787) by Dr. Heysham; the deaths from each class of disease were ascertained by simple proportion. The rate of mortality amongst persons assured by the Equitable Society agrees nearly with that of Carlisle; so the same absolute mortality was applied to Table VI. as to Tables IV. and VII. The mortality of the class of persons from whom the assured were selected was certainly higher. The observations made in Philadelphia, to which we shall refer, were for the 2 years 1833-1835; the total deaths amounted to 10,106, and were published in annual bills by the Board of Health. The mortality in the 3 years, 1833-35, was 2·4 per cent.; the deaths in 5 years out of 100 born, 31·3.

2. Of a thousand persons living at Carlisle, *fever* annually destroyed 3·6; *smallpox*, 2·8; the entire class of *eruptive fevers*, 4·5; fever and eruptive fevers, 8·1. The two groups constituted 32·4 per cent. of the fatal diseases; in Philadelphia they actually amount only to 14, in London to 10·7 per cent.

3. The *eruptive fevers* at Carlisle and at Philadelphia were most fatal under the age of 20; but this does not justify the current belief of medical men, that children are more susceptible of those diseases which affect the organisation only once than adults. Admit that of 100 children born 50 have smallpox before the age of 10, 26 between the ages 10-20, 14 between 20-30, &c.; is it not evident in this case, that although the absolute number diminishes, the relative number attacked of those who have never had smallpox increases? One who has lived 30 years in the world without an attack of measles is, perhaps, protected by some idiosyncrasy; but, *cæteris paribus*, is not a person aged 30 as liable to an attack of measles as a child? Would not smallpox, introduced into a country where it had never been before, attack persons of all ages indiscriminately?

4. Of 1615 deaths, Dr. Heysham ascribed only 20 to *inflammation*, and not one to an affection of the heart or large bloodvessels. This shows not so clearly that these diseases were uncommon, as that great ignorance of morbid anatomy prevailed among the most accomplished physicians at the close of the last century. In Philadelphia 14·4, in London, 10·8 per cent. of the deaths are attributed to inflammation: after the age of 20, in the Equitable Society 12 per cent., in Philadelphia 14 per cent. of the fatal cases were inflammations.

5. *Consumption and scrofula* at Carlisle and Philadelphia destroyed annually 3·4 per 1,000 of the inhabitants; and 3·8 per 1,000 of the persons aged 20 and upwards. One seventh part of the deaths were, consequently, from consumption; and above the age of 20, one fifth.

6. The violence of disease, Hippocrates somewhere says, is in proportion to the strength of the patient; and morbid anatomy proves that where there is great debility from age, or any other cause, inflammation runs through its course without manifesting distinctly its characteristic symptoms. The great number of deaths ascribed to natural decay, old age, and to weakness, are for this reason improperly considered

examples of death without disease; although death sometimes does happen without any apparent organic cause.

7. What is the effect of the selection exercised by the assurance companies? What class of diseases does it exclude? In the first place, the eruptive fevers. Among 4,095 deaths in the Equitable Society, only 1 was of smallpox. The deaths from consumption, instead of making 20, only amounted to 8·3 per cent. of the deaths, or 10·3 if those who died of ruptured blood-vessel be added. But by way of compensation, the deaths from dropsy are 22; from apoplexy and palsy 37 per 1,000; instead of 11, 12, and 11, 10·6, the proportions dying of these two classes of disease in Carlisle and Philadelphia. The advantage to the assurance offices of applying tables founded on a city population in the last century, and *including all the sick*, to a class of persons in good health, and little liable to the eruptive fevers or consumption, is obvious. With a little study, the selection of long-lived persons may be carried to a still greater extent.

8. In proportion as a population becomes civilised, and as its physical condition and mental life are ameliorated, the deaths from apoplexy appear to increase; while the fevers and plagues of the state of barbarism decrease in a much more rapid ratio. The persons assured by the Equitable Society represent the more intellectual order of people in this country; apoplexy is frequent among them; the numerous dropsies and inflammations mark their gastronomic excesses; the mortality from fever and erysipelas proves that they dwell in ill ventilated houses, and crowded cities, with bad sewers.

9. Life, divided into 5 vicennial periods, is most secure in the second; the fatality of nearly all diseases increases afterwards in a geometrical progression. The observations in Philadelphia show that consumption is not an exception to this law.

10. One of the most important results presented in this paper is, that the character of diseases changes in a determined ratio at different periods of existence. The tables indicate not only the degree, but the kind of danger, we have to encounter at all ages: for example, in the second vicennial period (20–40), the deaths from consumption at Carlisle constituted 50, at Philadelphia 34, in the Equitable Society 26 per cent. of the deaths from all causes *; in the third vicennium the nature of the danger has altered, for the deaths from consumption contribute but 23, 28, or 11 per cent. to the entire mortality. From tables of this description, the probability of death from each class of diseases can be calculated at all ages. We will add one instance of their practical application. In the first period of life (0–20) the eruptive fevers, inflammations, scrofulous and dropsical effusions, are most to be dreaded; in Philadelphia two fifths of the deaths were from affections of the brain and bowels. Who, with these facts before him, can fail to see the impropriety of giving children preparations of laudanum, spirits, or any food at first but the mother's bland milk? Cold often produces inflammation of the lungs in winter; but too much tenderness in this respect, and the accustoming of boys to a delicate diet, weaken the constitution. Between 20 and 40, *consumption*, inflammations, fevers, and epidemics, are the most deadly shafts of death, which, as Dr. Clark has shown, a judicious course of hygiene in this period may do much to disarm. The same class of diseases maintains the preponderance till 60; but, in the period following (60–80) *dropsies* and inflammations increase, while apoplexy gains a great ascendency. After 65 a man should undertake nothing requiring great intellectual exertion, or sustained energy: warmth, temperance, tranquillity, may prolong his years to the close of a century; a rude breath of the atmosphere, a violent struggle, or a shock, will suffice to terminate his existence. The apoplexy of the aged can, with care, be averted for several years; but it is, perhaps, the natural death, the euthanasia of the intellectual: their blood remains pure, the solids firm to the last, when a fragile artery gives way within the head,—the blood escapes, and by a gentle pressure dissolves sensibility at its source for ever. The life is no longer there,—the corporeal elements are given back to the universe!

---

* Dr. Clark had this period, probably, in view when he estimated the proportion of deaths from tuberculous diseases, after excluding the deaths in infancy, at a third part of the total mortality in this country.

Conclusions. — *On the Means of promoting Public Health in Great Britain.*

1. If governments can do little by *direct* enactments for the diminution of sickness, it is, nevertheless, their duty to determine, by statistical enumerations, the actual state of health, and the extent to which it is deteriorated in different circumstances. Returns of the diseases and deaths in the army, the navy, and all bodies of men employed in the public service, should be made annually ; and this, with the results of the general registration, would improve public health, by showing so distinctly the connection between diseases and their natural causes that men would either avoid or obviate the evils destructive of health by some invention.

2. Almost all classes of the people of this country are profoundly ignorant of the physiological laws which regulate their own existence ; health may consequently be improved by making a knowledge of the nature of the human organisation, and of the external agents by which it is influenced, an elementary part of the national education. The physical sciences are not, as Count Rumford maintained, the sole sources of human improvement ; but without their aid no solid advances can be made in civilisation. For this reason, the works and inventions of Rumford and Arnott will contribute more to the progress of society than many treatises written *ex professo* on the subject.

3. It has been shown that external agents have as great an influence on the frequency of sickness as on its fatality ; the obvious corollary is, that man has as much power to prevent as to cure disease. That prevention is better than cure, is a proverb ; that it is as easy, the facts we have advanced establish. Yet medical men, the guardians of public health, never have their attention called to the prevention of sickness ; it forms no part of their education. To promote health is apparently contrary to their interests : the public do not seek the shield of medical art against disease, nor call the surgeon, till the arrows of death already rankle in the veins. This may be corrected by modifying the present system of medical education, and the manner of remunerating medical men.

4. Public health may be promoted by placing the medical institutions of the country on a liberal scientific basis ; by the medical societies co-operating to collect statistical observations ; and by medical writers renouncing the notion that a science can be founded upon the limited experience of an individual. Practical medicine cannot be taught in books ; the science of medicine cannot be acquired in the sick room. The healing art may likewise be promoted by encouraging post-mortem examinations of diseased parts ; without which it is impossible to keep up in the body of the medical profession a clear knowledge of the internal changes indicated by symptoms during life. The practitioner who never opens a dead body must commit innumerable, and someties fatal, errors.

5. It has been proved that, in the present state of things, the mortality is greatly augmented wherever large masses of the people are brought together : it will be the duty of the government, the municipal corporations, and all classes of citizens, to render the towns of this country, and every establishment where large numbers are collected together, perfectly adapted to the wants of the human organisation, and compatible with the full enjoyment of health.

OBSERVATIONS

ON THE

RATE OF MORTALITY & SICKNESS

EXISTING AMONGST

FRIENDLY SOCIETIES:

PARTICULARISED FOR

VARIOUS TRADES, OCCUPATIONS, AND LOCALITIES,

WITH

A SERIES OF TABLES,

SHEWING

THE VALUE OF ANNUITIES, SICK GIFT, ASSURANCE FOR DEATH, AND
CONTRIBUTIONS TO BE PAID EQUIVALENT THERETO:

CALCULATED FROM

THE EXPERIENCE OF THE MEMBERS

COMPOSING

The Manchester Unity of the Independent Order of Odd Fellows.

BY HENRY RATCLIFFE,

CORRESPONDING SECRETARY.

Manchester:
PRINTED FOR THE ORDER BY GEORGE FALKNER, KING STREET.

1850.

[Entered at Stationers' Hall.]

Republished in 1974 by Gregg International, D. C. Heath Limited

PREFACE.

SOME years have elapsed since it was first attempted to obtain statistical information from the Lodges of the Manchester Unity. As might have been expected, every proposition was at first strenuously resisted, which had for its object the attainment of such information as alone could be relied upon as a safe guide to the successful financial management of so vast a body; the leaders of which were anxious to secure its permanent stability, as a Provident Association, by the application of every measure which the *experience of the Society itself* might demonstrate to be necessary to insure its safety.

At length the unanswerable arguments advanced by those desirous of profiting by past experience prevailed, and in the year 1846 it was determined that we should no longer decline to understand our true position, but that we should unhesitatingly avail ourselves of the advantages we possessed of acquiring information so practically valuable, upon a subject of the deepest interest to those whose position in life rendered it necessary that they should make some provision to mitigate the consequences arising from the loss of employment through sickness, and to ward off, as far as possible, that poverty which is too frequently the companion of declining years. Returns of the most ample kind for the years 1846-7-8 were required from all the Lodges composing the Unity; and thus was obtained all the information desirable to be possessed, relative to the Sickness and Mortality experienced by the Members of the Manchester Unity. From these returns, the Tables in this Work have been prepared.

It may be necessary to explain that the results thus shown were intended, in the first instance, for the use of the Members only, many of whom being unacquainted with the value of decimal fractions, the approximate values have been given in whole numbers.

The great object kept in view throughout the compilation of this Work, has been to test the correctness of the 'Data' supplied; and after the most careful investigation, and checking the results by independent and distinct means, there is every reason for placing the most implicit confidence in the accuracy of the stated Rates of Mortality and Average Sickness experienced by the Members of the Unity, as given in this Work. This confidence is further warranted by the fact, that the facilities possessed of comparing the present with former Returns obtained from the Unity, for other purposes, confirm their accuracy in the most important particulars.

It may not be out of place to remark, that the passing of the "Friendly Societies' Bill," almost simultaneously with the appearance of this Work, has rendered it highly probable that, in a few months, the Manchester Unity, as a Legalized Association, will enjoy the full security of the law for the protection of its accumulated capital.

The thanks of the Manchester Unity, and all similar societies, are eminently due to Lord Beaumont, J. H. S. Sotheron, Esq., J. B. Carter, Esq., C. B. Adderley, Esq., Lord Dudley Coutts Stuart, Wm. Scholefield, Esq., Richard Spooner, Esq., and other Members of the two Houses of Parliament, who have so successfully advocated the passing of a measure destined, it is hoped and believed, to confer incalculable advantages and privileges on such associations. This measure must be hailed as a most important recognition of the ability of the Working Classes to govern these great and useful combinations, in the prosperity of which they are so deeply interested; and the most sanguine belief is entertained that whatever adjustment of the rates of payments and benefits may be clearly shown to be necessary, by the experience here presented to the Members, will be cheerfully made by men whose intelligence and provident habits have won for them, despite the odd designation they bear, a consideration amongst all classes in the state.

The Tables and calculations are given in as simple and plain a manner as the subjects would permit; and it is to be hoped that, by careful attention, they will be fully understood by the great mass of persons interested in the welfare of Friendly Societies, and that the object sought to be gained by this Publication will thus be fully realised.

MANCHESTER, *September 27th,* 1850.

ERRATA.

Page 36, last line but two, *read* 9.4416 = 9 weeks, 3 days 2 hours, *in place of* 19.0002 = 19 weeks.
Page 40, Woolcombers, age 30, *read* 1.2171 = 1 1 12, *in place of* .7662 = 0 5 9.
Page 41, Woolcombers, age 20 to 30, *read* 11.2209 = 11 1 13, *in place of* 10.7539 = 10 5 7.
Page 41, Woolcombers, age 33 to 40, *read* 14.4130 = 14 2 20, *in place of* 9.4271 = 9 3 0.
Page 152, first portion of Table, *read* Rural, *in place of* City.

CONTENTS.

SECTION I.

SECTION II.

SECTION III.

SECTION IV.

———

SECTION V.

SECTION VI.

SECTION VII.

SECTION I.

VITALITY OF ENGLAND AND WALES,

AND

AVERAGE AMOUNT OF SICKNESS:

EXPERIENCED BY THE RESULTS OF MR. NEISON.

IN the second edition of the Fifth Report of the Registrar General for England and Wales, page 23, will be found a Table of the decrements of Male and Female Life, calculated upon the whole of the Population of England and Wales, as enumerated in the year 1841, and the number of deaths registered during the whole of the year. This Table may be considered one of the best measures of life in this country, including, as it does, every class of lives, in whatever state or position they may be existing.

This Table being calculated from the first year of life, and shewing, by the decrements through each year, that when the lives arrive at the eighteenth, the male have decreased 17,437, leaving 33,837 lives entering on the eighteenth year; it was thought that many persons interested in such inquiries, might be able more easily to trace the decrements of life if they were re calculated, commencing at age 18, with 100,000 lives. This has been done, and embodied in Table I. At age 18 it will be observed that there are 100,000 lives, and that 750 of these die off before attaining the nineteenth year. In passing through that year 765 die off, leaving 98,485 persons who enter on the twentieth year of life; and, in this manner, the numbers living, and the numbers dying out of those living, may be traced from year to year.

The fourth and ninth columns show the per-centage of deaths at each year of life; and, on examination, it will be seen that there is a regular increase in the rate of mortality until the age 55, when it becomes accelerated up to the age 94. After this year the rate of mortality does not appear so steady as previously, and may be accounted for in consequence of the small number of lives experienced upon above that age.

The fifth and tenth columns show the specific intensity, as existing in England and Wales, or, in other words, the number of persons living, out of which one would die annually at the age shown. Such as are unacquainted with decimal fractions can omit the two figures after the period, without impairing the utility of the Table for any purpose to which they may apply it; as, for instance, at age 18, by omitting the figures 21 after the period, it is seen that out of every 131 Members living at that age, one will die annually; again, at age 80, by leaving out the figures 14 after the period, it is found that out of every eight Members living at that age, one will die annually; and the same rule being applied throughout, the number of persons living, out of which one will die annually, may be easily ascertained.

B

TABLE I.

ENGLISH LIFE TABLE —MALES.

Age.	Living.	Dying.	Mortality per Cent.	Specific Intensity.	Age.	Living.	Dying.	Mortality per Cent.	Specific Intensity.
18	100000	750	.750	133.21	62	51985	1942	3.665	27.28
19	99250	765	.771	129.66	63	50043	1980	3.956	25.27
20	98485	780	.792	126.22	64	48063	2048	4.262	23.46
21	97705	792	.810	123.35	65	46015	2116	4.599	21.74
22	96913	806	.832	120.11	66	43899	2175	4.955	20.17
23	96107	821	.854	116.97	67	41724	2234	5.355	18.67
24	95286	836	.877	113.92	68	39490	2275	5.763	17.35
25	94450	848	.898	111.35	69	37215	2314	6.218	16.08
26	93602	863	.921	108.46	70	34901	2337	6.698	14.92
27	92739	877	.946	105.65	71	32564	2349	7.216	13.85
28	91862	892	.971	102.92	72	30215	2344	7.777	12.85
29	90970	907	.997	100.26	73	27871	2335	8.380	11.93
30	90063	922	1.023	97.66	74	25536	2306	9.030	11.07
31	89141	934	1.047	95.44	75	23230	2255	9.711	10.29
32	88207	948	1.075	92.97	76	20975	2194	10.460	9.55
33	87259	963	1.104	90.56	77	18781	2111	11.242	8.89
34	86296	978	1.133	88.21	78	16670	2016	12.099	8.26
35	85318	990	1.160	86.17	79	14654	1907	13.018	7.68
36	84328	1004	1.191	83.91	80	12747	1783	13.994	7.14
37	83324	1016	1.220	81.95	81	10964	1645	15.005	6.66
38	82308	1031	1.253	79.79	82	9319	1504	16.164	6.18
39	81277	1046	1.287	77.68	83	7815	1353	17.315	5.77
40	80231	1058	1.318	75.82	84	6462	1202	18.609	5.37
41	79173	1069	1.351	73.99	85	5260	1049	19.943	5.01
42	78104	1084	1.388	72.00	86	4211	898	21.333	4.68
43	77020	1097	1.424	70.18	87	3313	759	22.922	4.36
44	75923	1111	1.463	68.31	88	2554	626	24.537	4.07
45	74812	1120	1.497	66.78	89	1928	505	26.227	3.81
46	73692	1132	1.536	65.09	90	1423	399	28.066	3.56
47	72560	1146	1.580	63.27	91	1024	307	30.058	3.32
48	71414	1152	1.614	61.95	92	717	229	32.025	3.12
49	70262	1167	1.661	60.17	93	488	166	34.076	2.93
50	69095	1176	1.702	58.73	94	322	117	36.623	2.73
51	67919	1185	1.745	57.30	95	205	75	37.012	2.70
52	66734	1197	1.793	55.74	96	130	48	37.601	2.65
53	65537	1203	1.835	54.47	97	82	31	38.420	2.60
54	64334	1212	1.883	53.08	98	51	19	39.101	2.55
55	63122	1327	2.102	47.56	99	32	12	40.011	2.49
56	61795	1433	2.319	43.10	100	20	8	41.211	2.42
57	60362	1510	2.502	39.96	101	12	5	45.034	2.22
58	58852	1587	2.697	37.07	102	7	3	48.170	2.07
59	57265	1670	2.916	34.28	103	4	2	50.000	1.97
60	55595	1750	3.147	31.77	104	2	2	100.000	1.00
61	53845	1860	3.391	29.48					

The following Table (II.) shows the expectation of living calculated upon the mortality of England and Wales, for the year 1841, taken from the fifth Report of the Registrar General. Tables I. and II. have been given for the purpose of drawing comparisons between the value of life as existing in the whole of England and Wales, and in various classes engaged in various occupations:—

TABLE II.

EXPECTATION OF LIFE BY THE ENGLISH LIFE TABLES.—MALES.

Age.	Expecta-tion.	Age.	Expecta-tion.	Age.	Expecta-tion.	Age.	Expecta-tion.	Age.	Expecta-tion.	Age.	Expecta-tion.
18	41.26	31	32.47	44	23.96	57	15.40	70	8.51	83	4.11
19	40.57	32	31.80	45	23.30	58	14.78	71	8.08	84	3.87
20	39.88	33	31.14	46	22.65	59	14.18	72	7.67	85	3.64
21	39.19	34	30.49	47	22.00	60	13.59	73	7.28	86	3.42
22	38.51	35	29.83	48	21.34	61	13.01	74	6.90	87	3.22
23	37.83	36	29.17	49	20.68	62	12.45	75	6.53	88	3.03
24	37.15	37	28.52	50	20.02	63	11.91	76	6.18	89	2.85
25	36.47	38	27.87	51	19.36	64	11.38	77	5.85	90	2.68
26	35.80	39	27.21	52	18.70	65	10.86	78	5.52	91	2.53
27	35.13	40	26.56	53	18.03	66	10.36	79	5.21	92	2.40
28	34.46	41	25.91	54	17.36	67	9.87	80	4.92	93	2.30
29	33.79	42	25.26	55	16.68	68	9.40	81	4.64	94	2.23
30	33.13	43	24.61	56	16.03	69	8.95	82	4.37	95	2.22

In 1824, the Highland Society issued a Report showing the average amount of sickness experienced by persons at each respective age. Those tables show a very small amount of average sickness in comparison with others since published, and, for a length of time, no reliance whatever has been placed upon them.

Subsequently the Society for the Diffusion of Useful Knowledge obtained returns from Friendly Societies. These were placed in the hands of Mr. Ansell for compilation, and the results of the rate of mortality and sickness experienced in passing through 24,323 years of life, have been given in his treatise on Friendly Societies. The experience of sickness, given by him, approaches very closely to the results hereafter given of the experience of the Manchester Unity of the Independent Order of Odd Fellows; in fact, the variation of the aggregate sickness given by Mr. Ansell, in passing through a period of 50 years, from 20 to 70 years of age, is only six weeks' less sickness than the aggregate experienced during the same period of life by the members of the Unity. The aggregate sickness for each period of life will be hereafter given in a tabular form.

Mr. Neison having obtained the returns of sickness and deaths given by Friendly Societies for the years 1834-40, and the returns from Benefit Societies, has given the results of the experience of those societies, classifying it into three separate divisions, and by these means the rate of mortality and average amount of sickness may be seen for each separate division. The same results, deduced from that class of lives, in large towns and cities, and places purely rural, are also shown by Mr. Neison.

TABLE III.

AVERAGE SICKNESS PER ANNUM TO EACH PERSON,

AT THE FOLLOWING AGES, EXPRESSED IN WEEKS.—FROM MR. NEISON'S "VITAL STATISTICS."

Age.	Rural Districts.	Town Districts.	City Districts.	Rural, Town, and City Districts.	Age.	Rural Districts.	Town Districts.	City Districts.	Rural, Town, and City Districts.
10	.2257	1.2666	.3453	.4659	56	2.5240	3.4903	3.5246	2.8956
11	.4233	1.0820	.3453	.5616	57	2.7756	3.7450	3.7545	3.1371
12	.5969	.9392	.3453	.6412	58	3.0811	4.0670	3.9932	3.4293
13	.7205	.8382	.3453	.7046	59	3.4402	4.4564	4.2408	3.7722
14	.8041	.7788	.3453	.7520	60	3.8531	4.9132	4.4973	4.1657
15	.8437	.7612	.3453	.7833	61	4.3198	5.4373	4.7626	48.6099
16	.8414	.7853	.3453	.7984	62	4.9308	6.1219	5.0357	5.1904
17	.8397	.8069	.3674	.8117	63	5.6863	6.9670	5.3167	5.9073
18	.8387	.8259	.4115	.8230	64	6.5862	7.9726	5.6054	6.7605
19	.8384	.8424	.4777	.8324	65	7.6305	9.1387	5.9019	7.7501
20	.8387	.8564	.5659	.8398	66	8.8192	10.4652	6.2062	8.8760
21	.8397	.8678	.6762	.8453	67	10.0700	11.7646	6.7643	10.0679
22	.8426	.8746	.7713	.8515	68	11.3829	13.0368	7.5761	11.3257
23	.8475	.8767	.8511	.8585	69	12.7579	14.2817	8.6417	12.6494
24	.8542	.8741	.9157	.8661	70	14.1949	15.4995	9.9610	14.0391
25	.8630	.8649	.9650	.8744	71	15.6940	16.6901	11.5341	15.4947
26	.8736	.8551	.9991	.8834	72	17.1025	18.1368	13.5632	16.9652
27	.8802	.8504	1.0303	.8915	73	18.4205	19.8395	16.0483	18.4506
28	.8827	.8529	1.0584	.8988	74	19.6479	21.7984	18.9894	19.9509
29	.8810	.8626	1.0837	.9052	75	20.7848	24.0134	22.3864	21.4661
30	.8753	.8794	1.1059	.9107	76	21.8312	26.4844	26.2394	22.9963
31	.8655	.9035	1.1252	.9154	77	22.7113	28.6170	29.4479	24.3088
32	.8630	.9287	1.1480	.9250	78	23.4252	30.4112	32.0120	25.4036
33	.8677	.9551	1.1742	.9396	79	23.9730	31.8669	33.9315	26.2809
34	.8798	.9827	1.2040	.9591	80	24.3545	32.9841	35.2065	26.9405
35	.8991	1.0114	1.2372	.9836	81	24.5698	33.7629	35.8370	27.3825
36	.9257	1.0414	1.2740	1.0130	82	24.8912	34.6970	36.3375	27.9052
37	.9551	1.0819	1.3152	1.0474	83	25.3187	35.7864	36.7080	28.5086
38	.9872	1.1330	1.3611	1.0869	84	25.8523	37.0310	36.9484	29.1927
39	1.0221	1.1947	1.4114	1.1313	85	26.4920	38.4310	37.0588	29.9575
40	1.0677	1.2669	1.4663	1.1808	86	27.2378	39.9863	37.0392	30.8030
41	1.1002	1.3498	1.5258	1.2353	87	27.5232	41.0552	37.0235	31.0985
42	1.1398	1.4177	1.5901	1.2939	88	27.3481	41.8378	37.0118	30.8440
43	1.1786	1.5608	1.6593	1.3565	89	26.7126	42.3340	37.0039	30.0394
44	1.2166	1.6890	1.7335	1.4232	90	25.6167	42.5438	37.0000	28.6849
45	1.2537	1.8323	1.8125	1.4939	91	24.0603	42.6673	37.0000	26.7804
46	1.2900	1.9908	1.8964	1.5688	92	22.0610	42.9661	37.0000	24.4216
47	1.3417	2.1423	1.9954	1.6528	93	19.6187	43.2402	37.0000	21.6085
48	1.4089	2.2871	2.1095	1.7461	94	16.7334	43.4896	37.0000	18.3411
49	1.4915	2.4249	2.2388	1.8486	95	13.4051	43.7143	37.0000	14.6194
50	1.5896	2.5559	2.3831	1.9603	96	9.6339	43.7143	37.0000	10.4434
51	1.7031	2.6800	2.5426	2.0812	97	6.6169	43.7143	37.0000	7.1026
52	1.8335	2.8168	2.7144	2.2161	98	4.3541	43.7143	37.0000	4.5970
53	1.9808	2.9662	2.8985	2.3650	99	2.0914	43.7143	37.0000	2.0914
54	2.1450	3.1280	3.0949	2.5279	100	2.0914	43.7143	37.0000	2.0914
55	2.3260	3.3029	3.3036	2.7047					

On referring to Mr. Neison's "Vital Statistics," it will be found that the experience of the rate of mortality and average amount of sickness extends over a period of 1,147,143 years of life. Such a mass of experience has never been collected either before or since; and from the results there exhibited of the sickness in Benefit Societies, it considerably exceeds in amount the returns contained in any other statement heretofore given. But if the same presents a larger amount of sickness, the rate of mortality is more favourable than is shown to prevail in some other classes of society, and far more favourable than that which exists in the whole community. Many persons for whom this publication is intended, may not be in possession of Mr. Neison's work; but, to afford every one the means of comparing the average amount of sickness experienced by the three divisions of Mr. Neison with the three divisions of the Manchester Unity, Table III. has been inserted at page 12.

SECTION II.

DURATION OF LIFE IN THE UNITY.

THE Members of the Manchester Unity of the Independent Order of Odd Fellows being anxious to ascertain the rate of mortality and average sickness existing throughout their body, the Executive Government caused forms of returns to be issued to all the branches composing the Unity, requiring the Lodges to fill them up, by inserting the initials, the age, and amount of sickness (if any) experienced of each member, together with the deaths, if any had occurred; at the same time requesting them to notify, in a column left for that purpose, any member who, on whatever account, was not entitled to the benefits for any portion of time over which those returns extended. From the apparent care with which these returns have been prepared, and from the position of the Unity for obtaining this information, there is every reason to place the greatest reliance upon their correctness.

It must be understood that the Unity is composed of a large number of districts, each district being formed of a number of lodges, varying from one to eighty-four; and that the lodges of each district have one common fund, from which an allowance is paid at the death of any member. Having the means of testing the correctness of these returns, as far as mortality was concerned, the Corresponding Secretary availed himself of the opportunity, and required the secretaries of those common funds to furnish him with the number and age of such persons as had died during the period for which these returns were obtained, and found that the results agreed with the lodge returns; and thus, from an independent and distinct source, he obtained proof of the correctness of the general returns, as far as regarded mortality.

The returns received from lodges were then arranged into three classes:—

The first, or Rural Class, contained all lodges held in any township, village, or locality, the inhabitants of which numbered less than five thousand.

The second, or Town Class, included all lodges held in any town or city, the inhabitants of which numbered less than thirty and more than five thousand inhabitants; and also included all lodges held in townships bordering on large towns or cities, although they might not contain the stipulated population.

The third, or City Class, embraced all lodges held in any town or city, the population of which numbered more than thirty thousand inhabitants.

Each district of the Unity having been thus divided, each rural lodge in that district was analysed, by extracting the number of members at each age of life, the amount of sickness for such age, and the number of deaths that had taken place. These details were then entered on a sheet prepared for the purpose. The same course was continued until the whole of the rural lodges were extracted; they were then entered, each lodge separately, into a book, and headed with the name of the district, the totals forming the number of rural members, at the respective ages, the amount of sickness experienced for such year of life, and the number of deaths occurring at each age for that district.

Having thus obtained the number of members of each age, of every class, and of every district, the totals were transferred into another book, and every rural district in the same county was placed under the head of the county of which it formed a portion.

The whole of the counties were then entered under the head of "General Summary." Such general summary included the whole of the members at each age, the amount of sickness, and the number of deaths at each respective age, for every county, entered separately. The same plan was adopted for Ireland, Scotland, and Wales, and thus was obtained the sum total of all the members at each age of life, the amount of sickness for such age, and the number of deaths for every year in which they occurred.

The town and city districts were similarly arranged, and kept separate and distinct.

The totals of every age, amount of sickness, and number of deaths, for each of these three classes, will be found in Tables IV., V., and VI., and the general results of the whole combined, containing all the lives experienced upon, in rural, town, and city districts, in Table VII. In those tables the number of members, the amount of sickness, and the number of deaths, will be found in periods of years; and the rate of mortality per cent., and the average amount of sickness per annum, for that mean period of life opposite to which the same is placed.

RURAL DISTRICTS.

TABLE IV.

AGE.	No. OF MEMBERS.		DEATHS.			SICKNESS.		
	At each Age	In Periods.	At Each Age.	In Periods.		At Each Age.	In Periods.	
				Total.	Per Cent.		Total.	Per Annum.
18	849		5			261.571		
19	2096	6962	9	43	0.6176	890.000	3764.428	0.5407
20	4017		29			2612.857		
21	5936		47			3896.428		
22	8138		67			5656.142		
23	9566	46716	65	354	0.7577	6655.000	33581.140	0.7186
24	11085		85			8166.142		
25	11991		90			9207.428		
26	13237		82			9496.714		
27	13430		104			10418.142		
28	13814	68044	114	509	0.7480	10385.000	51290.712	0.7537
29	13195		93			10206.285		
30	14368		116			10784.571		

TABLE IV.—CONTINUED. 15

AGE.	No. OF MEMBERS.		DEATHS.			SICKNESS.		
	At each age.	In periods.	At Each Age.	In Periods. Total.	Per Cent.	At Each Age.	In Periods. Total.	Per Annum.
31	12322		89			9720.857		
32	12317		107			9913.142		
33	11024	58159	78	454	0.7806	8495.714	47451.140	0.8158
34	11267		94			9908.142		
35	11229		86			9413.285		
36	11352		86			9391.428		
37	9863		77			8723.285		
38	9088	45617	76	352	0.7716	8430.285	41329.568	0.9060
39	7478		48			7038.142		
40	7836		65			7746.428		
41	5584		58			5714.285		
42	5283		43			5583.142		
43	4299	22817	61	240	1.0518	4919.142	25070.425	1.0737
44	3906		42			4451.571		
45	3745		36			4402.285		
46	3437		43			5471.428		
47	2862		40			3866.571		
48	2532	12606	32	164	1.3009	3752.285	18725.283	1.4854
49	1915		28			2833.857		
50	1860		21			2801.142		
51	1167		14			2042.857		
52	889		15			1804.285		
53	668	3794	12	64	1.6868	1479.714	7707.998	2.0316
54	610		13			1469.000		
55	460		10			912.142		
56	400		8			856.285		
57	172		9			574.428		
58	241	1187	7	31	2.6116	701.714	3456.283	2.9117
59	165		4			697.571		
60	209		3			626.285		
61	125		6			698.714		
62	108		3			731.857		
63	84	469	8	20	4.2643	737.571	2894.570	6.1717
64	81		...▾			247.857		
65	71		3			478.571		
66	57		4			277.285		
67	45		?			335.142		
68	36	184	1	8	4.3468	280.571	1355.997	7.3695
69	29		1			289.142		
70	17		1			173.857		
71	25		2			346.000		
72	10		...			64.428		
73	9	62	...	3	4.8387	137.571	827.284	13.3419
74	10		1			175.285		
75	8		...			104.000		
76	3		...			3.285		
77	3		...			3.285		
78	3	11	...	0	0.0000	53.000	61.570	5.5972
79	1		...			2.000		
80	1		...			....		
81	1		...			52.000		
82	1		...			52.142		
83	2	5	1	1	20.0000	72.571	228.713	45.7426
84	...		...			....		
85	1		...			52.000		
86	...							
	266633		2243		8412	237745.111		.8916

TOWN DISTRICT.

TABLE V.

AGE.	No. OF MEMBERS.		DEATHS.			SICKNESS.		
	At each Age	In Periods.	At Each Age.	In Periods.		At Each Age.	In Periods.	
				Total.	Per Cent.		Total.	Per Annum.
18	393		2			88.857		
19	1176	3838	10	31	0.8077	509.142	1835.284	0.4781
20	2269		19			1237.285		
21	3475		24			2204.714		
22	4923		32			3376.285		
23	5993	29342	53	218	0.7429	4371.000	20793.855	0.7086
24	7248		46			4950.571		
25	7703		63*			5891.285		
26	8945		57			6866.571		
27	9112		69			6409.571		
28	9596	47505	92	361	0.6036	7559.714	36065.427	0.7600
29	9475		70			7057.571		
30	10377		73			8172.000		
31	9060		87			7643.428		
32	9059		86			7633.142		
33	8019	42810	58	393	0.9180	7823.000	38598.569	0.9016
34	8447		80			8168.571		
35	8225		82			7330.428		
36	8382		86			8361.714		
37	7103		79			6542.000		
38	6800	34560	59	342	0.9895	6911.857	34585.570	1.0007
39	5906		66			6013.285		
40	6369		52			6756.714		
41	4663		51			5086.714		
42	4622		52			5792.142		
43	3796	20016	34	217	1.0841	4073.428	23210.854	1.1596
44	3531		36			4160.142		
45	3404		44			4098.428		
46	3177		31			4157.571		
47	2627		35			3684.285		
48	2447	12391	35	173	1.3961	3546.142	19027.140	1.5355
49	2011		39			3603.428		
50	2129		33			4035.714		
51	1411		23			2471.714		
52	1300		19			2632.142		
53	1005	5388	20	103	1.9116	2583.000	11161.570	2.0715
54	971		20			1640.714		
55	701		21			1834.000		
56	746		20			2006.000		
57	478		12			1581.285		
58	516	2533	14	76	2.9980	1964.285	8373.427	3.3031
59	349		10			1321.857		
60	444		20			1500.000		
61	221		6			607.714		
62	182		11			1187.714		
63	180	878	13	45	5.1252	964.285	4291.855	4.8882
64	148		10			873.142		
65	147		5			659.000		
66	100		8			323.000		
67	72		4			275.428		
68	64	321	6	23	7.1651	649.142	1800.569	5.6092
69	37		3			288.571		
70	48		2			264.428		

TABLE V.—CONTINUED. 17

AGE.	No. OF MEMBERS.		DEATHS.			SICKNESS.		
	At each Age.	In Periods.	At Each Age.	In Periods.		At Each Age.	In Periods.	
				Total.	Per Cent.		Total.	Per Annum.
71	28		1			104.000		
72	15		2			173.142		
73	14	81	...	3	3.7037	274.000	888.427	10.9687
74	15		...			209.285		
75	9		...			128.000		
76	9		3			59.428		
77	4		...			71.142		
78	8	31	...	4	12.8032	204.142	590.140	19.0361
79	4		...			197.714		
80	6		1			57.714		
81	4		...			65.000		
82	4		...			98.000		
83	...	12	...	1	8.3333	......	169.000	14.0833
84	2		...			1.000		
85	1		1			5.000		
86	1		...			1.000		1.000
	199706		1990		.9964	201392.687		1.0084

CITY DISTRICTS.

TABLE VI.

AGE.	No. OF MEMBERS.		DEATHS.			SICKNESS.		
	At each Age.	In Periods.	At each Age.	In Periods.		At Each Age.	In Periods.	
				Total.	Per Annum.		Total.	Per Annum.
18	166		...			32.428		
19	554	1854	2	4	0.2157	235.428	780.998	0.4211
20	1134		2			513.142		
21	1921		15			1100.285		
22	2779		29			1701.428		
23	3847	19164	17	148	0.7722	2486.571	12720.283	0.6637
24	4935		42			3477.285		
25	5682		45			3954.714		
26	6485		60			5097.428		
27	7270		62			5218.000		
28	7496	37584	76	364	0.9685	5964.285	29829.570	0.7934
29	7928		72			6422.000		
30	8405		94			7127.857		
31	7978		66			6176.000		
32	7836		86			7069.142		
33	7244	37366	76	369	0.9875	5851.285	33047.855	0.8844
34	7210		71			6889.000		
35	7098		70			7062.428		
36	7216		63			6690.571		
37	6255		65			6448.857		
38	5672	29061	55	324	1.1148	6036.285	30957.569	1.0652
39	4894		70			5188.714		
40	5024		71			6593.142		
41	3859		51			5102.000		
42	3479		77			5139.285		
43	3020	15650	56	260	1.6613	4491.000	23503.570	1.5018
44	2727		43			4553.000		
45	2565		33			4218.285		

c

AGE.	No. OF MEMBERS.		DEATHS.			SICKNESS.		
	At each Age.	In Periods.	At Each Age.	In Periods.		At Each Age.	In Periods.	
				Total.	Per Annum.		Total.	Per Annum.
46	2422		46			4124.857		
47	1958		30			3619.142		
48	1802	8881	35	165	1.8578	3871.142	17296.283	1.9475
49	1407		29			2782.428		
50	1292		25			2898.714		
51	889		22			2398.857		
52	805		17			1936.571		
53	629	3450	29	109	3.1565	1375.285	8869.284	2.5708
54	660		20			1494.714		
55	467		21			1663.857		
56	433		9			2133.571		
57	292		8			949.142		
58	234	1400	7	37	2.6428	717.571	6008.140	4.2915
59	240		9			981.714		
60	201		4			1226.142		
61	176		10			1139.285		
62	128		4			975.857		
63	94	524	1	17	3.2142	511.285	3600.997	6.8721
64	74		2			391.285		
65	52		...			583.285		
66	67		7			349.571		
67	45		4			471.428		
68	29	195	2	17	8.7179	115.571	1091.998	8.6764
69	23		1			301.428		
70	31		3			454.000		
71	18		5			293.857		
72	19		3			228.000		
73	15	63	...	8	12.6984	300.571	1074.856	17.5123
74	10		...			252.428		
75	1		...					
76	5		...			28.428		
77	3		...			52.000		
78	3	21	1	2	9.5238	85.857	389.998	17.9795
79	4		...			144.428		
80	6		1			79.285		
81	2		...			15.000		
82	3		...			104.141		
83	...	8	...	1	12.5000	....	203.141	23.8177
84	3		1			84.000		
85	...		...			....		
86	1	.1	...			....		
	155222		1825		1.1757	169974.542		1.0950

RURAL, TOWN AND CITY DISTRICTS.

TABLE VII.

AGE.	No. OF MEMBERS.		DEATHS.			SICKNESS.		
	At each Age.	In Periods.	At Each Age.	In Periods. Total.	Per Cent.	At Each Age.	In Periods. Total.	Per Cent.
18	1408		7			382.856		
19	3806	12634	21	78	0.5018	1634.570	6380.710	0.5050
20	7420		50			4363.284		
21	11332		86			7201.427		
22	15840		128			10733.855		
23	19406	95222	135	720	0.7561	13512.571	67095.278	0.7046
24	23268		173			16593.998		
25	25376		198			19053.427		
26	28667		199			21460.713		
27	29812		235			22045.713		
28	30906	153133	282	1234	0.8058	23908.999	117185.709	0.7652
29	30598		235			23685.856		
30	33150		283			26084.428		
31	29360		242			23540.285		
32	29232		279			24615.426		
33	26287	138355	212	1216	0.8788	22170.000	119097.563	0.8607
34	26924		245			24965.711		
35	26552		238			23806.141		
36	26950		235			24443.713		
37	23221		221			21714.142		
38	21560	109238	190	1018	0.9340	21378.427	106872.707	0.9783
39	18278		184			18240.141		
40	19229		188			21096.284		
41	14106		160			15902.999		
42	13384		172			16514.569		
43	11115	58483	151	717	1.2259	13483.570	71784.849	1.2274
44	10164		121			13164.713		
45	9714		113			12718.998		
46	9036		120			13753.856		
47	7447		105			11169.998		
48	6781	33878	102	502	1.1818	11169.569	55048.706	1.6249
49	5333		96			9219.713		
50	5281		79			9735.570		
51	3467		59			6913.428		
52	2994		51			6372.998		
53	2302	12632	61	276	2.1849	5437.999	27738.852	2.1959
54	2241		53			4604.428		
55	1628		52			4409.999		
56	1579		37			4995.856		
57	942		29			3104.855		
58	991	5120	28	144	2.8282	3383.570	17837.850	3.4839
59	754		23			3001.142		
60	854		27			3352.427		
61	522		22			2445.713		
62	418		18			2895.428		
63	358	1871	22	82	4.5826	2213.141	10787.422	5.7655
64	303		12			1512.284		
65	270		8			1720.856		
66	224		19			949 856		
67	162		9			1081.998		
68	129	700	9	48	6.8571	1045.284	4818.564	6.9265.
69	89		5			879.141		
70	96		6			892.285		

AGE.	No. OF MEMBERS.		DEATHS.			SICKNESS.		
	At each Age.	In Periods.	At Each Age.	In Periods. Total.	In Periods. Per Cent.	At Each Age.	In Periods. Total.	In Periods. Per Cent.
71	71		8			743.857		
72	44		5			465.570		
73	38	206	...	14	6.7961	712.142		
74	74		1			636.998		
75	18		...			232.000	2790.567	13.5464
76	17		3			91.141		
77	10		...			126.427		
78	14	63	1	6	9.5237	342.999		
79	9		...			344.142	1041.708	16.5349
80	13		2			136.999		
81	7		...			132.000		
82	8		...			254.284		
83	2	24	·2	3	12.5000	72.571	600.855	25.0356
84	5		...			85.000		
85	2		1			57.000		
86	2					1.000	1.000	0.5000
	621561		6058		.9746	609112.340		.9799

In the returns received from lodges, the members were stated at their exact age on the first day of January for each year; therefore a member entered in the returns at 31 years and six months' old, would be placed on the sheets at 31 years of age, but the member would have six months' experience only in passing through his thirty-first year, and six months' experience in passing through his thirty-second year; and, as the rate of mortality, and average amount of sickness, for each period of life in the before-named tables, represented the mean period opposite to which the same was placed, it was thought that, for the purpose of adjusting the experience to each year of life, the following course would be sufficient : —

Let A 1 represent the first term,
A 2   ,,   ,, second ,,
A 3   ,,   ,, third ,,
A 4   ,,   ,, fourth ,,
A n   ,,   ,, n term; then

$$\frac{A1 + A2 + A3 + A4 + A5}{5} = A3$$

$$\frac{A2 + A3 + A4 + A5 + A6}{5} = A4$$

$$\frac{An-4 + An-3 + An-2 + An-1 + An}{5} = An-2$$

The adjusted results form the rate of mortality inserted in the fourth and ninth columns, Tables VIII., IX., X., and XI., and may be considered a fair expression of the rate of mortality for every year of life opposite to which the same is placed.

TABLE VIII.

MORTALITY.—RURAL DISTRICTS.

Age.	Living.	Dying.	Mortality per Cent.	Specific Intensity.	Age.	Living.	Dying.	Mortality per Cent.	Specific Intensity.
18	100000	645	.6456	154.89	60	61371	2014	3.2846	30.44
19	99355	655	.6596	151.60	61	59357	2141	3.6071	27.72
20	98700	664	.6736	148.45	62	57216	2216	3.8744	25.79
21	98036	687	.7016	142.53	63	55000	2243	4.0786	24.51
22	97349	704	.7236	138.19	64	52757	2236	4.2395	23.58
23	96645	714	.7396	135.20	65	50521	2171	4.2973	23.26
24	95931	719	.7497	133.38	66	48350	2085	4.3138	23.18
25	95212	717	.7537	132.67	67	46265	2020	4.3666	22.90
26	94495	710	.7518	133.01	68	44245	1945	4.3972	22.74
27	93785	704	.7515	133.06	69	42300	1887	4.4614	22.41
28	93081	701	.7530	132.80	70	40413	1836	4.4534	22.01
29	92380	698	.7561	132.25	71	38577	1790	4.6417	21.54
30	91682	697	.7610	131.40	72	36787	1783	4.8469	20.63
31	90985	698	.7675	130.29	73	35004	1806	5.1588	19.38
32	90287	697	.7723	129.48	74	33198	1851	5.5776	17.92
33	89590	695	.7755	128.94	75	31347	1913	6.1031	16.38
34	88895	691	.7771	128.68	76	29434	1982	6.7353	14.84
35	88204	685	.7770	128.71	77	27452	2032	7.4011	13.51
36	87519	678	.7752	128.70	78	25420	2058	8.1005	12.34
37	86841	681	.7848	127.42	79	23362	2063	8.8335	11.32
38	86160	694	.8060	124.06	80	21299	2044	9.6000	10.41
39	85466	717	.8388	119.21	81	19255	2002	10.4000	9.61
40	84749	748	.8831	113.10	82	17253	1915	11.1051	9.00
41	84001	807	.9391	104.05	83	15338	1797	11.7154	8.53
42	83194	827	.9940	100.60	84	13541	1655	12.2309	8.17
43	82367	863	1.0477	95.44	85	11886	1503	12.6496	7.90
44	81504	897	1.1002	90.89	86	10383	1317	12.9754	7.70
45	80607	928	1.1514	86.85	87	9036	1253	13.8742	7.20
46	79679	957	1.2012	83.25	88	7783	1194	15.3459	6.51
47	78722	989	1.2565	79.58	89	6589	1145	17.3906	5.75
48	77733	1024	1.3173	75.91	90	5444	1089	20.0101	4.99
49	76709	1061	1.3835	72.28	91	4355	1010	23.2007	4.31
50	75648	1101	1.4553	68.71	92	3345	883	26.4114	3.78
51	74547	1142	1.5324	65.25	93	2462	729	29.6421	3.37
52	73405	1197	1.6312	61.30	94	1733	571	32.8929	3.04
53	72208	1264	1.7514	57.09	95	1162	420	36.1638	2.76
54	70944	1343	1.8932	52.82	96	742	292	39.4547	2.53
55	69601	1431	2.0566	48.62	97	450	201	44.8838	2.22
56	68170	1528	2.2416	44.60	98	249	134	53.8711	1.85
57	66642	1636	2.4560	40.71	99	115	69	60.3517	1.65
58	65006	1755	2.7000	37.03	100	46	46	100.0000	1.00
59	63251	1886	2.9736	33.62					

TABLE IX.

MORTALITY.—TOWN DISTRICTS.

Age.	Living.	Dying.	Mortality per Cent.	Specific Intensity.	Age.	Living.	Dying.	Mortality per Cent.	Specific Intensity.
18	100000	794	.7946	125.84	60	58325	2244	3.8488	25.98
19	99206	781	.7881	126.01	61	56081	2397	4.2742	23.39
20	98425	769	.7816	127.97	62	53684	2521	4.6961	21.29
21	97656	750	.7687	130.09	63	51163	2616	5.1146	19.55
22	96906	729	.7527	132.91	64	48547	2683	5.5296	18.08
23	96177	706	.7338	136.27	65	45864	2715	5.9211	16.88
24	95471	679	.7119	140.46	66	43149	2739	6.3491	15.75
25	94792	651	.6870	145.56	67	40410	2640	6.5371	15.29
26	94141	620	.6592	152.04	68	37770	2457	6.5051	15.23
27	93521	607	.6495	153.96	69	35313	2208	6.2529	15.99
28	92914	611	.6580	152.32	70	33105	1913	5.7807	17.29
29	92303	631	.6846	146.07	71	31192	1587	5.0885	19.65
30	91672	668	.7294	137.09	72	29605	1450	4.8985	20.41
31	91004	721	.7922	126.52	73	28155	1467	5.2110	19.19
32	90283	763	.8454	118.28	74	26688	1608	6.0260	16.59
33	89520	795	.8888	112.51	75	25080	1841	7.3435	13.61
34	88725	818	.9226	108.38	76	23239	2129	9.1634	10.91
35	87907	831	.9466	105.63	77	21110	2244	10.6358	9.40
36	87076	836	.9609	104.06	78	18866	2219	11.7607	8.50
37	86240	841	.9761	102.44	79	16647	2085	12.5382	7.97
38	85399	847	.9923	100.77	80	14562	1888	12.9682	7.71
39	84552	853	1.0093	99.07	81	12674	1654	13.0507	7.66
40	83699	859	1.0273	97.34	82	11020	1446	13.1293	7.61
41	82840	866	1.0463	95.57	83	9574	1265	13.2158	7.56
42	81974	880	1.0739	93.11	84	8309	1104	13.2984	7.51
43	81094	900	1.1102	90.07	85	7205	964-	13.3810	7.47
44	80194	926	1.1552	86.56	86	6241	840	13.4635	7.42
45	79268	958	1.2089	82.71	87	5401	765	14.1677	7.05
46.	78310	995	1.2713	78.66	88	4636	718	15.4936	6.45
47	77315	1037	1.3418	74.52	89	3918	683	17.4410	5.73
48	76278	1083	1.4205	70.39	90	3235	647	20.0101	4.99
49	75195	1133	1.5073	66.34	91	2588	600	23.2007	4.31
50	74062	1186	1.6023	62.41	92	1988	525	26.4106	3.78
51	72876	1242	1.7054	58.64	93	1463	433	29.6399	3.37
52	71634	1311	1.8313	54.60	94	1030	338	32.8885	3.04
53	70323	1392	1.9800	50.50	95	692	250	36.1764	2.76
54	68931	1483	2.1516	46.47	96	442	174	39.4436	2.53
55	67448	1582	2.3461	42.62	97	268	120	44.9716	2.22
56	65866	1688	2.5634	39.01	98	148	78	52.7404	1.89
57	64178	1811	2.8223	35.43	99	70	42	60.5092	1.23
58	62367	1947	3.1228	32.02	100	28	28	100.0000	1.00
59	60420	2095	3.4650	28.92					

TABLE X.

MORTALITY—CITY DISTRICTS.

Age.	Living.	Dying.	Mortality per Cent.	Specific Intensity.	Age.	Living.	Dying.	Mortality per Cent.	Specific Intensity.
18	100000	215	.2157	463.60	60	52515	1514	2.8834	34.68
19	99785	382	.3826	261.36	61	51001	1532	3.0036	33.29
20	99403	435	.4383	228.15	62	49469	1740	3.5188	28.41
21	98968	543	.5496	182.01	63	47729	1827	3.8288	26.11
22	98425	636	.6464	154.70	64	45902	2081	4.5338	21.06
23	97789	713	.7289	137.19	65	43821	2381	5.4336	18.40
24	97076	773	.7969	125.48	66	41440	2705	6.5283	15.31
25	96303	819	.8506	117.56	67	38735	2929	7.5633	13.22
26	95484	849	.8898	112.38	68	35806	3057	8.5386	11.71
27	94635	872	.9220	108.45	69	32749	3096	9.4542	10.57
28	93763	888	.9471	105.59	70	29653	3057	10.3101	9.69
29	92875	896	.9651	103.61	71	26596	2954	11.1062	9.00
30	91979	898	.9761	102.44	72	23642	2740	11.6160	8.62
31	90181	892	.9799	102.05	73	20902	2474	11.8397	8.44
32	90189	891	.9880	101.21	74	18428	2170	11.7772	8.49
33	89298	893	1.0004	99.96	75	16258	1858	11.4285	8.75
34	88405	899	1.0172	98.30	76	14400	1554	10.7936	9.26
35	87506	908	1.0383	96.31	77	12846	1336	10.4047	9.61
36	86598	921	1.0637	94.01	78	11510	1181	10.2618	9.74
37	85677	947	1.1060	92.52	79	10329	1070	10.3650	9.64
38	84730	987	1.1650	85.83	80	9259	992	10.7142	9.33
39	83743	1039	1.2408	80.59	81	8267	934	11.3094	8.84
40	82704	1102	1.3334	74.99	82	7333	867	11.8308	8.45
41	81602	1174	1.4427	69.47	83	6466	794	12.2782	8.14
42	80428	1236	1.5380	65.01	84	5672	717	12.6518	7.90
43	79192	1283	1.6193	61.75	85	4955	641	12.9516	7.73
44	77909	1314	1.6866	59.29	86	4314	561	12.9738	7.69
45	76595	1332	1.7399	57.47	87	3753	525	13.9981	7.14
46	75263	1339	1.7792	56.20	88	3228	497	15.4078	6.49
47	73924	1377	1.8625	53.69	89	2731	475	17.4124	5.74
48	72547	1443	1.9900	50.23	90	2256	451	20.0101	4.99
49	71104	1537	2.1615	46.26	91	1805	418	23.2007	4.31
50	69567	1654	2.3772	42.06	92	1387	366	26.4114	3.78
51	67913	1790	2.6369	37.92	93	1021	302	29.6421	3.37
52	66123	1867	2.8241	35.40	94	719	236	32.8929	3.04
53	64256	1888	2.9388	34.02	95	483	174	36.1638	2.76
54	62368	1859	2.9811	33.54	96	309	121	39.4547	2.53
55	60509	1785	2.9509	33.88	97	188	84	44.9838	2.22
56	58724	1672	2.8482	35.10	98	104	54	52.7511	1.89
57	57052	1591	2.7901	35.83	99	50	30	60.5184	1.65
58	55461	1540	2.7766	36.01	100	20	20	100.0000	1.00
59	53921	1406	2.6077	38.34					

TABLE XI.

MORTALITY.—RURAL, TOWN AND CITY DISTRICTS.

Age.	Living.	Dying.	Mortality per Cent.	Specific Intensity.	Age.	Living.	Dying.	Mortality per Cent.	Specific Intensity.
18	100000	552	.5528	180.89	60	57520	2030	3.5293	28.33
19	99448	574	.5778	173.08	61	55490	2153	3.8808	25.76
20	98874	596	.6034	165.72	62	53337	2268	4.2525	23.51
21	98278	642	.6542	152.85	63	51069	2372	4.6450	21.52
22	97636	700	.7169	139.49	64	48697	2463	5.0583	19.76
23	96936	709	.7314	136.72	65	46234	2539	5.4924	18.20
24	96227	729	.7579	131.94	66	43695	2598	5.9473	16.81
25	95498	741	.7759	128.89	67	41097	2592	6.3087	15.85
26	94757	746	.7878	126.93	68	38505	2532	6.5768	15.20
27	94011	749	.7967	125.54	69	35973	2428	6.7515	14.81
28	93262	753	.8081	123.74	70	33545	2292	6.8327	14.63
29	92509	759	.8205	121.87	71	31253	2131	6.8205	14.66
30	91750	765	.8338	119.93	72	29122	2015	6.9198	14.45
31	90985	771	.8484	117.86	73	27107	1932	7.1307	14.02
32	90214	777	.8622	115.98	74	25175	1876	7.4531	13.41
33	89437	783	.8758	114.18	75	23299	1837	7.8871	12.67
34	88654	787	.8886	112.53	76	21462	1809	8.4326	11.85
35	87867	791	.9008	111.01	77	19653	1803	9.1777	10.89
36	87076	792	.9118	109.67	78	17850	1806	10.1225	9.87
37	86284	804	.9323	107.26	79	16044	1807	11.2670	8.87
38	85480	822	.9623	103.91	80	14237	1795	12.6111	7.92
39	84658	848	1.0018	99.82	81	12442	1761	14.1547	7.06
40	83810	880	1.0507	95.17	82	10681	1681	15.7446	6.34
41	82930	919	1.1091	90.16	83	9000	1564	17.3806	5.75
42	82011	956	1.1660	85.72	84	7436	1484	19.0627	5.00
43	81055	990	1.2215	81.86	85	5952	1237	20.7911	4.80
44	80065	1021	1.2756	78.39	86	4715	1063	22.5656	4.43
45	79044	1049	1.3282	75.28	87	3652	887	24.3057	4.11
46	77995	1073	1.3794	72.49	88	2765	719	26.0114	3.84
47	76922	1114	1.4484	69.04	89	2046	566	27.6827	3.61
48	75808	1164	1.5354	65.12	90	1480	433	29.3197	3.41
49	74644	1224	1.6402	60.96	91	1047	323	30.9222	3.23
50	73420	1294	1.7630	56.72	92	724	236	32.6805	3.05
51	72126	1346	1.9036	53.50	93	488	168	34.5948	2.30
52	70780	1445	2.0418	48.97	94	320	117	36.6649	2.72
53	69335	1513	2.1777	45.81	95	203	78	38.8910	2.57
54	67822	1567	2.3110	43.27	96	125	51	41.2729	2.42
55	66255	1618	2.4421	40.94	97	74	34	46.0747	2.17
56	64637	1662	2.5717	38.88	98	40	21	53.2905	1.87
57	62975	1727	2.7438	36.44	99	19	11	60.5183	1.65
58	61248	1813	2.9614	33.76	100	8	8	100.0000	1.00
59	59435	1915	3.2234	31.02					

Having thus obtained the rate of mortality at each year of life, it became a mere matter of arithmetic to form a mortality table, adopting the arbitrary number of 100,000 with which to commence ; and, having ascertained the rate of mortality, to multiply the persons then alive (100,000) by such rate of mortality, and divide the same by 100, the result showing the number of persons who would die in accordance with that rate of mortality, previous to their entering on the nineteenth year. This number, subtracted from the living, gives the number living and entering on the nineteenth year of life. Multiply the living at nineteen years of age by the rate of mortality, and divide the same, as before, by 100, and the number of persons who will die, according to that rate of mortality, in passing through their nineteenth year, is found ; subtract the number dying during the year from the living at nineteen years of age, and we obtain the number of persons who will be alive on entering upon the twentieth year of life. This course pursued for every year of life, until all the lives become exhausted, a table of mortality is obtained, showing the number of persons alive out of 100,000, commencement of the table, at every year of life, and the number of deaths occurring at each respective age, out of the number then living.

If attention be paid to the respective tables of mortality, commencing with Table VIII., Rural Districts, viewed in comparison with that previously given for the whole of England and Wales, it will be observed that out of 100,000 persons at age eighteen, 750 persons die in passing through that year, but that, in the rural districts, out of the same number of persons at that age, only 645 persons die during the year, and that, up to the age 54, the vitality is in favour of the rural districts ; but, from that period of life to age 64, the mortality of the rural districts of the Unity is greater than the whole community. After that period the same again becomes favourable to the rural class of the Unity. It will be observed from each table, England and Wales, and Rural Districts, commencing with 100,000 persons, that, in the former, half of that number die off at age 63-64, but the lives in the rural class attain the age 65-66 before half of them are exhausted. The experience of the lives in rural class, as shown by Mr. Neison, exhibits a superior vitality of four years, in comparison with the rural districts of the Unity. His tables of mortality commence at age ten, and, on arriving at the eighteenth year of age, he has then 97,093 lives, and, before half of these lives are exhausted, he shows that they attain the ages 69-70, exhibiting, consequently, a superior vitality of four years.

The Town Districts, at age eighteen, exhibit a higher rate of mortality than for the whole of the community of England and Wales, but a gradual decrease takes place up to age 27, when they show the lowest rate. From that age the rate of mortality increases until the arrival at 54, when it crosses, and becomes larger than in the whole community, and retains that position up to age 70, when it again becomes more favourable to the town districts of the Unity up to the termination of the table. As previously stated, half the lives die off in the whole community at ages 63-64, and the same rule applies to the town districts. Although this presents a fluctuating rate of mortality, still it is one nearly equal to that of the whole community ; but if the same be traced up to age 80, it will be found that the rate of mortality becomes superior to the whole community, for in the town districts, at that age, there are 14,562 lives existing, and in the whole community only 12,747 persons have lived to attain age 80.

In the City Districts half the lives die off before attaining age 62 ; thus showing a superior vitality in the whole community of two years over the city districts of the Unity, and although the rate of mortality of the city districts in the early portion of the table is very low, it increases so rapidly in comparison with the whole community, that it is exceeded at age 40, and maintains that increase up to 70 years of age.

D

The Rural, Town, and City Districts are composed of the whole of the Members, wherever located, and as many of them are inhabitants of the most densely populated cities, and follow both dangerous and unhealthful occupations, they may be considered a fair sample of the general community, but, on examination, it will be found that the rate of mortality is superior to that in the whole community at the early period of life, and retains that superiority up to age 40. From that time the rate decreases, until at the arrival of age 50 the mortality becomes more vital than in the whole community, and so remains up to age 71, when a change takes place in favour of the whole community. It will be noticed that, although the rate of mortality at the early period of life is favourable to the Unity, the mortality increases more rapidly in the middle ages of life, that half the lives become exhausted at the ages 63-64 ; the same takes place at this period in the whole community. From the tables of Mr. Neison it appears that half the lives living at age eighteen are exhausted at the ages 66-67, and this, for the three districts, composed of rural, town, and city, shows a superior vitality of three years more than the three districts of the Manchester Unity.

The Specific Intensity shows the number living, out of which one will die annually at the respective age. The specific intensity is obtained by dividing the numbers living at each age of life by the numbers dying in passing through such year, and shows very clearly the rapidity with which mortality increases. In the specific intensity of the whole of England and Wales, one gradual and uniform decrease takes place, from the beginning to the extreme of the table. In the rural districts the specific intensity decreases from the earliest to the last age in the table, with one slight exception at age 70 ; the same taking place with more rapidity than in the whole community up to 60 years of age. After that period a slow but regular decrease takes place, except at the age stated.

The specific intensity of the town districts is found, at the earliest age in the table, to be lower than in the whole community ; it increases up to age 27, then decreases to age 67, when another fluctuation takes place, which increases the intensity up to age 72. From that period of life a slow but regular decrease takes place until the extreme of the table.

In the city districts the specific intensity is the highest at the early ages, but decreases so rapidly, that at the age 41 it becomes less than in the whole community, and remains so up to age 50. At this period a favourable change takes place, which continues until the last age of the lives.

The Expectation of Life is the most interesting result presented, as it clearly shows the length of time one person has with another to participate in the pleasures and cares of existence. If reference be made to Mortality Table XI., Rural, Town, and City Districts, it will be seen that there are 203 persons alive at age 95 ; 125 persons alive at age 96 ; 74 persons alive at age 97 ; 40 persons alive at age 98 ; 19 persons alive at age 99 ; and 8 persons alive at age 100. The total number of these persons is 469, and if half the number alive at age 95 be subtracted from it, and the remainder divided by the number of persons living at age 95, the expectation of life will be found, which is shown to be 1.80 years ; and if the same course be taken for each age, viz. the number of members living at the age for which the expectation is wanted, added to those living at every year afterwards through the table, half the living at the age subtracted, and the remainder divided by the persons living at such age, a table of the expectation of life would be obtained. It has been previously stated that the expectation of life, at age 95, is 1.80 years. This is the average length of time that the 469 persons, aged 95, will live ; some of them would die during the year, others in the year following, but after the termination of life, if the number of years each person had lived after 95 years were placed together, and divided by the number of persons, it would be found that the average duration of their lives was 1.80 years.

The Expectation of Life, given in the English Life Table (III), calculated upon the experience of the whole community, can be read without the figures on the right side of the period ; as, at age 18 read 41, omitting the 26, and the 41 gives the expectation of life at age 18. In the Expectation Table (XII), as there are three decimal places on the right side of the period, omit three figures ; at age 18, rural districts, read 44, omitting the figures 901, although such a decimal fraction amounts to nearly a whole number, which would make the expectation 45.

The rate of mortality and average amount of sickness experienced in the Unity for the year 1849 was previously ascertained, and given to the Members immediately after that time. If reference be made to the expectation then shown to exist, and which was calculated from one year's experience, it will be found more favourable than what is now seen to prevail. The following difference in years shows the superiority as exhibited at that time from that experience :

At age 20 the expectation then shows .676 higher.

,,	30	,,	,,	.893	,,
,,	40	,,	,,	.910	,,
,,	50	,,	,,	1.052	,,
,,	60	,,	,,	.868	,,
,,	70	,,	,,	1.115	,,

From the following results, placed in a tabular form, it will be seen that in comparison with the whole community of England and Wales, in the rural districts, at each decennial period, there is a higher expectation of life.

Age 20 the difference is 3.598 years.

,,	30	,,	,,	3.292	,,
,,	40	,,	,,	2.468	,,
,,	50	,,	,,	1.823	,,
,,	60	,,	,,	2.058	,,
,,	70	,,	,,	2.705	,,

In the Town Districts there is a higher expectation of life at the periods of 20, 30, 40, and 70 years, and at the periods of 50 and 60 years the expectation is shown to be higher in the whole community. The following shows the difference of expectation and the class which it favours :—

Age 20, difference in favour of Unity, 1.565 years.

,,	30,	,,	,,	1.024	,,
,,	40,	,,	,,	.335	,,
,,	70,	,,	,,	1.537	,,
,,	50, difference in favour of Community,			.300	,,
,,	60,	,,	,,	.400	,,

In City Districts the expectation of life is less at every period than the expectation of the whole of England and Wales.

Age 20, the difference in favour of whole Community, .951 years

,,	30,	,,	,,	1.510	,,
,,	40,	,,	,,	1.968	,,
,,	50,	,,	,,	1.777	,,
,,	60,	,,	,,	988	,,
,,	70,	,,	,,	617	,,

When a comparison of the expectation of the whole Unity with that of England and Wales is made, the difference is not more than what might have been expected ; in fact, except at the period of 20 years, there is not any material difference, and this period, in appearance is

TABLE XII.

EXPECTATION.—RURAL, TOWN, AND CITY DISTRICTS,

AND THE

THREE DISTRICTS COMBINED.

Age.	Rural.	Town.	City.	Rural, Town and City.	Age.	Rural.	Town.	City.	Rural, Town and City.
18	44.901	42.776	40.689	42.453	60	15.648	13.550	12.602	13.292
19	44.189	42.114	39.775	41.691	61	15.159	13.072	11.961	12.761
20	43.478	41.445	38.929	40.920	62	14.707	12.634	11.317	12.252
21	42.779	40.759	38.095	40.172	63	14.279	12.231	10.710	11.781
22	42.068	40.070	37.294	39.433	64	13.865	11.864	10.113	11.334
23	41.371	39.462	36.542	38.712	65	13.457	11.528	9.573	10.902
24	40.675	38.658	35.807	37.994	66	13.032	11.222	9.094	10.504
25	39.979	37.931	35.090	37.284	67	12.604	10.949	8.695	10.141
26	39.278	37.190	34.387	36.576	68	12.156	10.679	8.365	9.791
27	38.572	36.434	33.691	35.854	09	11.692	10.387	8.099	9.451
28	37.856	35.557	33.000	35.142	70	11.215	10.047	7.893	9.092
29	37.143	34.905	32.510	34.422	71	10.725	9.633	7.743	8.721
30	36.422	34.154	31.620	33.702	72	10.223	9.122	7.648	8.331
31	35.598	33.393	30.909	32.984	73	9.632	8.567	7.585	7.912
32	34.970	32.656	30.228	32.263	74	9.217	8.010	7.536	7.481
33	34.238	31.930	29.504	31.531	75	8.734	7.491	7.475	7.043
34	33.502	31.212	28.818	30.812	76	8.267	7.045	7.394	6.586
35	32.760	30.499	28.109	30.084	77	7.830	6.706	7.207	6.165
36	32.020	29.784	27.456	29.353	78	7.416	6.449	6.985	5.737
37	31.259	29.068	26.687	28.614	79	7.026	6.236	6.727	5.327
38	30.502	28.349	25.980	27.885	80	6.641	6.057	6.446	4.947
39	29.745	27.628	25.280	27.143	81	6.312	5.885	6.160	4.589
40	29.028	26.895	24.592	26.412	82	5.986	5.694	5.881	4.253
41	28.243	26.178	23.917	25.693	83	5.671	5.478	5.602	3.954
42	27.516	25.449	23.259	24.971	84	5.357	5.236	5.316	3.686
43	26.787	24.720	22.614	24.263	85	5.034	4.962	5.014	3.472
44	26.065	23.992	21.978	23.552	86	4.690	4.651	4.684	3.251
45	25.350	23.266	21.347	22.856	87	4.315	4.297	4.310	3.057
46	24.639	22.545	20.716	22.155	88	3.932	3.924	3.930	2.878
47	23.933	21.829	20.082	21.452	89	3.551	3.551	3.554	2.713
48	23.231	21.119	19.453	20.763	90	3.174	3.196	3.197	2.559
49	22.571	20.416	18.838	20.083	91	2.866	2.869	2.871	2.411
50	21.843	19.720	18.243	19.402	92	2.580	2.592	2.586	2.262
51	21.109	19.033	18.097	18.743	93	2.326	2.333	2.334	2.111
52	20.603	18.354	17.140	18.091	94	2.094	2.103	2.105	1.965
53	19.811	17.687	16.625	17.465	95	1.878	1.887	1.889	1.813
54	19.155	17.035	16.112	16.834	96	1.659	1.671	1.671	1.626
55	18.515	16.398	15.592	16.226	97	1.451	1.430	1.425	1.405
56	17.893	15.780	15.050	15.615	98	1.146	1.162	1.173	1.175
57	17.292	15.182	14.477	15.014	99	.900	.900	.900	.921
58	16.715	14.608	13.878	14.423	100	.500	500	.500	.500
59	16.165	14.053	13.260	14.853					

affected by the higher expectation of the rural class, which causes the large difference at that period, in comparison with the other periods of life.

Age 20, the difference is in favour of the Unity, 1.04 years.

,, 30, ,, ,, .57 ,,

,, 70, ,, ,, .58 ,,

,, 40, the difference is in favour of whole Community, .15 ,,

,, 50, ,, ,, .57 ,,

,, 60, ,, ,, .30 ,,

EXPECTATION.—ENGLAND AND WALES,—MANCHESTER UNITY.

Mr. Neison.*

Age.	England and Wales.	MANCHESTER UNITY.				MR. NEISON'S TABLES.			
		Rural.	Town.	City.	Rural, Town and City.	Rural.	Town.	City.	Rural, Town and City.
20	39.88	43.47	41.44	38.92	40.92	45.35	42.27	40.01	43.77
30	33.13	36.42	34.15	31.62	33.70	38.40	34.57	32.86	36.60
40	26.56	29.02	26.89	24.59	26.41	30.97	27.15	26.08	29.33
50	20.02	21.84	19.72	18.24	19.40	23.47	19.97	19.92	22.19
60	13.59	15.64	13.55	12.60	13.29	16.65	13.76	13.76	15.69
70	8.51	11.21	10.04	7.89	9.09	10.71	8.70	8.76	10.20

From the above extracts of the expectation, taken from Mr. Neison's "Vital Statistics," it will be seen that in the rural districts, at each decennial period of life, there appears a higher expectation, except at the last period given, when the expectation of the Unity seems to be rather higher than the expectation given by Mr. Neison. In the town districts there does not appear that difference of expectation at any period of life which shows itself in either of the other two classes, or in the whole when combined. The high expectation of life showing itself in the rural districts is maintained in the city districts, and that at every period of life.

When the three districts of the Unity become combined, and the same of the districts of Mr. Neison, it will be seen that the difference in the expectation of the whole Unity, and the expectation of the whole of the lives of Mr. Neison, become greater than the expectation in any of the classes alone.

At Age 20, the difference in favour of Mr. Neison's Tables is 2.85.

,, 30, ,, ,, 2 96.

,, 40, ,, ,, 2.92.

,, 50, ,, ,, 2.79.

,, 60, ,, ,, 2.40.

,, 70, ,, ,, 1.11.

If reference be made to the best class of lives shown to exist in the Manchester Unity, it will be seen that the expectation shown for the rural class of Mr. Neison's lives is nearly equal to the expectation of any of those trades or classes.

---

* Mr. Neison gives the expectation to four places of decimals.

SECTION III.

AVERAGE AMOUNT OF SICKNESS EXPERIENCED

IN THE

MANCHESTER UNITY.

IF reference be again made to Tables IV., V., VI., and VII., the second column shows the number of persons at each year of life, and the ninth column, the amount of sickness experienced by those persons in passing through that year. The same results are given in weeks, and decimal fractions of a week. Of the columns next adjacent, one contains the number of persons at each period of five years, and the other the amount of sickness experienced amongst those persons for the same period of life. Such amount of sickness, being divided by the number of persons, gives the average amount of sickness per annum experienced for the mean age opposite to which it is placed. This average amount of sickness per annum conveys a just idea of the gradual increase of sickness to which persons are subject as they advance in years.

The mean average sickness per annum having been thus obtained, the same course was pursued as that previously explained, and the results give the average amount of sickness per annum experienced by the members of the Manchester Unity at each age, for the rural, town and city districts, and for the three districts combined. The results given in Table XIII., are shown in weeks and decimals of a week, and, for the convenience of those persons unacquainted with decimal fractions, they have been given in weeks, days, and hours. It must be observed that, in making any additions of the aggregate sickness, a slight discrepancy will appear, from the various reductions, and a small loss at each year of age by such reductions.

If an examination of the average amount of sickness be gone into as exhibited in Table XIII., Rural Districts, it will be seen that a very regular, but, at periods, an accelerating increase of sickness takes place from the earliest age in the table up to 73. At that period, and up to 77, a small decrease ensues, but after the age 77 the increase continues at a more rapid pace.

TABLE XIII.

AVERAGE SICKNESS PER ANNUM TO EACH PERSON,

EXPERIENCED IN

RURAL, TOWN, AND CITY DISTRICTS, AND THE THREE DISTRICTS COMBINED.

Age.	Rural.			Town.			City.			Rural, Town and City.		
	Weeks.	W.	D. H.	Weeks.	W.	D. H.	Weeks.	W.	D. H.	Weeks.	W.	D. H.
18	.5764 =	0	4 0	.5242 =	0	3 16	.4696 =	0	3 6	.5449 =	0	3 19
19	.5942 =	0	4 3	.5473 =	0	3 20	.4938 =	0	3 11	.5648 =	0	3 23
20	.6012 =	0	4 5	.5703 =	0	4 0	.5181 =	0	3 14	.5849 =	0	4 2
21	.6476 =	0	4 12	.6164 =	0	4 7	.5666 =	0	3 23	.6247 =	0	4 8
22	.6775 =	0	4 17	.6553 =	0	4 14	.6106 =	0	4 6	.6589 =	0	4 14
23	.7016 =	0	4 22	.6870 =	0	4 19	.6501 =	0	4 13	.6878 =	0	4 17
24	.7199 =	0	5 0	.7116 =	0	4 23	.6850 =	0	4 19	.7111 =	0	4 23
25	.7326 =	0	5 3	.7291 =	0	5 0	.7155 =	0	5 0	.7288 =	0	5 2
26	.7396 =	0	5 4	.7394 =	0	5 4	.7414 =	0	5 4	.7409 =	0	5 4
27	.7477 =	0	5 5	.7533 =	0	5 6	.7658 =	0	5 8	.7544 =	0	5 6
28	.7569 =	0	5 7	.7708 =	0	5 9	.7889 =	0	5 12	.7693 =	0	5 9
29	.7671 =	0	5 8	.7919 =	0	5 13	.8100 =	0	5 16	.7856 =	0	5 11
30	.7785 =	0	5 11	.8166 =	0	5 17	.8298 =	0	5 19	.8034 =	0	5 15

TABLE XIII.—CONTINUED.   31

Age.	Rural. Weeks.	W.	D.	H.	Town. Weeks.	W.	D.	H.	City. Weeks.	W.	D.	H.	Rural, Town and City. Weeks.	W.	D.	H.
31	.7909 =	0	5	12	.8449 =	0	5	22	.8480 =	0	5	23	.8225 =	0	5	18
32	.8042 =	0	5	15	.8715 =	0	6	2	.8697 =	0	6	2	.8424 =	0	5	21
33	.8184 =	0	5	17	.8964 =	0	6	6	.8951 =	0	6	6	.8633 =	0	6	1
34	.8334 =	0	5	20	.9196 =	0	6	10	.9240 =	0	6	11	.8850 =	0	6	4
35	.8494 =	0	5	23	.9412 =	0	6	14	.9566 =	0	6	16	.9077 =	0	6	8
36	.8674 =	0	6	1	.9610 =	0	6	17	.9927 =	0	6	23	.9312 =	0	6	12
37	.8888 =	0	6	5	.9832 =	0	6	21	1.0391 =	1	0	6	.9600 =	0	6	17
38	.9135 =	0	6	9	1.0078 =	1	0	1	1.0938 =	1	0	15	.9940 =	0	6	23
39	.9416 =	0	6	14	1.0348 =	1	0	5	1.1607 =	1	1	3	1.0333 =	1	0	5
40	.9730 =	0	6	19	1.0644 =	1	0	11	1.2379 =	1	1	15	1.0779 =	1	0	13
41	1.0065 =	1	0	1	1.0960 =	1	0	16	1.3252 =	1	2	6	1.1277 =	1	0	21
42	1.0498 =	1	0	8	1.1364 =	1	0	23	1.4129 =	1	2	21	1.1834 =	1	1	6
43	1.1029 =	1	0	17	1.1856 =	1	1	7	1.5029 =	1	3	12	1.2451 =	1	1	17
44	1.1657 =	1	1	3	1.2434 =	1	1	16	1.5912 =	1	4	3	1.3128 =	1	2	4
45	1.2388 =	1	1	16	1.3099 =	1	2	4	1.6800 =	1	4	18	1.3864 =	1	2	16
46	1.3206 =	1	2	5	1.3851 =	1	2	16	1.7691 =	1	5	6	1.4659 =	1	3	6
47	1.4088 =	1	2	20	1.4667 =	1	3	6	1.8653 =	1	6	1	1.5523 =	1	3	20
48	1.5014 =	1	3	12	1.5547 =	1	3	21	1.9687 =	1	6	18	1.6457 =	1	4	12
49	1.5999 =	1	4	4	1.6451 =	1	4	12	2.0791 =	2	0	13	1.7460 =	1	5	5
50	1.7038 =	1	4	23	1.7499 =	1	5	6	2.1967 =	2	1	9	1.8533 =	1	5	23
51	1.8130 =	1	5	16	1.8571 =	1	6	0	2.3213 =	2	2	6	1.9675 =	1	6	18
52	1.9356 =	1	6	13	1.9921 =	1	6	23	2.4897 =	2	3	10	2.1103 =	2	0	18
53	2.0716 =	2	0	12	2.1549 =	2	1	2	2.7023 =	2	4	22	2.2819 =	2	1	2
54	2.2209 =	2	1	13	2.3456 =	2	2	10	2.9582 =	2	6	17	2.4821 =	2	3	8
55	2.3836 =	2	2	16	2.5641 =	2	3	23	3.2590 =	3	1	19	2.7111 =	2	4	23
56	2.5596 =	2	3	22	2.8104 =	2	5	16	3.6031 =	3	4	4	2.9687 =	2	6	18
57	2.8308 =	2	5	19	3.0708 =	3	0	11	3.9816 =	3	6	20	3.2660 =	3	1	20
58	3.1972 =	3	1	5	3.3454 =	3	2	14	4.3946 =	4	2	18	3.6031 =	3	4	5
59	3.6588 =	3	4	14	3.6342 =	3	4	10	4.8419 =	4	5	21	3.9799 =	3	6	20
60	4.2157 =	4	1	12	3.9371 =	3	6	13	5.3237 =	5	2	6	4.3985 =	4	2	18
61	4.8677 =	4	6	1	4.2541 =	4	1	18	5.8398 =	5	5	21	4.8548 =	4	5	23
62	5.4372 =	5	3	1	4.5353 =	4	3	17	6.3248 =	6	2	6	5.2662 =	5	1	20
63	5.9242 =	5	6	11	4.7844 =	4	5	11	6.7788 =	6	5	10	5.6330 =	5	4	10
64	6.3287 =	6	2	7	4.9978 =	4	6	23	7.2018 =	7	1	9	5.9548 =	5	6	16
65	6.6507 =	6	4	13	5.1766 =	5	1	5	7.5933 =	7	4	3	6.2299 =	6	1	14
66	6.8902 =	6	6	5	5.3208 =	5	2	5	7.9545 =	7	6	16	6.4621 =	6	3	5
67	7.3208 =	7	2	5	5.6505 =	5	4	13	8.5966 =	8	4	4	6.9126 =	6	6	9
68	7.9423 =	7	6	14	6.1658 =	6	1	3	9.5200 =	9	3	15	7.5815 =	7	4	1
69	8.7549 =	8	5	7	6.8666 =	6	6	1	10.7247 =	10	5	1	8.4688 =	8	3	6
70	9.7585 =	9	5	7	7.7490 =	7	5	5	12.2106 =	12	1	11	9.5744 =	9	4	0
71	10.9529 =	10	6	16	8.8249 =	8	5	18	13.9777 =	13	6	20	10.8084 =	10	6	6
72	11.5987 =	11	4	4	10.0052 =	10	0	0	15.4102 =	15	2	20	12.0771 =	12	0	12
73	11.6958 =	11	4	20	11.0938 =	11	0	15	16.5073 =	16	3	13	13.1106 =	13	0	18
74	11.2442 =	11	1	7	12.6908 =	12	4	20	17.2708 =	17	1	21	13.9988 =	13	7	0
75	10.2439 =	10	1	16	14.1961 =	14	1	8	17.6991 =	17	4	21	14.7418 =	14	5	4
76	8.6950 =	8	4	20	15.8097 =	15	5	16	17.7925 =	17	5	13	15.3395 =	15	2	9
77	9.0616 =	9	0	10	16.9057 =	16	6	8	18.0888 =	18	0	14	16.1516 =	15	1	1
78	11.3439 =	11	2	9	17.4842 =	17	3	9	18.5879 =	18	4	2	17.1843 =	17	1	6
79	15.5417 =	15	3	19	17.5451 =	17	3	19	19.2898 =	19	2	0	18.4374 =	18	3	1
80	21.6552 =	21	4	14	17.0886 =	17	0	14	20.1946 =	20	1	8	19.9111 =	19	6	9
81	29.6842 =	29	4	18	16.1158 =	16	0	19	21.3022 =	21	2	2	21.6112 =	21	4	6
82	30.1075 =	30	0	18	15.3354 =	15	2	8	22.1884 =	22	1	7	22.9773 =	22	6	20
83	40.5250 =	40	3	16	14.7510 =	14	5	6	22.8530 =	22	5	23	24.0034 =	24	0	0
84	44.1367 =	44	0	22	14.3622 =	14	2	12	23.2961 =	23	2	1	24.6895 =	24	4	19
85	45.7426 =	45	5	4	14.1666 =	14	1	4	23.5177 =	23	3	14	25.0356 =	25	0	5
86	46.3526 =	46	2	11	13.9534 =	13	6	16	23.8314 =	23	5	19	25.3145 =	25	2	4

The experience of the town districts shows a less average amount of sickness than the rural districts, at the early ages in the table, but, increasing in amount, crosses the rural districts at age 27, and exhibits a higher amount of average sickness up to age 58. It then becomes more favourable to the town districts ; so much so, that the aggregate amount of sickness experienced by the town districts, in passing through the period 60-70 years, is only 51.6890 = 51 weeks, 4 days, 17 hours ; and, for the same period, the rural districts present an aggregate of sickness experienced, of 64.3324 = 64 weeks, 2 days, 5 hours. After this period has been passed, and by the time of attaining age 74, an increase in the average amount again takes place, more than equal to the decrease in the former period ; but as the same occurs at a later period in life than is shown in the rural districts, and the rate of mortality being greater in the town than in the rural districts, a less number of persons would live to claim the allowance for sickness at this period of life. The same results that occur here, between the ages 60 and 70, occurred in the results of the experience of 1849, thus showing that neither additional numbers, nor longer periods of time, have affected the experience.

The city districts present a still less average amount of sickness in the early period of the table, but the average increases with more rapidity than in the town districts, though quite at a regular and uniform rate, so that the average amount of sickness, at age 26, shows a larger amount than experienced in either of the districts before alluded to. Such increase continues from the very earliest to the extreme of the average given, but near the extremity decreases in the average amount, in comparison with the rural districts.

The three districts, when they become combined, exhibiting the average amount of sickness experienced in the Order, show one uniform and accelerating rate of increase in the average amount, from the first to the latest age given, and may be said to show the real average sickness experienced at each year, amongst the whole community of the Manchester Unity, including every trade and every class, whether resident in the densely crowded city, or located in the thinly populated places of the country.

The following table has been formed, to give a general idea of the average amount of sickness experienced at each decennial period of life, for the rural, town, and city districts, and the three districts combined, of the Manchester Unity, with the average sickness experienced by the lives of Mr. Neison for each of those classes, and the average sickness experienced by the lives of Mr. Ansell. Each class has been given separately, and if a comparison be instituted with the amount shown by Mr. Neison's tables, such comparison can be made of any one class with the same class in the Unity ; and should a comparison be drawn with the average sickness shown by Mr. Ansell, the experience of the whole Unity ought to be compared with it, as Mr. Ansell's experience does not show it to be of any one particular locality. It has been previously named, that little reliance has been placed, for some years back, on the Highland Society's Report, but to afford an opportunity of seeing the average amount experienced and taken from that report, the same is herewith given.

AVERAGE SICKNESS PER ANNUM TO EACH PERSON, AT DECENNIAL PERIODS OF LIFE.

MANCHESTER UNITY & MR. ANSELL'S TABLE.

Age	MANCHESTER UNITY						Rural, Town and City		Mr. Ansell's Table.	
	Rural.		Town.		City.					
	Weeks.	W. D. H.	Weeks.	W. D. H.	Weeks.	W. D. H.	Weeks.	W. D. H.	Weeks.	W. D. H.
20	.5942 =	0 4 3	.5703 =	0 4 0	.5181 =	0 3 14	.5849 =	0 4 2	.776 =	0 5 10
30	.7785 =	0 5 11	.8166 =	0 5 17	.8298 =	0 5 19	.8034 =	0 5 15	.861 =	0 6 0
40	.9730 =	0 6 19	1.0644 =	1 0 11	1.2379 =	1 1 15	1.0779 =	1 0 13	1.111 =	1 0 18
50	1.7088 =	1 4 23	1.7499 =	1 5 6	2.1067 =	2 1 9	1.8533 =	1 5 23	1.701 =	1 4 21
60	4.2157 =	4 1 12	3.9871 =	3 6 13	5.3237 =	5 2 6	4.3985 =	4 2 18	3.292 =	3 2 1
70	9.7585 =	9 5 7	7.7490 =	7 5 5	12.2106 =	12 1 11	9.5744 =	9 4 0	11.793 =	11 5 13
80	21.6552 =	21 4 14	17.0886 =	17 0 14	20.1946 =	20 1 8	19.9111 =	19 6 9		

AVERAGE SICKNESS PER ANNUM TO EACH PERSON, AT DECENNIAL PERIODS OF LIFE.

BY MR. NEISON'S TABLES & HIGHLAND SOCIETY.

Age	MR. NEISON'S TABLES.						Rural, Town and City.		Highland Society.	
	Rural.		Town.		City.					
	Weeks.	W. D. H.	Weeks.	W. D. H.	Weeks.	W. D. H.	Weeks.	W. D. H.	Weeks.	W. D. H.
20	.8387 =	0 5 21	.8564 =	0 6 0	.5659 =	0 3 23	.8398 =	0 5 21	.575 =	0 4 8
30	.8753 =	0 6 3	.8794 =	0 6 4	1.1059 =	1 0 18	.9107 =	0 6 9	.621 =	0 4 9
40	1.0677 =	1 0 11	1.2669 =	1 1 21	1.4663 =	1 3 6	1.1308 =	1 0 22	.758 =	0 5 0
50	1.5896 =	1 4 3	2.5559 =	2 3 21	2.3831 =	2 2 10	1.9603 =	1 6 17	1.361 =	1 2 12
60	3.8531 =	3 5 23	4.9132 =	4 6 9	4.4973 =	4 3 12	4.1657 =	4 1 4	2.346 =	2 2 10
70	14.1949 =	14 1 9	15.4995 =	15 3 12	9.9610 =	9 6 17	14.0391 =	14 0 7	10.701 =	10 4 21
80	24.3545 =	24 2 11	32.9841 =	32 6 21	35.2065 =	35 1 11	26.9405 =	26 6 14		

COMPARATIVE VIEW OF SICKNESS, IN VARIOUS PERIODS OF YEARS, FROM THE TABLES OF MR. NEISON, THE TABLES OF MR. ANSELL, AND THE EXPERIENCE OF THE UNITY.

AMOUNT OF SICKNESS IN EACH PERIOD OF YEARS, AS SHOWN BY MR. NEISON'S TABLES.

From Age	Rural		Town		City		Rural, Town, and City.		Excess for each period over Manchester Unity, R, T, and C.
	Weeks.	W. D. H.	Weeks.	W. D. H.	Weeks.	W. D. H.	Weeks.	W. D. H.	W. D. H.
20 to 30	8.6032 =	8 4 2	9.5149 =	9 3 14	8.9167 =	8 6 10	8.7145 =	8 5 0	1.0681 = 1 4 16
30 to 40	9.1405 =	9 0 20	10.4993 =	10 3 11	12.3562 =	12 2 11	9.9120 =	9 6 9	.8692 = 0 6 2
40 to 50	12.4887 =	12 3 10	16.7247 =	16 5 1	18.0276 =	18 0 4	14.7999 =	14 5 14	1.0567 = 1 0 10
50 to 60	23.3980 =	23 2 19	33.2085 =	33 1 11	32.4502 =	32 3 3	27.0894 =	27 0 14	
60 to 70	76.0367 =	76 0 6	90.0990 =	90 0 16	60.3079 =	60 2 3	77.3029 =	77 2 2	15.5407 = 15 3 18
70 to 80	197.7833 =	197 5 11	233.3572 =	233 2 10	214.0132 =	214 0 2	205.3562 =	205 2 11	63.8423 = 63 5 11

AMOUNT OF SICKNESS IN EACH PERIOD OF YEARS, AS SHOWN BY THE EXPERIENCE OF THE MANCHESTER UNITY, AND MR. ANSELL'S TABLES.

MANCHESTER UNITY.

From Age	Rural.		Town.		City.		Rural, Town, and City.		Excess for each period over Mr. Neison's		Mr. Ansell's Table.
	Weeks.	W. D. H.	Weeks.	W. D. H.	Weeks.	W. D. H.	Weeks.	W. D. H.	Weeks.	W. D. H.	
20 to 30	7.0917 =	7 0 15	7.0231 =	7 0 4	6.8520 =	6 5 23	7.0464 =	7 0 7			8.060 = 8 0 10
30 to 40	8.4561 =	8 3 9	9.2770 =	9 1 22	9.6095 =	9 4 6	9.0428 =	9 0 7			9.535 = 9 3 18
40 to 50	12.3664 =	12 2 13	13.0873 =	13 0 14	16.4323 =	16 3 0	13.7432 =	13 5 4			13.395 = 13 2 18
50 to 60	24.3049 =	24 2 3	25.5345 =	25 3 16	32.7484 =	32 5 5	27.2239 =	27 1 13			22.562 = 22 3 22
60 to 70	64.3321 =	61 2 7	51.6890 =	51 4 17	75.8580 =	75 6 0	61.7622 =	61 5 8			58.717 = 58 5 0
70 to 80	110.1362 =	110 0 22	132.3045 =	132 2 3	166.8847 =	166 5 20	141.5139 =	141 3 14	1845 =	0 0 22	

From the experience of the sickness shown by Mr. Neison's Table for the rural districts, it will be seen that, at the early ages, the average amount experienced in the same districts of the Unity is much less than what is given by that authority; that, from the ages 50 to 60 there appears a larger amount experienced in the Unity, but, from the ages 70 to 80, the average amount in the rural districts of Mr. Neison's Tables considerably exceeds the average amount experienced by the Unity members for the same districts.

The city districts of Mr. Neison, being compared with those here given, will show from age 20 to 50 a larger amount of sickness existing in the former than in the latter, but, from that age to age 74, the average amount in the Unity exceeds that shown by Mr. Neison's Tables. From this age a change again takes place, and the amount of Mr. Neison exceeds that of the Unity.

If the whole of the combined districts given by Mr. Neison be now taken in comparison with those of the Unity, it will be seen that at each of the periods given, with the exception of age 60, the average amount exceeds the results here shown, but, at the age 60, both rural and city districts of the Unity, being subject to an increased average amount over that of Mr. Neison, in like manner affect the whole when combined, so much as to cause the results in the whole districts to exceed those of Mr. Neison, although to a very small extent.

The comparative view of the sickness experienced, for the various periods of life it embraces, given in page 34, will give a clearer idea of the aggregate amount of sickness experienced by the Manchester Unity, Mr. Neison s Tables, and those of Mr. Ansell, than any heretofore given, and shows clearly the amount of sickness experienced from period to period.

If the aggregate amount of sickness, shown by these results to be experienced in passing from age 20 to 40, be compared with the experience shown by Mr. Ansell, it will be seen that, taking the three districts combined, and which embrace the whole Unity, they are not subject to the amount of sickness shown by Mr. Ansell. In the first period of 10 years they experience a less amount of sickness by .914 weeks, = 0 weeks, 6 days, 9 hours. In the next period, 30 to 40, the aggregate amount is .493 weeks, = 0 weeks, 3 days, 10 hours less than Mr. Ansell's; but, after those periods of life have been passed, the excess of aggregate sickness in the Unity over that shown by Mr. Ansell's Tables, becomes more than the deficiency previously occurring.

In comparing the rural districts with those of Mr. Neison, it will be observed that, in passing through each respective period, except from 50 60, there is an aggregate excess of sickness over the experience here given, and that, even at the period of life 50-60 years, the excess of the aggregate sickness of the Unity is only two and a half per cent. more than the aggregate sickness shown by Mr. Neison for that period of life.

The aggregate amount of sickness, in the town districts of Mr. Neison's Tables, shows a very considerable excess of aggregate sickness above the results here given in passing through every period of life, and the same accelerates after the period 30-40 for each period of years.

The city districts of the Manchester Unity for the periods of life 20-30, 30-40, and 40-50, show a less aggregate amount of sickness experienced for those respective periods than is evidenced by the results of Mr. Neison. In passing through the period 50-60, the aggregate amount approximates very closely, but in the next period, 60-70 years, the aggregate amount of the Unity is much larger than that given by Mr. Neison, and, after that period, for the next period, 70-80 years, Mr. Neison's aggregate of sickness again shows an excess over the Unity.

The whole of the districts, when combined, appear similar to the rural districts, showing a larger aggregate of sickness in the Tables of Mr. Neison than is seen to be experienced by the Unity at every period of life, except 50-60, and for that period they seem to approximate so closely that the difference is only one day for the whole period. In passing from 60-70 the excess of sickness in Mr. Neison's Tables for that period exceeds the excess of the Unity more than 25 per cent.

If the aggregate amount of sickness be examined for the periods 20-70 years, and for each of the three classes, rural, town, and city, as well as the three combined, it will be seen that the excess of rural in Mr. Neison's Tables, over that here given is 13.0865 = 13 weeks, 0 days, 14 hours, or about 10 per cent. more than the aggregate sickness here shown to be experienced. If the same be examined for the town districts, it will show an aggregate excess of 53.4435 = 53 weeks, 3 days, 2 hours, or 50 per cent. more than this amount. The city districts of the Unity show a larger amount of sickness experienced in those districts for that period than the aggregate of the city districts of Mr. Neison. The excess for the whole period is 9.4416 = 9 weeks, 3 days, 2 hours, or about seven per cent. more than the sickness of Mr. Neison, when the aggregate amount experienced by all the lives of Mr. Neison is compared with the aggregate amount of sickness experienced by the whole of the Unity; and, for the same period of years, it shows an excess of 19.0002 = 19 weeks of sickness experienced in that period by the lives of Mr. Neison more than in the Unity.

The following shows the aggregate sickness experienced by each class, separate and combined, for the period 20-70, also the excess in amount experienced by one over the other.

	RURAL.	TOWN.	CITY.	R. T. & C.
Aggregate amount of sickness—Mr. Neison's Tables	129.6680	160.0464	132.0586	137.8187
Ditto ditto Manchester Unity	116.5815	106.6029	141.5002	118.8185
Excess over Manchester Unity	13.0865	53.4435		19.0002
Excess over Mr. Neison's Tables			9.4416	

It must be apparent that these lives will be existing under very different circumstances, and be affected by a different combination of trades. Mr. Neison's agricultural labourers form 33 per cent., and in the experience here given, they form only 20 per cent. of the rural class, and if a larger per centage of similar trades, experiencing more than the average sickness, be combined in one more than in the other class, there will appear more average sickness existing in the first than in the other class, from not having that large per centage of those trades; other circumstances being similar.

In addition to being affected by a different combination of trades, the average sickness will vary according to locality; the persons resident in Glasgow and Liverpool, for example, experience such an average amount of sickness that by being included in the city districts, the bulk show an excess of aggregate sickness of 19.0002 = 19 weeks, over the same class of Mr. Neison's, but by being abstracted the remaining portion shews a much less aggregate sickness than the one just named.

SECTION IV.

DURATION OF LIFE, AND AVERAGE AMOUNT OF SICKNESS
OF VARIOUS TRADES.

On completing the previous portion of the subject, the whole of the return sheets from the rural districts were again analysed, and from such all gardeners and agricultural labourers, at each respective age, the amount of sickness experienced by them at that age, and the number of deaths occurring, were entered on sheets provided for that purpose. After the completion of the abstraction of agricultural labourers and gardeners, the same process was adopted for the abstraction of labourers from town and city districts. The following trades were then taken, without reference to locality:—Bakers, blacksmiths and farriers, bricklayers, plasterers and slaters, butchers, carpenters, clerks and schoolmasters, coopers, dyers, hatters, millwrights, operatives employed in cotton mills, miners, plumbers, painters and glaziers, potters, letter-press printers and compositors, sawyers, domestic servants, shoemakers, spinners, stonemasons, tailors, weavers, wheelwrights, and woolcombers.

The returns were divided into counties, and sheets having been prepared for every separate trade in each county, the total of such sheets formed the gross number of bakers, or any other trade in the county, which might have been extracted.

A book having been headed for each trade, all persons of that trade in the county of Bedford were entered under their respective age, the amount of sickness at each age, and the number of deaths occurring for that year. This course was followed with the next county, and pursued until each of the counties had been entered. The sum total then gave the number of persons at each age, the amount of sickness for such age, and the number of deaths occurring at such respective age for each trade, entered for each county. The same course was adopted for each of the trades, thus keeping not only every trade, but the persons in each county, of that trade, separate and distinct from every other county. Each trade was then classified into tables, similar to IV., V., VI., and VII., with regard to rural, town, and city districts, and comprise Tables XIV. to XXXIX. inclusive. By this method the mean rate of mortality, and the average amount of sickness for each mean period of life, were obtained.

The next step was to find the rate of mortality at every age of life. The same process was pursued as previously detailed at page 20, and from the rate of mortality were calculated the decrements of life, as given in Tables XL. to LXV. of the respective trades. To those tables of mortality are also appended columns showing the specific intensity and expectation of life for the different trades, calculated from such tables.

Previous to noticing the results arrived at respecting any separate trade or class, and for the purpose of forming comparisons of the expectations of the various trades or classes, the expectation of the whole of the rural, town, and city districts combined, has been given for each decennial period of life, and the same for every trade; and it must be borne in mind that the trade or class, of which comparisons are made in all the after process, form a portion of that general bulk with which such comparison is taking place. This mode of comparing one with the other is not strictly correct. The class in comparison ought to be first deducted from the general bulk; however, without making all these deductions of trade after trade, it is presumed that the same will be sufficient, by retaining the trade, to give a general idea of the sickness and mortality existing in each Trade.

———

EXPECTATION.—DECENNIAL PERIODS OF LIFE, ENGLAND AND WALES, MANCHESTER UNITY, AND VARIOUS TRADES.

England and Wales,—Rural, Town, and Cities, and various Trades.	AGE.				
	20	30	40	50	60
England and Wales	39.88	33.13	26.56	20.02	13.59
Manchester Unity	40.92	33.70	26.41	19.40	13.29
Bakers	41.92	34.05	26.58	20.09	14.12
Blacksmiths	37.96	30.34	23.52	18.11	13.02
Bricklayers	37.70	29.66	22.22	14.78	8.44
Butchers	41.60	33.49	26.33	20.32	14.89
Carpenters	45.28	38.47	31.65	25.07	18.88
Clerks...	34.99	27.77	20.61	14.18	12.11
Coopers	38.62	31.17	24.23	18.22	13.23
Dyers...	39.89	32.00	24.73	18.20	13.40
Hatters	38.91	34.29	27.93	19.87	12.89
Labourers, Town and City... ...	40.87	33.65	26.27	19.07	13.33
Ditto, Rural	45.32	37.71	29.91	22.18	15.82
Millwrights	40.32	33.38	27.37	19.60	13.69
Mill Operatives	38.09	30.45	22.61	15.55	10.61
Miners	38.22	31.65	24.28	17.82	12.27
Plumbers	38.13	31.59	24.67	18.24	12.67
Potters	36.59	30.51	23.80	18.74	13.71
Printers	36.66	28.86	20.55	14.67	12.04
Sawyers	40.02	33.06	26.05	18.04	13.11
Domestic Servants...	42.03	34.30	27.32	20.77	14.81
Shoemakers	40.87	33.99	26.23	19.04	13.05
Spinners	39.04	32.42	24.32	16.62	12.21
Stonemasons	38.19	30.41	24.16	18.15	14.79
Tailors	39.40	32.51	25.34	18.31	10.23
Weavers	41.92	35.55	28.53	22.01	15.61
Wheelwrights...	40.97	33.87	27.54	19.41	13.84
Woolcombers	38.56	33.73	25.96	17.64	13.22

On a general inspection of the extracts in the previous table, it will be seen that at the early period of life, age 20, the following trades, placed according to their expectation, show an inferior expectation in comparison with the general results of rural, town, and city districts combined:— Clerks, potters, letter-press printers, bricklayers, blacksmiths, mill operatives, plumbers, stonemasons, miners, woolcombers, coopers, hatters, spinners, tailors, dyers, sawyers, millwrights, town and city labourers, and shoemakers. The following trades show a superior expectation:— Wheelwrights, butchers, bakers, weavers, domestic servants, carpenters, and rural labourers.

At the next period of life, age 30, clerks, printers, bricklayers, blacksmiths, stonemasons, mill operatives, potters, coopers, plumbers, miners, spinners, tailors, dyers, sawyers, mill-wrights, butchers, and town labourers, show an inferior expectation; and woolcombers, wheelwrights, shoemakers, bakers, hatters, domestic servants, weavers, rural labourers, and carpenters, show a superior.

The decennial period of life, age 40, shows that letter-press printers, clerks, bricklayers, mill operatives, blacksmiths, potters, stonemasons, coopers, miners, spinners, plumbers, dyers, tailors, woolcombers, sawyers, shoemakers, town labourers, and butchers, have an inferior expectation; and that bakers, domestic servants, millwrights, wheelwrights, hatters, weavers, rural labourers, and carpenters, have a superior.

At the next period, age 50, clerks, letter-press printers, bricklayers, mill operatives, spinners, woolcombers, miners, sawyers, stonemasons, blacksmiths, coopers, dyers, plumbers, tailors, potters, shoemakers, and town labourers, show an inferior expectation; and wheelwrights, millwrights, hatters, bakers, butchers, domestic servants, weavers, rural labourers, and carpenters, exhibit a superior.

At the last period given in the table, bricklayers, tailors, mill operatives, printers, clerks, spinners, miners, plumbers, hatters, blacksmiths, shoemakers, woolcombers, coopers, and sawyers, show an inferior expectation; and dyers, town labourers, millwrights, potters, wheelwrights, bakers, stonemasons, domestic servants, butchers, weavers, rural labourers, and carpenters, show a superior expectation in comparison with the general results.

The average amount of sickness experienced by the members of different trades, at each respective age, will be found, on reference to Tables LXVI.-LXXII. inclusive. These results were arrived at in the same manner as already pointed out at page 20. The abstracts given in the following page will convey a general idea of the relative average amounts of sickness experienced by the members of those trades at the respective ages. An abstract of the average amount of sickness experienced in the rural, town, and city districts at the respective periods of life is presented for comparison.

The table inserted at page 40 shows the average amount of sickness experienced by each respective trade, for decennial periods of life, and the table on page 41 exhibits the aggregate amount of sickness experienced by each trade, and for each period. Particular attention is requested to this latter table, as reference will be made to it hereafter, in treating of the separate trades.

BAKERS.

Bakers form about .98 per cent. of all the lives whose experience has been previously given, and are residents of every part of the country from which the general results have been obtained. Mortality Table, No. XL., shows the numbers living and dying at each year in accordance with those results, and, from 100,000 persons living at age 18, it will be seen that on arrival at age 63-64 one half of this number dies off. The same occurs in the whole of the lives combined, and, for the whole of the population of England and Wales, at the same period. Bakers, therefore, show an equal vitality in comparison with the general results of the Unity, and the entire population.

On reference to the specific intensity, same table, it will be perceived that at age 18 out of 160.97 members living, one will die annually. From that age the intensity increases up to age 24. At that period one person dies out of 229.51 persons living. A decrease then commences, and continues until the age 43, when one person dies annually out of 56.27.

AVERAGE AMOUNT OF SICKNESS EXPERIENCED AT THE RESPECTIVE AGES OF LIFE.

	Age 20. Weeks.	Age 20. W. D. H.	Age 30. Weeks.	Age 30. W. D. H.	Age 40. Weeks.	Age 40. W. D. H.	Age 50. Weeks.	Age 50. W. D. H.	Age 60. Weeks.	Age 60. W. D. H.
Manchester Unity	.5849	= 0 4 2	.8034	= 0 5 15	1.0779	= 1 0 13	1.8533	= 1 5 23	4.3985	= 4 2 18
Bakers	.4738	= 0 3 8	.6036	= 0 4 5	1.2100	= 1 1 12	1.3187	= 1 2 6	3.0283	= 3 0 5
Blacksmiths	.6340	= 0 4 11	.8490	= 0 5 23	.9603	= 0 6 17	1.6722	= 1 4 17	4.3619	= 4 2 13
Bricklayers	.4863	= 0 3 10	.7999	= 0 5 14	.9861	= 0 6 22	1.7874	= 1 5 12	7.3116	= 7 2 4
Butchers	.3521	= 0 2 11	.4528	= 0 3 4	.8152	= 0 5 17	1.3363	= 1 2 9	3.3308	= 3 2 8
Carpenters	.5657	= 0 3 23	.8498	= 0 5 23	.9667	= 0 6 18	1.2473	= 1 1 18	3.8333	= 3 5 20
Clerks	.3402	= 0 2 9	.5206	= 0 3 16	.8360	= 0 5 20	1.4281	= 1 3 0	1.2296	= 1 1 15
Coopers	.5221	= 0 3 16	.7753	= 0 5 10	1.2398	= 1 1 16	3.5763	= 3 5 1	3.4242	= 3 0 21
Dyers	.3221	= 0 2 6	.7905	= 0 5 13	1.1644	= 1 1 4	1.9999	= 2 0 0	7.2143	= 7 1 12
Hatters	.4439	= 0 3 3	.6039	= 0 4 5	1.2573	= 1 1 19	1.9535	= 1 6 16	3.8582	= 3 5 23
Labourers, Town	.6103	= 0 4 7	.9638	= 0 6 18	1.2638	= 1 1 20	1.9477	= 1 6 15	4.1454	= 4 1 1
Ditto, Rural	.5818	= 0 4 2	.8845	= 0 6 5	1.1566	= 1 1 2	1.9471	= 1 6 15	3.8113	= 3 5 16
Millwrights	.4442	= 0 3 3	.7240	= 0 5 2	1.0715	= 1 0 12	1.5778	= 1 4 1	1.0527	= 1 0 9
Mill Operatives	.4585	= 0 3 5	.6645	= 0 4 16	.8721	= 0 6 3	1.6804	= 1 4 18	4.7024	= 4 5 13
Miners	.8546	= 0 6 0	1.3699	= 1 2 14	1.0257	= 1 0 12	3.2751	= 3 1 22	6.7598	= 6 5 8
Plumbers	.6804	= 0 4 18	.7869	= 0 5 12	1.1471	= 1 1 1	2.6696	= 2 4 17	3.9081	= 3 6 9
Potters	.4449	= 0 3 3	1.2589	= 1 1 20	1.6130	= 1 4 7	3.2268	= 3 1 14	10.3471	= 10 2 10
Printers	.3411	= 0 2 9	.6365	= 0 4 11	.9882	= 0 6 22	2.8991	= 2 6 7	4.9110	= 4 6 9
Sawyers	.6304	= 0 4 10	.8229	= 0 5 18	1.2117	= 1 1 12	4.5770	= 4 1 1	1.3166	= 1 2 5
Servants	.4677	= 0 3 7	.6254	= 0 4 9	.9206	= 0 6 11	1.2913	= 1 2 1	3.7022	= 3 4 22
Shoemakers	.6138	= 0 4 0	.7877	= 0 5 12	.9080	= 0 6 9	1.6275	= 1 4 10	2.7047	= 2 5 14
Spinners	.6179	= 0 4 13	.7999	= 0 5 14	1.3297	= 1 2 7	2.5904	= 2 4 3	4.7357	= 4 5 3
Stonemasons	.7264	= 0 5 2	.9371	= 0 6 13	1.3452	= 1 2 10	2.4802	= 2 3 9	6.3520	= 6 2 11
Tailors	.5037	= 0 3 13	.8353	= 0 5 20	1.1355	= 1 1 23	1.4595	= 1 3 5	2.9489	= 2 6 15
Weavers	.5757	= 0 4 1	.8874	= 0 6 5	1.1928	= 1 1 8	1.9984	= 2 0 0	4.5206	= 4 3 16
Wheelwrights	.4503	= 0 3 4	.9786	= 0 6 20	.8194	= 0 5 18	.7211	= 0 5 1	1.2427	= 1 1 17
Woolcombers	1.1680	= 1 1 4	.7662	= 0 5 9	1.5473	= 1 3 20	2.0187	= 2 0 3	6.1553	= 6 1 2

COMPARATIVE VIEW OF SICKNESS,

IN VARIOUS PERIODS OF YEARS,

FROM THE EXPERIENCE OF THE UNITY, AND THE VARIOUS TRADES IN THAT UNITY.

AGGREGATE OF SICKNESS IN EACH PERIOD OF YEARS.

	Age 20 to 30.		Age 30 to 40.		Age 40 to 50.		Age 50 to 60.	
	Weeks.	W. D. H.	Weeks.	W. D. H.	Weeks.	W. D. H.	Weeks.	W. D. H.
Manchester Unity	7.0463=	7 0 7	9.0428=	9 0 7	13.7432=13 5 4		27.2239=27 1 13	
Bakers ...	5.2569=	5 1 19	7.0361=	7 0 6	15.1195=15 0 20		27.2583=27 1 19	
Blacksmiths ...	7.8624=	7 6 1	8.5676=	8 3 23	13.2624=13 1 20		24.9970=24 6 23	
Bricklayers ...	6.8618=	6 6 1	8.8554=	8 6 0	12.8471=12 5 22		29.9609=29 6 17	
Butchers	4.6825=	4 4 19	5.4294=	5 3 0	10.5192=10 3 15		17.5256=17 3 16	
Cabinet Makers	7.5569=	7 3 21	9.0781=	9 0 13	10.8098=10 5 16		18.7644=18 5 9	
Clerks	4.1406=	4 1 0	6.5393=	6 3 19	11.1149=11 0 19		13.8887=13 6 5	
Coopers	6.9197=	6 6 10	10.6171=10 4 8		18.8044=18 5 15		34.3332=34 2 8	
Dyers	5.3085=	5 2 4	8.7410=	8 5 4	14.7541=14 5 7		31.1269=31 0 21	
Hatters	5.7684=	5 5 9	7.9460=	7 6 15	15.7743=15 5 10		32.0933=32 0 16	
Labourers, City	7.8339=	7 5 20	10.7897=10 5 13		14.9163=14 6 10		27.1400=27 1 0	
Ditto, Rural	7.5065=	7 3 13	10.1360=10 0 23		14.1457=14 1 1		23.7855=23 5 12	
Millwrights ...	6.3429=	6 2 8	8.2138=	8 1 12	13.3279=13 2 7		14.6301=14 4 10	
Mill Operatives	5.6229=	5 4 8	7.2435=	7 1 17	12.0533=12 0 9		28.3358=28 2 8	
Miners	11.2218=11 1 13		15.6215=15 4 8		25.5730=25 4 0		43.2810=43 1 23	
Plumbers ...	7.4899=	7 3 10	8.6707=	8 4 17	17.7194=17 5 1		33.7294=33 5 3	
Potters	8.6877=	8 4 19	12.2366=12 1 16		24.3465=24 2 10		44.0232=44 0 4	
Printers ...	5.3093=	5 2 4	7.8193=	7 5 18	16.4787=16 3 8		31.9852=31 6 21	
Sawyers	7.0864=	7 0 15	11.0546=11 0 9		14.2118=14 1 12		13.2466=13 1 17	
Servants ...	5.4257=	5 3 23	7.5761=	7 4 1	10.4663=10 3 6		22.4831=22 3 9	
Shoemakers ...	7.8701=	7 6 2	8.0200=	8 0 4	12.0175=12 0 3		22.4402=22 3 2	
Spinners ...	6.7656=	6 5 9	9.4789=	9 6 15	18.4460=18 3 3		35.4919=35 3 11	
Stonemasons ...	7.6076=	7 4 6	11.2959=11 2 2		16.4316=16 3 1		40.1647=40 1 4	
Tailors ...	7.0260=	7 0 4	9.6825=	9 4 19	12.0638=12 0 11		19.7493=19 5 6	
Weavers	7.5967=	7 4 4	10.5768=10 4 1		13.9304=13 6 12		31.3673=31 2 14	
Wheelwrights	7.7816=	7 5 11	9.4633=	9 3 6	8.0072=	8 0 1	9.4476=	9 3 3
Woolcombers ...	10.7539=10 5 7		9.4271=	9 3 0	16.9290=16 6 12		31.6463=31 4 13	

From the last named age up to 48 an increase again takes place, and one person dies out of 85.66 living. From this period of life a regular decrease takes place until the termination of the table.

The expectation of life, as given in the same table, shows a superior expectation, at each period, to that which appears from the general results of all the districts combined, and also shows a superior expectation when compared with that of the population of England and Wales. In Mr. Neison's work, he gives the expectation of bakers,* amongst other trades, and, for the purpose of comparison, it is herewith presented in decennial periods of life.

* Mr. Neison gives them to four places of decimals.

EXPECTATION OF THE FOLLOWING TRADES,

AT DECENNIAL PERIODS OF LIFE,

FROM THE EXPERIENCE OF THE UNITY, AND MR. NEISON'S TABLES.

Age.	MR. NEISON'S TABLES.					MANCHESTER UNITY.				
	Bakers.	Clerks.	Labourers Rural.	Miners.	Plumbers.	Bakers.	Clerks.	Labourers Rural.	Miners.	Plumbers.
20	40.32	31.83	47.90	40.67	36.90	41.92	34.99	45.32	38.22	38.13
30	32.35	27.57	40.59	34.00	30.50	34.05	27.77	37.71	31.65	31.59
40	24.47	21.85	32.76	24.92	24.30	26.57	20.61	29.91	24.28	24.67
50	19.09	16.04	25.07	17.53	17.09	20.09	14.18	22.18	17.82	18.24
60	14.06	12.42	17.82	11.85	12.16	14.12	12.11	15.82	12.27	12.67

The expectation of bakers, as experienced in the Manchester Unity, appears higher at every period, in comparison with the expectation of the same trade given by Mr. Neison; one experience may include a larger number of lives resident in large towns and cities, and, if so, it is very evident the class embracing these lives must show a less expectation than the other class combining a less number of those lives.

Bakers show a less average amount of sickness at each decennial period of life, with the exception of age 40, and at that period they exhibit an excess of sickness, as compared with the general results. In passing from periods 20-40, they have a less aggregate amount of sickness than is shown in the general results; but, for the whole period of 20-60 years, they experience a less aggregate sickness than the aggregate experience of all classes. Bakers, therefore, have a less aggregate amount of sickness, and a higher general expectation, than is evidenced from the general results of the whole of the lives combined,

BLACKSMITHS.

Blacksmiths form about 3.8 per cent. of all the lives, and are resident in all localities from which the experience has been obtained. One half reside in the counties of Lancashire, Middlesex, and Yorkshire. This class includes black and white smiths, and farriers.

Table XLI. shows that one half of this class of lives becomes extinct by the time of arrival at age 58-9. The specific intensity is much less at the earliest ages in the table than that shown in the general results. The specific intensity is highest at age 18, and from that age a regular decrease takes place until the termination of the lives.

From what has been previously stated it will appear that this class of lives must show a less expectation than the general results, and, with increase of years, the difference in the expectation becomes still more apparent.

At age 20 the difference in the expectation is 2.77 years, and from that period it gradually diminishes, so that at age 60 it is only .51 of a year, as compared with the whole of the general results.

At the early decennial periods of life blacksmiths are subject to a larger amount of sickness than is shown in the general results, but at the periods of life 40, 50 and 60 years, the average sickness is something less than the general lives. The aggregate of sickness experienced in passing from 20-30 years is more than the aggregate sickness of the general results, but, from 30-60, they have a less aggregate sickness than that which has been shown to exist in the whole of the general results. The aggregate of sickness experienced in passing from 20-60 is more than four per cent. less than the general aggregate for the same period, whilst at the same time there is a less general expectation.

BRICKLAYERS.

———

Bricklayers, Plasterers, and Slaters, have been grouped in one class, being parties supposed to be affected, so far as trade is concerned, in a similar manner. They exist in all parts enumerated in the general results, and form about 1.8 per cent. of the whole bulk of lives. On reference to Table XLII., the numbers living, &c., at each age will be seen, and it will be ascertained that half the number of persons forming this class die off at the age 60-1, thus affording evidence of an inferior vitality of three years to that stated in the general results, and to that of the whole of England and Wales.

The specific intensity of this class of trades appears not to be so steady and uniform as some others. The highest specific intensity is at age 18, when, out of each 211.46 persons living, one dies annually. From that age to 34 the intensity decreases, when one person dies annually out of 95.92 persons living. The intensity then increases for a short period, and up to age 38, when it will be seen that one person only dies out of 104.90 persons living. A regular decrease takes place from the last named age, and up to age 64, when one person dies annually out of 7.76 persons. A fluctuation again becomes apparent up to age 71, when one person dies out of 10.93, and, from that age, a decrease goes on until the termination of the table.

The same table shows that at age 20 the expectation of this class of lives is 37.70 years, and the general results show that the expectation at that age, and for the whole number of lives, is 40.92, giving a difference of 3.22 years ; and at each decennial period of life, as this class increases in years, the difference becomes greater, so that at 60 years the difference in the expectation of the general results and the class here given is 4.85 years, thus proving that the nature of their labours, and the circumstances attendant upon their performance, have a depreciatory effect upon life.

Although affording evidence of an inferior vitality, this class does not appear to experience the usual sickness, until far advanced in years. It seems that the persons of this class undergo a less average amount of sickness at the periods 20, 30, 40, and 50 years of age, but, at age 60, they experience far more average sickness than the general class of lives, for whilst the general results show an average sickness of 4.3985 weeks = 4 weeks, 2 days, 18 hours, to each person of that age, the experience of this class of lives shows an average sickness of 7.3116 Weeks = 7 weeks, 2 days, 4 hours. The aggregate sickness existing amongst this class, in passing from 20 to 50 years of age, is less than the aggregate of the general results, but the period 50-60 years gives an aggregate of sickness more than the general results, on the whole period of 20-60 years, of 25 per cent., and, at the period of an increase of sickness, the expectation becomes considerably less.

BUTCHERS.

Butchers do not form any particular part of the locality from which the experience has been collected, but are one portion of the general bulk, taken from each isolated part, and constitute about 1.2 per cent. of the general class of lives.

They will be found in years, and periods of years, and the sickness and mortality experienced for the respective ages and periods, at Table XVII.; and, on reference to Table XLIII., it will be seen that, in comparison with the general results, they show an equal vitality. Half the lives become extinct at ages 63-4; the same takes place at that period for the population of England and Wales.

The specific intensity of this class of lives will be seen on reference to the last named table, and at age 18 the experience shows that, out of 192.79 living, one will die annually, and that the intensity increases from that age to 23, when, out of 239.80 persons living, one will die annually; the intensity being greatest at that age for this class. It then decreases to age 50, when one person dies out of 38.71 persons living. For a short period and up to age 56, an increase again takes place, and at that age one person dies out of 40.54 persons living. The specific intensity then regularly decreases.

This class of lives, at each decennial period, when compared with the general results, shows an expectation similar, or higher. At the periods of life 20, 50, and 60, the expectation is higher than in the general mass, and at 30 and 40 it is nearly the same as given in previous results for the whole body.

Butchers experience a less amount of sickness at each period of life, and that to a considerable extent, than is shown to be experienced in lives generally, and, as they also experience less average sickness at each period, it necessarily follows that they have less aggregate sickness during the whole of their existence. The sickness experienced, in passing from 20-60 years, shows an aggregate of more than 30 per cent. less than the general aggregate, and, though a higher expectation of life is exhibited, it is still not to be compared with the large decrease of aggregate sickness.

CARPENTERS AND JOINERS.

Carpenters and Joiners are located in every place from which the general results have been obtained, and about 50 per cent. of them reside in Lancashire, Middlesex, and Yorkshire, and principally in the large towns and cities of those counties. The whole of this class constitutes about six per cent. of the general lives.

On reference to Table XLIV., it will be ascertained that one half of the lives die off at 69-70, showing the greatest vitality of any class whose experience has been here given, and, in comparison with the general results, and the whole population of England and Wales, a superior vitality of six years.

The specific intensity is the highest at 18. At that age one person dies out of 236.68 persons living. From that period the intensity decreases until arriving at 34 years, when the dying out of the living is one in 108.53 persons. An increase in the intensity then occurs for a very short period upwards, that is, for two years only. At the age 37 one person dies out of 110.02 persons living. The intensity then again decreases until age 47, when one person dies out of 76.97 persons living. Another increase now takes place, and continues up to age 52, when one person dies out of each 80.01 persons living. A third decrease in the intensity then occurs, and continues to age 59, when one person dies out of 40.90 persons living. After this a third increase begins, and continues up to age 61, when one person dies out of 50.07 persons living. From this age the intensity decreases until the end of the table.

Carpenters and joiners, at each decennial period of life, with the exception of age 20, show a higher expectation than any other class, and at age 20 the superiority of expectation appears in favour of agricultural labourers, though to a very limited extent. This class, so far as vitality is concerned, appears to be the best class of lives given in this experience. The expectation of life at age 20, as compared with the general results, shows a superiority of 4.55 years, and at other periods of life the superiority becomes increased.

At age 30 carpenters and joiners experience a larger amount of average sickness, but, at other decennial periods, a less amount than the general class of lives; consequently the sickness in passing through the period 20-30 years, shows a less aggregate of .5106 weeks = 3 days, 14 hours. During the period 30-40, the experience approaches very near the general results, but, from age 40-60, the aggregate sickness experienced is considerably less than that of the general class of lives. For the period 20-60 years, carpenters and joiners experience 19 per cent. less aggregate sickness than the general class. They have, therefore, not only a less aggregate of sickness, but, as before observed, show a superiority of vitality with that less aggregate sickness.

CLERKS AND SCHOOLMASTERS.

Clerks and Schoolmasters are inhabitants of all the localities from which the general results have been experienced. They constitute about 1.4 per cent. of the whole of the lives previously given in the rural, town, and city districts, and, relative to vitality, are the very worst class of lives shown in this experience. At Table XLV. it will be seen that one half of the persons forming this class die off on attaining the age 54-5, thus showing an inferior vitality of nine years, as compared with the general class of lives, and with those of England and Wales.

The specific intensity is less at every year of life than the general results. It increases from age 18 to 21, when the maximum has been attained, and one person dies annually out of 119.63 persons living. At this age a decrease in the intensity commences, and continues up to age 38, when one person dies out of 92 persons living. A second decrease now appears up to age 54, when one person dies out of 15.13 persons living; and at this age a third increase commences, and continues up to 60, at which latter age one person dies out of 19.50 persons living, and the intensity from this age decreases until the lives are exhausted.

Clerks and schoolmasters show a less expectation at the decennial periods of life, 20 and 30, than any other class of lives here experienced upon. At the other periods, 40, 50, and 60, they show the least expectation, with the exception of letter-press printers and compositors, and, at the latter periods, the last named class show a less inferior expectation, though to a very limited extent, than clerks and schoolmasters.

On reference to page 42, an abstract will be found of the expectation of clerks, drawn from Mr. Neison's " Vital Statistics;" also one from the experience here given of clerks and schoolmasters. At age 20 it will be seen that the expectation from this experience shows a superiority of 3.16 years. At age 30 they approach very near to each other. At age 40 the difference is 1.24 in favour of Mr. Neison's lives. At 50 and 60 the superiority still remains with the latter's lives, the difference at 50 being 1.86 years, and at 60 years .31. On the general expectation for these periods the difference is only 05 of a year.

This class of lives experiences a less average amount of sickness than any other class here given. Butchers alone approach closely to it The last named class, in passing the period, 30-50, experiences a less aggregate sickness than clerks, and for the periods 20-30, 50-60, clerks experience a less aggregate sickness than butchers. The aggregate sickness, as compared with the general results, shows an amount of 37 per cent. less, and an aggregate of 6 per cent. less than the next lowest class (butchers), so that clerks and schoolmasters experience a less aggregate sickness, and a less general expectation, than any class of lives given in this experience.

COOPERS.

Coopers, a few of whom are in the agricultural districts, in various counties, but the greater portion of whom reside in towns and cities, form about .35 per cent. of the general class of lives, and, on reference to Table XLVI., it will be seen that half of them die off at age 59-60, thus showing an inferior vitality of four years, in comparison with the general results, and with the population of England and Wales.

The specific intensity of this class, commencing at the early age of 18, when one person dies out of 219.61 persons living, decreases to age 32, when one dies out of each 85.22. From this age it increases to age 37, at which time one person dies annually out of 104.03. From that age the intensity decreases till the conclusion of the table.

The expectation of coopers, in comparison with the general results, shows an inferior expectation at each decennial period of life up to 60, the difference being greatest at the early period, and becoming less for each period of life until the age of 70. The expectation, at this age, shows itself to be superior to that of the general class of lives.

This class also appears to be subject to a less amount of average sickness at the periods of 20, 30, and 60 years, but is subject to an excessive amount at the other periods of 40 and 50, and to such an extent as to cause the aggregate sickness for every period, except 20-30, to exceed the aggregate sickness of the general class of lives. At the period 20-30 the aggregate sickness seems to approach very near to that of the general class, but for the whole period 20-60 the excess of aggregate sickness is 19 per cent. more than that of the general results, showing in this class of lives a larger aggregate sickness and a less general expectation.

DYERS.

Dyers form about .54 per cent. of the general class of lives, and 70 per cent. of this trade reside in the manufacturing districts of Lancashire and Yorkshire. They show an inferior vitality of three years in comparison with the general results, and with the population of England and Wales. On reference to Table XLVII., it will be seen that half the lives die off by the time of attaining age 60-1.

The specific intensity appears the greatest at the earliest age in the Table, viz. 18. At that age one person dies annually out of 217.62 persons living, and from that period the intensity decreases to age 28, when one person dies out of every 105.82. From this age to

34 the intensity increases, and, at the latter age, one person dies annually out of 159.03. A second decrease then takes place, and continues to age 44, when one person dies annually out of every 57.24. A second increase commences after this age, and continues to 47, when one person dies annually out of 60.23. From this age the intensity decreases to the end of the table.

The expectation of dyers is below the general results, and the difference at each decennial period is nearly equal. The greatest difference is at age 40, when the expectation of dyers is 1.68 years less than the general class of lives.

Dyers, at the first decennial period in the table, experience a less average amount of sickness than any class of lives here given; at the next period of life they approach very near the general results; at the following period the amount of average sickness exceeds that of the general results. In the next period, age 50, the excess of average sickness becomes greater, and, at the last period in the table, age 60, the average sickness is 64 per cent. more than the general results, showing in this class of lives, with advanced years, an increase of sickness, at a higher accelerating rate than in the general class. In the first period of life, 20-30, dyers experience an aggregate of sickness very much less than the general class. At the next period, 30-40, the aggregate sickness is still less; but, as in the average sickness, the difference is not so great as at the first period. In the next period of life, 40-60, the aggregate sickness exceeds that of the general class. In comparison with the whole period, dyers show an excess in aggregate sickness of five per cent. over the general class, thus showing an excess of aggregate sickness, and a less general expectation of life.

HATTERS.

Hatters constitute about .58 per cent. of the general class of lives, and 50 per cent. of them are located in the counties of Lancashire and Middlesex. They exhibit an inferior vitality of one year, as compared with that of the general results, and with the population of England and Wales. Half the lives of this class, it will be seen on reference to Table XLVIII, die off at the age of 62-3.

The specific intensity of this class of lives is very low at the early ages of the table. At age 18, one person will die annually out of 38.57 persons living. From this age, to age 26, the intensity increases, and at that age one person will die out of every 87.07. It decreases until age 32, when one person will die out of every 66.23 persons living. It again increases, and, on arriving at 45 years of age, it is seen to be the highest in the table, one person dying out of every 182 persons living. From this age the intensity decreases until the end of the table.

From the lowness of the specific intensity, it must be apparent that, at the early age, this class of lives will show an inferior expectation, and, in comparison with the general class, the expectation at age 20 is 2.01 years less. At the periods of life 30, 40, and 50, the expectation is superior to the general class, but at the next period of life, age 60, it becomes inferior to it. On the whole of the period, the general expectation between one class and the other, does not vary one year.

Hatters, as well as dyers, at the periods of life 20 and 30 years, experience a less average amount of sickness than the general class of lives. At the next periods of life, 40 and 50, they experience about the same average sickness as dyers, and more than the general class. At the next period, age 60, hatters experience a less average amount of sickness than appears in the general results, and considerably less than dyers, at this age of life. The aggregate amount of sickness, in passing the periods 20-30, 30-40, is less than the aggregate sickness experienced by the general class for the same periods, but, for the periods 40-50, 50-60, the aggregate sickness experienced by this class exceeds that of the general class more than seven per cent., showing, at the early ages of life, an increased rate of mortality, and a low average sickness, and, at the middle ages of life, a low rate of mortality, and an increased rate of sickness.

LABOURERS.

TOWN AND CITY DISTRICTS.

This class of lives is located in the large cities and towns only, and includes about 12 per cent. of the two classes, town and city districts. On reference to Table L., it will be seen that one half the lives die away at the age 62-3, showing a superior vitality of one year in comparison with city districts, and a lower vitality of one year in comparison with town districts.

The specific intensity in this class increases from 18, at which age one person dies out of 106.47 persons living, up to age 24, when one person dies out of 146.01, this being the highest specific intensity attained throughout the table. From the last named age the intensity decreases until 34, when one person dies out of every 114.22 persons living. A very small increase in the intensity again appears for two years of life. At age 36 one person dies out of every 116.22, and from the latter age a decrease takes place until the termination of the table.

The expectation of this class of lives approaches very close to the general class of rural, town, and city districts combined; at no period in the table does the difference in expectation appear to the extent of .25 of a year. If a comparison be made with town and city districts, the folowing extracts from those tables show the expectation at each decennial period, and also that of this class, giving the difference of expectation for each of the classes.

Age.	Expectation. Town Districts.	Expectation. City Districts.	Expectation. Labourers, Town and City.	Expectation. in favour of Town Districts.	Expectation in favour of Labourers, compared with City Districts.
20	41.44	38.92	40.87	.57	1.95
30	34.15	31.62	33.65	.50	2.03
40	26.89	24.59	26.27	.62	1.68
50	19.72	18.24	19.07	.65	.83
60	13.55	12.60	13.33	.22	.73

It will be seen that the town districts exhibit an expectation almost uniformly superior to the labourers of town and city districts, showing that labourers, as far as vitality is concerned, may be classed as nearly equal to the great bulk of all the trades combined which form this class, and that the expectation of the labourers, in town and city districts, is of a higher value than the expectation of the general mass of trades composing the city districts.

This class of lives experiences more average sickness, at each decennial period of life, than that experienced by the general lives comprised in the town districts; and, at the first period, 20 and 30 years, the average sickness of this class exceeds that of the lives comprised in the city class for those periods of life. At 40, 50, and 60, the city districts experience a larger average sickness than this class.

The following extracts show the aggregate amount of sickness experienced by each of the classes, at one view.

COMPARATIVE VIEW OF THE AMOUNT OF SICKNESS, FOR VARIOUS PERIODS OF YEARS.

TOWN AND CITY DISTRICTS, AND THE LABOURERS OF THOSE DISTRICTS.

Age.	Town Districts.	City Districts.	Labourers, Town and City.	Difference in favour of Town Districts.	Difference in favour of City Districts.	Difference against City Districts.
20 to 30	7.0251 = 7 0 4	6.9520 = 6 6 15	7.8339 = 7 5 20	.8188 = 0 5 16	.8819 = 0 6 5	
30 to 40	9.2710 = 9 1 21	9.6095 = 9 4 6	10.7897 = 10 5 12	1.5187 = 1 3 15	1.1802 = 1 1 6	
40 to 50	13.0873 = 13 0 14	16.4325 = 16 3 0	14.9163 = 14 6 10	1.8290 = 1 5 20		1.5160 = 0 3 14
50 to 60	25.5245 = 25 3 16	32.7484 = 32 5 5	27.1400 = 27 0 23	1.6155 = 1 4 7		5.6084 = 0 4 0

The above shows that, for every period given, the labourers in the town and city districts experience an aggregate sickness greater than the town districts; that, for two of the periods, 20-30, and 30-40, they experience an aggregate of sickness greater than the bulk of lives comprised in the city districts; but, for the periods 40-50, 50-60, the city districts experience more aggregate sickness than the labourers of the town and city districts, for those periods of years. For the whole period, 20-60, the labourers of the town and city districts experience an aggregate amount of sickness of 10.5 per cent. more than that of the town districts, and of 7.7 per cent. less than the aggregate of the city districts, for that period.

LABOURERS.

RURAL DISTRICTS.

All the persons constituting this class are located in the rural districts, and form more than 20 per cent. of the persons composing the rural districts, previously given. As such a large per centage of the rural districts consists of labourers, if any one class or trade required to be deducted from the general bulk, for the purpose of forming a comparison with those lives in the same district, and not including the lives under comparison, this class, more than any other, requires that such a course should be adopted. However, as previously stated, something like a fair idea may be formed, without the separation of the labourers from the other trades of the district.

On reference to Table XLIX., it will be seen that half the lives in this class die off at age 67-8, showing the highest vitality of any class given, with the exception of carpenters and joiners, and displaying a superior vitality, in comparison with the rural districts; of one year, half of the lives in those districts dying off at age 65-6.

This class of lives shows the highest specific intensity at age 18, when one person dies out of 374.50 persons living, showing a very low rate of mortality at the early ages. From 18 to 33, the intensity decreases, and at that age one person dies out of every 147.27 persons living. At this age it increases for the short period of two years, and at age 35 one person dies out of every 160.12 persons living. Thence it decreases until the termination of the table.

Agricultural labourers have the highest general expectation of any of the classes here given, with the exception of carpenters and joiners, and, if compared with the rural districts, of which they themselves form a large portion, it will be seen that, at every decennial period of life, they show a superior expectation. The following exhibits, in a tabular form, the expectation of rural labourers, and that of all classes in the rural districts, and also the difference for those respective periods.

Age.	Expectation. Rural Labourers.	Expectation. Rural Classes.	Difference in favour of Labourers.
20	45.32	43.47	1.85
30	37.71	36.42	1.29
40	29.91	29.02	.89
50	22.18	21.84	.34
60	15.82	15.64	.18

This class of lives, at age 20, experiences a less average amount of sickness than that which is experienced by the whole of the rural class, and again, at age 60, a less average amount is experienced; but, for the other decennial ages, 30, 40, and 50, agricultural labourers undergo a larger average sickness than the whole of the lives composing the rural class. For the periods 20-30, 30-40, 40-50, it is greater than that experienced by the whole of the rural class; but, for the period 50-60, this class experiences a less aggregate of sickness than the class before named, and for the whole period, 20-60, agricultural labourers experience an aggregate amount of sickness of 6.2 per cent. more than the whole of the lives of the rural districts.

MILLWRIGHTS.

Millwrights are located, more or less, throughout every part inhabited by the general class. They form about .39 per cent. of the whole of the lives, and 50 per cent. of them are resident in Lancashire, Yorkshire, and Scotland. The specific intensity is highest at the first age (18) in the table, when one person dies out of every 181.06 persons living. From that age it decreases to age 34. At this year of life one person dies out of every 71.71 persons living. It then increases from the last-mentioned age up to 46, when one person dies out of every 122.02. From this period of life the intensity decreases until the termination of the table.

Millwrights display an expectation approaching that of the general class of lives, and it is very remarkable that, with such a small number of lives, the approximation should continue at every decennial period. It might have been expected that, at one of the periods, it would have been more or less affected, so as to have shown a much higher or lower expectation than the general results, which include so large a number, and consequently would not be affected by one or two additional deaths. At the periods of life, 20 and 30, the expectation in the general bulk is more favourable than in this class, the greatest difference being .60 of a year ; but, at the periods 40, 50, and 60, the expectation of millwrights is higher than that of the general class of lives, the greatest difference being .96 of a year, at the period 40 years of age. At the other periods the expectation is nearly equal.

Millwrights do not appear to experience much sickness at the early, or farther advanced periods of life, but from the limited number of those, after 40 years of age, whose experience has been obtained, they may not show the sickness in so satisfactorily a manner as could have been desired. In the period of life where larger numbers have been given, the sickness appears less, but not to a very much greater extent. It is also less at each period, and the aggregate sickness, from period to period, is shown to be less than in the general class of lives.

MILL OPERATIVES.

This class is composed of all persons employed in cotton mills, with the exception of spinners, and embraces carders, slubbers, rovers, &c., &c. They form about 2.17 per cent. of the general class of lives, and are principally resident in the counties of Chester, Derby, Lancaster, and York, and in Scotland. A few of the number are located in the counties of Leicester and Nottingham, and in Wales. On reference to Table LII., it will be seen that half the lives die off at the age 59-60, showing, in comparison with the general class of lives, an inferior vitality of three years, and the same with that of England and Wales.

The highest specific intensity appears at the first age in the table, when one person dies out of every 198.68 persons. From that age to 29 it decreases, and at the latter age one person dies out of every 109.03 persons living. At this period an increase in the intensity commences, and continues to age 35, when one person dies out of every 136.40, and from the latter age it decreases until the end of the table. In comparing the specific intensity of this class with the general results, it will be seen that it appears favourable for a very short period only, viz., up to 25 years. After that a much less intensity exhibits itself at every year, the difference becoming greater with advanced years, and showing a less specific intensity than the general class.

An inferior expectation is also found to exist at every period given, the difference increasing up to 50. At the next period (60) the expectation is not quite so unfavourable as at age 50, the greatest difference, as compared with the general class, being 3.85 years ; but the general expectation is much less.

Mill operatives do not appear to experience as much average sickness as the general class of lives. At the periods 20, 30, 40, and 50, it is much less than the general results, but at the period 60 they experience more sickness; in the aggregate, and for the period 20-30, they experience 1.4234 weeks = 1 week, 2 days, 13 hours, less sickness. In the period 30-40, they experience 1.7993 weeks = 1 week, 5 days, 14 hours less; and in the period 50-60, they experience 1.1119 weeks = 1 week, 0 days, 18 hours, more sickness; and for the whole period, 20-60, they show an aggregate sickness of about 6.6 per cent. less than the general class of lives, so that in mill operatives there appears a less expectation of life, and, at the same time, a less amount of average sickness.

MINERS.

Miners form about 4.93 per cent. of the general class of lives, and are located in 16 counties of England, where mining is carried on, and also a portion in Scotland and Wales. They show a less vitality of three years than the general class, for, on reference to Table LIII., it will be found that one half of the lives die off at age 60-1, being also a less vitality of three years than that of England and Wales.

It will be perceived that, at 18 years of age, the specific intensity of this class is lower than at 31. At the former age one person dies out of every 96.95 persons living. It increases up to the latter age, showing then the highest intensity in the table, one person dying annually out of every 117.31 persons living. From that time it decreases until the end of the table. It is also lower at the commencement of the table than that of the general class. At age 31 they approach very near each other, but in a short period afterwards the difference becomes greater, until age 45. From this age the difference becomes less, and, at age 55-6, they cross each other, and this class shows a higher specific intensity up to age 61. From this age there is a less specific intensity until the conclusion of the table.

The expectation of life appears inferior to that of the general class at each decennial period, the greatest difference being 2.70 years, at the first period in the table, age 20, and the least difference being 1.02 years at age 60.

As the expectation of miners has been given by Mr. Neison, for decennial periods, and inserted under the head when treating of the experience of bakers, if reference be made thereto, it will be seen that at the periods 20, 30, and 40, the expectation given by Mr. Neison exceeds that of this experience, and, at the other periods, 50 and 60, it is inferior.

At age 20 the difference appears in favour of Mr. Neison's lives 2.45 years.

,,	30	,,	,,	,,	2.35	,,
,,	40	,,	,,	,,	0.25	,,
,,	50	the difference is in favour of this experience ...	...		0.71	,,
,,	60	,,	,,	,,	... ...	0.82	,,

The mortality in this class appears greater in some counties, than in others; no doubt this arises, to some extent, from the peculiarity of their places of employment, or residences.

This class of lives shows a very large amount of average sickness at every period, and an increased sickness with advance of years. From the very nature of the employment this must have been anticipated, but not to such an extent as appears from these results. At age 20 miners experience an average sickness of 46 per cent. more than the general class. At age 30 they have 70 per cent., at 40 years 78 per cent., at 50 years 76 per cent., and at 60 years 53 per cent. more average sickness than the general class of lives. The aggregate amount of sickness experienced by miners for the period of life 20-60 is 95.6973 weeks = 95 weeks, 4 days, 21 hours, showing an excess of about 67 per cent. more than the general results. Had these lives, which form 4.93 per cent. of the general class, been first extracted therefrom (and which should have been the case), it would have shown a less amount of average sickness experienced by the general class, and consequently would have proved that miners are subject to more average sickness per annum in excess of the general class than appears to exist.   It would have reduced the aggregate sickness of the class as existing without miners, and, therefore, would have shown a larger difference between the two.

PLUMBERS.

Plumbers, Glaziers, and Painters, of which this class is composed, form about 1.89 per cent. of the general class, and are resident in all localities which the general class comprises. On reference to Table LIV., it will be seen that half the lives die off at age 59-60, showing an inferior vitality to miners.   In comparison with the general class, and with the population of England and Wales, they exhibit an inferior vitality of four years.

The specific intensity of this class appears to be very changeable, increasing and decreasing at various periods of life, and commencing at age 18, when one person dies out every 62.58 persons living.   The intensity increases until it appears the highest in the table at age 25, when one person dies annually out of every 119.20.   From that age it decreases until age 38, when one person dies out of every 67.29.   It then increases to age 42, at which age one person dies out of 99.34.   Another decrease now commences, and continues to age 48.   At this age one person dies out of every 38.40 persons living.   The last increase now takes place, and on arriving at age 52 one person dies out of every 53.73.   From this latter age it decreases until the last age in the table.   The specific intensity remains below that of the general class up to age 52.   At that period it becomes greater than in the general class, and retains its superiority up to 55.   After this a lower rate is exhibited at every age.

This class of lives shows an inferior expectation at every decennial period of life, the difference being greatest at age 20, viz., 2.79 years, and least at age 60, viz., .62 years.   At each decennial period of life the difference decreases.   The expectation of life for plumbers, glaziers, and painters, from Mr. Neison's "Vital Statistics," is given at page 42, and also the expectation of this class of lives.   From Mr. Neison's experience, on reference thereto, it will be seen that a superior expectation is apparent at each period given.

At age 20 the superiority of expectation is by Mr. Neison 1.23
,,   30   ,,   ,,   ,,   1.09
,,   40   ,,   ,,   ,,   0.37
,,   50   ,,   ,,   ,,   1.15
,,   60   ,,   ,,   ,,   0.51

Showing the least variation in the expectation at age 40, and the next least difference at age 60; the greatest difference appears at the earliest period; with a very superior expectation, this class of lives experience far more aggregate sickness than the general class.

This class experiences more average sickness at the first period, age 20; at the third age, 40, and at the fourth age, 50, than the general class of lives.   At the other periods of life, ages 30 and 60, a less amount is experienced.   For the period 20-30 they experience a larger aggregate amount of sickness; for the period 30-40 a less amount; for the period 40-60 a greater amount, and, for the whole period, 20-60, they experience about 18 per cent. more aggregate sickness than the general class of lives.

POTTERS.

Potters constitute about .41 per cent. of the general class of lives, and 50 per cent. of them are located in the county of Stafford.   The remainder are spread over various other counties.

With the exception of clerks and letter-press printers, they have the lowest vitality of any class here given. On reference to Table LV., it will be seen that half the lives die off at age 56-7, showing an inferior vitality of seven years, as compared with the general class, and with the population of England and Wales.

The expectation is very much inferior to that of the general class. At the early age of 18 the difference is 4.33 years, and at each respective period afterwards the difference decreases, until at 50 the difference is only .66 of a year. The general expectation is, therefore, far below the united class of lives.

Potters, at age 20, experience less average sickness than the general class, but, for a limited period only, for, at age 23, the average amount of sickness is more than that of the general class, and for each year of life it increases, so that, at age 60, it is considerably more than that of the general class.

In the period 20-30, as compared with the general class, the aggregate sickness shows an excess of about 23 per cent.; for period 30-40 about 36 per cent.; for period 40-50 about 77 per cent.; for period 50-60 about 61 per cent. ; and, for the whole period, 20-60, about 56 per cent. over and above the aggregate amount of sickness of the general class of lives, so that this class experiences a less general expectation and a larger aggregate amount of sickness than the general class.

LETTER-PRESS PRINTERS AND COMPOSITORS.

This class forms about .78 per cent. of the general class. Letter-press printers and compositors are located principally in large towns and cities. On reference to Table LVI., it will be seen that half the lives die off at age 55-6, showing the most inferior vitality, with the exception of clerks, of any class here given, and, as compared with the general results, and the population of England and Wales, an inferior vitality of eight years.

This class of lives shows a very inferior expectation at the early ages. At age 20 the difference, in comparison with the general class, is 4.26 years of an inferiority. At the next period, age 30, the difference is 4.84 years ; at the following period, age 40, it is 5.86 years ; at age 50 it is 4.73 years ; and, at age 60, it is reduced to 1.25 years, showing a less general expectation for every period given in the table.

Printers and compositors appear to experience a less average amount of sickness at the three first periods, 20, 30, and 40, but, at the remaining given periods of life, they have more average sickness than the general class. The aggregate amount of sickness, for the periods 20-30 and 30-40, is less than the aggregate amount of the general class, but an increase being experienced before arriving at 50 years of age, it causes the period 50-60 to show an excess of aggregate sickness more than the general results for that period. For the period 50-60, it is about 17 per cent. more than that of the general class of lives ; and for the whole period, 20-60, this class experiences an aggregate sickness of about 7.9 per cent. more than the class just named, showing a less general expectation, and a larger aggregate of sickness.

SAWYERS.

Sawyers form about 66 per cent. of the general class of lives, and are located in all parts of the country. They have an inferior vitality to the general class. On reference to Table LVII., it will be seen that half the lives die off at age 61-2, showing two years of inferior vitality.

Sawyers show a less specific intensity, at age 18, than the general class of lives. At that age one dies annually out of 149.49 persons living, and the intensity from that age to 27 decreases, so that, at the last age named, one person dies out of 108.75. It then begins to increase, and continues to do so until age 32, at which age one person dies out of every 138.04 persons living. A second decrease now appears up to age 38, when one person dies out of 71.06. The third increase now takes place, and continues up to age 46, when one person dies out of every 176.89, this being the highest intensity throughout the table. From this age it decreases until the end of the table. The specific intensity of this class is lower than that of the general class, up to age 29-30. At that time it crosses the intensity of the general class, and remains higher up to age 34-5. At this age it again crosses, and becomes less, as in the earlier ages, but at age 41-2 it again becomes greater, and is increased to age 50-1, when it crosses that of the general class, and shows less to the conclusion of the table.

The expectation of sawyers is less than that of the general class of lives. The greatest difference is at the period of life age 50, showing then a superior expectation to that of the general class, of 1.36 years. At the remaining periods of life, the superiority of the expectation of the general class is not to a great extent.

The average amount of sickness experienced by this class of lives, at the periods 20, 30, and 40, is more than that experienced by the general class. At the later periods, 50 and 60, it is less than that of the general class, but when reference is made to Table XXXI., containing the number of lives, it will be seen that, after age 50, the experience is more limited, on account of the number of persons being less, so that it is very probable that, with more lives, the average sickness might have shown itself to have been more than here given.

The aggregate sickness, for period 20-30, is nearly the same as in the general class, the difference being only .0401 = 6 hours ; for 30-40 an excess of sickness is experienced, and if the whole period, 20-40, be compared, there appears an excess of 12.7 per cent. sickness experienced by this class, and with that excess of aggregate sickness, appears a less general expectation of life.

DOMESTIC SERVANTS.

This class includes livery servants, waiters at inns, and all other descriptions of servants generally resident with those by whom they are employed. They constitute something like 2.61 per cent. of the general class of lives, and about 20 per cent. of them are located in London for a portion of the year. For the other part of the year they breathe the refreshing atmosphere of the country. On reference to Table LVIII., it will be seen that half of the lives die away at age 63-4, showing an equal vitality, in comparison with the general class, and with the population of England and Wales.

The specific intensity of this class is highest at age 18, when one person dies annually out of every 321.44 persons living. It increases from that age to age 43, when one person dies out of every 67.17. At this age it increases to age 47, a very short period ; and, at the latter age, one person dies out of every .75.18. After this age the intensity decreases until the conclusion of the table.

In comparison with the general class of lives a higher intensity is maintained from the first age in the table to age 31-2, when the intensity of the general class crosses that of this class, and shows a higher specific intensity up to age 45-6. It then again crosses, and shows a less specific intensity than that of the general class throughout the table. This class of lives, in comparison with the general class, appears to have the highest rate of mortality, and far exceeds that class from age 33 to age 45.

Domestic servants show a superior expectation at every decennial period of life. At age 20 the difference is 1.11 year; at age 30 it is .60 year; at age 40 it is .91 year; at age 50 it is 1.37 years; and, at age 60 it is 1.52 year, showing a general superior expectation of life, in comparison with the general class.

This class experiences a less average amount of sickness at every decennial period of life than the general class, the least difference being at age 20, and the greatest at age 60; consequently it must experience a less aggregate amount of sickness. The aggregate sickness experienced by domestic servants, for period 20-60, is 19 per cent. less than the aggregate of the general class, showing a less aggregate sickness, and a superior general expectation.

SHOEMAKERS.

Shoemakers form about 3.9 per cent. of the general class of lives, and, from the nature of their employment, it will at once be assumed that they are located in every portion of the Unity; in fact, there was scarcely an instance of any locality from which the returns were received in which shoemakers and tailors were not found. Agricultural labourers and carpenters show the highest vitality, weavers the next, and then shoemakers. It will be seen, on reference to Table LIX., that half the lives of this class die off at age 65-6, showing a superior vitality of two years, as compared with the general class, and with England and Wales.

The specific intensity of this class of lives fluctuates more than any other with the exception of tailors. The highest intensity is attained at age 18, when one person dies annually out of every 172.83 persons, and from that age it decreases to age 24, when one person dies out of every 199.37 persons living. At that age the intensity commences to increase, and so continues to age 35, when one person dies out of every 144.73 persons living. The second decrease now takes place in the intensity, and continues until age 53, at which age one person dies out of every 33.76 persons living. At this age the second increase commences, and continues to age 61, when one person dies out of every 67.77 persons living. The third decrease is continued from the latter age to age 69, when one person dies out of every 8.71 persons living. At 69 years of age the last increase occurs, and goes on to age 74, when one person dies out of every 12.96 persons living. From the last age the intensity decreases until the end of the table.

If the specific intensity be compared with that of the general class, it will be seen that a higher intensity exists in this class of lives from age 28-9 to age 47-8; from age 54-5 to age 64-5; and again, from age 75-6 to 81-2; consequently at the other periods the intensity is lower than that of the general class, and shows a higher rate of mortality for those periods of time than that which exists amongst the general class of lives.

The expectation of life, at the various decennial periods, approaches very near to that of the general class, in none of the periods differing more than .5 of a year. Although the specific intensity appears to increase and decrease so often, yet at each decennial period it becomes so regulated as to vary to a small extent only from the general class of lives.

At the first period in the table, age 20, this class experiences more than the average amount of sickness of the general class. At the next periods, ages 30, 40, 50, and 60, a less average amount of sickness is experienced. The average amount of sickness, at the early age, causes more aggregate to be experienced in passing the period 20-30, but, at each subsequent period, 30-40, 40-50, and 50-60, it is less than that of the general class, and, for the whole period, 20-60 years, the aggregate of sickness experienced by this class is 11 per cent. less than that of the general class for the same period, showing a less aggregate sickness, and an equal general expectation.

SPINNERS.

Spinners constitute about 1.82 per cent. of the general class, and are principally located in the counties of Chester, Derby, Lancaster, and York, and in Scotland.   Some few are located in other counties, and about 70 per cent. of them reside in the county of Lancaster alone, and principally in the large towns and cities.   On reference to Table LX., it will be seen that half the lives die off at age 59-60, showing an inferior vitality of four years, as compared with the general class.

The specific intensity of this class increases from age 18, at which epoch one person dies annually out of every 73.38, to age 33, when one person dies out of every 176.02.   It then decreases to age 60, when one person dies out of every 16.83 persons living.   It again increases at this age, for a period of two years, and at age 62 one person dies out of every 17.25.   From the latter age the intensity decreases to the end of the table.

The specific intensity of this class is lower from age 18 to 27-8.   From the latter age to 49-50 it is higher, and, from 49-50 it is lower, until the end of the table ; thus showing that, in the early and late periods of life, this class is subject to a higher rate of mortality, than that which is experienced in the general class.

Spinners show an inferior expectation at every decennial period, the most inferior becoming apparent at 50 years of age, when the difference is 2.88.   The least difference of expectation is 1.38, at age 60, so that the general expectation is far below that of all the classes.

Spinners experience more than the average amount of sickness at the decennial periods of 20, 40, 50, and 60, and, at the age 30, approach very near the average amount experienced by the general class.   The aggregate amount of sickness experienced for the period 20-30 is less than that of the general class ; but, at other periods, 30-40, 40-50, and 50-60, it is much more than that of the general class, and, for the whole period, 20-60, it exceeds by 23 per cent. the aggregate sickness experienced by the general class of lives, so that in this class appear more aggregate sickness, and an inferior expectation.

STONEMASONS.

Stonemasons form about 2.96 per cent of the general class of lives, and are located in every part of the country.   Next to clerks, potters, and letter-press printers, they have the most inferior vitality, half the lives dying off at age 57-8.   They exhibit an inferior vitality of six years, as compared with the general class, and with the population of England and Wales.

The specific intensity is the highest at 18 years of age, when one person dies annually out of every 154.99 persons living.   From that age it decreases to age 58, when one person dies out every 20.80.   An increase then commences, and continues to age 63.   At this age one person dies out of every 25.60.   The intensity then decreases until the conclusion of the table.

In comparing the specific intensity with that of the general class, it will be observed that, from the commencement of the table to age 61, a lower rate is apparent in this class of lives ; and, at age 61-2, and up to age 77-8, a higher specific intensity appears.   After this age the intensity again is less than in the general class, showing a higher rate of mortality to exist amongst stonemasons for all the years of life, except from age 61-2 to age 77-8, than that which exists in the general class of lives.

H

The expectation of life amongst this class of persons is less than that of the general class of lives, at the periods 20, 30, 40, and 50 ; but, at age 60, there appears a superior expectation of 1.48 years. The difference at the first period is 2.73 years ; at the second period, age 30, it is 3.29 years ; at the third period, age 40, it is 2.25 years ; and, at the fourth period, age 50, it is 1.25 years ; thus showing that the greatest difference exists at the early ages given.

The average amount of sickness experienced by this class, at each decennial period, is more than that experienced by the general class. The aggregate sickness of stonemasons, for the period 20-30, is 7.9 per cent. more than the general aggregate ; for the period 30-40 it is 24.9 per cent. ; for the period 40-50 it is 19.5 per cent. more ; and, for the whole period, it is 51.9 per cent. more than that experienced by the general class, showing in this class of lives an inferior expectation, and, with the exception of miners, the largest aggregate amount of sickness for those periods of life.

TAILORS.

Tailors form about 3.4 per cent. of the general class, and, as was observed of shoemakers, there is scarcely a locality which contributes to the general class of lives where one or more tailors will not be found to exist. It will be seen, on reference to Table LXII., that half of the lives die off at age 63-4, showing an equal vitality with the general class, and with the population of England and Wales.

This class of lives shows a change in the specific intensity at seven different periods of life, whilst that of shoemakers change at six different periods. From age 18, when one person dies annually out of every 110.59 persons living, the intensity increases up to age 28, at which period one person dies out of 129.76. After that time a decrease takes place, and continues to age 34, when one person dies out of every 100.22. The intensity then increases up to age 36, at which age one person dies out of every 104.65. A second decrease takes place up to 43, at which age one person dies out of every 60.62, and at that epoch the third increase in the intensity takes place, and continues to age 49, when one person dies out of 109.37. It then decreases to age 68, at which period one person dies out of every 7.04. The last increase takes place at the latter age, and continues to 74, when one person dies in every 13.85. After this the intensity decreases to the last age in the table.

In comparing the specific intensity with that of the general class of lives, it will be observed that a higher specific intensity appears in the general class from age 18 to 26-7 ; from 29-30 to 45-6 ; from 60 to 73-4 ; and, from age 76-7 to the termination of the table, showing a higher rate of mortality at those ages in this class than that which exists in the general class of lives.

The expectation of life is inferior to the general class. At the decennial period of life, age 20, the difference is 1.52 years ; at 30 it is 1.29 years ; at 40 it is 1.07 years ; at 50 it is 1.09 years ; and at 60 it is 3.06 years, showing an inferior expectation in this class of the above amount at each period named.

The average amount of sickness experienced at the periods 20, 50, and 60, is less, and, at the periods 30 and 40, it is more, than the average amount experienced by the general class of lives. For the period 20-30 years the aggregate sickness approaches very near ; for 40-50, and 50-60, it is less ; for 30-40 it is more ; and, for the whole period, 20-60, it is 17.5 per cent. less than the aggregate sickness experienced by the general class for that period, so that this class of lives shows a less aggregate amount of sickness, and an inferior general expectation of life, in comparison with the general class.

WEAVERS.

Weavers constitute about three per cent. of the general class, and are principally located in the manufacturing counties, 70 per cent. of them being in the counties of Lancashire and Yorkshire. They show a superior vitality of two years, in comparison with the general class of lives. On reference to Table LXIII., it will be seen that half the lives die off at age 65-6, showing a superior vitality of two years, when contrasted with the vitality of the population of England and Wales.

The specific intensity of this class of lives from age 18, when one person dies annually out of every 98.69 persons living, increases up to age 29, at which period one person dies out of every 130.37. From that age it decreases to the end of the table. The specific intensity, if compared with that of the general class, appears higher from age 27-8 to 32-5, and again from age 47-8 to 84-5, showing that the rate of mortality for those periods of life is higher than in the general class.

Weavers show a superior expectation at each decennial period of life; at age 20 they have a superiority of 1.00 year; at age 30 of 1.85 years; at age 40 of 2.12 years; at age 50 of 2.61 years; and at age 60 of 2.32 years; thus exhibiting a far superior general expectation for each period.

The average amount of sickness at the first period, age 20, is less than that of the general class, and, at each of the other periods, it is greater. In the aggregate amount of sickness for each period, 20-30, 30-40, 40-50, and 50-60, it is more than in the general class, the greatest excess being in the last period, 50-60. For the whole period, 20-60, there appears an excess of aggregate sickness of about 11 per cent. more than that of the general class of lives. This class, therefore, shows a superior general expectation, and more aggregate sickness than the general class.

WHEELWRIGHTS.

Wheelwrights form about .74 per cent. of the general class, and are found in every part over which the calculations have extended. On reference to Table LXIV., it will be seen that half the lives die off at age 62-3, showing an inferior vitality to that of the general class, and of the population of England and Wales.

The specific intensity, from 18 years of age, at which period one person dies annually out of every 105.48 persons living, increases up to age 23. At this latter age one person dies out of every 156.07. It then decreases to age 36. At this age one person dies out of every 77.15. A second increase then takes place up to age 43, the highest specific intensity being attained at this age, one person dying out of every 182.71. From this age it decreases to the end of the table.

The specific intensity is less at the commencement of the table, and up to age 39-40, showing a higher rate of mortality. From that age to 55 a higher specific intensity is seen, and from 55 years of age an intensity approximating to that of the general class appears until the conclusion of the table, showing for the early period a higher rate; for the middle period a lower rate; and, for the latter period of life, an equal mortality with the general class of lives.

The expectation of wheelwrights approaches very near to that of the general class, the greatest difference being at 40 years of age, when a superiority is shown in this class of 1.13 years.   At the other periods a superior expectation is shown, but to a very limited extent.

The average sickness experienced by wheelwrights is less at each decennial period, with the exception of age 30, than the general class of lives, and this exception so affects the general results, as to cause the aggregate sickness, for period 30-40 years, to exceed that of the general class for that period only.   For the other periods the aggregate sickness is so much less as to cause it, for the whole period 20-60 to be 60 per cent. less than the aggregate of the general class.

WOOLCOMBERS.

Woolcombers form .68 per cent. of the general class of lives, 83 per cent. of which are located in the county of York, and the remaining portion in a few other counties.   Half of the lives, it will be seen, on reference to Table LXV., die off at the age 59-60, showing an inferior vitality of four years, in comparison with the general class, and with the population of England and Wales.

The specific intensity of this class of lives is the lowest of any yet given, at age 18, at which time one person dies annually out of every 26.97 persons living.   From this age it increases up to 37, when one person dies out of every 150.19.   It then decreases to 42, at which age one person dies out of every 109.44.   It again increases until 47, when the maximum is attained, one person dying out of every 188.82.   A second decrease in the intensity commences at this age, and continues to 59, when one person dies out of every 16.43.   The last increase now takes place, and continues to age 63, when one person dies out of every 21.63.   From this age the intensity decreases until the conclusion of the table.

The specific intensity is lower in this class of lives, as compared with the general class, from age 19 to 29-30; from age 52-3 to 62-3; and again from 71-2 to the end of the table : thus showing a high rate of mortality for those periods of life.   At the other periods of life it is more favourable in this than in the general class.   The expectation is inferior to the general class at each decennial period except age 30.   At that period woolcombers show a superiority of .24 years.   At the period 20 the expectation is 2.17 years less; at 40 it is .92 years less; at 50 it is 1.55 years less ; and at 60 it is .31 years less than the expectation of the general class of lives.

The same rule that governs the rate of mortality appears to show itself in this class of lives with reference to sickness.   At the first period in the table the average sickness per annum appears more than in the general class, and the expectation less; at the next period, with a superior expectation, a less average amount of sickness appears.   At the other periods of life, with an inferior expectation, woolcombers experience more average sickness than the general class of lives ; but the aggregate sickness for all the periods 20-30, 30-40, 40-50, and 50-60, shows a great amount experienced by this class in comparison with the general one, the excess being, for the whole period 20-60, 20 per cent. more than the aggregate sickness of the general class of lives.

In some of the following tables, which should present the number of persons, amount of sickness and deaths (if any) at *each* age, it was found to be a matter of some difficulty to insert every separate age; it will be seen, in a few instances at the end of the tables, that they have been condensed in periods, giving the number of persons, amount of sickness, &c., for a series of years. Whenever the tables begin to be so condensed, it must be understood that the same includes all the persons, sickness and deaths (if any) for that period, as for instance at Table XIV., age 68 would have included the number of persons, amount of sickness and number of deaths for the period 64-70 had there been any of those ages.

TABLE XIv.—BAKERS.

AGE	No. OF MEMBERS.		DEATHS.			SICKNESS.		
	At each age.	In periods.	At Each Age.	In Periods.		At Each Age.	In Periods.	
				Total.	Per Cent.		Total.	Per Annum.
18	13		...			1.428		
19	42	147	...	1	.6802	15.571	71.141	.4840
20	92		1			54.142		
21	188		1			61.428		
22	211		1			118.857		
23	267	1298	...	5	.3852	117.714	595.998	.4591
24	305		1			116.142		
25	327		2			181.857		
26	347		2			247.142		
27	361		1			206.142		
28	366	1828	4	10	.5470	204.000	1136.426	.6216
29	380		2			270.285		
30	374		1			208.857		
31	333		2			175.428		
32	317		4			193.142		
33	274	1464	...	8	.6722	137.571	844.568	.5769
34	274		1			200.285		
35	266		1			138.142		
36	246		3			219.428		
37	212		3			129.428		
38	192	918	2	12	1.0383	176.285	692.283	.7541
39	141		1			73.857		
40	127		3			93.285		
41	98		3			120.000		
42	70		...			111.142		
43	59	300	2	6	2.0000	151.285	568.855	1.8961
44	38		1			100.571		
45	35		...			85.857		
46	32		1			99.571		
47	24		...			30.714		
48	31	113	...	1	.9026	13.714	151.570	1.3411
49	14		...			4.571		
50	12		...			3.000		
51	4		...			1.000		
52	6		...			....		
53	4	18	...	0	0.0000	6.000	7.000	.3888
54	2		...			....		
55	2		...			....		
56	2		1			2.714		
57	2		...			....		
58	2	6	...	1	16.6666	....	2.714	.4523
59	...		...			....		
60	...		...			....		
61	1		...			4.571		
62	1		...			20.000		
63	...	4	...	0	0.0000	....	27.571	6.8927
64	1		...			3.000		
65	1		...			....		
66	...		...			....		
67	...		...			....		
68	...	0	...	0	0.0000	....	0.000	0.0000
69	...		...			....		
70	...		...			....		
71	...		...			....		
73	1	1	...	0	0.0000	0.000	0.000	0.0000
78	1	1	...	0	0.0000	13.000	13.000	13.0000
	6098		44		.7215	4111.126		.6741

TABLE XV.—BLACKSMITHS. 63

AGE.	No. of Members. At each Age	In Periods.	Deaths. At Each Age.	In Periods. Total.	Per Cent.	Sickness. At Each Age.	In Periods. Total.	Per Annum.
18	52		...			1.142		
19	159	502	2	3	.5976	93.571	253.141	.5042
20	291		1			158.428		
21	480		1			279.714		
22	709		4			550.000		
23	880	4259	9	27	.6339	721.142	3529.998	.8288
24	1037		6			896.428		
25	1153		7			1082.714		
26	1199		10		—	867.285		
27	1252		10			939.571		
28	1236	6275	13	49	.7808	1124.714	5225.426	.8318
29	1258		11			1122.714		
30	1330		5			1171.142		
31	1154		10			1027.714		
32	1097		13			874.571		
33	996	5188	12	52	1.1023	785.428	4538.712	.8748
34	1013		10			1044.142		
35	928		7			806.857		
36	1001		9			684.714		
37	869		5			699.285		
38	846	4081	4	33	1.2987	644.428	3290.712	.8063
39	630		10			591.857		
40	735		5			670.428		
41	497		6			495.714		
42	479		8			525.285		
43	382	1996	9	33	2.6553	506.000	2378.569	1.1916
44	328		5			451.428		
45	310		5			400.142		
46	281		7			431.000		
47	225		2			373.714		
48	197	1014	5	18	1.8164	301.714	1615.998	1.5936
49	176		3			325.428		
50	135		1			184.142		
51	85		2			184.142		
52	74		5			85.428		
53	72	353	1	10	2.8328	172.571	631.997	1.7903
54	79		2			114.285		
55	43		...			75.571		
56	48		...			169.714		
57	23		1			4.000		
58	26	149	2	6	4.0268	36.000	506.713	3.4007
59	29		2			199.285		
60	23		1			97.714		
61	21		3			167.571		
62	9		2			59.714		
63	6	47	...	5	10.6382	64.000	343.427	5.8041
64	4		...			52.142		
65	7		...			....		
66	5		1			3.000		
67	3		1			10.000		
68	1	12	...	2	16.6666	....	14.285	1.1904
69	2		...			1.285		
70	1		...			....		
71	2	2	...					
	23878		238		.9967	22328.978		.9351

AGE.	No. OF MEMBERS.		DEATHS.			SICKNESS.		
	At each Age.	In Periods.	At Each Age.	In Periods.		At Each Age.	In Periods.	
				Total.	Per Cent.		Total.	Per Annum.
18	29		...			2.000		
19	67	238	...	0	.0000	8.285	78.285	.3289
20	142		...			68.000		
21	212		2			107.857		
22	328		...			204.571		
23	357	1844	2	9	.4880	274.571	1332.427	.7225
24	477		...			284.428		
25	470		5			461.000		
26	555		4			370.857		
27	611		2			522.142		
28	531	2845	6	20	.7029	390.428	2160·855	.7595
29	574		6			418.000		
30	574		2			459.428		
31	548		5			266.000		
32	517		4			506.714		
33	476	2509	4	28	1.1159	418.428	2106.142	.8609
34	486		9			482.000		
35	482		6			433.000		
36	513		5			332.000		
37	431		5			371.428		
38	411	2048	1	18	.8789	414.857	1939.427	.9491
39	338		2			379.000		
40	355		5			442.142		
41	262		3			283.428		
42	232		2			177.000		
43	169	951	1	12	1.2618	133.571	990.570	1.0416
44	146		5			169.857		
45	142		1			226.714		
46	159		2			288.285		
47	104		2			169.714		
48	104	522	2	9	1.7241	175.000	859.570	1.6466
49	84		2			45.571		
50	71		1			181.000		
51	41		1			82.000		
52	33		2			62.571		
53	30	153	...	3	1.9607	44.285	305.856	1.9990
54	28		...			24.000		
55	21		...			93.000		
56	17		...			49.000		
57	11		2			61.000		
58	10	42	...	2	4.7619	14.000	124.000	3.7168
59	1		...			... ...		
60	3		...			... ...		
61	2		...			4.000		
62	1		...			15.714		
63	7	14	1	2	14.2857	134.571	177.856	12.7040
64	1		...			... ...		
65	3		1			23.571		
66	4		1			30.142		
67	3		...			8.000		
68	2	11	...	1	9.9999	3.000	60.142	5.4674
69	...		...			... ...		
70	2		...			19.000		
73	7	7	2	2	28.5742	318.141	318.141	45.4487
78	1	1	...	0	.0000	52.142	52.142	52.1420
	11185		106		.9476	10505.413		.9409

TABLE XVII.—BUTCHERS. 65

AGE.	No. OF MEMBERS.		DEATHS.			SICKNESS.		
	At each Age.	In Periods.	At each Age.	In Periods.		At Each Age.	In Periods.	
				Total.	Per Cent.		Total.	Per Annum.
18	24 ⎫		...			....		
19	54 ⎬	179	1 ⎬	1	.5586	5.000 ⎬	35.714	.1995
20	101 ⎭		...			30.714 ⎭		
21	169 ⎫		1 ⎫			74.714 ⎫		
22	222 ⎪		... ⎪			53.714 ⎪		
23	283 ⎬	1387	2 ⎬	5	.3604	321.714 ⎬	805.998	.5811
24	359 ⎪		1 ⎪			194.571 ⎪		
25	354 ⎭		1 ⎭			161.285 ⎭		
26	375 ⎫		2 ⎫			126.428 ⎫		
27	400 ⎪		3 ⎪			208.857 ⎪		
28	423 ⎬	2049	3 ⎬	13	.6344	204.714 ⎬	873.284	.4262
29	411 ⎪		3 ⎪			146.428 ⎪		
30	440 ⎭		2 ⎭			186.857 ⎭		
31	372 ⎫		4 ⎫			219.142 ⎫		
32	377 ⎪		3 ⎪			215.000 ⎪		
33	348 ⎬	1760	4 ⎬	16	.9090	124.428 ⎬	867.712	.4930
34	336 ⎪		3 ⎪			132.285 ⎪		
35	327 ⎭		2 ⎭			176.857 ⎭		
36	320 ⎫		8 ⎫			248.285 ⎫		
37	266 ⎪		1 ⎪			141.428 ⎪		
38	251 ⎬	1230	3 ⎬	14	1.1123	109.571 ⎬	717.855	.5836
39	182 ⎪		... ⎪			115.000 ⎪		
40	211 ⎭		2 ⎭			103.571 ⎭		
41	138 ⎫		2 ⎫			88.428 ⎫		
42	129 ⎪		1 ⎪			117.571 ⎪		
43	106 ⎬	583	... ⎬	7	1.2006	112.000 ⎬	677.856	1.1626
44	107 ⎪		1 ⎪			179.000 ⎪		
45	103 ⎭		3 ⎭			180.857 ⎭		
46	106 ⎫		2 ⎫			134.571 ⎫		
47	74 ⎪		3 ⎪			52.571 ⎪		
48	73 ⎬	343	3 ⎬	9	2.6239	70.857 ⎬	345.569	1.0075
49	48 ⎪		1 ⎪			54.428 ⎪		
50	42 ⎭		... ⎭			33.142 ⎭		
51	27 ⎫		... ⎫			8.000 ⎫		
52	31 ⎪		1 ⎪			72.000 ⎪		
53	20 ⎬	119	... ⎬	3	2.5210	41.714 ⎬	217.713	1.8295
54	22 ⎪		1 ⎪			49.428 ⎪		
55	19 ⎭		1 ⎭			46.571 ⎭		
56	16 ⎫		... ⎫			33.000 ⎫		
57	8 ⎪		1 ⎪			2.000 ⎪		
58	8 ⎬	41	... ⎬	1	2.4390	3.000 ⎬	59.714	1.4564
59	5 ⎪		... ⎪			6.000 ⎪		
60	4 ⎭		... ⎭			15.714 ⎭		
61	3 ⎫		... ⎫			.... ⎫		
62	1 ⎪		... ⎪			.... ⎪		
63	1 ⎬	7	... ⎬	0	0.0000	.... ⎬	43.000	6.1428
64	... ⎪		... ⎪			.... ⎪		
65	2 ⎭		... ⎭			43.000 ⎭		
66	1	1	1	1	100.0000	50.142	50.142	50.1420
	7699		70		.9090	4694.557		.6097

I

AGE.	No. OF MEMBERS.		DEATHS.			SICKNESS.		
	At each Age.	In Periods.	At Each Age.	In Periods. Total.	Per Cent.	At Each Age.	In Periods. Total.	Per Annum.
18	66		...			17.142		
19	199	666	1	2	.3003	66.285	267.998	.4023
20	401		1			184.571		
21	615		11			610.142		
22	1140		9			801.142		
23	1403	6801	7	62	.9116	941.428	5515.854	.8110
24	1741		17			1364.285		
25	1902		18			1798.857		
26	2075		14			1604.571		
27	2045		15			1620.428		
28	2094	10257	19	75	.7312	1899.285	8263.283	.8056
29	1984		9			1511.428		
30	2059		18			1627.571		
31	1761		14			1244.142		
32	1782		21			1724.571		
33	1599	8351	4	79	.9459	1504.428	7651.997	.9165
34	1623		21			1823.285		
35	1586		19			1355.571		
36	1655		16			1300.428		
37	1375		8			1103.285		
38	1299	6477	11	57	.8800	1422.285	5977.854	.9229
39	1107		16			976.714		
40	1041		6			1175.142		
41	690		6			809.142		
42	624		9			731.857		
43	488	2728	9	33	1.2093	412.142	2816.998	1.0326
44	475		6			402.857		
45	451		3			461.000		
46	414		4			542.285		
47	335		6			257.714		
48	291	1420	6	19	1.3380	411.571	1666.998	1.1739
49	206		1			217.857		
50	174		2			237.571		
51	128		...			127.142		
52	95		2			106.142		
53	73	440	2	5	1.1363	121.000	597.426	1.3577
54	77		1			65.142		
55	67		...			178.000		
56	50		1			141.000		
57	29		1			64.571		
58	24	145	1	4	2.7586	40.857	340.427	2.3477
59	16		...			10.142		
60	26		1			83.857		
61	10		...			112.857		
62	10		1			94.857		
63	13	59	...	1	1.6949	63.142	357.569	6.0018
64	13		...			35.285		
65	13		...			51.428		
66	13		2			27.428		
67	4		...			... ...		
68	2	22	1	3	2.8679	14.000	41.428	1.8830
69	3		...			... ...		
70	...		...			... ...		
73	13	13	...	0	0.0000	107.285	107.285	8.2526
78	1	1	...	0	0.0000	1.000	1.000	1.0000
	37380		340	0	.9095	33606.117		.8990

TABLE XIX.—CLERKS AND SCHOOLMASTERS. 67

AGE.	No. OF MEMBERS.		DEATHS.			SICKNESS.		
	At each Age.	In Periods.	At Each Age.	In Periods.		At Each Age.	In Periods.	
				Total.	Per Cent.		Total.	Per Annum.
18	29		...			3.000		
19	74	234	1	2	.8547	20.428	71.570	.3058
20	131		1			.48.142		
21	171		1			76.714		
22	259		2			113.142		
23	294	1470	1	14	.8235	147.714	666.426	.3920
24	385		4			96.285		
25	361		6			232.571		
26	408		3			209.428		
27	438		5			152.142		
28	438	2149	6	20	.9306	223.571	995.855	.4634
29	410		3			163.857		
30	455		3			246.857		
31	424		8			284.571		
32	410		3			200.285		
33	367	1939	6	26	1.3408	264.142	1175.997	.6064
34	389		6			262.714		
35	349		3			164.285		
36	352		4			194.571		
37	306		5			308.428		
38	266	1419	...	14	.9866	155.142	1071.711	.7552
39	241		2			164.142		
40	254		3			249.428		
41	161		1			148.714		
42	156		5			97.142		
43	124	676	2	10	1.4792	159.285	647.283	.9575
44	121		...			58.714		
45	114		2			183.428		
46	101		3			149.857		
47	88		2			150.428		
48	86	383	2	11	2.8720	140.714	539.283	1.4080
49	55		2			69.142		
50	53		2			29.142		
51	34		...			33.000		
52	42		...			58.714		
53	25	136	1	1	7.3529	22.000	198.142	1.4569
54	16		...			13.428		
55	19		...			71.000		
56	14		...			39.571		
57	13		1			8.142		
58	14	60	...	3	5.0000	4.000	79.712	1.3285
59	7		1			16.714		
60	12		1			11.285		
61	2		...			2.000		
62	2		...			1.000		
63	6	17	...	0	0.0000	... ...	18.285	1.0814
64	3		...			1.285		
65	4		...			14.000		
66	1		...			1.000		
67	4		...			2.000		
68	...	5	...	0	0.0000	... ...	3.000	6.000
69	...		...			... ...		
70	...		...			... ...		
	8488		101		1.1899	5467.264		.6440

TABLE XX.—COOPERS.

AGE.	No. OF MEMBERS.		DEATHS.			SICKNESS.		
	At each Age.	In Periods.	At each Age.	In Periods.		At Each Age.	In Periods.	
				Total.	Per Cent.		Total.	Per Annum.
18	3 ⎫		... ⎫			1.714 ⎫		
19	9 ⎬	35	... ⎬	0	.0000	7.000 ⎬	12.714	.3631
20	23 ⎭		... ⎭			4.000 ⎭		
21	38 ⎫		... ⎫			12.571 ⎫		
22	49 ⎪		1 ⎪			33.714 ⎪		
23	74 ⎬	318	... ⎬	2	.6288	44.285 ⎬	241.997	.7609
24	62 ⎪		1 ⎪			64.142 ⎪		
25	95 ⎭		... ⎭			87.285 ⎭		
26	115 ⎫		... ⎫			50.000 ⎫		
27	130 ⎪		... ⎪			98.714 ⎪		
28	129 ⎬	632	3 ⎬	6	.9493	92.714 ⎬	450.327	.7125
29	117 ⎪		2 ⎪			102.328 ⎪		
30	141 ⎭		1 ⎭			106.571 ⎭		
31	116 ⎫		1 ⎫			122.285 ⎫		
32	120 ⎪		2 ⎪			95.571 ⎪		
33	114 ⎬	551	1 ⎬	7	1.2704	90.571 ⎬	479.283	.8698
34	110 ⎪		2 ⎪			139.571 ⎪		
35	91 ⎭		1 ⎭			31.285 ⎭		
36	98 ⎫		2 ⎫			112.428 ⎫		
37	84 ⎪		... ⎪			64.142 ⎪		
38	81 ⎬	388	... ⎬	3	.7731	185.000 ⎬	566.426	1.4599
39	58 ⎪		1 ⎪			156.142 ⎪		
40	67 ⎭		... ⎭			48.714 ⎭		
41	43 ⎫		1 ⎫			35.714 ⎫		
42	30 ⎪		... ⎪			55.428 ⎪		
43	24 ⎬	160	1 ⎬	4	2.5000	4.714 ⎬	145.569	.9098
44	28 ⎪		1 ⎪			24.142 ⎪		
45	35 ⎭		1 ⎭			25.571 ⎭		
46	26 ⎫		1 ⎫			62.714 ⎫		
47	18 ⎪		... ⎪			70.428 ⎪		
48	14 ⎬	76	... ⎬	1	1.3182	21.714 ⎬	227.998	2.9999
49	9 ⎪		... ⎪			73.142 ⎪		
50	9 ⎭		... ⎭			... ... ⎭		
51	12 ⎫		... ⎫			75.000 ⎫		
52	8 ⎪		... ⎪			13.428 ⎪		
53	7 ⎬	34	1 ⎬	1	2.9411	26.857 ⎬	150.999	4.4411
54	4 ⎪		... ⎪			25.714 ⎪		
55	3 ⎭		... ⎭			10.000 ⎭		
56	3 ⎫		... ⎫			3.714 ⎫		
57	1 ⎪		1 ⎪			7.285 ⎪		
58	... ⎬	5	... ⎬	1	20.0000	... ... ⎬	10.999	2.1998
59	... ⎪		... ⎪			... ... ⎪		
60	1 ⎭		... ⎭			... ... ⎭		
61	1 ⎫		... ⎫			... ... ⎫		
62	... ⎪		... ⎪			... ... ⎪		
63	... ⎬	1	... ⎬	0	0.0000	... ... ⎬	.0000	0.0000
64	... ⎪		... ⎪			... ... ⎪		
65	... ⎭		... ⎭			... ... ⎭		
66	... ⎫	1	... ⎫	0	.0000	... ... ⎫	0.0000	0.0000
67	1 ⎭		... ⎭			... ... ⎭		
	2201		25		1.1358	2286.312		1.0387

TABLE XXI.—DYERS. 69

AGE.	No. OF MEMBERS.		DEATHS.			SICKNESS.		
	At each Age.	In Periods.	At Each Age.	In Periods.		At Each Age.	In Periods.	
				Total.	Per Cent.		Total.	Per Annum.
18	12 ⎫		... ⎫			1.000 ⎫		
19	16 ⎬	53	... ⎬	0	0.0000	4.428 ⎬	14.142	.2668
20	25 ⎭		... ⎭			8.714 ⎭		
21	50 ⎫		... ⎫			26.857 ⎫		
22	86 ⎪		... ⎪			26.142 ⎪		
23	76 ⎬	465	1 ⎬	3	.6451	21.857 ⎬	188.712	.4058
24	105 ⎪		1 ⎪			51.428 ⎪		
25	148 ⎭		1 ⎭			62.428 ⎭		
26	144 ⎫		1 ⎫			130.714 ⎫		
27	158 ⎪		3 ⎪			149.142 ⎪		
28	156 ⎬	764	3 ⎬	8	1.0471	108.142 ⎬	580.283	.7595
29	140 ⎪		... ⎪			45.571 ⎪		
30	166 ⎭		1 ⎭			146.714 ⎭		
31	140 ⎫		1 ⎫			59.285 ⎫		
32	163 ⎪		1 ⎪			110.428 ⎪		
33	125 ⎬	687	1 ⎬	4	.5822	100.857 ⎬	575.141	83.71
34	144 ⎪		1 ⎪			109.857 ⎪		
35	115 ⎭		... ⎭			194.714 ⎭		
36	132 ⎫		1 ⎫			172.571 ⎫		
37	131 ⎪		1 ⎪			57.857 ⎪		
38	106 ⎬	572	1 ⎬	4	.6993	64.857 ⎬	507.856	.8878
39	93 ⎪		... ⎪			107.000 ⎪		
40	110 ⎭		1 ⎭			105.571 ⎭		
41	89 ⎫		... ⎫			136.714 ⎫		
42	77 ⎪		3 ⎪			165.285 ⎪		
43	68 ⎬	368	1 ⎬	7	1.9021	42.000 ⎬	581.284	1.5795
44	71 ⎪		2 ⎪			139.571 ⎪		
45	63 ⎭		1 ⎭			97.714 ⎭		
46	47 ⎫		2 ⎫			114.000 ⎫		
47	61 ⎪		1 ⎪			76.000 ⎪		
48	65 ⎬	274	... ⎬	4	1.4598	52.285 ⎬	387.856	1.4155
49	48 ⎪		... ⎪			38.857 ⎪		
50	53 ⎭		1 ⎭			106.714 ⎭		
51	36 ⎫		... ⎫			49.571 ⎫		
52	30 ⎪		... ⎪			45.000 ⎪		
53	30 ⎬	142	1 ⎬	4	2.8169	48.142 ⎬	408.426	2.8762
54	22 ⎪		... ⎪			88.571 ⎪		
55	24 ⎭		3 ⎭			177.142 ⎭		
56	12 ⎫		... ⎫			11.428 ⎫		
57	13 ⎪		2 ⎪			73.000 ⎪		
58	7 ⎬	43	... ⎬	2	4.6511	2.285 ⎬	124.713	2.9003
59	4 ⎪		... ⎪			31.000 ⎪		
60	7 ⎭		... ⎭			7.000 ⎭		
61	5 ⎫		... ⎫			17.142 ⎫		
62	3 ⎪		... ⎪			15.428 ⎪		
63	... ⎬	10	... ⎬	0	0.0000	... ... ⎬	136.854	13.6854
64	1 ⎪		... ⎪			52.142 ⎪		
65	1 ⎭		... ⎭			52.142 ⎭		
66	... ⎫		... ⎫			52.142 ⎫		
67	... ⎪		... ⎪			... ... ⎪		
68	2 ⎬	2	1 ⎬	1	50.0000	26.000 ⎬	78.142	39.0710
69	... ⎪		... ⎪			... ... ⎪		
70	... ⎭		... ⎭			... ... ⎭		
73	4	4	0		0.0000	11.142	11.142	2.7850
	3384		37		1.0933	3594.551		1.0622

TABLE XXII.—HATTERS.

AGE.	No. OF MEMBERS. At each age.	No. OF MEMBERS. In periods.	DEATHS. At Each Age.	DEATHS. In Periods. Total.	DEATHS. In Periods. Per Cent.	SICKNESS. At Each Age.	SICKNESS. In Periods. Total.	SICKNESS. In Periods. Per Annum.
18	5		...			... ...		
19	11	34	1	1	2.9411	10.428	11.428	.3059
20	18		...			1.000		
21	41		...			25.000		
22	60		1			40.572		
23	73	334	1	4	1.1976	68.714	217.430	.6509
24	79		2			36.572		
25	81		...			46.572		
26	121		2			46.142		
27	118		2			57.000		
28	158	717	1	8	1.1156	104.285	418.427	.5835
29	151		1			104.428		
30	169		2			106.572		
31	159		5			99.142		
32	158		3			150.000		
33	127	767	1	13	1.6949	29.000	486.855	.6347
34	160		1			105.285		
35	163		3			103.428		
36	169		2			289.000		
37	135		...			102.000		
38	139	732	1	4	.5464	123.285	720.570	.9843
39	143		1			75.285		
40	146		...			131.000		
41	124		...			56.142		
42	108		...			150.857		
43	93	458	...	2	.5497	294.857	763.570	1.6671
44	70		2			180.000		
45	63		...			81.714		
46	72		2			101.142		
47	76		1			119.000		
48	61	313	...	4	1.2779	122.572	498.285	1.5919
49	57		...			57.857		
50	47		1			97.714		
51	40		...			95.714		
52	44		...			163.000		
53	38	178	1	2	1.1234	45.000	444.285	2.4959
54	32		...			49.857		
55	24		1			90.714		
56	19		...			170.285		
57	17		1			49.714		
58	15	73	...	2	2.7397	70.857	351.141	4.8100
59	15		1			38.285		
60	7		...			22.000		
61	9		1			34.000		
62	9		...			15.285		
63	6	34	1	2	5.8823	19.000	77.285	2.2730
64	5		...			6.000		
65	5		...			3.000		
66	4		...			9.000		
67	3		1			11.000		
68	1	9	...	1	11.1111	15.000	87.142	9.6825
69	...		...			... ...		
70	1		...			52.142		
73	3	3	...	0	0.0000	104.285	104.285	34.761
78	6	6	1	1	16.6666	276.854	276.854	46.1423
	3658		44		1.2028	4457.557		1.2185

TABLE XXIII.—LABOURERS, AGRICULTURAL.   71

AGE.	No. OF MEMBERS.		DEATHS.			SICKNESS.		
	At each Age	In Periods.	At Each Age.	In Periods.		At Each Age.	In Periods.	
				Total.	Per Cent.		Total.	Per Annum.
18	198		...			65.428		
19	533	1562	...	2	.1280	226.285	756.141	.4840
20	831		2			464.428		
21	1229		12			789.714		
22	1649		12			1227.714		
23	1931	9441	8	62	.6567	1362.000	7114.427	.7535
24	2262		18			1748.714		
25	2370		12			1986.285		
26	2706		15			2450.714		
27	2723		25			2306.285		
28	2662	13660	18	87	.6368	2002.285	11334.855	.8297
29	2737		16			2098.857		
30	2832		13			2476.714		
31	2319		18			2321.571		
32	2382		16			2147.571		
33	2265	11426	15	77	.6739	2069.285	11046.569	.9667
34	2212		14			2188.000		
35	2248		14			2320.142		
36	2102		12			2244.571		
37	1846		8			2121.714		
38	1691	8682	15	53	.6104	1916.285	9757.569	1.1238
39	1436		5			1399.285		
40	1607		13			2075.714		
41	1139		6			1329.000		
42	1170		7			1469.142		
43	913	4892	11	38	.7767	967.285	5900.712	1.2061
44	857		8			1157.428		
45	813		6			977.857		
46	776		7			1211.428		
47	617		7			736.285		
48	539	2772	4	29	1.0461	905.142	4709.425	1.6989
49	431		6			751.285		
50	409		5			1105.285		
51	229		4			602.571		
52	200		1			429.428		
53	136	766	5	12	1.5665	413.142	1776.712	2.3195
54	121		...			212.714		
55	80		2			118.857		
56	87		...			126.714		
57	55		...			81.285		
58	44	256	1	2	.7812	111.857	591.141	2.3091
59	34		...			94.714		
60	36		1			176.571		
61	24		1			176.714		
62	19		...			58.714		
63	14	84	2	4	4.7619	139.142	509.426	6.0646
64	14		...			106.428		
65	13		1			28.428		
66	7		...			15.000		
67	10		...			46.285		
68	11	35	...	0	0.0000	19.428	223.426	6.3836
69	5		...			124.285		
70	2		...			18.428		
71	4		...			66.142		
72	1	8	...	0	0.0000	35.571	201.713	25.2141
73	3		...			104.000		
	53584		366		.6830	53922.116		1.0063

AGE.	No. OF MEMBERS.		DEATHS.			SICKNESS.		
	At each Age.	In Periods.	At Each Age.	In Periods. Total.	Per Cent.	At Each Age.	In Periods. Total.	Per Annum.
18	92		...			45.142		
19	234	823	2	8	.9720	98.428	434.855	.5283
20	497		6			.291.285		
21	705		4			409.000		
22	909		4			692.428		
23	1057	5436	5	35	.6438	814.571	3988.426	.7337
24	1301		10			1046.142		
25	1464		12			1026.285		
26	1649		12			1253.285		
27	1820		16			1648.428		
28	1909	9339	15	71	.7602	1912.714	8583.426	.9190
29	1805		14			1720.714		
30	2156		14			2048.285		
31	1923		16			2229.142		
32	1928		19			1940.142		
33	1711	9239	16	83	.8983	1565.428	9528.568	1.0313
34	1829		16			2065.285		
35	1848		16			1728.571		
36	1918		15			2192.000		
37	1616		16			1841.000		
38	1518	8020	13	67	.8354	1626.571	9346.856	1.1654
39	1384		13			1499.857		
40	1584		10			2187.428		
41	1143		12			1635.000		
42	1085		20			1624.285		
43	942	4858	9	61	1.2556	1162.571	7016.426	1.4114
44	894		9			1292.285		
45	794		11			1302.285		
46	895		8			1345.857		
47	672		9			1121.714		
48	604	3152	8	40	1.2690	1120.857	5090.427	1.6149
49	480		7			643.571		
50	501		8			858.428		
51	333		7			690.142		
52	256		5			693.571		
53	211	1190	8	32	2.6890	544.000	2912.141	2.4471
54	230		7			616.857		
55	160		5			367.571		
56	166		4			398.000		
57	115		1			226.142		
58	86	538	2	15	2.7945	399.142	1699.854	3.1595
59	71		2			354.142		
60	100		6			322.428		
61	38		4			184.571		
62	52		1			294.714		
63	34	193	3	11	5.6994	187.142	1085.569	5.6249
64	46		2			284.428		
65	23		1			134.714		
66	24		...			61.714		
67	11		...			21.857		
68	13	69	1	2	2.8985	163.000	502.570	5.7855
69	7		1			87.857		
70	14		...			168.142		
73	21	21	3	3	14.2857	165.855	165.855	7.8978
78	6	6	...	0	0.0000	54.856	54.856	9.1426
83	3	3	...	0	0.0000	67.000	67.000	22.3333
	42887		428		.9979	50476.829		1.1769

TABLE XXV.—MILLWRIGHTS. 73

AGE.	No. OF MEMBERS.		DEATHS.			SICKNESS.		
	At each Age.	In Periods.	At each Age.	In Periods. Total.	In Periods. Per Cent.	At Each Age.	In Periods. Total.	In Periods. Per Annum.
18	6		...			... ...		
19	11	39	...	0	.0000	1.142	10.999	.2810
20	22		...			9.857		
21	46		...			45.142		
22	57		3			26.142		
23	84	419	...	3	.7159	53.857	288.855	.6893
24	119		...			80.857		
25	113		...			82.857		
26	133		2			135.857		
27	122		1			49.857		
28	148	659	3	7	1.0622	145.714	451.570	.6852
29	132		...			63.571		
30	124		1			56.571		
31	106		1			81.857		
32	91		1			69.714		
33	93	476	...	7	1.4705	50.571	372.427	.7823
34	94		...			41.571		
35	92		5			128.714		
36	101		2			103.428		
37	94		1			91.857		
38	79	409	1	5	1.2224	33.571	352.283	.8613
39	59		1			46.285		
40	76		...			77.142		
41	59		...			107.571		
42	51		1			132.857		
43	34	221	1	2	.9040	27.571	306.570	1.3871
44	43		...			30.714		
45	34		...			7.857		
46	45		...			48.285		
47	31		...			34.000		
48	24	131	...	1	.7633	73.285	181.855	1.3882
49	17		1			21.285		
50	11		...			5.000		
51	17		...			31.142		
52	14		1			29.142		
53	4	51	...	1	1.9630	15.428	94.997	1.8626
54	7		...			9.000		
55	9		...			10.285		
56	7		...			8.714		
57	3		...			... ...		
58	7	22	...	0	0.0000	... ...	23.714	1.0715
59	2		...			... ...		
60	3		...			15.000		
61	...		...			... ...		
62	...		...			... ...		
63	2	4	...	0	0.0000	... ...	0.000	0.0000
64	2		...			... ...		
65	...		...			... ...		
	2431		26		1.0695	2083.270		.8569

K

AGE.	No. OF MEMBERS.		DEATHS.			SICKNESS.		
	At each Age.	In Periods.	At Each Age.	In Periods.		At Each Age.	In Periods.	
				Total.	Per Cent.		Total.	Per Annum.
18	22		...			2.142		
19	57	200	...	1	5000	6.857	80.427	.4021
20	121		1			71.428		
21	181		3			70.857		
22	245		1			163.142		
23	314	1549	1	8	.5164	196.857	841.998	.5435
24	371		...			222.857		
25	438		3			188.285		
26	498		7			314.285		
27	505		4			287.857		
28	540	2677	7	27	1.0085	416.714	1692.713	.6323
29	563		5			322.000		
30	571		4			351.857		
31	554		6			374.571		
32	597		2			462.571		
33	502	2816	4	20	.7103	462.000	2007.427	.7128
34	586		4			375.714		
35	577		4			332.571		
36	558		3			395.571		
37	546		5			432.142		
38	499	2476	3	19	.7673	402.714	1822.141	.7359
39	443		2			245.000		
40	430		6			346.714		
41	366		6			458.571		
42	403		7			387.571		
43	351	1725	8	30	1.7391	482.142	1856.855	1.0764
44	316		3			309.000		
45	289		6			219.571		
46	300		5			368.857		
47	261		2			408.857		
48	254	1192	3	15	1.2583	390.571	1748.427	1.4668
49	182		3			340.571		
50	195		2			239.571		
51	112		5			161.000		
52	109		4			241.714		
53	101	494	5	20	4.0485	200.571	944.141	2.0012
54	114		3			257.571		
55	58		3			83.285		
56	84		2			242.714		
57	58		2			173.428		
58	51	273	2	12	4.3956	173.000	1117.998	4.0952
59	35		1			208.714		
60	45		5			320.142		
61	24		4			57.142		
62	18		...			228.571		
63	13	84	1	7	8.3333	70.000	490.426	5.8384
64	18		1			72.571		
65	11		1			62.142		
66	8		2			23.000		
67	3		...			1.000		
68	5	21	...	2	9.5238	... ...	37.000	1.7619
69	4		...			13.000		
70	1		...			... ...		
73	3	3	...	0	0.0000	72.142	72.142	24.0473
78	1	1	...	0	0.0000	... ...	0.000	0.0000
	13511		161		1.1916	12711.695		.9407

TABLE XXVII.—MINERS. 75

AGE.	No. OF MEMBERS: At each Age.	In Periods.	DEATHS. At Each Age.	In Periods. Total.	Per Cent.	SICKNESS. At Each Age.	In Periods. Total.	Per Annum.
18	170		...			34.571		
19	431	1258	5	13	1.0333	331.000	887.713	.7056
20	657		8			522.142		
21	832		10			939.000		
22	1017		10			946.714		
23	1096	5355	11	55	1.0270	1273.857	5773.713	1.0781
24	1208		10			1224.142		
25	1202		14			1390.000		
26	1396		3			1847.285		
27	1383		14			1683.428		
28	1352	7018	13	63	.8976	1842.285	9136.997	1.3019
29	1381		11			1720.142		
30	1506		22			2043.857		
31	1330		6			1905.285		
32	1315		14			1959.428		
33	1134	6102	12	51	.8357	1512.714	8983.140	1.4721
34	1146		11			1571.285		
35	1177		8			2034.428		
36	1160		14			1955.857		
37	996		13			2011.571		
38	917	4725	6	49	1.0370	1596.428	8037.141	1.7009
39	773		7			1118.428		
40	879		9			1354.857		
41	644		7			1206.000		
42	656		10			1677.142		
43	561	2935	13	47	1.6013	1286.857	6042.998	2.2033
44	539		6			1059.571		
45	538		11			1413.428		
46	459		8			1338.571		
47	415		8			1364.571		
48	366	1905	6	39	2.0471	1092.285	6036.855	3.1689
49	305		9			859.000		
50	360		8			1382.428		
51	230		8			630.571		
52	198		3			811.714		
53	132	780	3	22	2.8205	528.857	2679.141	3.4347
54	115		3			242.571		
55	105		5			435.428		
56	97		2			554.571		
57	61		3			266.142		
58	73	364	3	12	3.2967	564.428	1976.140	5.4289
59	59		2			303.142		
60	74		2			287.857		
61	35		2			222.857		
62	39		2			374.285		
63	22	130	1	6	4.6153	269.571	1138.284	8.7557
64	16		...			57.571		
65	18		1			214.000		
66	12		...			76.285		
67	11		...			145.285		
68	12	51	2	5	9.8039	116.142	730.711	14.3276
69	5		...			160.714		
70	11		3			232.285		
73	26	26	2	2	7.6922	620.855	620.855	23.8790
78	4	4	...	0	0.0000	2.000	2.000	0.5000
83	1	1	...	0	0.0000	52.142	52.142	52.1428
	30654		364		1.1874	52697.830		1.7190

AGE.	No. OF MEMBERS.		DEATHS.			SICKNESS.		
	At each Age.	In Periods.	At each Age.	In Periods.		At Each Age.	In Periods.	
				otal.	Per Cent.		Total.	Per Annum.
18	18		...			6.571		
19	59	222	1	·4	1.8018	21.571	143.284	.6454
20	145		3			115.142		
21	155		...			161.428		
22	376		3			203.000		
23	476	2173	8	17	.7823	409.142	1592.712	.7329
24	548		3			341.428		
25	618		3			477.714		
26	700		8			546.000		
27	662		5			490.428		
28	685	3355	5	31	.9239	520.428	2716.712	.8007
29	614		4			520.428		
30	694		9			639.428		
31	632		3			417.142		
32	631		4			471.857		
33	561	2904	3	21	.7231	439.142	2186.997	.7530
34	573		5			402.428		
35	507		6			456.428		
36	510		8			472.857		
37	431		9			345.000		
38	372	1892	5	33	1.7441	406.857	1846.428	.9759
39	305		4			274.714		
40	274		7			347.000		
41	221		1			261.571		
42	157		1			238.857		
43	151	778	2	5	.6426	159.142	1077.426	1.4041
44	132		1			210.285		
45	117		...			207.571		
46	85		3			230.000		
47	94		2			176.142		
48	60	321	2	10	3.1152	200.142	794.569	2.4752
49	46		2			128.857		
50	36		1			59.428		
51	27		1			63.000		
52	11		...			28.714		
53	12	78	...	1	1.2820	15.714	230.999	2.9615
54	17		...			94.714		
55	11		...			28.857		
56	15		1			54.571		
57	8		...			60.857		
58	6	42	1	2	4.7619	9.571	178.284	4.2448
59	8		...			11.428		
60	5		...			41.857		
61	6		1			22.428		
62	5		...			7.000		
63	5	17	...	1	5.8223	28.428	57.856	3.4032
64	...		...			... ...		
65	1		...			... ...		
68	1	1	1	1	100.0000	11.000	11.000	11.0000
	11783		126		1.0693	10836.267		.9196

TABLE XXIX.—POTTERS. 77

AGE.	No. OF MEMBERS. At each Age	In Periods.	DEATHS. At Each Age.	In Periods. Total.	Per Annum.	SICKNESS. At Each Age.	In Periods. Total.	Per Annum.
18	8		...			5.428		
19	8	32	...	0	.0000	... ...	10.713	.3347
20	16		...			5.285		
21	25		...			2.142		
22	39		...			16.285		
23	48	283	...	3	1.0600	23.571	198.854	.7026
24	82		1			104.714		
25	89		2			52.142		
26	110		3			148.142		
27	119		2			92.142		
28	121	601	1	10	1.6638	123.714	747.140	1.2431
29	127		3			235.000		
30	124		1			148.142		
31	121		...			100.285		
32	111		1			110.571		
33	130	586	...	5	.8532	159.142	751.711	1.2827
34	116		2			194.142		
35	108		2			187.571		
36	122		...			114.428		
37	85		1			54.285		
38	91	461	2	6	1.3015	108.000	612.140	1.3278
39	90		3			262.285		
40	73		...			73.142		
41	71		4			186.857		
42	90		3			199.714		
43	58	301	1	8	2.6581	150.000	614.427	2.0412
44	44		...			39.285		
45	38		...			38.571		
46	50		1			130.285		
47	35		1			79.285		
48	31	167	2	6	3.5928	77.285	549.568	3.2908
49	27		2			117.571		
50	24		...			145.142		
51	18		...			34.142		
52	14		...			47.000		
53	15	71	...	0	0.0000	91.571	222.855	3.1388
54	16		...			49.142		
55	8		...			1.000		
56	12		...			5.857		
57	3		...			... ...		
58	8	37	1	1	2.7027	75.571	183.284	4.9537
59	9		...			16.714		
60	5		...			85.142		
61	2		...			... ...		
62	6		...			176.857		
63	3	16	...	0	0.0000	52.142	294.999	18.4374
64	2		...			45.000		
65	3		...			21.000		
68	1	1	...	0	0.0000	52.142	52.142	52.1428
73	1	1	...	0	0.0000	52.000	52.000	52.0000
78	1	1	1	1	100.0000	3.000	3.000	3.0000
83	2	2	...	0	0.0000	104.284	104.284	52.1420
	2560			40	1.5625	4397.117		1.7175

AGE.	No. OF MEMBERS.		DEATHS.			SICKNESS.		
	At each age.	In periods.	At Each Age.	In Periods.		At Each Age.	In Periods.	
				Total.	Per Cent.		Total.	Per Annum.
18	7		...			... ...		
19	22	95	...	0	.0000	3.428	22.856	.2405
20	66		...			19.428		
21	106		1			43.571		
22	136		1			63.285		
23	178	854	...	6	.7025	94.571	492.140	.5762
24	211		2			173.428		
25	223		2			117.285		
26	292		3			137.714		
27	273		3			126.714		
28	278	1346	1	9	.6686	176.571	756.712	.5621
29	229		2			183.285		
30	274		...			132.428		
31	218		1			173.142		
32	214		1			157.571		
33	175	1011	1	6	.5934	175.285	756.426	.7481
34	218		2			147.428		
35	186		1			103.000		
36	185		2			99.000		
37	164		...			163.142		
38	151	748	2	5	.6684	200.428	649.283	.8680
39	112		1			95.142		
40	136		...			91.571		
41	104		...			63.000		
42	85		3			81.428		
43	75	402	2	8	1.9900	123.714	469.856	1.1687
44	66		2			147.000		
45	72		1			54.714		
46	55		2			132.285		
47	60		...			140.857		
48	51	241	4	8	3.3195	25.000	561.570	2.3301
49	43		1			220.714		
50	32		1			42.714		
51	19		...			42.571		
52	31		1			95.714		
53	19	108	1	6	5.5555	123.428	405.284	3.7526
54	22		...			78.000		
55	17		4			65.571		
56	18		...			47.857		
57	8		...			6.000		
58	9	51	1	1	1.9607	36.285	111.713	2.1830
59	9		...			19.571		
60	7		...			‹2.000		
61	4		2			29.142		
62	10		2			83.571		
63	6	26	...	5	19.2307	110.000	234.141	9.0054
64	3		1			9.428		
65	3		...			2.000		
66	1		...			... ...		
67	1		...			52.000		
68	1	6	...	0	0.0000	... ...	52.000	8.6666
69	1		...			... ...		
70	2		...			... ...		
73	1	1	...	0	0.0000	... ...		
78	4	4	...	0	0.0000	156.284	156.284	39.0710
	4893		54		1.1036	4668.265		.9540

TABLE XXXI.—SAWYERS.　　79

AGE.	No. OF MEMBERS.		DEATHS.			SICKNESS.		
	At each Age.	In Periods.	At Each Age.	In Periods. Total.	Per Cent.	At Each Age.	In Periods. Total.	Per Annum.
18	9		...			15.000		
19	30	81	...	0	.0000	12.142	49.284	.6084
20	42		...			22.142		
21	52		1			44.000		
22	81		1			48.857		
23	101	495	...	4	.8080	59.142	328.141	.6634
24	118		...			90.142		
25	143		2			86.000		
26	183		...			102.857		
27	171		2			184.428		
28	174	923	2	9	.9750	112.428	725.998	.7865
29	175		2			186.285		
30	220		3			140.000		
31	201		2			123.428		
32	204		...			145 142		
33	190	1015	...	6	.5911	172.857	890.711	.8775
34	209		2			229.142		
35	211		2			220.142		
36	200		5			261.142		
37	169		4			205.571		
38	164	800	2	13	1.6250	240.000	966.855	1.2085
39	121		1			142.714		
40	146		1			117.428		
41	94		1			110.428		
42	103		...			80.571		
43	100	473	1	4	.8456	164.714	575.569	1.2168
44	93		2			90.571		
45	83		...			129.285		
46	84		...			93.571		
47	59		...			144.428		
48	53	264	...	1	.3787	76.571	470.427	1.7819
49	37		1			132.000		
50	31		...			23.857		
51	25		...			30.142		
52	15		...			17.142		
53	8	64	1	2	3.1250	3.857	81.426	1.2722
54	8		1			15.285		
55	8		...			15.000		
56	9		...			5.714		
57	3		1			11.571		
58	5	22	...	1	4.5454	4.000	26.285	1.1946
59	3		...			3.000		
60	2		...			2.000		
61	3		...			4.000		
62	1		...			7.000		
63	3	10	...	0	0.0000	... ...	15.000	1.5000
64	2		...			4.000		
65	1		...			... ...		
66	1		...			... ...		
67	2		...			2.000		
68	3	6	1	1	16.6666	53.714	55.714	9.2856
69	...		...			... ...		
70	...		...			... ...		
	4153		41		.9872	4185.410		1.0218

AGE.	No. OF MEMBERS.		DEATHS.			SICKNESS.		
	At each Age.	In Periods.	At Each Age.	In Periods.		At Each Age.	In Periods.	
				Total.	Per Cent.		Total.	Per Annum.
18	39		...			2.000		
19	153	412	1	1	.2427	63.571	173.428	.4209
20	220		...			107.857		
21	383		1			199.285		
22	520		5			196.000		
23	636	3248	3	19	.5849	286.000	1747.284	.5379
24	821		4			601.428		
25	888		6			464.571		
26	933		6			575.142		
27	963		5			381.428		
28	1006	4948	9	36	.7275	651.571	2866.140	.5792
29	974		9			644.714		
30	1072		7			613.285		
31	874		8			590.857		
32	878		9			543.142		
33	726	3860	8	35	.9067	558.000	2682.855	.6949
34	702		2			403.571		
35	680		8			587.285		
36	663		12			481.428		
37	560		4			589.000		
38	442	2117	5	27	1.1170	425.571	2134.427	.8830
39	384		4			312.714		
40	368		2			325.714		
41	234		3			165.714		
42	213		4			258.857		
43	169	879	3	14	1.5927	166.428	858.855	.9770
44	131		2			158.428		
45	132		2			109.428		
46	95		1			62.000		
47	86		1			84.857		
48	67	330	1	4	1.2012	76.142	360.284	1.0819
49	39		1			23.285		
50	43		...			114.000		
51	28		...			50.428		
52	26		...			18.857		
53	21	96	...	0	0000	6.000	154.142	1.6056
54	14		...			74.857		
55	7		...			4.000		
56	14		...			65.857		
57	4		...			2.000		
58	3	34	1	1	2.9411	44.142	111.999	3.2940
59	5		...			... ...		
60	8		...			... ...		
61	5	8	1	1	12.5000	59.857	163.999	20.4999
62	3		...			104.142		
68	1		...			... ...		
69	1	3	...	0	0.0000	... ...	0.000	0.0000
70	1		...			... ...		
	16235		138		.8500	11253.413		.6931

TABLE XXXIII.—SHOEMAKERS. 81

AGE.	No. OF MEMBERS.		DEATHS.			SICKNESS.		
	At each Age.	In Periods.	At Each Age.	In Periods. Total.	Per Cent.	At Each Age.	In Periods. Total.	Per Annum.
18	37		...			7.428		
19	119	415	1	2	.4819	35.285	175.570	.4230
20	259		1			132.857		
21	374		1			357.285		
22	543		5			340.000		
23	693	3418	6	33	.9654	704.142	3076.712	.9001
24	812		6			676.285		
25	996		15			999.000		
26	1196		9			1100.000		
27	1274		13			986.285		
28	1188	6360	13	53	.8333	1010.714	4983.284	7835
29	1263		9			853.714		
30	1439		9			1032.571		
31	1266		9			1026.000		
32	1195		8			875.571		
33	1069	5612	6	38	.6769	727.142	4455.998	.7940
34	1005		5			907.428		
35	1077		10			919.857		
36	1120		4			927.714		
37	994		8			779.714		
38	860	4493	6	32	.7122	651.285	3539.855	.7878
39	752		8			618.000		
40	767		6			563.142		
41	524		9			484.428		
42	536		8			542.571		
43	431	2305	3	28	1.2147	574.428	2509.569	1.0887
44	422		7			473.000		
45	392		1			435.142		
46	378		2			423.142		
47	306		4			410.857		
48	280	1394	4	18	1.2912	414.000	1988.998	1.4267
49	217		4			408.428		
50	213		4			332.571		
51	135		5			274.428		
52	131		...			183.428		
53	87	494	5	17	3.4413	216.428	952.855	1.9288
54	77		3			114.571		
55	64		4			164.000		
56	62		1			99.714		
57	38		...			84.000		
58	35	188	2	3	1.5957	183.857	549.999	2.9255
59	23		...			105.857		
60	30		...			76.571		
61	20		...			46.285		
62	20		1			85.428		
63	11	72	...	1	1.3888	11.142	187.140	2.5991
64	14		...			26.428		
65	7		...			17.857		
66	3		1			3.000		
67	3		...			7.000		
68	4	27	1	4	14.8148	29.000	138.142	5.1163
69	10		2			90.142		
70	7		...			9.000		
71	4		...			23.000		
72	3	10	1	1	10.0000	1.000	32.000	3.2000
73	3		...			8.000		
	24788		230		.9278	22590.122		.9109

L

TABLE XXXIV.—SPINNERS.

AGE.	No. OF MEMBERS.		DEATHS.			SICKNESS.		
	At each age.	In periods.	At Each Age.	In Periods.		At Each Age.	In Periods.	
				Total.	Per Cent.		Total.	Per Annum.
18	15		...			... ...		
19	58	203	1	3	1.4778	23.000	137.571	.6776
20	130		2			114.571		
21	197		2			106.714		
22	243		2			131.714		
23	341	1551	3	14	.9026	228.714	936.141	.6035
24	366		2			180.285		
25	404		5			288.714		
26	452		2			391.428		
27	521		8			300.000		
28	521	2493	3	20	.8022	397.857	1863.141	.7473
29	482		3			387.714		
30	517		4			386.142		
31	488		1			397.285		
32	519		4			442.142		
33	473	2426	1	12	.4946	363.571	2132.998	.8790
34	495		4			485.000		
35	451		2			445.000		
36	470		3			491.857		
37	379		2			302.571		
38	406	1999	2	16	.8004	456.571	2039.712	1.0203
39	330		4			399.428		
40	414		5			389.285		
41	261		5			617.571		
42	290		4			555.142		
43	280	1251	2	14	1.1191	394.571	2244.569	1.7942
44	219		2			359.714		
45	201		1			317.571		
46	202		...			350.285		
47	147		2			198.857		
48	150	755	2	8	1.0596	280.142	1554.141	2.0584
49	133		4			332.000		
50	123		...			392.857		
51	93		2			428.857		
52	67		3			106.714		
53	78	384	3	12	3.1250	215.000	1301.285	3.3887
54	88		2			277.000		
55	58		2			273.714		
56	50		1			119.428		
57	35		1			102.428		
58	35	179	4	11	6.1451	162.428	733.140	4.0957
59	34		4			183.428		
60	25		1			165.428		
61	19		1			96.428		
62	17		...			52.857		
63	22	71	3	4	5.6338	96.285	404.426	5.6961
64	7		...			106.285		
65	6		...			52.571		
66	2		...			52.000		
67	3		1			32.285		
68	4	14	1	2	14.2857	27.142	137.427	9.8162
69	2		...			26.000		
70	3		...			... ...		
71	1		...			20.000		
72	...	3	...	0	0.0000	... ...	98.142	32.7047
73	2		...			78.142		
	11329		116		1.0239	13582.693		1.1988

TABLE XXXV.—STONEMASONS. 83

AGE.	No. of Members. At each Age.	No. of Members. In Periods.	Deaths. At Each Age.	Deaths. In Periods. Total.	Deaths. In Periods. Per Cent.	Sickness. At Each Age.	Sickness. In Periods. Total.	Sickness. In Periods. Per Annum.
18	36		...			16.571		
19	132	430	...	2	.5855	79.142	317.713	.7388
20	262		2			222.000		
21	356		7			155.000		
22	495		1			207.000		
23	599	2941	7	26	.8840	485.714	2082.714	.7081
24	733		5			616.000		
25	758		6			619.000		
26	879		7			686.285		
27	873		8			663.857		
28	874	4403	4	39	.8857	647.714	3492.998	.7933
29	872		7			719.428		
30	905		13			775.714		
31	732		12			841.000		
32	801		8			942.857		
33	737	3829	2	39	1.0185	677.142	4415.856	1.1532
34	763		5			1053.857		
35	796		12			901.000		
36	803		9			807.285		
37	703		9			932.428		
38	698	3456	9	42	1.2124	923.571	4074.854	1.1790
39	601		6			657.285		
40	651		9			754.285		
41	459		7			788.714		
42	437		8			698.000		
43	360	1924	6	36	1.8710	385.428	3068.284	1.5947
44	335		7			631.142		
45	333		8			565.000		
46	262		4			430.428		
47	234		5			277.285		
48	192	1017	2	20	1.9665	261.000	1683.570	1.6554
49	173		9			433.000		
50	156		...			281.857		
51	94		4			308.714		
52	62		2			236.857		
53	63	312	1	12	3.8461	203.000	1112.856	3.7177
54	59		5			175.571		
55	34		...			188.714		
56	33		3			252.428		
57	24		2			105.714		
58	17	97	...	5	5.1546	30.000	465.427	4.7982
59	12		...			15.714		
60	11		...			61.571		
61	4		...			28.000		
62	10		...			123.285		
63	6	28	1	1	3.5714	68.142	243.140	8.6831
64	6		...			21.428		
65	2		...			2.285		
66	1		...			9.000		
67	...		...			... ...		
68	2	8	...	0	0.0000	4.000	54.285	6.7856
69	2		...			2.000		
70	3		...			39.285		
73	3	3	1	1	33.3333	5.285	5.285	1.7616
78	1	1	...	0	0.0000	... ...	0.000	0.0000
	18449			223	1.2087	21016.982		1.1391

TABLE XXXVI.—TAILORS.

AGE	No. OF MEMBERS.		DEATHS.			SICKNESS.		
	At each Age.	In Periods.	At Each Age.	In Periods. Total.	In Periods. Per Cent.	At Each Age.	In Periods. Total.	In Periods. Per Annum.
18	21		...			.571		
19	106	335	...	3	.8955	30.428	120.713	.3603
20	208		3			89.714		
21	400		2			265.000		
22	669		2			470.714		
23	711	3620	11	34	.9392	584.428	2602.284	.7188
24	876		11			687.285		
25	964		8			594.857		
26	1104		5			989.428		
27	1198		7			958.428		
28	1229	6140	10	43	.7003	969.285	4872.426	.7935
29	1286		10			937.714		
30	1323		11			1017.571		
31	1134		12			893.285		
32	1098		9			863.428		
33	960	5050	12	53	1.0495	1041.857	4536.997	.8984
34	940		6			915.285		
35	918		14			823.142		
36	947		6			1133.142		
37	844		9			976.571		
38	706	3583	6	32	.8931	724.571	3947.426	1.1017
39	550		7			608.142		
40	536		4			505.000		
41	354		9			447.571		
42	319		5			372.000		
43	253	1362	4	26	1.9089	316.714	1616.141	1.1865
44	219		3			240.285		
45	217		5			239.571		
46	191		...			245.000		
47	153		...			138.428		
48	104	-684	2	5	7.3099	140.714	822.141	1.2019
49	115		1			102.142		
50	121		2			195.857		
51	73		1			168.142		
52	52		...			52.285		
53	32	231	...	3	1.2987	23.428	426.426	1.8459
54	43		1			133.571		
55	31		1			49.000		
56	29		1			70.571		
57	17		...			28.142		
58	10	84	...	1	1.1904	51.428	185.569	2.2091
59	15		...			34.428		
60	13		...			1.000		
61	6		...			56.000		
62	7		...			23.000		
63	9	29	1	2	6.8965	22.285	117.713	4.0590
64	6		1			4.000		
65	1		...			12.428		
66	4		1			28.571		
67	3		...			... ...		
68	3	12	1	2	16.6666	28.857	57.428	4.7856
69	1		...			... ...		
70	1		...			... ...		
73	3	3	...	0	0.0000	... ...	0.000	0.0000
78	6	6	1	1	16.6666	31.000	31.000	51.6666
	21139		205		.6697	19336.264		.9147

TABLE XXXVII.—WEAVERS. 85

AGE.	No. OF MEMBERS.		DEATHS.			SICKNESS.		
	At each Age.	In Periods.	At each Age.	In Periods. Total.	In Periods. Per Cent.	At Each Age.	In Periods. Total.	In Periods. Per Annum.
18	42		1			1.000		
19	128	410	1	4	.9983	49.000	170.857	.4167
20	240		2			120.857		
21	377		1			198.714		
22	536		6			348.000		
23	610	2982	4	32	1.0731	416.428	2429.427	.8145
24	718		10			700.000		
25	741		11			766.285		
26	790		1			543.285		
27	817		3			775.000		
28	774	3976	6	28	.7040	606.714	3154.856	.7934
29	746		5			554.000		
30	849		13			675.857		
31	719		8			654.428		
32	716		9			790.714		
33	627	3424	5	31	.9053	597.714	3522.570	1.0287
34	689		5			733.000		
35	673		4			746.714		
36	681		8			746.571		
37	616		5			665.285		
38	544	2858	6	29	1.0146	675.857	3374.569	1.1806
39	487		4			660.142		
40	530		6			626.714		
41	410		4			495.142		
42	379		6			414.285		
43	425	1982	6	27	1.3622	594.428	2400.283	1.2110
44	390		6			433.714		
45	378		5			462.714		
46	353		3			472.000		
47	341		6			501.714		
48	309	1556	3	23	1.4781	587.000	2442.713	1.5698
49	273		5			420.428		
50	280		6			461.571		
51	241		4			494.142		
52	221		4			583.285		
53	175	915	3	17	1.8579	454.285	2415.425	2.6416
54	166		4			530.428		
55	112		2			353.285		
56	122		2			420.857		
57	78		2			338.000		
58	83	445	3	9	2.0224	263.285	1853.998	4.1662
59	79		1			346.714		
60	83		1			485.142		
61	65		2			251.142		
62	40		2			170.857		
63	33	191	2	6	3.1413	278.285	965.140	5.0530
64	28		...			120.142		
65	25		...			144.714		
66	16		1			49.428		
67	12		...			7.000		
68	11	55	2	3	5.4545	125.285	238.713	4.3401
69	8		...			49.000		
70	8		...			8.000		
73	23	23	...	0	0.0000	220.855	220.855	9.6023
78	8	8	...	0	0.0000	59.000	59.000	7.3750
83	5	5	...	0	0.0000	57.856	57.856	11.5712
	18830		209		1.1094	23306.262		1.2377

TABLE XXXVIII.—WHEELWRIGHTS.

AGE.	No. OF MEMBERS.		DEATHS.			SICKNESS.		
	At each Age.	In Periods.	At Each Age.	In Periods. Total.	Per Cent.	At Each Age.	In Periods. Total.	Per Annum.
18	15		1			... ...		
19	19	95	...	1	1.0526	2.000	18.142	.1909
20	61		...			16.142		
21	107		...			50.571		
22	177		...			78.571		
23	187	942	3	5	.5307	274.428	790.997	.8397
24	243		2			212.142		
25	228		...			175.285		
26	278		4			173.714		
27	272		5			256.571		
28	259	1295	1	12	.9266	347.857	1154.570	.8916
29	235		1			159.000		
30	251		1			217.628		
31	196		2			225.285		
32	209		4			334.142		
33	165	967	4	12	1.2409	141.571	1072.712	1.1092
34	211		1			235.714		
35	186		1			136.000		
36	204		2			180.428		
37	170		3			165.000		
38	140	750	1	10	1.3333	78.142	568.997	.7586
39	119		2			100.142		
40	117		2			45.285		
41	76		1			31.000		
42	65		...			95.714		
43	61	300	...	1	.3333	32.714	273.284	.9109
44	56		...			41.428		
45	42		...			72.428		
46	40		1			29.142		
47	33		1			26.142		
48	39	179	...	2	1.1173	20.428	121.426	.6783
49	35		...			21.000		
50	32		...			24.714		
51	14		...			4.714		
52	15		...			13.000		
53	14	60	...	0	0.0000	8.285	47.141	.7856
54	8		...			16.571		
55	9		...			4.571		
56	6		...			5.428		
57	2		...			12.000		
58	2	16	...	0	0.0000	... ...	19.428	1.2142
59	2		...			... ...		
60	4		...			2.000		
61	3		...			... ...		
62	2		...			6.428		
63	...	5	...	0	0.0000	... ...	6.428	1.2856
64	...		...			... ...		
65	...		...			... ...		
81	1	1	....	0	0.0000	4.000	4.000	4.0000
	4610		43		.9327	4077.125		.8814

TABLE XXXIX.—WOOLCOMBERS. 87

AGE.	No. OF MEMBERS.		DEATHS.			SICKNESS.		
	At each Age	In Periods.	At Each Age.	In Periods.		At Each Age.	In Periods.	
				Total.	Per Annum.		Total.	Per Annum.
18	9		...			15.714		
19	18	68	...	3	4.4117	10.428	79.142	1.1638
20	41		3			53.000		
21	70		2			63.571		
22	104		1			162.571		
23	110	559	1	5	.8944	127.000	656.427	1.1742
24	135		1			196.714		
25	140		...			106.571		
26	155		1			129.428		
27	161		1			209.428		
28	160	830	1	7	.8451	164.714	826.283	.9955
29	165		3			150.142		
30	189		1			172.571		
31	181		2			204.428		
32	182		2			252.142		
33	175	887	2	7	.7891	312.571	1374.711	1.5497
34	173		...			226.428		
35	176		1			379.142		
36	152		2			198.571		
37	129		...			215.857		
38	112	663	...	4	.6033	170.142	1004.284	1.5146
39	135		2			220.000		
40	135		...			199.714		
41	111		2			153.857		
42	123		...			202.285		
43	113	569	2	6	1.0544	150.571	908.426	1.5965
44	117		1			199.142		
45	105		1			202.571		
46	83		...			218.857		
47	71		1			106.000		
48	84	404	...	1	.2475	90.000	725.428	1.7955
49	84		...			140.000		
50	82		...			170.571		
51	73		3			237.714		
52	43		1			101.857		
53	34	203	...	5	2.4630	47.428	477.856	2.3539
54	27		...			26.000		
55	26		1			64.857		
56	15		2			69.714		
57	7		...			11.714		
58	8	43	...	3	6.9767	10.000	174.141	4.0497
59	5		1			14.428		
60	8		...			68.285		
61	8		...			108.142		
62	6		...			31.000		
63	5	25	...	1	4.0000	46.000	232.856	9.3140
64	4		1			47.714		
65	2		...			... ...		
66	...		...			... ...		
67	1		...			1.428		
68	2	3	...	0	0.0000	... ...	1.428	.4760
69	...		...			... ...		
70	...		...			... ...		
73	2	2	1	1	50.0000	16.285	16.285	8.1425
78	...	0	...	0	0.0000	... ...	0.000	0.0000
83	3	3	...	0	0.0000	156.426	156.426	52.1420
	4259		43		1.0096	6633.693		1.5575

TABLE XL.

MORTALITY AND EXPECTATION.—BAKERS.

Age.	Living.	Dying.	Mortality per cent.	Specific Intensity.	Expecta-tion.	Age.	Living.	Dying.	Mortality per cent.	Specific Intensity	Expecta-tion.
18	100000	621	.6212	160.97	43.66	60	58195	2187	3.7636	26.60	14.12
19	99379	561	.5917	176.96	42.82	61	56008	2221	3.9664	25.21	13.66
20	98818	555	.5622	177.87	41.92	62	53787	2259	4.2015	23.80	13.20
21	98263	494	.5032	198.72	41.15	63	51528	2303	4.4699	22 37	12.76
22	97769	452	.4624	216.26	40.61	64	49225	2348	4.7706	20.95	12.33
23	97317	428	.4399	227.37	39.79	65	46877	2392	5.1039	19.59	11.92
24	96889	422	.4357	229.51	38.97	66	44485	2432	4.4697	18.28	11.54
25	96467	433	.4494	222.51	38.13	67	42053	2429	5.7766	17.31	11.18
26	96034	460	.4821	208.38	37.30	68	39624	2387	6.0245	16.59	10.83
27	95574	490	.5130	194.93	36.48	69	37237	2313	6.2135	16.09	10.49
28	95084	515	.5425	184.33	35.67	70	34924	2215	6.3434	15.76	10.16
29	94569	539	.5705	175.28	34.86	71	32709	2097	6.4147	15.58	9.82
30	94030	561	.5971	167.47	34.05	72	30612	2007	6.5502	15.26	9.45
31	93469	581	.6221	160.74	33.26	73	28607	1931	6.7501	14.81	9.08
32	92888	610	.6572	152.16	32.46	74	26676	1862	7.0143	14.25	8.70
33	92278	648	.7022	142.40	31.67	75	24814	1822	7.3429	13.61	8.31
34	91630	694	.7574	132.03	30.89	76	22992	1778	7.7358	12.92	7.93
35	90936	746	.8206	121.86	30.12	77	21214	1740	8.2092	12.20	7.56
36	90190	807	.8938	111.67	29.37	78	19474	1706	8.7632	11.41	7.19
37	89383	888	.9940	100.83	28.56	79	17768	1669	9.3974	10.64	6.83
38	88495	992	1.1212	89.19	27.91	80	16099	1626	10.1129	9.89	6.49
39	87503	1142	1.2754	74.62	27.22	81	14473	1578	10.9085	9.16	6.16
40	86361	1228	1.4229	70.27	26.58	82	12895	1495	11.5942	8.62	5.85
41	85133	1343	1.6150	63.36	25.95	83	11400	1387	12.1699	8.21	5.56
42	83790	1445	1.7253	57.96	25.36	84	10013	1265	12.6357	7.91	5.26
43	82345	1463	1.7769	56.27	24.80	85	8748	1136	12.9915	7.69	4.95
44	80882	1373	1.6982	58.59	24.24	86	7612	1007	13.2373	7.55	4.61
45	79509	1241	1.5611	64.20	23.65	87	6605	931	14.1021	7.09	4.24
46	78268	1050	1.3417	74.53	23.01	88	5674	884	15.5859	6.41	3.85
47	77218	935	1.2103	82.62	22.31	89	4790	847	17.6866	5.65	3.47
48	76283	890	1.1673	85.66	21.59	90	3943	804	20.4063	4.90	3.11
49	75393	914	1.2126	82.46	20.84	91	3139	745	23.7470	4.21	2.78
50	74479	1002	1.3462	74.28	20.09	92	2394	675	27.0888	3.69	2.50
51	73477	1152	1.5680	63.77	19.35	93	1719	522	30.3765	3.29	2.28
52	72325	1301	1.7992	55.58	18.65	94	1197	402	33.6273	2.97	2.06
53	71024	1449	2.0400	49.00	17.99	95	795	292	36.8342	2.71	1.86
54	69575	1593	2.2903	43.86	17.35	96	503	200	39.9550	2.50	1.65
55	67982	1747	2.5701	38.90	16.75	97	303	137	45.3080	2.20	1.41
56	66235	1840	2.7794	35.97	16.19	98	166	87	52.9333	1.88	1.16
57	64395	1990	3.0954	32.35	15.62	99	79	47	60.5183	1.31	.90
58	62405	2058	3.2981	30.32	15.10	100	32	32	100.0000	1.00	.50
59	60347	2152	3.5675	28.03	14.60						

TABLE XLI.

MORTALITY AND EXPECTATION.—BLACKSMITHS, &c.

Age.	Living.	Dying.	Mortality per cent.	Specific Intensity.	Expecta-tion.	Age.	Living.	Dying.	Mortality per cent.	Specific Intensity	Expecta-tion.
18	100000	604	.6048	165.34	39.49	60	47325	2067	4.3690	22.88	13.02
19	99396	604	.6084	164.36	38.73	61	45258	2054	4.5401	22.02	12.62
20	98792	604	.6120	163.39	37.96	62	43204	2054	4.7556	21.02	12.20
21	98188	608	.6192	161.49	37.19	63	41150	2063	5.0155	19.93	11.78
22	97580	615	.6309	158.50	36.42	64	39087	2079	5.3198	18.79	11.38
23	96965	627	.6470	154.55	35.65	65	37008	2097	5.6684	17.64	10.99
24	96338	643	.6675	149.81	34.88	66	34911	2116	6.0633	16.49	10.62
25	95695	662	.6925	144.50	34.11	67	32795	2103	6.4150	15.58	10.27
26	95033	686	.7218	138.54	33.35	68	30692	2076	6.7656	14.78	9.94
27	94347	715	.7582	131.89	32.58	69	28616	2001	6.9929	14.30	9.63
28	93632	750	.8016	124.75	31.83	70	26615	1920	7.2171	13.85	9.31
29	92882	791	.8520	117.37	31.08	71	24695	1825	7.3940	13.52	9.00
30	92091	837	.9094	109.96	30.34	72	22870	1741	7.6104	13.13	8.68
31	91254	888	.9737	102.70	29.62	73	21129	1661	7.8643	12.71	8.35
32	90366	931	1.0329	96.81	28.97	74	19468	1592	8.1777	12.22	8.02
33	89435	972	1.0872	91.97	28.20	75	17876	1517	8.4905	11.77	7.69
34	88463	1005	1.1364	88.00	27.54	76	16359	1450	8.8647	11.28	7.36
35	87458	1031	1.1807	84.69	26.82	77	14909	1385	9.2937	10.75	7.03
36	86427	1054	1.2199	81.97	26.13	78	13524	1322	9.7775	10.22	6.63
37-	85373	1114	1.3056	76.59	25.45	79	12202	1258	10.3161	9.69	6.37
38	84259	1211	1.4378	69.55	24.78	80	10944	1193	10.9095	9.16	6.04
39	83048	1342	1.6164	61.86	24.13	81	9751	1126	11.5577	8.65	5.72
40	81706	1504	1.8414	54.30	23.52	82	8625	1058	12.2668	8.15	5.40
41	80202	1694	2.1128	47.33	23.00	83	7567	984	13.0368	7.68	5.09
42	78508	1802	2.2962	43.55	22.43	84	6583	912	13.8678	7.21	4.77
43	76706	1834	2.3918	41.80	21.95	85	5671	838	14.7797	6.76	4.46
44	74872	1796	2.3996	41.67	21.47	86	4833	760	15.7325	6.35	4.15
45	73076	1695	2.3195	43.11	20.99	87	4073	694	17.0518	5.86	3.83
46	71381	1535	2.1518	46.47	20.48	88	3379	633	18.7375	5.33	3.52
47	69846	1437	2.0582	48.58	19.92	89	2746	570	20.7896	4.81	3.21
48	68409	1394	2.0390	49.04	19.82	90	2176	504	23.1882	4.31	2.93
49	67015	1403	2.0938	47.76	18.72	91	1672	434	25.9731	3.85	2.66
50	65612	1458	2.2229	44.98	18.11	92	1238	357	28.8651	3.46	2.42
51	64154	1556	2.4262	41.21	17.51	93	881	280	31.8640	3.13	2.20
52	62598	1650	2.6366	37.92	16.92	94	601	210	34.9699	2.85	1.99
53	60948	1739	2.8541	35.03	16.37	95	391	149	38.1828	2.61	1.80
54	59209	1822	3.0787	32.48	15.84	96	242	100	41.5026	2.40	1.60
55	57387	1904	3.3104	30.20	15.33	97	142	66	46.8442	2.13	1.34
56	55483	1969	3.5492	28.17	14.84	98	76	41	54.2077	1.84	1.14
57	53514	2073	3.7744	25.81	14.33	99	35	21	61.5712	1.62	.90
58	51441	2050	3.9861	25.08	13.92	100	14	14	100.0000	1.00	.50
59	49391	2066	4.1843	23.89	13.48						

M

TABLE XLII.

MORTALITY AND EXPECTATION.—BRICKLAYERS, PLASTERERS, AND SLATERS.

Age.	Living.	Dying.	Mortality per cent.	Specific Intensity.	Expectation.	Age.	Living.	Dying.	Mortality per cent.	Specific Intensity	Expectation.
18	100000	473	.4729	211.46	39.34	60	51766	4437	8.5713	11.66	8.44
19	99527	472	.4750	210.52	38.52	61	47329	4958	10.4760	9.54	8.18
20	99055	472	.4771	209.59	37.70	62	42371	5011	11.8284	8.45	8.08
21	98583	472	.4793	208.63	36.88	63	37360	4717	12.6283	7.91	8.10
22	98111	483	.4925	203.04	36.06	64	32643	4203	12.8760	7.76	8.20
23	97628	499	.5119	195.35	35.23	65	28440	3575	12.5712	7.95	8.34
24	97129	523	.5390	185.52	34.41	66	24865	2912	11.7141	8.53	8.47
25	96606	554	.5739	174.24	33.59	67	21953	2408	10.9713	9.11	8.52
26	96052	592	.6169	162.10	32.79	68	19545	2016	10.3430	9.66	8.52
27	95460	637	.6678	149.74	31.99	69	17529	1722	9.8290	10.17	8.44
28	94823	689	.7266	137.62	31.20	70	15807	1490	9.4295	10.60	8.30
29	94134	747	.7934	126.03	30.42	71	14317	1309	9.1444	10.93	8.11
30	93387	810	.8681	115.19	29.66	72	13008	1119	9.0303	11.59	7.90
31	92577	880	.9507	105.28	28.92	73	11889	1079	9.0872	11.00	7.57
32	91697	923	1.0073	99.26	28.19	74	10810	1007	9.3152	10.73	7.28
33	90744	942	1.0379	96.34	27.47	75	9803	952	9.7142	10.29	6.98
34	89832	936	1.0425	95.92	26.75	76	8851	912	10.3042	9.70	6.66
35	88896	908	1.0211	97.93	26.03	77	7939	865	10.9038	9.17	6.39
36	87988	856	.9737	102.70	25.29	78	7074	814	11.5131	8.68	6.11
37	87132	846	.9710	102.98	24.54	79	6260	759	11.1321	8.24	5.84
38	86286	822	.9532	104.90	23.77	80	5501	701	12.7607	7.83	5.57
39	85464	837	.9802	102.02	23.00	81	4800	642	13.3789	7.47	5.31
40	84627	873	1.0320	96.89	22.22	82	4158	583	14.0340	7.12	5.06
41	83754	928	1.1086	90.20	21.45	83	3575	526	14.7260	6.79	4.80
42	82826	984	1.1883	84.15	20.68	84	3049	471	15.4549	6.47	4.61
43	81842	1040	1.2712	78.66	19.92	85	2578	418	16.2208	6.16	4.29
44	80802	1096	1.3573	73.67	19.17	86	2160	367	17.0235	5.87	4.02
45	79706	1153	1.4466	69.12	18.43	87	1793	322	17.9837	5.56	3.74
46	78553	1209	1.5390	64.95	17.69	88	1471	289	19.7016	5.07	3.45
47	77344	1254	1.6225	61.63	16.96	89	1182	255	21.5750	4.63	3.34
48	76090	1291	1.6969	58.93	16.23	90	927	219	23.6061	4.23	2.91
49	74799	1318	1.7623	56.74	15.51	91	708	186	26.3961	3.78	2.69
50	73481	1336	1.8187	54.98	14.78	92	522	151	29.0914	3.43	2.41
51	72145	1346	1.8660	53.59	14.05	93	371	118	31.8902	3.13	2.22
52	70799	1427	2.0159	49.60	13.30	94	253	88	34.7951	2.87	2.02
53	69372	1573	2.2684	44.08	12.56	95	165	62	37.8041	2.64	1.83
54	67799	1778	2.6234	38.11	11.84	96	103	42	40.9151	2.44	1.63
55	66021	2034	3.0811	32.45	11.15	97	61	28	46.1902	2.16	1.41
56	63987	2329	3.6413	27.46	10.48	98	33	17	53.4494	1.87	1.19
57	61658	2756	4.4704	22.36	10.10	99	16	9	61.0687	1.63	1.03
58	58902	3279	5.5685	17.95	9.30	100	7	7	100.0000	1.00	.50
59	55623	3857	6.9354	14.41	8.85						

TABLE XLIII.

MORTALITY AND EXPECTATION.—BUTCHERS.

Age.	Living.	Dying.	Mortality per cent.	Specific Intensity.	Expecta- tion.	Age.	Living.	Dying.	Mortality per cent.	Specific Intensity.	Expecta- tion.
18	100000	518	.5188	192.79	43.16	60	55342	1586	2.8678	34.87	14.89
19	99482	496	.4990	200.40	42.49	61	53756	1656	3.0822	32.44	14.31
20	98986	474	.4792	208.68	41.60	62	52100	1733	3.3349	30.06	13.75
21	98512	433	.4396	227.47	40.80	63	50367	1826	3.6260	27.57	13.21
22	98079	410	.4188	238.77	39.97	64	48541	1920	3.9554	25.28	12.69
23	97669	407	.4170	239.80	39.32	65	46621	2015	4.3231	23.13	12.19
24	97262	422	.4340	230.41	38.30	66	44606	2109	4.7291	21.14	11.72
25	96840	455	.4700	212.27	37.46	67	42497	2160	5.0848	19.66	11.27
26	96385	504	.5248	190.54	36.72	68	40337	2174	5.3902	18.55	10.85
27	95881	555	.5796	172.53	35.83	69	38163	2149	5.6453	17.71	10.44
28	95326	604	.6344	157.62	35.04	70	36014	2106	5.8502	17.09	10.03
29	94722	653	.6892	145.09	34.26	71	33908	2036	6.0047	16.65	9.63
30	94069	700	.7441	134.39	33.49	72	31872	1989	6.2407	16.02	9.21
31	93369	746	.7990	125.15	32.74	73	29883	1959	6.5580	15.25	8.79
32	92623	788	.8511	117.49	31.99	74	27924	1942	6.9568	14.37	8.37
33	91835	826	.9003	111.07	31.27	75	25982	1932	7.4369	13.75	7.96
34	91009	861	.9467	105.63	30.59	76	24050	1923	7.9983	12.50	7.54
35	90148	892	.9902	101.10	29.83	77	22127	1908	8.6240	11.59	7.18
36	89226	920	1.0308	97.02	29.13	78	20219	1883	9.3139	10.73	6.80
37	88336	942	1.0649	93.72	28.42	79	18336	1846	10.0682	9.93	6.45
38	87394	960	1.0983	91.04	27.73	80	16490	1795	10.8868	9.18	6.12
39	86434	972	1.1252	88.87	27.03	81	14695	1729	11.7693	8.49	5.81
40	85462	980	1.1475	87.34	26.33	82	12966	1633	12.5947	7.93	5.52
41	84482	984	1.1651	85.82	25.63	83	11333	1514	13.3630	7.48	5.24
42	83498	1032	1.2362	80.89	24.93	84	9819	1381	14.0740	7.10	4.98
43	82466	1122	1.3606	73.49	24.22	85	8438	1238	14.7278	6.80	4.72
44	81344	1249	1.5385	65.14	23.55	86	7200	1102	15.3246	6.52	4.41
45	80095	1418	1.7608	56.50	22.91	87	6098	987	16.2042	6.17	4.14
46	78677	1613	2.0544	48.67	22.37	88	5111	886	17.3665	5.75	3.84
47	77064	1752	2.2780	43.89	21.77	89	4225	794	18.8116	5.31	3.54
48	75312	1838	2.4406	40.97	21.27	90	3431	704	20.5394	4.86	3.24
49	73474	1868	2.5422	39.33	20.79	91	2727	615	22.5493	4.43	2.95
50	71606	1849	2.5827	38.71	20.32	92	2112	528	25.0358	3.99	2.66
51	69757	1787	2.5621	39.03	19.85	93	1584	443	27.9977	3.57	2.39
52	67970	1728	2.5423	39.33	19.45	94	1141	358	31.4349	3.18	2.12
53	66242	1671	2.5234	39.62	18.85	95	783	276	35.3478	2.82	1.86
54	64571	1617	2.5054	39.91	18.33	96	507	201	39.7362	2.51	1.61
55	62954	1562	2.4882	40.18	17.83	97	306	143	46.8957	2.13	1.34
56	61392	1514	2.4718	40.54	17.22	98	163	92	56.8261	1.75	1.08
57	59878	1497	2.5015	39.97	16.65	99	71	47	66.7567	1.49	.83
58	58381	1504	2.5774	38.79	16.06	100	24	24	100.0000	1.00	.50
59	56877	1537	2.6995	37.04	15.47						

TABLE XLIV.

MORTALITY AND EXPECTATION.—CABINET MAKERS, CARPENTERS, AND JOINERS.

Age.	Living.	Dying.	Mortality per cent.	Specific Intensity.	Expectation.	Age.	Living.	Dying.	Mortality per cent.	Specific Intensity	Expectation.
18	100000	422	.4225	236.68	46.86	60	62091	1452	2.3334	42.76	18.88
19	99578	481	.4836	206.78	46.05	61	60639	1286	2.1207	47.04	18.32
20	99097	539	.5447	183.58	45.28	62	59353	1185	1.9970	50.07	17.70
21	98558	657	.6669	149.94	44.52	63	58168	1141	1.9632	50.93	17.06
22	97901	741	.7574	132.03	43.81	64	57027	1151	2.0189	49.53	16.39
23	97160	793	.8163	122.50	43.14	65	55876	1209	2.1641	46.20	15.72
24	96367	813	.8436	118.53	42.49	66	54667	1311	2.3987	41.68	15.05
25	95554	802	.8392	119.16	41.85	67	53356	1414	2.6505	37.72	14.41
26	94752	761	.8031	124.51	41.20	68	51942	1516	2.9195	34.25	13.79
27	93991	753	.7829	124.82	40.53	69	50426	1616	3.2057	31.19	13.19
28	93238	726	.7785	128.45	39.85	70	48810	1712	3.5091	28.46	12.61
29	92512	730	.7898	126.61	39.17	71	47098	1806	3.8297	26.13	12.05
30	91782	749	.8170	122.39	38.47	72	45292	1873	4.1368	23.62	11.51
31	91033	782	.8599	116.29	37.79	73	43419	1923	4.4302	22.57	10.98
32	90251	804	.8916	112.15	37.11	74	41496	1954	4.7101	21.23	10.47
33	89447	819	.9161	109.15	36.44	75	39542	1967	4.9764	20.09	9.96
34	88628	816	.9214	108.53	35.77	76	37575	1964	5.2290	19.12	9.46
35	87812	807	.9195	108.75	35.10	77	35611	1963	5.5135	18.13	8.95
36	87005	788	.9063	110.33	34.42	78	33648	1961	5.8300	17.15	8.44
37	86217	783	.9089	110.02	33.73	79	31687	1957	6.1784	16.18	7.94
38	85434	792	.9273	107.84	33.03	80	29730	1950	6.5588	15.25	7.43
39	84642	813	.9615	104.00	32.34	81	27780	1936	6.9711	14.34	6.91
40	83829	848	1.0116	98.85	31.65	82	25844	1967	7.6140	13.13	6.32
41	82981	894	1.0774	92.81	30.97	83	23877	2026	8.4872	11.78	5.88
42	82087	932	1.1353	88.08	30.30	84	21851	2095	9.5909	10.42	5.38
43	81155	961	1.1851	84.38	29.64	85	19756	2158	10.9251	9.15	4.89
44	80194	984	1.2269	81.49	28.99	86	17598	2203	12.4897	8.00	4.43
45	79210	998	1.2607	79.32	28.34	87	15395	2226	14.4591	6.91	4.00
46	78212	1006	1.2864	77.73	27.70	88	13169	2216	16.8274	5.95	3.59
47	77206	1002	1.2991	76.97	27.05	89	10953	2146	19.6007	5.10	3.22
48	76204	989	1.2985	77.01	26.40	90	8807	2005	22.7769	4.00	2.88
49	75215	966	1.2847	77.83	25.74	91	6802	1792	26.3559	3.79	2.59
50	74249	934	1.2576	79.51	25.07	92	5010	1493	29.7991	3.35	2.34
51	73315	892	1.2173	82.14	24.38	93	3517	1164	33.1065	2.88	2.13
52	72423	905	1.2497	80.01	23.73	94	2353	853	36.2781	2.75	1.93
53	71518	969	1.3552	73.78	22.94	95	1500	589	39.3140	2.54	1.74
54	70549	1081	1.5336	65.20	22.28	96	911	384	42.2140	2.36	1.54
55	69468	1240	1.7851	56.01	21.61	97	527	254	48.2347	2.07	1.31
56	68228	1439	2.1095	47.40	21.00	98	273	156	57.2346	1.74	1.16
57	66789	1554	2.3269	42.97	20.44	99	117	79	66.5104	1.48	.82
58	65235	1589	2.4365	41.06	19.92	100	38	38	100.0000	1.00	.50
59	63646	1555	2.4387	40.90	19.40						

TABLE XLV.

MORTALITY AND EXPECTATION.—CLERKS AND SCHOOLMASTERS.

Age.	Living.	Dying.	Mortality per cent.	Specific Intensity.	Expecta-tion.	Age.	Living.	Dying.	Mortality per cent.	Specific Intensity	Expecta-tion.
18	100000	848	.8483	117.88	36.38	60	35370	1812	5.1256	19.50	12.11
19	99152	838	.8452	118.31	35.68	61	33558	1741	5.1883	19.27	11.73
20	98314	827	.8421	119.04	34.99	62	31817	1685	5.2979	18.87	11.34
21	97487	814	.8359	119.63	34.28	63	30132	1643	5.4542	18.33	10.98
22	96673	811	.8392	119.15	33.56	64	28489	1611	5.6571	17.67	10.56
23	95862	805	.8400	119.04	32.84	65	26878	1587	5.9068	16.92	10.15
24	95057	808	.8504	117.59	32.12	66	25291	1568	6.2031	16.12	9.77
25	94249	816	.8663	115.43	31.39	67	23723	1553	6.5494	15.26	9.38
26	93433	829	.8877	112.65	30.66	68	22170	1539	6.9454	14.39	9.00
27	92604	853	.9212	108.55	29.93	69	20631	1524	7.3913	13.52	8.64
28	91751	887	.9669	103.43	29.20	70	19107	1506	7.8871	12.67	8.29
29	90864	931	1.0247	97.58	28.48	71	17601	1484	8.4326	11.85	7.96
30	89933	984	1.0946	91.35	27.77	72	16117	1455	8.9880	11.07	7.64
31	88949	1046	1.1766	85.00	27.07	73	14662	1400	9.5534	10.46	7.35
32	87903	1079	1.2280	81.43	26.39	74	13262	1343	10.1288	9.87	7.08
33	86824	1048	1.2489	80.07	25.71	75	11919	1277	10.7141	9 33	6.82
34	85740	1062	1.2392	80.69	25.03	76	10642	1203	11.3093	8.84	6.58
35	84678	1015	1.1990	83.40	24.34	77	9439	1116	11.8307	8.45	6.35
36	83663	943	1.1282	88.63	23.63	78	8323	1021	12.2781	8.14	6.14
37	82720	902	1.0912	91.64	22.89	79	7302	934	12.6517	7.90	5.85
38	81818	889	1.0881	92.00	22.14	80	6368	824	12.9515	7.72	5.75
39	80929	905	1.1189	89.37	21.37	81	5544	730	13.1773	7.58	5.50
40	80024	947	1.1836	84.48	20.61	82	4814	650	13.5093	7.40	5.24
41	79077	1013	1.2821	77.99	19.85	83	4164	580	13.9476	7.16	5.00
42	78064	1105	1.4166	70.60	19.10	84	3584	519	14.4922	6.89	4.73
43	76959	1221	1.5871	63.00	18.37	85	3065	464	15.1429	6.60	4.45
44	75738	1388	1.7936	55.75	17.62	86	2601	413	15.8999	6.28	4.15
45	74350	1513	2.0362	49.11	16.98	87	2188	373	17.0728	5.85	3.84
46	72837	1685	2.3147	43.20	16.32	88	1815	338	18.6614	5.35	3.52
47	71152	1935	2.7204	36.76	15.69	89	1477	305	20.6657	4.83	3.29
48	69217	2246	3.2460	30.80	15.12	90	1172	270	23.0859	4.33	2.93
49	66971	2608	3.8951	25.67	14.61	91	902	233	25.9217	3.85	2.66
50	64363	3004	4.6678	21.42	14.18	92	669	193	28.8671	3.46	2.42
51	61359	3413	5.5639	17.97	13.85	93	476	151	31.9222	3.14	2.20
52	57946	3582	6.1831	16.17	13.64	94	325	114	35.0870	2.85	1.99
53	54364	3551	6.5326	15.30	13.50	95	211	80	38.3614	2.60	1.80
54	50813	3358	6.6087	15.13	13.41	96	131	54	41.7456	2.39	1.60
55	47455	3042	6.4115	15.59	13.33	97	77	36	47.1012	2.12	1.38
56	44413	2638	5.9410	16.83	13.21	98	41	22	54.4289	1.83	1.15
57	41775	2329	5.5771	17.93	13.01	99	19	11	61.7567	1.61	.92
58	39446	2148	5.3219	18.36	12.75	100	8	8	100.0000	1.00	.50
59	37298	1928	5.1694	19.34	12.46						

TABLE XLVI.

MORTALITY AND EXPECTATION.—COOPERS.

Age.	Living.	Dying.	Mortality per cent.	Specific Intensity.	Expecta- tion.	Age.	Living.	Dying.	Mortality per cent.	Specific Intensity	Expecta- tion.
18	100000	455	.4564	219.61	40.26	60	49129	2233	4.5464	21.99	13.23
19	99544	475	.4779	209.24	39.44	61	46896	2215	4.7251	21.16	12.84
20	99069	494	.4995	200.20	38.62	62	44681	2195	4.9146	20.34	12.45
21	98575	534	.5426	184.29	37.82	63	42486	2173	5.1150	19.55	12.07
22	98041	578	.5899	169.52	37.12	64	40313	2147	5.3263	18.77	11.69
23	97463	625	.6414	155.90	36.24	65	38166	2117	5.5484	18.02	11.32
24	96838	675	.6971	143.78	35.47	66	36049	2084	5.7813	17.29	10.96
25	96163	728	.7570	132.10	34.71	67	33965	2039	6.0053	16.65	10.60
26	95435	783	.8211	121.78	33.97	68	31926	1985	6.2205	16.07	10.25
27	94652	837	.8852	112.96	33.25	69	29941	1923	6.4267	15.56	9.89
28	93815	890	.9493	105.34	32.54	70	28018	1855	6.6241	15.09	9.54
29	92925	941	1.0135	98.21	31.85	71	26163	1783	6.8125	14.66	9.18
30	91984	991	1.0777	92.79	31.17	72	24380	1724	7.0734	14.13	8.82
31	90993	1039	1.1419	87.57	30.50	73	22656	1678	7.4068	13.50	8.45
32	89954	1055	1.1733	85.26	29.85	74	20978	1638	7.8127	12.79	8.08
33	88899	1041	1.1720	85.32	29.20	75	19340	1603	8.2910	12.06	7.73
34	87858	999	1.1380	87.87	28.54	76	17737	1568	8.8417	11.31	7.38
35	86859	930	1.0713	93.34	28.39	77	16169	1520	9.4023	10.63	7.05
36	85929	835	.9719	102.89	27.16	78	14649	1460	9.9727	10.02	6.73
37	85094	818	.9614	104.03	26.42	79	13189	1391	10.5530	9.47	6.42
38	84276	876	1.0399	96.16	25.67	80	11798	1314	11.1432	8.97	6.12
39	83400	1006	1.2074	82.82	24.94	81	10484	1231	11.7432	8.51	5.82
40	82394	1206	1.4638	68.32	24.23	82	9253	1143	12.3580	8.09	5.53
41	81188	1468	1.8092	55.27	23.60	83	8110	1053	12.9877	7.69	5.24
42	79720	1624	2.0382	49.06	23.01	84	7057	962	13.6322	7.32	4.95
43	78096	1675	2.1508	46.60	22.50	85	6095	871	14.2916	6.99	4.66
44	76421	1640	2.1471	46.57	21.96	86	5224	780	14.9658	6.69	4.34
45	74781	1515	2.0271	49.33	21.43	87	4444	713	16.0519	6.22	4.02
46	73266	1312	1.7908	55.84	20.87	88	3731	654	17.5499	5.69	3.69
47	71954	1199	1.6666	60.00	20.24	89	3077	598	19.4610	5.13	3.37
48	70755	1170	1.6547	60.43	19.57	90	2479	540	21.7818	4.59	3.07
49	69585	1221	1.7549	56.98	18.89	91	1939	475	24.5156	4.07	2.79
50	68364	1338	1.9673	50.83	18.22	92	1464	400	27.3648	3.65	2.53
51	67026	1536	2.2919	43.53	17.58	93	1064	322	30.3294	3.29	2.29
52	65490	1703	2.6014	38.44	16.98	94	742	247	33.4133	2.99	2.07
53	63787	1847	2.8960	34.53	16.42	95	495	181	36.6127	2.73	1.86
54	61940	1966	3.1756	31.49	15.89	96	314	125	39.9234	2.50	1.65
55	59974	2063	3.4402	29.06	15.39	97	189	85	45.4182	2.20	1.41
56	57911	2136	3.6898	27.10	14.93	98	104	55	53.0973	1.88	1.15
57	55755	2189	3.9252	25.47	14.46	99	49	29	60.7350	1.64	.90
58	53586	2221	4.1464	24.11	14.03	100	20	20	100.0000	1.00	.50
59	51365	2236	4.3533	22.97	13.61						

TABLE XLVII.

MORTALITY AND EXPECTATION.—DYERS.

Age.	Living.	Dying.	Mortality per cent.	Specific Intensity.	Expecta- tion.	Age.	Living.	Dying.	Mortality per cent.	Specific Intensity	Expecta- tion.
18	100000	459	.4595	217.62	41.50	60	51408	2418	4.7034	21.26	13.40
19	99541	485	.4876	205.08	40.60	61	48990	2317	4.7296	21.14	13.03
20	99056	501	.5058	197.71	39.89	62	46673	2242	4.8056	20.80	12.66
21	98555	544	.5521	181.12	39.09	63	44431	2191	4.9313	20.27	12.27
22	98011	595	.6073	164.66	38.30	64	42240	2157	5.1008	19.58	11.88
23	97416	648	.6654	150.28	37.54	65	40083	2137	5.3321	18.75	11.49
24	96768	708	.7322	136.57	36.78	66	37946	2127	5.6070	17.83	11.11
25	96060	774	.8059	124.08	36.05	67	35819	2098	5.8586	17.07	10.74
26	95286	844	.8863	112.82	35.34	68	33721	2054	6.0928	16.41	10.38
27	94442	880	.9320	107.29	34.65	69	31667	1996	6.3036	15.86	10.02
28	93562	884	.9450	105.82	33.97	70	29671	1926	6.4931	15.40	9.66
29	92678	852	.9194	108.76	33.29	71	27745	1848	6.6611	15.01	9.39
30	91826	790	.8611	116.13	32.60	72	25897	1787	6.9041	14.48	8.93
31	91036	699	.7681	130.19	31.87	73	24110	1740	7.2222	13.85	8.55
32	90337	631	.6984	143.18	31.12	74	22370	1703	7.6154	13.13	8.18
33	89706	584	.6520	153.37	30.33	75	20667	1670	8.0836	12.37	7.81
34	89122	560	.6288	159.03	29.53	76	18997	1638	8.6208	11.59	7.45
35	88562	557	.6290	158.98	28.71	77	17359	1593	9.1814	10.89	7.11
36	88005	574	.6524	153.26	27.89	78	15766	1536	9.7472	10.25	6.78
37	87431	628	.7192	139.04	27.07	79	14230	1469	10.3244	9.46	6.46
38	86803	720	.8294	120.56	26.26	80	12761	1392	10.9129	9.16	6.14
39	86083	846	.9830	101.72	25.49	81	11369	1308	11.5126	8.68	5.83
40	85237	1005	1.1800	84.74	24.73	82	10061	1223	12.1567	8.22	5.53
41	84232	1196	1.4206	70.39	24.02	83	8838	1135	12.8451	7.78	5.22
42	83036	1324	1.5954	62.68	23.35	84	7703	1045	13.5779	7.36	4.92
43	81712	1392	1.7044	58.67	22.72	85	6658	955	14.3551	6.96	4.62
44	80320	1403	1.7476	57.24	22.11	86	5703	865	15.1776	6.58	4.31
45	78917	1361	1.7250	57.97	21.49	87	4838	791	16.3544	6.11	3.99
46	77556	1269	1.6366	61.10	20.86	88	4047	723	17.8823	5.50	3.67
47	76287	1266	1.6601	60.23	20.20	89	3324	657	10.7665	5.05	3.36
48	75021	1257	1.6756	59.68	19.53	90	2667	586	22.0050	4.54	3.07
49	73764	1344	1.8231	54.85	18.86	91	2081	511	24.5976	4.06	2.79
50	72420	1450	2.0026	49.93	18.20	92	1570	429	27.3227	3.65	2.54
51	70970	1613	2.2740	43.97	17.56	93	1141	344	30.1801	3.31	2.31
52	69357	1778	2.5645	38.99	16.96	94	797	264	33.1700	3.01	2.09
53	67579	1942	2.8741	34.79	16.39	95	533	193	36.2923	2.75	1.88
54	65637	2102	3.2027	31.22	15.86	96	340	134	39.5869	2.52	1.66
55	63535	2255	3.5505	28.16	15.37	97	206	92	45.1010	2.21	1.42
56	61280	2400	3.9173	25.52	14.91	98	114	60	52.8466	1.89	1.16
57	58880	2482	4.2160	23.71	14.51	99	54	32	60.6281	1.64	.90
58	56398	2507	4.4466	22.48	14.12	100	22	22	100.0000	1.00	.50
59	53891	2483	4.6091	21.69	13.76						

TABLE XLVIII.

MORTALITY AND EXPECTATION.—HATTERS.

Age.	Living.	Dying.	Mortality per cent.	Specific Intensity.	Expecta-tion.	Age.	Living.	Dying.	Mortality per cent.	Specific Intensity	Expecta-tion.
18	100000	2592	2.5924	38.57	38.90	60	55475	2218	3.9967	25.02	12.89
19	97408	2355	2.4180	41.35	38.96	61	53257	2464	4.6252	21.62	12.37
20	95053	2132	2.2437	44.56	38.91	62	50793	2616	5.1502	19.41	11.95
21	92921	1760	1.8950	52.77	38.75	63	48177	2685	5.5717	17.94	11.57
22	91161	1470	1.6127	62.00	38.53	64	45492	2679	5.8896	16.97	11.23
23	89691	1253	1.3969	71.58	38.15	65	42813	2613	6.1041	16.38	10.90
24	88438	1106	1.2476	79.96	37.69	66	40200	2498	6.2151	16.08	10·50
25	87332	1018	1.1648	85.85	37.16	67	37702	2392	6.3454	15.75	10.24
26	86314	991	1.1484	87.07	36.59	68	35310	2293	6.4951	15.39	9.85
27	85323	988	1.1580	86.35	36.01	69	33017	2200	6.6641	15.00	9.55
28	84335	1008	1.1949	83.68	35.43	70	30817	2111	6.8526	14.59	9.20
29	83327	1049	1.2578	79.49	34.85	71	28706	2026	7.0604	14.16	8.84
30	82278	1109	1.3472	74.22	34.29	72	26680	1960	7.3465	13.61	8.48
31	81169	1188	1.4630	68.35	33.75	73	24720	1906	7.7110	12.96	8.11
32	79981	1207	1.5098	66.23	33.25	74	22814	1860	8.1539	12.26	7.74
33	78774	1172	1.4874	67.23	32.75	75	20954	1817	8.6751	11.52	7.39
34	77602	1084	1.3960	71.63	32.23	76	19137	1774	9.2746	10.78	7.03
35	76518	946	1.2355	80.93	31.68	77	17363	1716	9.8832	10.11	6.71
36	75572	760	1.0058	99.42	31.01	78	15647	1643	10.5010	9.52	6.39
37	74812	615	.8221	121.63	30.32	79	14004	1558	11.1280	8.98	6.08
38	74197	508	.6845	146.02	29.56	80	12446	1464	11.7641	8.50	5.78
39	73689	437	.5930	168.63	28.76	81	10982	1362	12.4093	8.05	5.48
40	73252	401	.5476	182.61	27.93	82	9620	1260	13.1087	7.62	5.20
41	72851	400	.5483	182.80	27.02	83	8360	1158	13.8622	7.21	4.90
42	72451	419	.5779	173.04	26.23	84	7202	1056	14.6698	6.81	4.59
43	72032	459	.6366	157.08	25.62	85	6146	954	15.5316	6.43	4.32
44	71573	518	.7242	138.08	24.54	86	5192	854	16.4473	6.08	4.01
45	71055	598	.8409	118.92	23.72	87	4338	770	17.7501	5.63	3.72
46	70457	695	.9865	101.36	22.91	88	3568	693	19.4398	5.14	3.42
47	69762	765	1.0968	91.17	22.14	89	2875	618	21.5164	4.64	3.12
48	68997	809	1.1719	85.33	21.37	90	2257	541	23.9801	4.17	2.84
49	68188	826	1.2116	82.53	20.62	91	1716	460	26.8307	3.72	2.58
50	67362	820	1.2161	82.23	19.87	92	1256	374	29.8354	3 35	2.34
51	66542	789	1.1852	84.37	19:11	93	882	291	32.9941	3.03	2.12
52	65753	819	1.2451	80.31	18.33	94	591	214	36.3069	2.77	1.92
53	64934	868	1 3358	74.86	17.52	95	377	149	39.7738	2.51	1.74
54	64066	972	1.5174	65.90	16.79	96	228	98	43.3947	2.30	1.55
55	63094	1117	1.7698	56 50	16.04	97	130	63	48.7278	2.05	1.34
56	61977	1298	2.0930	47.76	15.32	98	67	36	53.7731	1.85	1.14
57	60679	1504	2.4773	40.36	14.64	99	31	19	62.8184	1.59	.80
58	59175	1730	2.9227	34.21	14.00	100	12	12	100.0000	1.00	.50
59	57445	1970	3.4292	29.16	13.40						

TABLE XLIX.

MORTALITY AND EXPECTATION.—LABOURERS & GARDENERS.
(AGRICULTURAL.)

Age.	Living.	Dying.	Mortality per cent.	Specific Intensity.	Expecta-tion.	Age.	Living.	Dying.	Mortality per cent.	Specific Intensity	Expecta-tion.
18	100000	267	.2670	374.50	47.80	60	65719	2021	3.0617	32.66	15.82
19	99733	285	.2865	349.04	46.20	61	63698	2038	3.2004	31.24	15.39
20	99448	337	.3394	294.63	45.32	62	61660	2070	3.3586	29.77	14.88
21	99141	441	.4451	224.66	44.47	63	59590	2108	3.5382	28.26	14.38
22	98670	522	.5289	189.07	43.67	64	57482	2148	3.7372	26.75	13.89
23	98148	580	.5908	169.26	42.90	65	55334	2188	3.9556	25.28	13.41
24	97568	614	.6300	158.73	42.15	66	53146	2227	4.1913	23·85	12.94
25	96954	629	.6488	154.13	41.41	67	50919	2242	4.4034	22.70	12.49
26	96325	621	.6448	155.08	40.68	68	48677	2214	4.5498	21.97	12.04
27	95704	615	.6431	155.49	39.95	69	46463	2208	4.7525	21.04	11.59
28	95089	612	.6436	155.37	39.21	70	44255	2164	4.8916	20.44	11.14
29	94477	610	.6464	154.70	38.46	71	42091	2108	5.0089	19.96	10.69
30	93867	611	.6516	153.46	37.71	72	39983	2086	5.2175	19.16	10.23
31	93256	614	.6590	151.74	36.95	73	37897	2090	5.5174	18.12	9.76
32	92642	612	.6608	151.33	36.19	74	35807	2115	5.9085	16.92	9.30
33	92030	625	.6590	147.27	35.43	75	33692	2085	6.1909	16.15	8.86
34	91465	597	.6535	153.00	34.66	76	31607	2138	6.7645	14.78	8.39
35	90808	567	.6245	160.12	33.89	77	29469	2161	7.3356	13.63	7.98
36	90241	570	.6320	158.22	33.10	78	27308	2156	7.8981	12.66	7.58
37	89671	564	.6298	158.77	32.31	79	25152	2127	8.4580	11.82	7.18
38	89017	567	.6367	157.05	31.51	80	23025	2121	9.2133	10.85	6.80
39	88540	577	.6523	153.30	30.71	81	20901	2041	9.7639	10.48	6.44
40	87963	595	.6769	147.73	29.91	82	18863	1953	10.3580	9.65	6.08
41	87368	620	.7100	140.84	29.11	83	16910	1852	10.9554	9.12	5.73
42	86478	648	.7474	133.79	28.31	84	15058	1758	11.6762	8.56	5.37
43	86100	679	.7889	126.75	27.52	85	13300	1649	12.4004	8.06	5.02
44	85421	713	.8345	119.83	26.74	86	11651	1534	13.1678	7.59	4.66
45	84708	749	.8843	113.08	25.96	87	10117	1446	14.2968	6.90	4.20
46	83959	787	.9381	106.59	25.19	88	8671	1368	15.7869	6.33	3.91
47	83172	833	1.0021	99.79	24.44	89	7303	1288	17.6384	5.66	3.56
48	82339	886	1.0760	92.93	23.66	90	6015	1193	19.8512	5.15	3.22
49	81453	944	1.1600	86.20	22.91	91	4822	1170	24.4252	4.09	2.89
50	80509	1009	1.2541	79.73	22.18	92	3652	921	25.2341	4.96	2.66
51	79500	1079	1:3581	73.63	21.45	93	2731	772	28.2778	3.53	2.39
52	78421	1168	1.4901	67.10	20.74	94	1959	618	31.5564	3.16	2.13
53	77253	1274	1.6502	60.59	20.05	95	1341	470	35.0698	3.85	1 89
54	75979	1396	1.8378	54.41	19.37	96	871	338	38.8180	2.57	1.64
55	74583	1531	2.0535	48.69	18.73	97	533	243	45.6351	2.18	1.37
56	73052	1678	2.2970	43.53	18.07	98	290	161	55.6711	2.79	1.10
57	71374	1798	2.5196	39.68	17.52	99	129	84	65.6572	1.52	.84
58	69576	1893	2.7213	36.74	16.96	100	45	45	100.0000	1.00	.50
59	67683	1964	2.9019	34.46	16.42						

N

TABLE L.

MORTALITY AND EXPECTATION.—LABOURERS (TOWN AND CITY.)

Age.	Living.	Dying.	Mortality per cent.	Specific Intensity.	Expecta- tion.	Age.	Living.	Dying.	Mortality per cent.	Specific Intensity	Expecta- tion.
18	100000	939	.9391	106.47	42.10	60	56322	2228	3.9563	25.27	13.33
19	99061	897	.9062	110.36	41.50	61	54094	2454	4.5372	22.04	12.86
20	98164	825	.8406	118.97	40.87	62	51640	2589	5.0145	19.94	12.44
21	97339	754	.7750	129.03	40.21	63	49051	2643	5.3881	18.55	12.08
22	96585	702	.7274	137.47	39.52	64	46408	2626	5.6580	17.67	11.75
23	95883	668	.6972	143.41	38.81	65	43782	2550	5.8242	17.16	11.41
24	95215	652	.6849	146.01	38.08	66	41232	2427	5.8866	16.98	11.08
25	94563	652	.6903	144.86	37.34	67	38805	2319	5.9759	16.73	10.75
26	93911	670	.7136	140.13	36.59	68	36486	2223	6.0921	16.41	10.40
27	93241	687	.7376	136.51	35.85	69	34263	2136	6.2352	16.04	10.04
28	92554	705	.7626	131.13	35.20	70	32127	2058	6.4052	15.61	9.67
29	91849	724	.7886	126.81	34.38	71	30069	1985	6.6021	15.14	9.30
30	91125	743	.8154	122.63	33.65	72	28084	1929	6.8688	14.55	8.93
31	90382	762	.8430	118.62	32.92	73	26155	1885	7.2051	13.87	8.55
32	89620	773	.8625	115.94	32.20	74	24270	1847	7.6112	13.13	8.17
33	88847	776	.8740	114.41	31.97	75	22423	1813	8.0871	12.36	7.80
34	88071	771	.8755	114.22	30.75	76	20610	1779	8.6326	11.58	7.45
35	87300	761	.8729	114.56	30.02	77	18831	1730	9.1885	10.88	7.11
36	86539	745	.8604	116.22	29.27	78	17101	1668	9.7548	10.25	6.77
37	85794	744	.8674	115.28	28.52	79	15433	1594	10.3314	9.67	6.45
38	85050	760	.8933	111.94	27.70	80	13889	1511	10.9181	9.15	6.16
39	84290	791	.9387	106.53	27.01	81	12328	1420	11.5159	8.68	5.83
40	83499	838	1.0034	99.66	26.27	82	10908	1330	12.1980	8.19	5.52
41	82661	899	1.0874	91.96	25.53	83	9578	1230	12.8447	7.78	5.23
42	81762	945	1.1552	86.56	24.80	84	8348	1133	13.5760	7.36	4.92
43	80817	975	1.2066	82.87	24.09	85	7215	1035	14.3519	6.96	4.62
44	79842	991	1.2418	80.52	23.38	86	6180	937	15.1723	6.59	4.31
45	78851	994	1.2608	79.31	22.66	87	5243	857	16.3474	6.11	4.09
46	77857	883	1.2634	79.14	21.95	88	4386	784	17.8772	5.59	3.69
47	76974	1017	1.3212	75.70	21.19	89	3602	711	19.7614	5.06	3.36
48	75957	1089	1.4376	69.72	20.47	90	2891	636	22.0060	4.54	3.11
49	74868	1204	1.6092	62.14	19.76	91	2255	554	24.5942	4.06	2.79
50	73664	1353	1.8370	54.43	19.07	92	1701	464	27.3273	3.65	2.54
51	72311	1533	2.1210	47.12	18.42	93	1237	373	30.1999	3.31	2.30
52	70778	1664	2.3524	42.50	17.81	94	864	286	33.2121	3.01	2.09
53	69114	1749	2.5312	39.50	17.23	95	578	210	36.3638	2.75	1.87
54	67365	1790	2.6575	37.62	16.66	96	368	145	39.6550	2.52	1.60
55	65575	1786	2.7312	36.69	16.10	97	223	100	45.1642	2.21	1.41
56	63789	1756	2.7523	36.33	15.54	98	123	65	52.8514	1.89	1.15
57	62033	1790	2.8853	34.65	14.97	99	58	35	60.6187	1.64	.90
58	60243	1886	3.1303	31.94	14.44	100	23	23	100.0000	1.00	.50
59	58357	2035	3.4873	28.73	13.80						

TABLE LI.

MORTALITY AND EXPECTATION.—MILLWRIGHTS.

Age.	Living.	Dying.	Mortality per cent.	Specific Intensity.	Expecta- tion.	Age.	Living.	Dying.	Mortality per cent.	Specific Intensity	Expecta- tion.
18	100000	552	.5523	181.06	41.87	60	55997	2318	4.1405	24.15	13.69
19	99448	569	.5727	174.61	41.09	61	53679	2319	4.3212	23.14	13.25
20	98879	586	.5932	168.57	40.32	62	51360	2319	4.5167	22.14	12.83
21	98293	623	.6341	157.70	39.56	63	49041	2318	4.7271	21.15	12.41
22	97670	664	.6806	146.92	38.81	64	46723	2313	4.9523	20.66	12.01
23	97006	710	.7328	136.46	38.07	65	44410	2305	5.1924	19.25	11.61
24	96296	761	.7907	126.47	37.35	66	42105	2293	5.4473	18.35	11.21
25	95535	816	.8543	117.05	36.64	67	39812	2264	5.6888	17.57	10.83
26	94719	874	.9235	108.28	35.95	68	37548	2221	5.9109	16.90	10.46
27	93845	896	.9553	104.67	35.28	69	35327	2166	6.1315	16.30	10.08
28	92949	994	1.0695	93.50	34.62	70	33161	2100	6.3328	15.79	9.71
29	91955	1053	1.1462	87.24	33.99	71	31061	2025	6.5206	15.33	9.33
30	90902	1113	1.2254	81.60	33.38	72	29036	1967	6.7759	14.75	8.95
31	89789	1173	1.3070	76.50	32.78	73	27069	1921	7.0098	14.08	8.56
32	88616	1207	1.3624	73.39	32.21	74	25148	1883	7.4892	13.35	8.18
33	87409	1216	1.3916	71.85	31.65	75	23265	1848	7.9472	12.58	7.80
34	86193	1201	1.3945	71.71	31.09	76	21417	1814	8.4727	11.80	7.43
35	84992	1165	1.3712	72.92	30.52	77	19603	1773	9.0486	11.05	7.07
36	83827	1107	1.3216	75.66	29.94	78	17830	1724	9.6750	10.33	6.72
37	82720	1049	1.2691	78.79	29.33	79	16106	1667	10.3519	9.66	6.39
38	81671	991	1.2138	82.38	28.70	80	14439	1599	11.0792	9.02	6.07
39	80680	932	1.1557	86.52	28.05	81	12840	1522	11.8569	8.43	5.76
40	79748	873	1.0948	91.34	27.37	82	11318	1426	12.5991	7.93	5.47
41	78875	795	1.0312	99.24	26.67	83	9892	1316	13.3059	7.51	5.19
42	78080	761	.9746	102.60	25.94	84	8576	1198	13.9773	7.15	4.91
43	77319	715	.9252	108.08	25.19	85	7378	1078	14.6133	6.84	4.63
44	76604	676	.8828	113.27	24.42	86	6300	958	15.2138	6.57	4.33
45	75928	643	.8476	117.98	23.69	87	5342	866	16.2206	6.16	4.02
46	75285	616	.8195	122.02	22.83	88	4476	789	17.6336	5.67	3.70
47	74669	631	.8450	118.34	22.01	89	3687	717	19.4527	5.14	3.39
48	74038	677	.9241	109.21	21.20	90	2970	643	21.6785	4.61	3.09
49	73361	777	1.0568	94.40	20.39	91	2327	565	24.3103	4.11	2.81
50	72584	902	1.2431	80.44	19.60	92	1762	477	27.0782	3.69	2.55
51	71682	1063	1.4830	67.43	18.84	93	1285	385	29.9821	3.33	2.31
52	70619	1234	1.7476	57.22	18.12	94	900	297	33.0220	3.02	2.09
53	69385	1413	2.0369	49.09	17.43	95	603	218	36.1980	2.76	1.87
54	67972	1597	2.3508	42.53	16.78	96	385	152	39.5099	2.53	1.66
55	66375	1785	2.6894	37.18	16.17	97	233	104	45.0461	2.22	1.42
56	64590	1971	3.0526	32.75	15.61	98	129	68	52.8065	1.89	1.16
57	62619	2116	3.3793	29.59	15.08	99	61	36	60.5610	1.65	.90
58	60503	2220	3.6695	27.25	14.59	100	25	25	100.0000	1.00	.50
59	58283	2286	3.9232	25.48	14.13						

TABLE LII.

MORTALITY AND EXPECTATION.—MILL OPERATIVES.

Age.	Living.	Dying.	Mortality per cent.	Specific Intensity.	Expectation.	Age.	Living.	Dying.	Mortality per cent.	Specific Intensity	Expectation.
18	100000	503	.5033	198.68	39.70	60	48676	2899	5.9706	16.78	10.61
19	99497	502	.5049	198.05	38.89	61	45777	3093	6.7581	14.79	10.25
20	98995	501	.5066	197.39	38.09	62	42684	3165	7.4158	13.48	9.96
21	98494	502	.5098	196.15	37.28	63	39519	3139	7.9435	12.58	9.71
22	97992	521	.5321	187.93	36.47	64	36380	3034	8.3414	11.98	9.51
23	97471	559	.5735	174.36	35.56	65	33346	2870	8.6094	11.61	9.33
24	96912	614	.6338	157.77	34.86	66	30476	2665	8.7476	11.43	9.16
25	96298	686	.7132	140.21	34.08	67	27811	2469	8.8786	11.26	8.99
26	95612	776	.8116	123.21	33.32	68	25342	2281	9.0025	11.10	8.82
27	94836	833	.8784	113.84	32.59	69	23061	2103	9.1192	10.96	8.64
28	94003	858	.9135	109.46	31.88	70	20958	1934	9.2292	10.83	8.46
29	93145	854	.9171	109.03	31.16	71	19024	1775	9.3319	10.71	8.27
30	92291	820	.8891	112.58	30.45	72	17249	1623	9.4135	10.62	8.07
31	91471	758	.8295	120.55	29.72	73	15626	1480	9.4740	10.55	7.85
32	90713	711	.7841	127.53	28.96	74	14146	1345	9.5134	10.51	7.63
33	90002	677	.7529	132.81	28.19	75	12801	1220	9.5318	10.49	7.39
34	89325	657	.7359	135.88	27.40	76	11581	1103	9.5291	10.49	7.10
35	88668	650	.7331	136.40	26.60	77	10478	1017	9.7104	10.29	6.79
36	88018	655	.7445	134.31	25.79	78	9461	953	10.0758	9.92	6.47
37	87363	692	.7924	126.20	24.98	79	8508	909	10.6252	9.41	6.14
38	86671	760	.8769	114.03	24.17	80	7599	863	11.3587	8.80	5.82
39	85911	857	.9980	100.20	23.38	81	6736	827	12.2762	8.14	5.55
40	85054	982	1.1557	86.52	22.61	82	5909	778	13.1720	7.59	5.20
41	84072	1135	1.3501	74.08	21.87	83	5131	720	14.0459	7.11	4.91
42	82937	1232	1.4863	67.28	21.11	84	4411	656	14.8941	6.71	4.63
43	81705	1278	1.5645	63.91	20.48	85	3755	589	15.7086	6.36	4.35
44	80427	1274	1.5846	63.10	19.79	86	3166	523	16.5372	6.04	4.07
45	79153	1224	1.5466	64.65	19.06	87	2643	468	17.7133	5.64	3.78
46	77929	1130	1.4505	68.94	18.39	88	2175	418	19.2629	5.19	3.49
47	76799	1140	1.4852	67.33	17.66	89	1757	372	21.1800	4.72	3.20
48	75659	1248	1.6507	60.59	16.92	90	1385	325	23.4665	4.26	2.92
49	74411	1448	1.9471	51.47	16.19	91	1060	276	26.1224	3.82	2.67
50	72963	1732	2.3743	42.11	15.55	92	784	226	28.8746	3.46	2.44
51	71231	2088	2.9323	34.10	14.87	93	558	177	31.7233	3.15	2.22
52	69143	2345	3.3926	29.47	14.30	94	381	132	34.6683	2.88	2.02
53	66798	2508	3.7552	26.62	13.79	95	249	93	37.7097	2.65	1.83
54	64290	2584	4.0201	24.87	13.51	96	156	63	40.8475	2.44	1.63
55	61706	2583	4.1873	23.88	12.84	97	93	43	46.3554	2.15	1.40
56	59123	2575	4.2567	22.95	12.35	98	50	26	53.8134	1.85	1.18
57	56548	2527	4.4697	22.37	11.93	99	24	14	61.4115	1.62	.91
58	54021	2607	4.8264	20.71	11.46	100	10	10	100.0000	1.00	.50
59	51414	2738	5.3267	18.77	11.02						

TABLE LIII.

MORTALITY AND EXPECTATION.—MINERS.

Age.	Living.	Dying.	Mortality per cent.	Specific Intensity.	Expectation.	Age.	Living.	Dying.	Mortality per cent.	Specific Intensity.	Expectation.
18	100000	1031	1.0319	96.95	39.41	60	50393	1927	3.8241	26.15	12.27
19	98969	1020	1.0313	96.96	38.82	61	48466	1981	4.0878	24.46	11.74
20	97949	1009	1.0306	97.03	38.22	62	46485	2094	4.5063	22.19	11.22
21	96940	998	1.0924	97.12	37.61	63	44391	2254	5.0796	19.68	10.73
22	95942	984	1.0232	97.50	36.92	64	42137	2450	5.8157	17.19	10.28
23	94958	961	1.0121	98.80	36.37	65	39687	2655	6.6907	14.94	9.88
24	93997	936	.9961	100.39	35.74	66	37032	2861	7.7284	12.93	9.55
25	93061	907	.9752	102.54	35.09	67	34171	2895	8.4741	11.80	9.31
26	92154	874	.9493	105.34	34.43	68	31276	2792	8.9277	11.20	9.13
27	91280	845	.9261	107.97	33.76	69	28484	2589	9.0894	11.00	8.97
28	90435	819	.9056	110.42	33.07	70	25895	2319	8.9591	11.16	8.82
29	89616	795	.8878	112.63	32.37	71	23576	2012	8.5368	11.71	8.64
30	88821	775	.8727	114.58	31.65	72	21564	1790	8.3009	12.04	8.40
31	88046	757	.8603	117.31	30.93	73	19774	1631	8.2508	12.12	8.11
32	87289	749	.8584	116.49	30.12	74	18143	1521	8.3869	11.92	7.80
33	86540	750	.8671	115 32	29.45	75	16622	1447	8.7092	11.48	7.47
34	85790	760	.8862	112.84	28.57	76	15175	1398	9.2179	10.84	7.13
35	85030	778	.9159	109.18	27.95	77	13777	1344	9.7594	10.24	6.78
36	84252	805	.9562	104.58	27.21	78	12433	1284	10.3337	9.67	6.49
37	83447	843	1.0110	198.91	26.46	79	11149	1242	11.1411	8.97	6.18
38	82604	875	1.0603	94.31	25.73	80	9907	1147	11.5812	8.63	5.89
39	81729	918	1.1242	88.95	25.00	81	8760	1073	12.2541	8.16	5.59
40	80811	971	1.2026	83.15	24 28	82	7687	995	12.9532	7.72	5.31
41	79840	1050	1.3154	76.02	23.57	83	6692	915	13.6784	7.31	5.02
42	78790	1121	1.4235	70.24	22.87	84	5787	835	14.4299	6.93	4.64
43	77669	1201	1.5469	64 64	22.20	85	4942	751	15.2076	6.57	4.46
44	76468	1273	1.6656	60.03	21.54	86	4191	671	16.0113	6.24	4.17
45	75195	1338	1.7795	56.19	20.89	87	3520	604	17.1741	5.82	3.87
46	73857	1380	1.8686	53.51	20.26	88	2916	545	18.6960	5.34	3.56
47	72477	1428	1.9709	50.73	19.63	89	2371	487	20.5768	4.85	3.27
48	71049	1482	2.0859	47.73	19.02	90	1884	429	22.8167	4.38	2.99
49	69567	1540	2.2148	45.15	18.42	91	1455	369	25.4096	3.93	2.72
50	68027	1603	2.3564	42.43	17.82	92	1036	305	28.1448	3.55	2.48
51	66424	1668	2.5111	39.82	17.24	93	781	242	31.0224	3.22	2.25
52	64756	1718	2.6539	37.68	16.67	94	539	183	34.0423	2.93	2.04
53	63038	1755	2.7847	35.91	16.11	95	356	132	37.2046	2.68	1.84
54	61283	1779	2.9037.	34.43	15.56	96	224	90	40.5152	2.46	1.63
55	59504	1795	3.0107	33.14	15.01	97	134	61	45.9499	2.17	1.40
56	57709	1792	3.1061	32.19	14.47	98	73	39	53.5090	1.86	1.15
57	55917	1808	3.2349	30.91	13.91	99	34	20	61.0680	1.63	.91
58	54109	1838	3.3976	29.43	13.36	100	14	14	100.0000	1.00	.50
59	52271	1878	3.5940	27.82	12.82						

TABLE LIV.

MORTALITY AND EXPECTATION.—PLUMBERS AND PAINTERS.

Age.	Living.	Dying.	Mortality per cent.	Specific Intensity.	Expectation.	Age.	Living.	Dying.	Mortality per cent.	Specific Intensity	Expectation.
18	100000	1597	1.5979	62.58	38.93	60	48829	2543	5.2099	19.19	12.67
19	98403	1472	1.4959	66.84	38.55	61	46286	2515	5.4339	18.40	12.34
20	96931	1351	1.3940	71.73	38.13	62	43771	2464	5.6304	17.76	12.02
21	95580	1137	1.1901	84.02	37.66	63	41307	2395	5.7994	17.24	11.70
22	94443	975	1.0326	26.84	37.11	64	38912	2311	5.9408	16.83	11.40
23	93468	861	.9216	108.50	36.49	65	36601	2216	6.0547	16.51	11.08
24	92607	793	.8570	116.68	35.83	66	34385	2111	6.1411	16.28	10.77
25	91814	770	.8389	119.20	35.13	67	32274	2016	6.2491	16.00	10·44
26	91044	789	.8672	115.31	34.43	68	30258	1930	6.3788	15.67	10.10
27	90255	795	.8818	113.40	33.72	69	28328	1849	6.5302	15.31	9.75
28	89460	789	.8827	113.02	33.02	70	26479	1774	6.7033	14.91	9.40
29	88671	771	.8699	114.95	32.31	71	24705	1704	6.8979	14.50	9.04
30	87900	741	.8434	118.57	31.59	72	23001	1649	7.1722	13.94	8.67
31	87159	700	.8033	124.48	30.85	73	21352	1607	7.5263	13.28	8.30
32	86459	702	.8120	123.15	30.10	74	19745	1571	7.9601	12.56	7.94
33	85757	745	.8696	114.99	29.34	75	18174	1540	8.4737	11.80	7.58
34	85012	829	.9761	102.44	28.59	76	16634	1508	9.0670	11.02	7.24
35	84183	952	1.1315	88.37	27.87	77	15126	1460	9.6571	10.35	6.91
36	83231	1111	1.3357	74.86	27.18	78	13666	1399	10.2441	9.76	6.60
37	82120	1194	1.4550	68.72	26.54	79	12267	1328	10.8278	9.23	6.29
38	80926	1202	1.4894	67.29	25.93	80	10939	1245	11.4083	8.78	6.00
39	79724	1147	1.4389	69.49	25.31	81	9694	1161	11.9857	8.34	5.71
40	78577	1024	1.3035	76.71	24.67	82	8533	1075	12.6065	7.93	5.41
41	77553	838	1.0832	92.53	23.99	83	7458	989	13.2706	7.53	5.12
42	76715	772	1.0066	99.34	23 25	84	6469	904	13.9782	7.32	4.83
43	75943	815	1.0738	93.12	22.48	85	5565	819	14.7291	6.78	4.54
44	75128	963	1.2848	77.97	21.72	86	4746	738	15.5231	6.42	4.23
45	74165	1216	1.6395	60.99	20.99	87	4008	668	16.6770	5.99	3.93
46	72949	1553	2.1341	46.85	20.38	88	3340	607	18.1910	5.49	3.61
47	71396	1753	2 4555	40.72	19.77	89	2733	553	20.2649	4.93	3.30
48	69643	1813	2.6040	38.40	19.25	90	2180	489	22.4989	4.45	3.01
49	67830	1749	2.5794	38.76	18.75	91	1691	424	25.0928	3.98	2.73
50	66081	1573	2 3818	41.98	18.24	92	1267	352	27.8263	3 59	2.48
51	64508	1299	2.0152	49.62	17.67	93	915	279	30.4989	3.27	2.36
52	63209	1176	1.8611	53.73	17.02	94	636	213	33.5114	2.98	2.02
53	62033	1190	1.9195	52.09	16.33	95	423	155	36.6362	2.72	1.86
54	60843	1332	2.1904	45.65	15.64	96	268	107	39.9543	2.50	1.64
55	59511	1591	2.6738	37.40	14.98	97	161	73	45.4335	2.20	1.41
56	57920	1951	3.3697	29.67	14.38	98	88	46	53.1009	1.88	1.17
57	55969	2222	3.9713	25.18	13.87	99	42	25	60·7683	1.64	.90
58	53767	2407	4.4786	22.32	13.42	100	17	17	100.0000	1.00	.50
59	51340	2511	4:8914	20.44	13.02						

TABLE LV.

MORTALITY AND EXPECTATION.—POTTERS.

Age.	Living.	Dying.	Mortality per cent.	Specific Intensity.	Expectation.	Age.	Living.	Dying.	Mortality per cent.	Specific Intensity	Expectation.
18	100000	672	.6723	148.74	38.07	60	45137	1700	3.7658	26.55	13.71
19	99328	715	.7207	138.75	37.32	61	43437	1771	4.0781	24.52	13.23
20	98613	758	.7692	130.00	36.59	62	41666	1826	4.3842	22.80	12.77
21	97855	847	.8661	115.46	35.87	63	39840	1866	4.6843	21.34	12.34
22	97008	938	.9678	103.32	35.18	64	37974	1890	4.9782	20.08	11.92
23	96070	1032	1.0742	93.09	34.51	65	36084	1900	5.2661	18.98	11.50
24	95038	1126	1.1854	84.35	33.89	66	34184	1896	5.5478	18.02	11.13
25	93912	1222	1.3014	76.84	33.29	67	32288	1875	5.8092	17.21	10.75
26	92690	1318	1.4221	70.31	32.72	68	30413	1840	6.0502	16.52	10.39
27	91372	1358	1.4863	67.28	32.18	69	28573	1792	6.2709	15.94	10.02
28	90014	1344	1.4939	66.93	31.66	70	26781	1733	6.4712	15.45	9.66
29	88670	1281	1.4450	69.20	31.13	71	25048	1670	6.6511	15.03	9.29
30	87389	1170	1.3395	74.65	30.51	72	23378	1614	6.9052	14.48	8.92
31	86219	1015	1.1774	84.93	29.99	73	21764	1574	7.2835	13.82	8.55
32	85204	908	1.0656	93.84	29.20	74	20190	1541	7.6358	13.09	8.18
33	84296	846	1.0042	99.58	28.65	75	18649	1482	8.1124	12.32	7.81
34	83450	778	.9331	107.16	27.94	76	17167	1487	8.6629	11.54	7.44
35	82672	853	1.0324	96.86	27.20	77	15680	1446	9.2230	10.84	7.10
36	81819	918	1.1220	89.13	26.48	78	14234	1394	9.7925	10.21	6.77
37	80901	999	1.2360	80.90	25.77	79	12840	1332	10.3716	9.64	6.45
38	79902	1098	1.3744	72.75	25.09	80	11508	1232	10.7601	9.29	6.14
39	78804	1211	1.5370	65.06	24.43	81	10276	1187	11.5581	8.65	5.82
40	77593	1368	1.5640	56.68	23.80	82	9089	1108	12.2009	8.19	5.52
41	76225	1475	1.9354	51.66	23.22	83	7981	1028	12.8885	7.77	5.20
42	74750	1580	2.1138	47.24	22.67	84	6953	947	13.6209	7.34	4.91
43	73170	1653	2.2594	44.25	22.15	85	6006	864	14.3981	6.94	4.61
44	71517	1696	2.3721	42.15	21.65	86	5142	782	15.2201	6.57	4.30
45	69821	1711	2.4519	40.78	21.16	87	4360	714	16.3964	6.09	3.98
46	68110	1702	2.4988	40.40	20.68	88	3646	653	17.9270	5.57	3.66
47	66408	1693	2.5493	39.22	20.20	89	2993	593	19.8118	5.04	3.36
48	64715	1685	2.6031	38.41	19.71	90	2400	529	20.0510	4.53	3.06
49	63030	1677	2.6604	37 58	19.23	91	1871	461	24.6444	4.05	2.79
50	61353	1670	2.7212	36.74	18.74	92	1410	385	27.3734	3.65	2.54
51	59683	1663	2.7854	35.90	18.25	93	1025	309	30.2378	3.30	2.30
52	58020	1651	2.8459	35.13	17.76	94	716	237	33.2378	3.00	2.09
53	56369	1636	2.9027	34.45	17.27	95	479	173	36.3732	2.75	1.87
54	54733	1618	2.9556	33.83	16.58	96	306	121	39.6643	2.52	1.65
55	53115	1596	3.0049	33.27	16.26	97	185	83	45.1725	2.21	1.41
56	51519	1572	3.0503	32.78	15.75	98	102	54	52.8978	1.89	1.15
57	49947	1573	3.1491	31.74	15.23	99	48	29	60.6433	1.64	.89
58	48374	1597	3.3013	30.29	14.73	100	19	19	100.0000	1.00	.50
59	46777	1640	3.5068	28.51	14.22						

TABLE LVI.

MORTALITY AND EXPECTATION.—PRINTERS AND COMPOSITORS.

Age.	Living.	Dying.	Mortality per cent.	Specific Intensity.	Expecta-tion.	Age.	Living.	Dying.	Mortality per cent.	Specific Intensity	Expecta-tion.
18	100000	608	.6088	164.25	38.20	60	38502	2391	6.2109	16.10	12.04
19	99392	616	.6205	161.16	37.43	61	36111	2279	6.3113	15.84	11.80
20	98776	624	.6322	158.17	36.66	62	33832	2170	6.4159	15.58	11.57
21	98152	643	.6557	152.50	35.89	63	31662	2065	6.5249	15.32	11.32
22	97509	656	.6730	148.58	35.13	64	29597	1964	6.6381	15.06	11.13
23	96853	662	.6842	146.15	34.36	65	27633	1866	6.7557	14.80	10.82
24	96191	663	.6895	145.03	33.59	66	25767	1772	6.8775	14.54	10.57
25	95528	657	.6887	145.20	32.82	67	23995	1670	6.9620	14.36	10.33
26	94871	647	.6820	146.62	32.05	68	22325	1564	7.0090	14.26	10.06
27	94224	634	.6736	148.45	31.26	69	20761	1457	7.0188	14.24	9.78
28	93590	620	.6635	150.71	30.47	70	19304	1349	6.9911	14.30	9.48
29	92970	606	.6518	153.42	29.67	71	17955	1243	6.9261	14.43	9.16
30	92364	589	.6384	156.64	28.86	72	16712	1170	7.0067	14.27	8.80
31	91775	572	.6234	160.41	28.05	73	15542	1124	7.2329	13.82	8.43
32	91203	560	.6144	162.76	27.22	74	14418	1096	7.6047	13.19	8.05
33	90643	554	.6114	163.55	26.38	75	13322	1082	8.1221	12.31	7.67
34	90089	553	.6144	162.76	25.54	76	12240	1075	8.7851	11.38	7.30
35	89536	552	.6234	160.41	24.98	77	11165	1053	9.4356	10.59	6.96
36	88984	568	.6384	156.64	23.85	78	10112	1018	10.0734	9.92	6.63
37	88416	621	.7032	142.20	23.00	79	9094	972	10.6987	9.34	6.32
38	87795	735	.8379	119.34	22.16	80	8122	918	11.3115	8.84	6.01
39	87060	872	1.0025	99.75	21.34	81	7204	858	11.9116	8.39	5.72
40	86188	1031	1.1970	83.54	20.55	82	6346	796	12.5517	7.96	5.42
41	85157	1244	1.4613	68.43	19.79	83	5550	734	13.2318	7.55	5.13
42	83913	1448	1.7259	57.94	19.08	84	4816	671	13.9517	7.16	4.83
43	82465	1641	1.9909	50.22	18.41	85	4145	609	14.7117	6.82	4.54
44	80824	1823	2.2562	44.32	17.77	86	3536	548	15.5115	6.44	4.23
45	79001	1992	2.5218	39.65	17.17	87	2988	498	16.6710	5.99	3.92
46	77009	2146	2.7877	35.87	16.65	88	2490	453	18.1902	5.49	3.65
47	74863	2313	3.0898	32.36	16.06	89	2037	408	20.0698	4.98	3.30
48	72550	2487	3.4282	29.16	15.56	90	1629	363	22.3074	4.48	3.00
49	70063	2664	3.8029	26.29	15.09	91	1266	315	24.9054	4.01	2.71
50	67399	2840	4.2139	23.73	14.67	92	951	262	27.6412	3.62	2.45
51	64559	3009	4.6611	21.45	14.29	93	689	210	30.5149	3.27	2.19
52	61550	3100	5.0370	19.85	13.97	94	479	160	33.5264	2.98	1.94
53	58450	3122	5.3417	18.72	13.68	95	319	147	36.6758	2.72	1.66
54	55328	3084	5.5751	18.07	13.43	96	172	68	39.9630	2.50	1.65
55	52244	2997	5.7373	17.43	13.19	97	104	47	45.4390	2.20	1.32
56	49247	2870	5.8282	17.15	12.96	98	57	30	53.1038	1.88	1.16
57	46377	2745	5.9210	16.88	12.73	99	27	16	60.7607	1.64	.90
58	43632	2624	6.0157	16.62	12.50	100	11	11	100.0000	1.00	.50
59	41008	2506	6.1123	16.36	12.27						

TABLE LVII.

MORTALITY AND EXPECTATION.—SAWYERS.

Age.	Living.	Dying.	Mortality per cent.	Specific Intensity.	Expectation.	Age.	Living.	Dying.	Mortality per cent.	Specific Intensity	Expectation.
18	100000	668	.6689	149.49	41.47	60	53362	2501	4.6882	21.33	13.11
19	99332	681	.6862	146.06	40.74	61	50861	2420	4.7596	21.05	12.67
20	98651	694	.7036	142.45	40.02	62	48441	2364	4.8805	20.48	12.31
21	97957	723	.7383	135.44	39.30	63	46077	2327	5.0510	19.79	11.91
22	97234	751	.7728	129.39	38.59	64	43750	2306	5.2709	18.97	11.52
23	96483	778	.8071	123.90	37.89	65	41444	2296	5.5404	18.02	11.13
24	95705	804	.8410	118.97	37.19	66	39148	2293	5.8593	17.06	10.76
25	94901	830	.8748	114.31	36.50	67	36855	2264	6.1451	16.27	10.40
26	94071	854	.9082	110.10	35.82	68	34591	2213	6.3980	15.62	10.04
27	93217	857	.9195	108.75	35.15	69	32378	2152	6.6178	15.00	9.70
28	92360	839	.9087	110.30	34.46	70	30226	2056	6.8047	14.69	9.35
29	91521	801	.8760	114.15	33.77	71	28170	1960	6.9585	14.37	9.00
30	90720	745	.8212	121.77	33.06	72	26210	1886	7.1986	13.89	8.63
31	89975	669	.7445	134.31	32.34	73	24324	1830	7.5251	13.28	8.26
32	89306	647	.7244	138.04	31.58	74	22494	1785	7.9379	12.60	7.89
33	88659	674	.7611	131.38	30.80	75	20709	1747	8.4371	11.85	7.53
34	87985	751	.8544	117.04	30.04	76	18962	1710	9.0226	11.08	7.18
35	87234	876	1.0045	99.55	29.29	77	17252	1659	9.6180	10.39	6.85
36	86358	1045	1.2112	82.56	28.58	78	15593	1595	10.2234	9.77	6.52
37	85313	1147	1.3454	74.32	27.93	79	13998	1517	10.8388	9.22	6.21
38	84166	1184	1.4071	71.06	27.36	80	12481	1430	11.4641	8.72	5.90
39	82982	1158	1.3963	71.61	26.68	81	11051	1337	12.0993	8.24	5.60
40	81824	1074	1.3130	76.16	26.05	82	9714	1241	12.7839	7.82	5.30
41	80750	934	1.1572	86.41	25.39	83	8473	1145	13.5177	7.39	5.01
42	79816	809	1.0138	98.63	24.68	84	7328	1047	14.3009	6.69	4.71
43	79007	697	.8829	113.26	23.93	85	6281	950	15.1334	6.60	4.42
44	78310	598	.7645	130.80	23.14	86	5331	853	16.0151	6.24	4.12
45	77712	511	.6586	151.82	22.31	87	4478	773	17.2739	5.78	3.81
46	77101	436	.5653	176.89	21.46	88	3705	700	18.9096	5.28	3.55
47	76765	461	.6005	166.52	20.58	89	3005	627	20.9224	4.77	3.20
48	76304	583	.7642	130.85	19.70	90	2378	554	23.3121	4.28	2.91
49	75721	799	1.0564	94.66	18.85	91	1824	475	26.0787	3.83	2.64
50	74922	1106	1.4771	67.70	18.04	92	1349	391	28.9930	3.44	2.40
51	73816	1566	2.0263	47.12	17.31	93	958	307	32.0549	3.11	2.18
52	72250	1822	2.5225	39.64	16.67	94	651	229	35.2645	2.83	1.97
53	70428	2088	2.9657	33.71	16.09	95	422	163	38.6218	2.58	1.77
54	68340	2293	3.3559	29.79	15.57	96	259	109	42.1267	2.37	1.58
55	66047	2439	3.6930	27.07	15.08	97	150	71	47.5170	2.19	1.36
56	63608	2529	3.9770	25.14	14.65	98	79	43	54.7927	1.82	1.14
57	61079	2576	4.2186	23.70	14.24	99	36	21	62.0684	1.61	.98
58	58503	2584	4.4176	22.63	13.84	100	15	15	100.0000	1.00	.50
59	55919	2557	4.5742	21.86	13.46						

o

TABLE LVIII.

MORTALITY AND EXPECTATION.—SERVANTS, FOOTMEN, AND WAITERS.

Age.	Living.	Dying.	Mortality per cent.	Specific Intensity.	Expectation.	Age.	Living.	Dying.	Mortality per cent.	Specific Intensity	Expectation.
18	100000	311	.3111	321.44	43.75	60	58034	1995	3.4381	29.09	14.81
19	99689	344	.3453	289.60	42.88	61	56039	2066	3.6866	27.12	14.32
20	99345	377	.3795	263.50	42.03	62	53973	2120	3.9291	25.45	13.85
21	98968	443	.4479	223.26	41.19	63	51853	2180	4.2057	23.77	13.40
22	98525	501	.5084	196.69	40.37	64	49673	2184	4.3963	22.74	12.96
23	98024	549	.5608	178.31	39.58	65	47489	2194	4.6021	21.64	12.53
24	97475	590	.6053	165.20	38.80	66	45295	2192	4.8397	20.66	12.12
25	96885	622	.6419	155.78	38.03	67	43103	2176	5.0486	19.80	11.71
26	96263	645	.6704	149.16	37.27	68	40927	2147	5.2477	19.05	11.31
27	95618	669	.7004	142.77	36.52	69	38780	2108	5.4371	18.39	10.90
28	94949	694	.7318	136.64	35.77	70	36672	2059	5.6167	17.80	10.49
29	94255	720	.7647	130.77	35.04	71	34613	2002	5.7865	17.28	10.10
30	93535	747	.7991	125.14	34.30	72	32611	1964	6.0222	16.60	9.69
31	92788	774	.8349	119.77	33.57	73	30647	1938	6.3239	15.81	9.28
32	92014	802	.8716	114.73	32.85	74	28709	1921	6.6915	14.94	8.87
33	91212	830	.9103	109.85	32.13	75	26788	1908	7.1251	14.03	8.47
34	90382	858	.9499	105.27	31.43	76	24880	1897	7.6246	13.11	8.08
35	89524	887	.9907	100.93	30.72	77	22983	1870	8.1392	12.28	7.71
36	88637	915	1.0327	96.84	30.02	78	21113	1830	8.6690	11.53	7.34
37	87722	952	1.0854	92.13	29.33	79	19283	1776	9.2140	10.85	7.00
38	86770	996	1.1487	87.05	28.58	80	17507	1711	9.7741	10.23	6.66
39	85774	1048	1.2226	81.79	27.98	81	15796	1634	10.3493	9.66	6.32
40	84726	1107	1.3072	76.49	27.32	82	14162	1548	10.9342	9.14	6.00
41	83619	1172	1.4023	71.31	26.67	83	12614	1454	11.5288	8.67	5.67
42	82447	1206	1.4628	68.36	26.04	84	11160	1354	12.1331	8.24	5.34
43	81241	1209	1.4886	67.17	25.42	85	9806	1250	12.7470	7.84	5.01
44	80032	1181	1.4797	67.73	24.80	86	8556	1144	13.3704	7.47	4.67
45	78851	1132	1.4361	69.63	24.16	87	7412	1066	14.3837	6.95	4.32
46	77719	1055	1.3578	73.64	23.51	88	6346	1001	15.7863	6.33	3.96
47	76664	1019	1.3299	75.18	22.82	89	5345	939	17.5785	5.88	3.61
48	75645	1023	1.3524	73.91	22.12	90	4406	870	19.7603	5.06	3.28
49	74622	1063	1.4253	70.16	21.42	91	3536	789	22.3315	4.47	2.96
50	73559	1139	1.5486	64.72	20.77	92	2747	690	25.1348	3.97	2.74
51	72420	1247	1.7223	58.06	20.04	93	2057	579	28.1702	3.54	2.40
52	71173	1349	1.8962	52.73	19.38	94	1478	464	31.4374	3.18	2.14
53	69824	1445	2.0701	48.31	18.74	95	1014	354	34.9370	2.86	1.89
54	68379	1533	2.2442	44.59	18.14	96	660	255	38.6684	2.58	1.65
55	66846	1592	2.4184	41.34	17.52	97	405	184	45.5404	2.19	1.37
56	65254	1691	2.5926	38.57	16.95	98	221	122	55.5530	1.80	1.10
57	63563	1768	2.7827	35.93	16.39	99	99	65	65.5657	1.52	.84
58	61795	1840	2.9856	33.57	15.89	100	34	34	100.0000	1.00	.50
59	59955	1921	3.2044	31.20	15.32						

TABLE LIX.

MORTALITY AND EXPECTATION.—SHOEMAKERS.

Age.	Living.	Dying.	Mortality per cent.	Specific Intensity.	Expecta-tion.	Age.	Living.	Dying.	Mortality per cent.	Specific Intensity	Expecta-tion.
18	100000	578	.5786	172.83	42.36	60	58335	882	1.5127	66.10	13.05
19	99422	622	.6269	159.76	41.60	61	57453	847	1.4754	67.77	12.24
20	98800	667	.6753	148.08	40.87	62	56606	1090	1.9273	51.88	11.41
21	98133	757	.7720	129.53	40.14	63	55516	1599	2.8806	34.71	10.62
22	97376	821	.8440	118.48	39.36	64	53917	2335	4.3311	23.08	9.93
23	96555	860	.8915	112.06	38.87	65	51582	3238	6.2790	15.92	9.35
24	95695	875	.9143	109.37	38.12	66	48344	4217	8.7241	11.46	8.95
25	94820	865	.9125	109.58	37.35	67	44127	4591	10.4053	9.61	8.75
26	93955	832	.8861	112.85	36.81	68	39536	4476	11.3226	8.83	8.71
27	93123	800	.8588	116.44	36.14	69	35060	4023	11.4761	8.71	8.78
28	92323	766	.8302	120.45	35.44	70	31037	3372	10.8658	9.20	8.83
29	91557	733	.8009	124.85	34.74	71	27665	2625	9.4916	10.53	8.85
30	90824	699	.7705	129.78	33.99	72	25040	2029	8.1082	12.33-	8.72
31	90125	666	.7393	135.26	33.27	73	23011	1821	7.9156	12.63	8.44
32	89459	640	.7157	139.80	32.52	74	21190	1634	7.7138	12.96	8.13
33	88819	621	.6998	142.89	31.67	75	19556	1545	7.9028	12.65	7.77
34	88198	610	.6915	144.64	30.97	76	18011	1527	8.4826	11.78	7.40
35	87588	605	.6909	144.73	30.18	77	16484	1494	9.0872	11.00	7.00
36	86983	607	.6979	142.95	29.39	78	14990	1455	9.7106	10.29	6.68
37	86376	625	.7237	138.17	28.59	79	13535	1401	10.3587	9.65	6.35
38	85751	658	.7681	130.19	27.79	80	12134	1338	11.0297	9.06	6.03
39	85093	707	.8315	120.26	27.12	81	10796	1265	11.7234	8.52	5.71
40	84386	770	.9132	109.50	26.23	82	9531	1185	12.4417	8.03	5.41
41	83616	847	1.0137	98.64	25.47	83	8346	1100	13.1783	7.58	5.11
42	82769	907	1.0971	91.14	24.72	84	7246	1010	13.9395	7.17	4.81
43	81862	952	1.1635	85.91	23.99	85	6236	920	14.7231	6.77	4.55
44	80810	981	1.2129	82.44	23.27	86	5316	825	15.5291	6.43	4.25
45	79929	995	1.2453	80.30	22.55	87	4491	752	16.7500	5.97	3.88
46	78934	995	1.2606	79.40	21.82	88	3739	687	18.3856	5.13	3.56
47	77939	1059	1.3588	73.59	21.10	89	3052	623	20.4360	4.89	3.25
48	76880	1183	1.5400	64.93	20.38	90	2429	556	22.9012	4.36	2.91
49	75697	1365	1.8041	55.42	19.69	91	1873	482	25.7811	3.87	2.68
50	74332	1599	2.1512	46.48	19.04	92	1391	399	28.7079	3.48	2.38
51	72733	1877	2.5812	38.74	18.45	93	992	313	31.6815	3.16	2.22
52	70856	2020	2.8514	35.07	17.93	94	679	235	34.7019	2.88	2.02
53	68836	2038	2.9617	33.76	17.44	95	444	166	37.7692	2.64	1.83
54	66798	1945	2.9125	34.33	16.96	96	278	112	40.8832	2.47	1.63
55	64853	1752	2.7030	36.99	16.45	97	166	76	46.1532	2.16	1.39
56	63101	1473	2.3339	43.04	15.89	98	90	48	53.6094	1.86	1.15
57	61628	1251	2.0302	49.25	15.23	99	42	25	61.0556	1.63	.90
58	60377	1082	1.7922	55.79	14.53	100	17	17	100.0000	1.00	.50
59	59295	960	1.6197	61.73	13.82						

TABLE LX.

MORTALITY AND EXPECTATION.—SPINNERS.

Age.	Living.	Dying.	Mortality per cent.	Specific Intensity	Expectation.	Age.	Living.	Dying.	Mortality per cent.	Specific Intensity	Expectation.
18	100000	1362	1.3626	73.38	39.98	60	48945	2907	5.9404	16.83	12.21
19	98638	1287	1.3051	76.62	39.51	61	46038	2687	5.8382	17.12	11.95
20	97351	1211	1.2476	80.33	39.04	62	43341	2516	5.7957	17 25	11.66
21	96140	1088	1.1326	88.29	38.52	63	40830	2383	5.8372	17.13	11 35
22	95052	985	1.0365	96.47	37.87	64	38447	2283	5.9384	16.83	11.02
23	94067	902	.9594	104.23	37.35	65	36164	2209	6.1074	16.37	10.69
24	93165	839	.9013	110.95	36.71	66	33955	2154	6.3442	15.76	10 35
25	92326	796	.8622	115.98	36.03	67	31811	2090	6.5704	15.21	10.02
26	91530	771	.8422	118.73	35.34	68	29721	2016	6.7859	14.73	9.69
27	90759	738	.8138	122.86	34.64	69	27705	1936	6.9907	14.30	9.36
28	90021	699	.7772	128.66	33.92	70	25769	1851	7.1849	13.91	9.02
29	89322	654	.7323	136.55	33.19	71	23918	1762	7.3683	13.57	8.68
30	88668	602	.6791	147.25	32.42	72	22156	1691	7.6346	13.09	8.33
31	88066	540	.6136	162.97	31.64	73	20465	1633	7.9838	12.53	7.98
32	87526	508	.5806	172.23	30.83	74	18832	1584	8.4157	11.88	7 63
33	87018	494	.5681	176.02	30.01	75	17248	1540	8.9306	11.19	7.28
34	86524	502	.5802	172.35	29.18	76	15708	1493	9.5282	10.49	6.97
35	86022	530	.6168	162.12	28.35	77	14215	1441	10.1374	9.86	6.63
36	85492	579	.6779	147.51	27.52	78	12774	1374	10.7581	9.29	6.32
37	84913	628	.7396	135.20	26.70	79	11400	1298	11.3903	8.77	6.02
38	84285	675	.8018	124.71	25.90	80	10102	1215	12.0341	8.30	5.74
39	83610	723	.8645	115.67	25.09	81	8887	1127	12.6893	7.88	5.45
40	82887	769	.9278	107.78	24.32	82	7760	1038	13.3862	7.47	5.17
41	82118	814	.9915	100.85	23.54	83	6722	949	14.1248	7.08	4.77
42	81304	845	1.0401	96.14	22.77	84	5773	860	14.9049	6.70	4.51
43	80459	863	1.0736	93.14	22.01	85	4913	772	15.7268	6.35	4.33
44	79596	869	1.0920	91.57	21.24	86	4141	687	16.5902	6.02	4.05
45	78727	860	1.0953	91.50	20.47	87	3454	615	17.8181	5.61	3.76
46	77867	843	1.0834	92.30	19.69	88	2839	551	19.4102	5.15	3.46
47	77024	890	1.1564	86.47	18.90	89	2288	488	21.3667	4.68	3.18
48	76134	1006	1.3225	75.61	18.11	90	1800	426	23.6876	4.22	2.90
49	75128	1172	1.5575	64.20	17.35	91	1374	362	26.3727	3.79	2.65
50	73956	1394	1.8856	53.03	16.62	92	1012	294	29.1364	3.43	2 42
51	72562	1740	2.2986	41.71	15.93	93	718	229	31.9785	3.12	2.21
52	70822	1947	2.7499	36.36	15.31	94	489	170	34.8997	2.86	2.01
53	68875	2231	3.2394	30.86	14.73	95	319	120	37.8984	2.63	1.82
54	66644	2510	3.7671	26.54	14.23	96	199	81	40.9760	2.43	1.62
55	64134	2778	4.3330	23.07	13.71	97	118	54	46.2250	2.16	1.39
56	61356	3029	4.9370	20.25	13.34	98	64	34	53.6453	1.86	1.15
57	58327	3149	5.3997	18.51	13.00	99	30	18	61.0657	1.63	.90
58	55178	3163	5.7212	17.44	12.75	100	12	12	100.0000	1.00	.50
59	52015	3070	5.9014	16.94	12.43						

TABLE LXI.

MORTALITY AND EXPECTATION.—STONEMASONS.

Age.	Living.	Dying.	Mortality per cent.	Specific Intensity.	Expectation.	Age.	Living.	Dying.	Mortality per cent.	Specific Intensity.	Expectation.
18	100000	645	.6452	154.99	39.68	60	44347	2005	4.5212	22.11	14.79
19	99355	655	.6750	151.59	38.93	61	42342	1864	4.4026	22.71	14.47
20	98700	695	.7049	141.86	38.19	62	40478	1619	3.9995	25.00	14.11
21	98005	749	.7646	130.78	37.45	63	38859	1517	3.9060	25.60	13.68
22	97256	790	.8124	123.09	36.74	64	37342	1465	3.9241	25.48	13.21
23	96466	816	.8484	118.14	36.04	65	35877	1454	4.0538	24.66	12.73
24	95650	834	.8724	114.57	35.34	66	34423	1478	4.2950	23.28	12.25
25	94816	839	.8847	113.03	34.65	67	32945	1484	4.5057	22.19	11.78
26	93977	831	.8850	112.99	33.95	68	31461	1474	4.6860	21.34	11.31
27	93146	829	.8906	112.28	33.25	69	29987	1450	4.8359	20.67	10.86
28	92317	832	.9014	110.93	32.54	70	28537	1414	4.9554	20.18	10.36
29	91485	839	.9175	108.99	31.83	71	27123	1368	5.0445	19.82	9.88
30	90646	851	.9387	106.53	31.12	72	25755	1364	5.2995	18.86	9.38
31	89795	866	.9653	103.57	30.41	73	24391	1395	5.7209	17.47	8.87
32	88929	884	.9942	100.58	29.71	74	22996	1450	6.3083	15.85	8.38
33	88045	903	1.0257	97.49	29.00	75	21546	1521	7.0620	14.16	7.91
34	87142	923	1.0596	94.37	28.29	76	20025	1598	7.9818	12.52	7.48
35	86219	947	1.0960	91.03	27.59	77	18427	1629	8.8413	11.31	7.08
36	85272	967	1.1348	88.12	26.89	78	16798	1613	9.6406	10.37	6.72
37	84305	1007	1.1921	83.88	26.20	79	15179	1575	10.3796	9.63	6.39
38	83298	1056	1.2681	78.85	25.51	80	13604	1500	11.0584	9.04	6.08
39	82242	1120	1.3626	73.38	24.84	81	12104	1413	11.6769	8.56	5.76
40	81122	1197	1.4758	67.75	24.16	82	10691	1319	12.3398	8.10	5.45
41	79925	1284	1.6075	62.20	23.52	83	9372	1222	13.0469	7.66	5.15
42	78641	1350	1.7167	58.25	22.89	84	8150	1124	13.7984	7.24	4.85
43	77291	1393	1.8034	55.45	22.29	85	7026	1023	14.5942	6.86	4.55
44	75898	1417	1.8675	53.54	21.68	86	6003	926	15.4342	6.33	4.24
45	74481	1425	1.9002	52.25	21.09	87	5077	845	16.6451	6.00	3.92
46	73056	1408	1.9283	51.85	20.49	88	4232	771	18.2269	5.48	3.60
47	71648	1446	2.0187	49.53	19.88	89	3461	698	20.1797	4.95	3.29
48	70202	1530	2.1805	45.84	19.28	90	2763	621	22.5034	4.44	3.00
49	68672	1658	2.4137	41.41	18.70	91	2142	539	25.1980	3.87	2.73
50	67014	1821	2.7184	36.78	18.15	92	1603	449	28.0315	3.56	2.48
51	65193	2017	3.0943	32.31	17.60	93	1154	357	31.0022	3.22	2.25
52	63176	2177	3.4474	29.00	17.19	94	797	271	34.1110	2.93	2.04
53	60999	2304	3.7777	26.47	16.79	95	526	196	37.3650	2.67	1.83
54	58695	2395	4.0811	24.55	16.43	96	330	134	40.7558	2.45	1.62
55	56300	2460	4.3695	22.88	16.11	97	196	90	46.2117	2.16	1.39
56	53840	2493	4.6312	21.59	15.82	98	106	56	53.7387	1.86	1.16
57	51347	2452	4.7772	20.93	15.56	99	50	30	61.2657	1.63	.89
58	48895	2350	4.8075	20.80	15.32	100	20	20	100.0000	1.00	.50
59	46545	2198	4.7222	21.17	15.07						

TABLE LXII.

MORTALITY AND EXPECTATION.—TAILORS.

Age.	Living.	Dying.	Mortality per cent.	Specific Intensity.	Expectation.	Age.	Living.	Dying.	Mortality per cent.	Specific Intensity	Expectation.
18	100000	904	.9042	110.59	40.68	60	62088	2156	3.4728	28.79	10.23
19	99096	900	.9085	110.07	40.04	61	59932	2765	4.6140	21.67	9.58
20	98196	896	.9129	109.54	39.40	62	57167	3383	5.9178	16.89	9.02
21	97300	896	.9216	108.50	38.77	63	53784	3971	7.3840	13.54	8.56
22	96404	905	.9390	106.49	38.14	64	49813	4500	9.0129	11.06	8.20
23	95499	864	.9051	110.48	37.48	65	45313	4895	10.8040	9.25	7.97
24	94635	832	.8799	113.64	36.81	66	40418	5156	12.7584	7.83	7.87
25	93803	791	.8434	118.56	36.13	67	·35262	4897	13.8867	7.20	7.95
26	93012	740	.7957	125.67	35.44	68	30365	4308	14.1894	7.04	8.15
27	92272	712	.7715	129.61	34.71	69	26057	3561	13.6663	7.31	8.42
28	91560	705	.7706	129.76	33.98	70	22496	2764	12.3176	8.11	8.70
29	90855	720	.7934	126.03	33.24	71	19732	2001	10.1445	9.85	8.82
30	90135	757	.8397	119.09	32.51	72	17731	1519	8.5682	11.67	8.76
31	89378	813	.9095	109.92	31.78	73	16212	1230	7.5931	13.16	8.53
32	88565	849	.9591	104.26	31.06	74	14982	1080	7.2176	13.85	8.19
33	87716	867	.9886	101.15	30.36	75	13902	1034	7.4419	13.43	7.77
34	86849	866	.9978	100.22	29.66	76	12868	1063	8.2658	12.09	7.38
35	85983	848	.9867	101.34	28.95	77	11805	1066	9.0529	11.04	7.02
36	85135	813	.9555	104.65	28.24	78	10739	1052	9.8033	10.20	6.64
37	84322	820	.9731	102.76	27.50	79	9687	1018	10.5170	9.50	6.31
38	83502	866	1.0376	96.35	26.77	80	8669	972	11.1939	8.91	6.00
39	82636	940	1.1190	87.83	26.04	81	7697	910	11.8340	8.45	5.69
40	81696	1068	1.3073	76.49	25.34	82	6787	849	12.5182	7.98	5.39
41	80628	1217	1.5104	66.20	24.67	83	5738	786	13.2466	7.54	5.09
42	79411	1289	1.6238	61.58	24.04	84	5152	722	14.0192	7.13	4.79
43	78122	1289	1.6495	60.62	23 42	85	4430	657	14.8360	6.74	4.49
44	76833	1219	1.5875	62.99	22.82	86	3773	592	15.6969	6.37	4.18
45	75614	1085	1.4377	69.64	22.17	87	3181	538	16.9322	5.90	3.87
46	74529	896	1.2021	83.18	21.48	88	2643	490	18.5418	5.39	3.55
47	73633	767	1.0423	95.94	20.74	89	2153	442	20.5258	4.87	3.25
48	72866	685	.9403	106.34	19.95	90	1711	391	22.8841	4.36	2.96
49	72181	660	.9142	109.37	19.14	91	1320	338	25.6167	3.90	2.69
50	71521	685	.9579	104.39	18.31	92	982	279	28.4881	3 51	2.44
51	70836	758	1.0714	93.33	17.48	93	703	221	31.4982	3.17	2.22
52	70078	811	1.1579	86.36	16.67	94	482	167	34.6471	2.88	2.01
53	69267	843	1 2174	82.14	15.86	95	315	119	37.9348	2.63	1.81
54	68424	855	1.2498	80.01	15.04	96	196	81	41.3612	2.41	1.61
55	67569	848	1.2552	79.66	14.23	97	115	53	46.7809	2.13	1.39
56	66721	823	1.2336	81.07	13.34	98	62	33	54.1940	1.84	1.16
57	65898	951	1.4145	69.22	12.56	99	29	17	61.6071	1.62	.91
58	64947	1226	1.8880	52.96	11.74	100	12	12	100.0000	1.00	.50
59	63721	1633	2.5641	39.00	10.96						

TABLE LXIII.

MORTALITY AND EXPECTATION.—WEAVERS.

Age.	Living.	Dying.	Mortality per cent.	Specific Intensity.	Expecta-tion.	Age.	Living.	Dying.	Mortality per cent.	Specific Intensity	Expecta-tion.
18	100000	1013	1.0132	98.69	43.05	60	58355	1441	2.4698	40.48	15.61
19	98987	1010	1.0206	97.98	42.49	61	56914	1532	2.6935	37.12	14.99
20	97977	1006	1.0281	97.26	41.92	62	55382	1642	2.9651	33.88	14.39
21	96971	1011	1.0430	95.87	41.35	63	53740	1765	3.2844	30.44	13.82
22	95960	998	1.0402	96.35	40.78	64	51975	1897	3.6516	27.38	13.27
23	94962	968	1.0197	98.06	40.21	65	50078	2036	4.0665	24.59	12.75
24	93994	922	.9814	101.89	39.62	66	48042	2175	4.5291	22.07	12.27
25	93072	861	.9254	108.06	39.00	67	45867	2255·	4.9175	20.33	11.83
26	92211	785	.8516	117.42	38.36	68	43612	2281	5.2318	19.11	11.42
27	91426	731	.8006	124.99	37.69	69	41331	2261	5.4718	18.35	11.02
28	90695	700	.7724	129.46	36.99	70	39070	2202	5.6377	17.73	10.63
29	89995	690	.7670	130.37	36.27	71	36868	2112	5.7293	17.45	10.23
30	89305	700	.7844	127.48	35.55	72	34756	2049	5.8975	16.95	9.82
31	88605	730	.8246	121.27	34.82	73	32707	2009	6.1424	16.28	9.41
32	87875	756	.8612	116.11	34.11	74	30698	1984	6.4638	15.47	8.99
33	87119	779	.8941	111.84	33.40	75	28714	1970	6.8619	14.57	8.54
34	86340	797	.9233	108.30	32.70	76	26744	1962	7.3363	13.63	8.17
35	85543	811	.9489	105.38	32.00	77	24782	1937	7.8197	12.78	7.78
36	84732	822	.9707	103.01	31.30	78	22845	1898	8.3116	12.03	7.40
37	83910	840	1.0021	99 79	30.60	79	20947	1841	8.8121	11.34	7.04
38	83070	866	1.0431	95.86	29.91	80	19106	1780	9.3213	10.72	6.65
39	82204	899	1.0935	91.44	29.22	81	17326	1704	9.8391	10.16	6.29
40	81305	935	1.1536	84.90	28.53	82	15622	1634	10.4632	9.55	5.92
41	80370	983	1.2231	81.75	27.86	83	13988	1565	11.1934	8.93	5.55
42	79387	1018	1.2833	77.92	27.20	84	12423	1494	12.0298	8.31	5.19
43	78369	1045	1.3343	74.94	26.55	85	10929	1417	12.9724	7.70	4.83
44	77324	1064	1.3760	72 67	25.90	86	9512	1333	14.0211	7.13	4.48
45	76260	1074	1.4084	71.00	25.25	87	8179	1257	15.3587	6.50	4.13
46	75186	1076	1.4315	69.86	24.61	88	6922	1175	16.9850	5.88	3.79
47	74110	1085	1.4653	68.24	23.96	89	5747	1086	18.9002	5.29	3.46
48	73025	1102	1.5096	66.24	23.30	90	4661	983	21.1041	4.73	3.15
49	71923	1125	1.5644	63.92	22.65	91	3678	891	23.5967	4.23	2.77
50	70798	1151	1.6299	61.49	22.01	92	2787	731	26.2601	3.80	2.54
51	69647	1188	1.7058	58.62	21.36	93	2056	598	29.0942	3.43	2.37
52	68459	1213	1.7732	56.42	20.72	94	1458	468	32.0991	3.11	2.14
53	67246	1231	1.8319	54.58	20.09	95	990	349	35.2748	2.83	1.91
54	66015	1242	1.8821	53.13	19.45	96	641	247	38.6212	2.58	1.69
55	64773	1246	1.9237	51.98	18.82	97	394	174	44.2669	2.25	1.43
56	63527	1243	1.9566	51.10	18.18	98	220	114	52.2120	1.91	1.17
57	62284	1262	2.0276	49.31	17.53	99	106	63	60.1571	1.66	.90
58	61022	1303	2.1368	46.79	16.88	100	43	43	100.0000	1.00	.50
59	59719	1364	2.2842	43.77	16.24						

TABLE LXIV.

MORTALITY AND EXPECTATION.—WHEELWRIGHTS.

Age.	Living.	Dying.	Mortality per cent.	Specific Intensity.	Expecta-tion.	Age.	Living.	Dying.	Mortality per cent.	Specific Intensity	Expecta-tion.
18	100000	948	.9480	105.48	42.20	60	56308	2311	4.1056	24.35	13.84
19	99052	887	.8958	111.63	41.60	61	53997	2302	4.2643	23·45	13.41
20	98165	828	.8436	118.53	40.97	62	51695	2296	4.4424	22.51	12.98
21	97337	719	.7393	135.26	40.31	63	49399	2292	4.6398	21.55	12.56
22	96618	648	.6716	148.89	39.61	64	47107	2287	4.8565	20.59	12.15
23	95970	614	.6407	156.07	38.87	65	44820	2282	5.0924	19.63	11.74
24	95356	616	.6464	154.70	38.12	66	42538	2274	5.3473	18.70	11.35
25	94740	652	.6889	145.15	37.36	67	40264	2249	5.5875	17.89	10.96
26	94088	722	.7680	130.20	36.62	68	38015	2211	5.8168	17.19	10.58
27	93366	788	.8440	118.48	35.90	69	35804	2159	6.0315	16.57	10.20
28	92578	848	.9166	106.09	35.20	70	33645	2097	6.2327	16.04	9.83
29	91730	904	.9860	101.41	34.52	71	31548	2025	6.4205	15.57	9.45
30	90826	955	1.0522	95.03	33.87	72	29523	1972	6.6798	14.97	9.06
31	89871	1002	1.1150	89.68	33.21	73	27551	1931	7.0107	14.26	8.67
32	88869	1038	1.1690	85.54	32.58	74	25620	1899	7.4131	13.48	8.29
33	87831	1066	1.2141	82.36	31.96	75	23721	1870	7.8871	12.67	7.91
34	86765	1084	1.2503	79.98	31.35	76	21851	1842	8.4326	11.85	7.55
35	85681	1094	1.2777	78.26	30.74	77	20009	1798	8.9880	11.12	7.20
36	84587	1096	1.2961	77.15	30.13	78	18211	1739	9.5534	10.46	6.97
37	83491	1061	1.2709	78.68	29.52	79	16472	1668	10.1288	9.82	6.53
38	82430	988	1.2021	83.36	28.89	80	14804	1586	10.7141	9.33	6.21
39	81442	887	1.0895	91.78	28.24	81	13218	1494	11.3093	8.64	5.90
40	80555	751	.9333	107.14	27.54	82	11724	1401	11.9503	8.36	5.58
41	79804	585	.7333	136.36	26.80	83	10323	1304	12.6370	7.91	5.27
42	79219	479	.6046	165.39	25.99	84	9019	1207	13.3894	7.46	4.97
43	78740	431	.5473	182.71	25.15	85	7812	1105	14.1475	7.06	4.66
44	78309	439	.5614	178.12	24.28	86	6707	1004	14.9713	6.67	4.34
45	77870	505	.6469	154.37	23.42	87	5703	921	16.1488	0.19	4.02
46	77365	621	.8037	124.42	22.57	88	4782	845	17.6802	5.65	3.70
47	76744	745	.9718	102.90	21.74	89	3937	770	19.5653	5.11	3.39
48	75999	875	1.1513	86.85	20.95	90	3167	690	21.8041	4.58	3.09
49	75124	1008	1.3421	74.51	20.19	91	2477	604	24.3964	4.09	2.81
50	74116	1144	1.5443	64.75	19.41	92	1873	508	27.1290	3.68	2.56
51	72972	1282	1.7578	56.88	18.76	93	1365	403	30.0009	3.37	2.33
52	71690	1428	1.9928	50.18	18.08	94	962	317	33.0125	3.02	2.09
53	70262	1576	2.2492	44.56	17.44	95	645	233	36.1638	2.76	1 88
54	68686	1735	2.5271	39.57	16.87	96	412	162	39.4551	2.53	1.66
55	66951	1892	2.8265	35.37	16.25	97	250	112	44.9838	2.22	1.42
56	65059	2047	3.1473	31.77	15.75	98	138	72	52.7511	1.89	1.17
57	63012	2164	3.4355	29.10	15.21	99	66	39	60.5184	1.65	.90
58	60848	2246	3.6913	27.09	14.73	100	27	27	100.0000	1.00	.50
59	58602	2294	3.9146	25.54	14.27						

TABLE LXV.

MORTALITY AND EXPECTATION.—WOOLCOMBERS.

Age.	Living.	Dying.	Mortality per cent.	Specific Intensity.	Expecta- tion.	Age.	Living.	Dying.	Mortality per cent.	Specific Intensity	Expecta- tion.
18	100000	3707	3.7071	26.97	37.82	60	47105	2725	5.7859	17.28	13 22
19	96293	3231	3.3563	29 79	38.25	61	44380	2303	5.1906	19.26	13.00
20	93062	2796	3.0046	33.28	38.56	62	42077	2016	4.8026	20.82	12.71
21	90266	2077	2 3012	43.45	38.74	63	40061	1851	4.6220	21.63	12.30
22	88189	1531	1.7364	57.59	38.64	64	38210	1776	4.6487	21.51	11.87
23	86658	1135	1.3104	76.31	38.32	65	36434	1778	4.8828	20.48	11.42
24	85523	875	1.0231	97.74	37.82	66	34656	1845	5.3242	18.78	10.98
25	84648	740	.8745	114.35	37.21	67	32811	1875	5.7172	17.49	10.57
26	83908	725	.8647	115.64	36.53	68	30936	1875	6.0617	16.49	10.18
27	83183	710	.8546	117.01	35.84	69	29061	1847	6.3578	15.76	9.81
28	82473	696	.8442	118.45	35.15	70	27214	1797	6.6055	15.13	9.44
29	81777	681	.8336	119.96	34.44	71	25417	1729	6.8047	14.69	9.07
30	81096	667	.8227	121.55	33.73	72	23688	1677	7.0796	14.12	8.70
31	80429	652	.8115	123.22	33.00	73	22011	1635	7.4304	13.45	8.32
32	79777	634	.7950	125.78	32.28	74	20376	1601	7.8569	12.72	7.95
33	79143	611	.7734	129.29	31.53	75	18775	1569	8.3593	11.96	7.59
34	78532	586	.7466	133.94	30.77	76	17206	1537	8.9374	11.18	7.23
35	77946	556	.7146	139.93	30.00	77	15669	1492	9.5261	10.49	6.90
36	77390	524	.6775	147.60	29.21	78	14177	1435	10.1255	9.87	6.57
37	76866	511	.6658	150.19	28.34	79	12742	1367	10.7355	9.31	6.25
38	76355	518	.6796	147.14	27.60	80	11375	1291	11.3561	9.03	5.96
39	75837	545	.7189	139.10	26.77	81	10084	1208	11.9873	8.34	5.64
40	75292	590	.7837	127.60	25.96	82	8876	1124	12.6667	7.89	5.34
41	74702	652	.8739	114.42	25.16	83	7752	1038	13.3941	7.46	5.05
42	74050	676	.9137	109.44	24.38	84	6714	951	14.1697	7.05	4.75
43	73374	662	.9033	110.70	23.60	85	5763	864	14.9934	6.66	4.45
44	72712	612	.8425	118.69	22.81	86	4899	777	15.8651	6.30	4.15
45	72100	527	.7314	136.72	22.00	87	4122	705	17.1055	5.84	3.81
46	71573	408	.5701	175.40	21.16	88	3417	641	18.7104	5.32	3.58
47	71165	376	.5296	188.82	20.28	89	2776	574	20.6920	4.83	3.23
48	70789	431	.6101	163.90	19.38	90	2202	507	23.0381	4.34	2.94
49	70358	570	.8114	123.24	18.50	91	1695	436	25.7527	3.88	2.67
50	69788	791	1.1337	88.20	17.64	92	1259	360	28.6290	3.49	2.43
51	68997	1087	1.5768	63.41	16.84	93	899	284	31.6669	3.15	2.20
52	67910	1434	2.1118	47.35	16.10	94	615	214	34.8665	2.86	2.07
53	66476	1820	2.7387	36.51	15.44	95	401	153	38.2278	2.61	1.79
54	64656	2230	3.4576	28.98	14.86	96	248	103	41.7507	2.39	1.59
55	62426	2664	4.2684	23.42	14.37	97	145	68	47.1894	2.11	1.36
56	59762	3090	5.1711	19.33	13.99	98	77	42	54.5439	1.83	1.13
57	56672	3272	5.7742	17.31	13.76	99	35	21	61.8984	1.61	.90
58	53400	3245	6.0777	16.45	13.54	100	14	14	100.0000	1.00	.50
59	50155	3050	6.0816	16.43	13.38						

P

TABLE LXVI.—TRADES' SICKNESS.

Age.	BAKERS. Weeks	W. D. H.	BLACKSMITHS. Weeks.	W. D. H.	BRICKLAYERS. Weeks.	W. D. H.	BUTCHERS. Weeks.	W. D. H.
18	.4788 =	0 3 8	.5691 =	0 4 0	.4076 =	0 2 21	.2758 =	0 1 22
19	.4763 =	0 3 8	.6015 =	0 4 5	.4469 =	0 3 3	.3139 =	0 2 5
20	.4738 =	0 3 7	.6340 =	0 4 11	.4863 =	0 3 10	.3521 =	0 2 11
21	.4689 =	0 3 7	.6989 =	0 4 21	.5650 =	0 3 23	.4284 =	0 3 0
22	.4714 =	0 3 7	.7509 =	0 5 6	.6294 =	0 4 10	.4832 =	0 3 9
23	.4815 =	0 3 9	.7901 =	0 5 13	.6796 =	0 4 18	.5165 =	0 3 15
24	.4990 =	0 3 12	.8165 =	0 5 17	.7156 =	0 5 0	.5285 =	0 3 17
25	.5241 =	0 3 16	.8300 =	0 5 19	.7373 =	0 5 4	.5189 =	0 3 15
26	.5566 =	0 3 21	.8306 =	0 5 20	.7447 =	0 5 5	.4880 =	0 3 10
27	.5807 =	0 4 2	.8328 =	0 5 20	.7546 =	0 5 7	.4659 =	0 3 6
28	.5966 =	0 4 3	.8366 =	0 5 21	.7671 =	0 5 9	.4527 =	0 3 4
29	.6043 =	0 4 5	.8420 =	0 5 22	.7822 =	0 5 11	.4483 =	0 3 3
30	.6036 =	0 4 6	.8490 =	0 5 23	.7999 =	0 5 14	.4528 =	0 3 4
31	.6347 =	0 4 11	.8576 =	0 6 0	.8201 =	0 5 18	.4661 =	0 3 6
32	.5946 =	0 4 4	.8617 =	0 6 1	.8399 =	0 5 21	.4804 =	0 3 9
33	.6034 =	0 4 5	.8614 =	0 6 1	.8591 =	0 6 0	.4957 =	0 3 11
34	.6211 =	0 4 9	.8566 =	0 6 0	.8779 =	0 6 3	.5120 =	0 3 14
35	.6477 =	0 4 13	.8474 =	0 5 22	.8961 =	0 6 7	.5292 =	0 3 17
36	.6831 =	0 4 19	.8337 =	0 5 20	.9137 =	0 6 9	.5473 =	0 3 20
37	.7571 =	0 5 7	.8381 =	0 5 21	.9315 =	0 6 12	.5849 =	0 4 2
38	.8698 =	1 6 2	.8607 =	0 6 0	.9495 =	0 6 16	.6421 =	0 4 12
39	1.0210 =	1 0 4	.9014 =	0 6 8	.9677 =	0 6 19	.7189 =	0 5 1
40	1.2109 =	1 1 12	.9603 =	0 6 17	.9861 =	0 6 22	.8152 =	0 5 17
41	1.4393 =	1 3 1	1.0373 =	1 0 6	1.0046 =	1 0 1	.9310 =	0 6 12
42	1.5998 =	1 4 4	1.1151 =	1 0 19	1.0436 =	1 0 7	1.0174 =	1 0 3
43	1.6924 =	1 4 20	1.1935 =	1 1 8	1.1031 =	1 0 17	1.0744 =	1 0 12
44	1.7172 =	1 5 0	1.2726 =	1 1 22	1.1831 =	1 1 7	1.0981 =	1 0 16
45	1.6741 =	1 4 17	1.3524 =	1 2 11	1.2836 =	1 2 0	1.1005 =	1 0 17
46	1.5631 =	1 3 23	1.4328 =	1 3 1	1.4046 =	1 2 20	1.0695 =	1 0 12
47	1.4720 =	1 3 7	1.5049 =	1 3 13	1.5154 =	1 3 15	1.0775 =	1 0 13
48	1.4009 =	1 2 20	1.7689 =	1 5 9	1.6162 =	1 4 7	1.1247 =	1 0 21
49	1.3498 =	1 2 10	1.6246 =	1 4 9	1.7068 =	1 4 23	1.2109 =	1 1 12
50	1.3187 =	1 2 5	1.6722 =	1 4 17	1.7874 =	1 5 12	1.3363 =	1 2 8
51	1.3077 =	1 2 4	1.7155 =	1 5 0	1.8578 =	1 6 0	1.5007 =	1 3 12
52	1.2675 =	1 1 20	1.8074 =	1 5 16	1.9829 =	1 6 21	1.6172 =	1 4 8
53	1.1943 =	1 1 9	1.9598 =	1 6 17	2.1627 =	2 1 3	1.6860 =	1 4 19
54	2.3970 =	2 2 19	2.1328 =	2 0 22	2.3970 =	2 2 19	1.7070 =	1 4 23
55	2.6858 =	2 4 19	2.4343 =	2 3 1	2.6858 =	2 4 19	1.6802 =	1 4 18
56	3.0295 =	3 0 5	2.7563 =	2 5 7	3.0295 =	3 0 5	1.6056 =	1 4 6
57	3.6639 =	3 4 16	3.1101 =	3 0 18	3.6639 =	3 4 15	1.7333 =	1 5 3
58	4.5890 =	4 4 3	3.4957 =	3 3 11	4.5890 =	4 4 3	2.0634 =	2 0 11
59	5.8049 =	5 5 15	3.9129 =	3 6 9	5.8049 =	5 5 15	2.5959 =	2 4 4
60	7.3116 =	7 2 4	4.3619 =	4 2 13	7.3116 =	7 2 4	3.3308 =	3 2 7
61	8.9290 =	8 6 12	4.8425 =	4 5 21	8.9290 =	8 6 12	4.2680 =	4 1 21
62	10.2577 =	10 1 22	5.2910 =	5 2 1	10.2577 =	10 1 19	4.2680 =	4 1 21
63	10.7574 =	10 5 7	5.7072 =	5 4 23	10.7574 =	10 5 7	4.2680 =	4 1 21
64	10.6082 =	10 4 6	6.0911 =	6 0 15	10.6082 =	10 4 6	4.2680 =	4 1 21
65	9.8101 =	9 5 16	6.4428 =	6 3 2	9.8101 =	9 5 16	4.2680 =	4 1 21
66	8.3628 =	8 2 13	6.9622 =	6 6 18	8.3628 =	8 2 13	4.2680 =	4 1 21
67	8.8040 =	8 5 16	7.0816 =	7 0 14	8.8040 =	8 5 15	4.2680 =	4 1 21
68	11.1339 =	11 0 23	7.5212 =	7 3 16	11.1339 =	11 0 23	4.2680 =	4 1 21
69	15.3525 =	15 2 11	7.9608 =	7 6 17	15.3525 =	15 2 11	4.2680 =	4 1 21
70	21.4598 =	21 3 5	8.4405 =	8 3 2	21.4598 =	21 3 5	4.2680 =	4 1 21
	178.4129		126.5628		182.1667		84.7572	

TABLE LXVII.—TRADES' SICKNESS.

Age.	CABINET MAKERS, &c.				CLERKS AND SCHOOLMASTERS.				COOPERS.				DYERS.			
	Weeks.	W.	D.	H.	Weeks.	W.	D.	H.	Weeks.	W.	D.	H.	Weeks.	W.	D.	H.
18	.4840 =	0	3	9	.3230 =	0	2	6	.4426 =	0	3	2	.2946 =	0	2	1
19	.5248 =	0	3	16	.3316 =	0	2	8	.4823 =	0	3	9	.3085 =	0	2	4
20	.5657 =	0	3	23	.3402 =	0	2	9	.5221 =	0	3	16	.3224 =	0	2	6
21	.6454 =	0	4	12	.3574 =	0	2	12	.6016 =	0	4	5	.3502 =	0	2	11
22	.7125 =	0	5	0	.3740 =	0	2	15	.6633 =	0	4	15	.3865 =	0	2	17
23	.7611 =	0	5	8	.3901 =	0	2	18	.7071 =	0	4	23	.4315 =	0	3	1
24	.7931 =	0	5	13	.4055 =	0	2	20	.7331 =	0	5	3	.4850 =	0	3	9
25	.8086 =	0	5	16	.4204 =	0	2	23	.7413 =	0	5	5	.5472 =	0	3	20
26	.8076 =	0	5	16	.4346 =	0	3	1	.7317 =	0	5	3	.6179 =	0	4	8
27	.8112 =	0	5	16	.4518 =	0	3	4	.7303 =	0	5	3	.6776 =	0	4	18
28	.8194 =	0	5	18	.4718 =	0	3	7	.7371 =	0	5	4	.7263 =	0	5	2
29	.8323 =	0	5	20	.4948 =	0	3	11	.7521 =	0	5	7	.7639 =	0	5	8
30	.8498 =	0	5	23	.5206 =	0	3	16	.7753 =	0	5	10	.7905 =	0	5	13
31	.8719 =	0	6	2	.5492 =	0	3	20	.8067 =	0	5	15	.8060 =	0	5	16
32	.8899 =	0	6	5	.5780 =	0	4	1	.8555 =	0	6	0	.8204 =	0	5	18
33	.9038 =	0	6	8	.6070 =	0	4	6	.9216 =	0	6	11	.8338 =	0	5	20
34	.9134 =	0	6	10	.6363 =	0	4	11	1.0050 =	1	0	1	.8461 =	0	5	22
35	.9189 =	0	6	11	.6662 =	0	4	16	1.1058 =	1	0	18	.8573 =	0	6	0
36	.9209 =	0	6	11	.6955 =	0	4	21	1.2238 =	1	1	13	.8674 =	0	6	2
37	.9256 =	0	6	12	.7274 =	0	5	2	1.2962 =	1	2	2	.9032 =	0	6	8
38	.9351 =	0	6	13	.7615 =	0	5	8	1.3230 =	1	2	6	.9646 =	0	6	18
39	.9488 =	0	6	15	.7976 =	0	5	14	1.3042 =	1	2	3	1.0517 =	1	0	9
40	.9667 =	0	6	18	.8360 =	0	5	20	1.2398 =	1	1	16	1.1644 =	1	1	4
41	.9886 =	0	6	22	.8764 =	0	6	3	1.1298 =	1	0	22	1.3027 =	1	2	3
42	1.0118 =	1	0	2	.9268 =	0	6	12	1.1254 =	1	0	21	1.4068 =	1	2	21
43	1.0363 =	1	0	6	.9872 =	0	6	22	1.2266 =	1	1	14	1.4767 =	1	3	8
44	1.0620 =	1	0	11	1.0576 =	1	0	10	1.4334 =	1	3	1	1.5124 =	1	3	14
45	1.0890 =	1	0	15	1.1379 =	1	0	23	1.7458 =	1	5	5	1.5139 =	1	3	14
46	1.1172 =	1	0	20	1.2281 =	1	1	14	2.1638 =	2	1	3	1.4811 =	1	3	9
47	1.1472 =	1	1	1	1.3023 =	1	2	3	2.5558 =	2	3	21	1.5132 =	1	3	14
48	1.1788 =	1	1	6	1.3603 =	1	2	13	2.9219 =	2	6	11	1.6104 =	1	4	7
49	1.2122 =	1	1	12	1.4023 =	1	2	20	3.2621 =	3	1	20	1.7725 =	1	5	10
50	1.2473 =	1	1	18	1.4281 =	1	3	0	3.5763 =	3	4	1	1.9999 =	2	0	0
51	1.2840 =	1	2	0	1.4377 =	1	3	1	3.8645 =	3	6	1	2.2918 =	2	2	1
52	1.3530 =	1	2	11	1.4402 =	1	3	2	4.0054 =	4	0	1	2.5265 =	2	3	17
53	1.4543 =	1	3	4	1.4357 =	1	3	1	3.9990 =	4	0	0	2.7037 =	2	4	22
54	1.5879 =	1	4	3	1.4241 =	1	2	23	3.8454 =	3	5	22	2.8235 =	2	5	18
55	1.7537 =	1	5	7	1.4055 =	1	2	20	3.5444 =	3	3	19	2.8858 =	2	6	5
56	1.9517 =	1	6	10	1.3798 =	1	2	16	3.0962 =	3	0	16	2.8906 =	2	6	6
57	2.2586 =	2	1	19	1.3493 =	1	2	11	2.8300 =	2	5	20	3.3258 =	3	2	7
58	2.6745 =	2	4	17	1.3141 =	1	2	5	2.7280 =	2	5	2	4.1916 =	4	1	8
59	3.1994 =	3	1	10	1.2742 =	1	1	22	2.8440 =	2	5	22	5.4877 =	5	3	10
60	3.8333 =	3	5	20	1.2296 =	1	1	15	3.1242 =	3	0·21		7.2143 =	7	1	13
61	4.5761 =	4	4	1	1.1802 =	1	1	6	3.5865 =	3	4	3	9.3713 =	9	2	15
62	5.0031 =	5	0	1	1.1419 =	1	1	0	4.0603 =	4	0	10	12.1123 =	12	0	19
63	5.1145 =	5	0	19	1.1147 =	1	0	19	4.5457 =	4	3	20	15.4374 =	15	3	2
64	4.9102 =	4	6	9	1.0987 =	1	0	16	5.0427 =	5	0	7	19.3465 =	19	2	10
65	4.3901 =	4	2	18	1.0398 =	1	0	7	5.5511 =	5	3	21	23.8396 =	23	5	21
66	3.5544 =	3	3	21	1.0999 =	1	0	16	6.0512 =	6	0	9	28.9167 =	28	6	10
67	3.1406 =	3	1	0	1.1129 =	1	0	19	6.5833 =	6	4	2	31.5270 =	31	3	17
68	3.1487 =	3	1	1	1.1326 =	1	0	22	7.0874 =	7	0	15	31.6700 =	31	4	17
69	3.5788 =	3	4	1	1.1590 =	1	1	3	7.5836 =	7	4	2	29.3470 =	29	2	10
70	4.4308 =	4	3	0	1.1918 =	1	1	8	8.0718 =	8	0	12	24.5568 =	24	3	22
	92.8986				48.8392				132.8871				293.8725			

TABLE LXVIII.—TRADES' SICKNESS.

Age.	HATTERS. Weeks.	W.	D.	H.	LABOURERS. Town and City.) Weeks.	W.	D.	H.	LABOURERS. (Agricultural.) Weeks.	W.	D.	H.	MILLWRIGHTS. Weeks.	W.	D.	H.
18	.3749 =	0	2	15	.5693 =	0	4	0	.5379 =	0	3	18	.3626 =	0	2	13
19	.4094 =	0	2	21	.5898 =	0	4	3	.5648 =	0	3	23	.4034 =	0	2	20
20	.4439 =	0	3	3	.6103 =	0	4	7	.5818 =	0	4	2	.4442 =	0	3	3
21	.5129 =	0	3	14	.6513 =	0	4	13	.6457 =	0	4	12	.5258 =	0	3	16
22	.5650 =	0	3	23	.6916 =	0	4	20	.6918 =	0	4	20	.5910 =	0	4	3
23	.6006 =	0	4	5	.7311 =	0	5	3	.7302 =	0	5	3	.6397 =	0	4	12
24	.6197 =	0	4	8	.7698 =	0	5	9	.7609 =	0	5	8	.6719 =	0	4	17
25	.6223 =	0	4	9	.8077 =	0	5	16	.7839 =	0	5	12	·6876 =	0	4	19
26	.6088 =	0	4	6	.8447 =	0	5	22	.7991 =	0	5	14	.6868 =	0	4	19
27	.6004 =	0	4	5	.8789 =	0	6	4	.8168 =	0	5	17	.6900 =	0	4	20
28	.5968 =	0	4	3	.9101 =	0	6	9	.8369 =	0	5	21	.6973 =	0	4	21
29	.5980 =	0	4	5	.9384 =	0	6	14	.8594 =	0	6	0	.7086 =	0	4	23
30	.6039 =	0	4	5	.9638 =	0	6	18	.8845 =	0	6	5	.7246 =	0	5	2
31	.6141 =	0	4	7	.9862 =	0	6	22	.9119 =	0	6	9	.7434 =	0	5	5
32	.6363 =	0	4	11	1.0096 =	1	0	2	.9401 =	0	6	14	.7621 =	0	5	8
33	.6704 =	0	4	17	1.0338 =	1	0	6	.9691 =	0	6	19	.7801 =	0	5	11
34	.7165 =	0	5	0	1.0589 =	1	0	10	.9989 =	1	0	0	.7973 =	0	5	14
35	.7745 =	0	5	10	1.0849 =	1	0	14	1.0295 =	1	0	5	.8139 =	0	5	17
36	.8444 =	0	5	22	1.1117 =	1	0	19	1.0609 =	1	0	10	.8297 =	0	5	19
37	.9276 =	0	6	12	1.1430 =	1	1	0	1.0893 =	1	0	15	.8633 =	0	6	1
38	1.0242 =	1	0	4	1.1788 =	1	1	6	1.1147 =	1	0	19	.9158 =	0	6	10
39	1.1341 =	1	0	23	1.2190 =	1	1	13	1.1371 =	1	0	23	.9842 =	0	6	21
40	1.2573 =	1	1	19	1.2638 =	1	1	20	1.1566 =	1	1	2	1.0715 =	1	0	12
41	1.3938 =	1	2	18	1.3130 =	1	2	5	1.1730 =	1	1	5	1.1766 =	1	1	6
42	1.5000 =	1	3	12	1.3605 =	1	2	12	1.2059 =	1	1	10	1.2608 =	1	1	20
43	1.5760 =	1	4	1	1.4063 =	1	2	20	1.2552 =	1	1	19	1.3240 =	1	2	6
44	1.6216 =	1	4	8	1.4504 =	1	3	4	1.3029 =	1	2	3	1.3662 =	1	2	14
45	1.6369 =	1	4	11	1.4928 =	1	3	11	1.4031 =	1	2	20	1.3875 =	1	2	17
46	1.6216 =	1	4	8	1.5335 =	1	3	18	1.5016 =	1	3	12	1.3877 =	1	2	17
47	1.6460 =	1	4	13	1.5993 =	1	4	5	1.6053 =	1	4	6	1.4008 =	1	2	20
48	1.7093 =	1	4	23	1.6903 =	1	4	20	1.7141 =	1	5	0	1.4449 =	1	3	3
49	1.8118 =	1	5	16	1.8064 =	1	5	16	1.8280 =	1	5	19	1.5019 =	1	3	12
50	1.9535 =	1	6	16	1.9477 =	1	6	15	1.9471 =	1	6	15	1.5778 =	1	4	1
51	2.1343 =	2	0	23	2.1141 =	2	0	19	2.0712 =	2	0	12	1.6726 =	1	4	17
52	2.3701 =	2	2	14	2.2757 =	2	1	22	2.1700 =	2	1	5	1.7169 =	1	5	0
53	2.6651 =	2	4	16	2.4326 =	2	3	1	2.2436 =	2	1	17	1.7106 =	1	4	23
54	3.0151 =	3	0	3	2.5846 =	2	4	2	2.2920 =	2	2	1	1.6536 =	1	4	14
55	3.4215 =	3	2	23	2.7319 =	2	5	3	2.3151 =	2	2	5	1.5461 =	1	3	20
56	3.9043 =	3	6	8	2.8743 =	2	6	3	2.3131 =	2	2	5	1.3879 =	1	2	17
57	4.1891 =	4	1	8	3.0869 =	3	0	15	2.4617 =	2	3	6	1.2297 =	1	1	15
58	4.2758 =	4	1	22	3.3697 =	3	2	14	2.7609 =	2	5	8	1.0715 =	1	0	12
59	4.1645 =	4	1	4	3.7225 =	3	5	1	3.2108 =	3	1	12	1.0634 =	1	0	11
60	3.8532 =	3	5	23	4.1454 =	4	1	0	3.8113 =	3	5	16	1.0527 =	1	0	9
61	3.3278 =	3	2	7	4.6385 =	4	4	11	4.3625 =	4	2	13				
62	3.2022 =	3	1	10	5.0394 =	5	0	7	5.1760 =	5	1	6				
63	3.4745 =	3	3	8	5.3480 =	5	2	11	5.6522 =	5	4	14				
64	4.1567 =	4	1	2	5.5645 =	5	3	23	5.9909 =	5	6	22				
65	5.2368 =	5	1	16	5.6889 =	5	4	20	6.1922 =	6	1	8				
66	6.7187 =	6	5	1	5.7210 =	5	5	1	6.2560 =	6	1	19				
67	7.9414 =	7	6	14	5.8312 =	5	5	20	7.0602 =	7	0	10				
68	8.9050 =	8	6	8	6.0195 =	6	0	3	8.6049 =	8	4	6				
69	9.6095 =	9	4	6	6.2859 =	6	2	0	10.7701 =	10	5	10				
70	10.0548 =	10	0	9	6.6303 =	6	4	10	13.9158 =	13	6	10				
	128.8469				122.7516				134.4685				44.3334			

TABLE LXIX.—TRADES' SICKNESS.

Age.	MILL OPERATIVES.		MINERS.		PLUMBERS & PAINTERS.		POTTERS.	
	Weeks.	W. D. H.	Weeks.	W. D. H.	Weeks.	W. D. H.	Weeks.	W. D. H.
18	.4303 =	0 3 0	.7801 =	0 5 11	.6629 =	0 4 15	.4082 =	0 2 21
19	.4444 =	0 3 3	.8173 =	0 5 17	.6716 =	0 4 17	.4449 =	0 3 3
20	.4585 =	0 3 5	.8546 =	0 6 0	.6804 =	0 4 18	.4817 =	0 3 9
21	.4867 =	0 3 10	.9291 =	0 6 12	.6979 =	0 4 21	.5552 =	0 3 21
22	.5129 =	0 3 14	.9976 =	0 7 0	.7149 =	0 5 0	.6357 =	0 4 11
23	.5370 =	0 3 18	1.0602 =	1 0 10	.7315 =	0 5 3	.7232 =	0 5 2
24	.5590 =	0 3 22	1.1168 =	1 0 19	.7477 =	0 5 6	.8175 =	0 5 17
25	.5789 =	0 4 1	1.1675 =	1 1 4	.7635 =	0 5 8	.9188 =	0 6 10
26	.5966 =	0 4 4	1.2122 =	1 1 12	.7788 =	0 5 11	1.0269 =	1 0 5
27	.6141 =	0 4 7	1.2548 =	1 1 19	.7888 =	0 5 13	1.1149 =	1 0 19
28	.6312 =	0 4 10	1.2953 =	1 2 2	.7935 =	0 5 14	1.1829 =	1 1 7
29	.6480 =	0 4 13	1.3337 =	1 2 8	.7929 =	0 5 13	1.2309 =	1 1 15
30	.6645 =	0 4 16	1.3699 =	1 2 14	.7869 =	0 5 12	1.2589 =	1 1 19
31	.6806 =	0 4 18	1.4039 =	1 2 20	.7756 =	0 5 10	1.2668 =	1 1 21
32	.6944 =	0 4 21	1.4403 =	1 3 2	.7754 =	0 5 10	1.2749 =	2 1 22
33	.7059 =	0 4 23	1.4790 =	1 3 9	.7864 =	0 5 12	1.2833 =	1 2 0
34	.7151 =	0 5 0	1.5201 =	1 3 16	.8086 =	0 5 16	1.2919 =	1 2 1
35	.7220 =	0 5 1	1.5635 =	1 3 23	.8420 =	0 5 21	1.3007 =	1 2 3
36	.7266 =	0 5 2	1.6092 =	1 4 6	.8865 =	0 6 5	1.3097 =	1 2 4
37	.7439 =	0 5 5	1.6683 =	1 4 16	.9393 =	0 6 14	1.3454 =	1 2 10
38	.7739 =	0 5 10	1.7408 =	1 5 4	1.0004 =	1 0 0	1.4079 =	1 2 21
39	.8166 =	0 5 17	1.8265 =	1 5 19	1 0696 =	1 0 12	1.4971 =	1 3 12
40	.8721 =	0 6 3	1.9257 =	1 6 12	1.1471 =	1 1 1	1.6130 =	1 4 7
41	.9262 =	0 6 12	2.0381 =	2 0 7	1.2327 =	1 1 15	1.7556 =	1 5 7
42	1.0102 =	1 0 2	2.1644 =	2 1 4	1.1441 =	1 1 0	1.9198 =	1 6 10
43	1.0883 =	1 0 15	2.3043 =	2 2 3	1.4811 =	1 3 9	2.1054 =	2 0 18
44	1.1563 =	1 1 2	2.4580 =	2 3 5	1.6439 =	1 4 12	2.3124 =	2 2 5
45	1.2324 =	1 1 15	2.6255 =	2 4 9	1.8325 =	1 5 20	2.5410 =	2 3 19
46	1.3104 =	1 2 4	2.8066 =	2 5 15	2.0467 =	2 0 8	2.7909 =	2 5 13
47	1.3943 =	1 2 18	2.9621 =	2 6 18	2.2375 =	2 1 16	2.9844 =	2 6 23
48	1.4839 =	1 3 9	3.0920 =	3 0 16	2.4049 =	2 2 20	3.1216 =	3 0 20
49	1.5792 =	1 4 2	3.1963 =	3 1 9	2.5489 =	2 3 20	3.2024 =	3 1 10
50	1.6804 =	1 4 18	3.2751 =	3 1 22	2.6696 =	2 4 17	3.2268 =	3 1 14
51	1.7872 =	1 5 12	3.3282 =	3 2 7	2.7668 =	2 5 9	3.1948 =	3 1 9
52	1.9565 =	1 6 17	3.4505 =	3 3 4	2.8960 =	2 6 7	3.0421 =	3 0 7
53	2.1880 =	2 1 8	3.6420 =	3 4 12	3.0570 =	3 0 10	3.3759 =	3 2 15
54	2.4823 =	2 3 9	3.9025 =	3 6 8	3.2499 =	3 1 18	3.5746 =	3 4 1
55	2.8388 =	2 5 21	4.2323 =	4 1 15	3.4747 =	3 3 8	3.8598 =	3 6 0
56	3.2576 =	3 1 19	4.6311 =	4 4 10	3.7313 =	3 5 3	4.2243 =	4 1 14
57	3.6623 =	3 4 15	5.0832 =	5 0 14	3.9030 =	3 6 8	5.0554 =	5 0 9
58	4.0530 =	4 0 9	5.5887 =	5 4 3	3.9897 =	3 6 22	6.3528 =	6 2 11
59	4.4297 =	4 3 0	6.1474 =	6 1 1	3.9914 =	3 6 23	8.1167 =	8 0 20
60	4.7924 =	4 5 13	6.7595 =	6 5 8	3.9081 =	3 6 9	10.3471 =	10 2 10
61	5.1410 =	5 1 0	7.4248 =	7 3 23	3.7398 =	3 5 4	13.0438 =	13 0 7
62	5.2569 =	5 1 19	8.1800 =	8 1 6	3.7570 =	3 5 7	15.5037 =	15 3 13
63	5.1399 =	5 1 0	9.0249 =	9 0 4	3.9597 =	3 6 17	17.7268 =	17 5 2
64	4.7902 =	4 5 13	9.9597 =	9 6 17	4.3479 =	4 2 10	19.7130 =	19 5 0
65	4.2078 =	4 1 11	10.9843 =	10 6 21	4.9216 =	4 6 11	21.4264 =	21 3 6
66	3.3925 =	3 2 18	12.0986 =	12 0 17	5.7609 =	5 5 8	22.9749 =	22 6 20
67	3.6316 =	3 4 10	13.3722 =	13 2 15	6.4404 =	6 3 2	25.2249 =	25 1 14
68	4.9252 =	4 6 12	14.8049 =	14 5 15	7.2001 =	7 1 10	28.2124 =	28 1 12
69	7.2733 =	7 1 22	16.3969 =	16 2 19	7.9600 =	7 6 17	31.9374 =	31 6 14
70	10.6759 =	10 4 18	18.1480 =	18 1 1	8.7600 =	8 5 8	36.4000 =	36 2 20
	113.3569		224.4485		129.6994		333.6935	

TABLE LXX.—TRADES' SICKNESS.

Age.	PRINTERS AND COM-POSITORS. Weeks.	W. D. H.	SAWYERS. Weeks.	W. D. H.	SPINNERS. Weeks.	W. D. H.	SERVANTS, FOOTMEN, &c. Weeks.	W. D. H.
18	.3076 =	0 2 4	.6194 =	0 4 8	.6627 =	0 4 15	.4443 =	0 3 3
19	.3411 =	0 2 9	.6249 =	0 4 9	.6553 =	0 4 14	.4560 =	0 3 5
20	.3747 =	0 2 15	.6304 =	0 4 10	.6479 =	0 4 13	.4677 =	0 3 7
21	.4418 =	0 3 2	.6414 =	0 4 12	.6331 =	0 4 11	.4911 =	0 3 10
22	.4949 =	0 3 11	.6551 =	0 4 14	.6270 =	0 4 9	.5114 =	0 3 14
23	.5341 =	0 3 18	.6715 =	0 4 17	.6296 =	0 4 10	.5287 =	0 3 17
24	.5593 =	0 3 22	.6908 =	0 4 20	.6409 =	0 4 12	.5430 =	0 3 19
25	.5705 =	0 4 0	.7127 =	0 5 0	.6609 =	0 4 15	.5543 =	0 3 21
26	.5677 =	0 3 23	.7377 =	0 5 4	.6896 =	0 4 20	.5625 =	0 3 23
27	.5729 =	0 4 0	.7607 =	0 5 8	.7179 =	0 5 1	.5738 =	0 4 0
28	.5861 =	0 4 3	.7827 =	0 5 12	.7457 =	0 5 5	.5880 =	0 4 3
29	.6073 =	0 4 6	.8034 =	0 5 15	.7730 =	0 5 10	.6052 =	0 4 6
30	.6365 =	0 4 11	.8229 =	0 5 18	.7999 =	0 5 14	.6254 =	0 4 9
31	.6737 =	0 4 17	.8411 =	0 5 21	.8262 =	0 5 19	.6485 =	0 4 13
32	.7082 =	0 4 23	.8689 =	0 6 2	.8529 =	0 5 23	.6745 =	0 4 17
33	.7401 =	0 5 4	.9063 =	0 6 8	.8800 =	0 6 4	.7035 =	0 4 22
34	.7693 =	0 5 9	1.0613 =	1 0 10	.9075 =	0 6 9	.7353 =	0 5 4
35	.7959 =	0 5 14	1.2259 =	1 1 14	.9354 =	0 6 13	.7701 =	0 5 10
36	.8198 =	0 5 18	1.2921 =	1 2 1	.9636 =	0 6 18	.8077 =	0 5 16
37	.8511 =	0 5 23	1.3453 =	1 2 10	1.0172 =	1 0 3	.8415 =	0 5 21
38	.8895 =	0 6 6	1.3857 =	1 2 17	1.0960 =	1 0 16	.8716 =	0 6 2
39	.9352 =	0 6 13	1.3051 =	1 2 3	1.2002 =	1 1 10	.8980 =	0 6 7
40	.9882 =	0 6 22	1.2117 =	1 1 12	1.3297 =	1 2 7	.9206 =	0 6 11
41	1.0483 =	1 0 8	1.2133 =	1 1 12	1.4844 =	1 3 9	.9394 =	0 6 14
42	1.1429 =	1 1 0	1.2373 =	1 1 16	1.6188 =	1 4 8	.9586 =	0 6 17
43	1.2718 =	1 1 22	1.2835 =	1 2 0	1.7329 =	1 5 3	.9782 =	0 6 20
44	1.4352 =	1 3 1	1.3520 =	1 2 11	1.8265 =	1 5 19	.9983 =	0 6 23
45	1.6331 =	1 4 11	1.4428 =	1 3 2	1.8998 =	1 6 7	1.0188 =	1 0 3
46	1.8653 =	1 6 1	1.5558 =	1 3 21	1.9526 =	1 6 16	1.0397 =	1 0 6
47	2.1681 =	2 0 18	1.6258 =	1 4 9	2.0481 =	2 0 8	1.0775 =	1 0 13
48	2.3611 =	2 2 13	1.6528 =	1 4 14	2.1862 =	2 1 7	1.3320 =	1 2 8
49	2.6247 =	2 4 9	1.6368 =	1 4 11	2.3670 =	2 2 14	1.2032 =	1 1 10
50	2.8991 =	2 6 7	1.5779 =	1 4 1	2.5904 =	2 4 3	1.2913 =	1 2 1
51	3.1836 =	3 1 7	1.4760 =	1 3 8	2.8564 =	2 6 0	1.3960 =	1 2 19
52	3.3484 =	3 2 11	1.3913 =	1 2 18	3.0976 =	3 0 16	1.5473 =	1 3 20
53	3.3935 =	3 2 18	1.3240 =	1 2 6	3.3138 =	3 2 5	1.7452 =	1 5 5
54	3.3189 =	3 2 6	1.2739 =	1 1 22	3.5051 =	3 3 13	1.9897 =	1 6 22
55	3.1247 =	3 0 21	1.2411 =	1 1 16	3.6715 =	3 4 17	2.2808 =	2 1 23
56	2.8108 =	2 5 16	1.2256 =	1 1 14	3.8129 =	3 5 17	2.6184 =	2 4 8
57	2.8325 =	2 5 20	1.2254 =	1 1 14	3.9900 =	3 6 22	2.9294 =	2 6 12
58	3.1899 =	3 1 8	1.2405 =	1 1 16	4.2028 =	4 1 10	3.2137 =	3 1 12
59	3.8838 =	3 6 5	1.2709 =	1 1 21	4.4514 =	4 3 4	3.4713 =	3 3 7
60	4.9118 =	4 6 9	1.3166 =	1 2 5	4.7357 =	4 5 4	3.7022 =	3 4 22
61	6.2762 =	6 1 23	1.3776 =	1 2 15	5.0557 =	5 0 9	3.9063 =	3 6 8
62	7.3542 =	7 2 12	1.7379 =	1 5 4	5.4766 =	5 3 8	4.7169 =	4 5 0
63	8.1458 =	8 1 1	2.3975 =	2 2 19	5.9983 =	5 6 23	6.1342 =	6 0 23
64	8.6510 =	8 4 13	3.3562 =	3 2 12	6.6208 =	6 4 8	8.1580 =	8 1 3
65	8.8697 =	8 6 2	4.6142 =	4 4 7	7.3441 =	7 2 10	10.7885 =	10 5 13
66	8.8020 =	8 5 15	6.5713 =	6 4 0	8.1681 =	8 1 4	14.0255 =	14 0 4
67	9.6514 =	9 4 14	7.3970 =	7 2 19	9.7428 =	9 5 5	14.0255 =	14 0 4
68	11.4180 =	11 2 22	8.3513 =	8 2 11	12.0683 =	12 0 12	14.0255 =	14 0 4
69	14.1017 =	14 0 17	8.8142 =	8 5 17	15.1446 =	15 1 0	14.0255 =	14 0 4
70	17.7026 =	17 4 22	9.2856 =	9 2 0	18.9716 =	18 6 19	14.0255 =	14 0 4
	168.1256		102.0631		170.8270		154.3851	

TABLE LXXI.—TRADES' SICKNESS.

Age.	SHOEMAKERS.		SHOEMAKERS. W. D. H.	STONEMASONS.		STONEMASONS. W. D. H	TAILORS.		TAILORS. W. D. H.	WEAVERS.		WEAVERS. W. D. H.
	Weeks	W.	D. H.	Weeks.	W.	D. H	Weeks.	W.	D. H.	Weeks.	W.	D. H.
18	.5184 =	0	3 15	.7325 =	0	5 3	.4320 =	0	3 1	.4962 =	0	3 11
19	.5661 =	0	3 23	.7295 =	0	5 2	.4678 =	0	3 7	.5359 =	0	3 18
20	.6138 =	0	4 7	.7264 =	0	5 2	.5037 =	0	3 13	.5757 =	0	4 1
21	.7092 =	0	4 23	.7203 =	0	5 1	.5754 =	0	4 1	.6552 =	0	4 14
22	.7808 =	0	5 11	.7188 =	0	5 1	.6357 =	0	4 11	.7180 =	0	5 1
23	.8288 =	0	5 19	.7219 =	0	5 1	.6847 =	0	4 19	.7641 =	0	5 8
24	.8529 =	0	5 23	.7297 =	0	5 3	.7223 =	0	5 1	.7934 =	0	5 13
25	.8534 =	0	5 23	.7421 =	0	5 5	.7486 =	0	5 6	.8060 =	0	5 16
26	.8301 =	0	5 20	.7591 =	0	5 8	.7635 =	0	5 8	.8018 =	0	5 15
27	.8118 =	0	5 16	.7871 =	0	5 12	.7796 =	0	5 11	.8078 =	0	5 16
28	.7987 =	0	5 14	.8261 =	0	5 19	.7970 =	0	5 14	.8241 =	0	5 18
29	.7906 =	0	5 13	.8761 =	0	6 3	.8155 =	0	5 17	.8506 =	0	5 23
30	.7877 =	0	5 12	.9371 =	0	6 14	.8353 =	0	5 20	.8874 =	0	6 5
31	.7898 =	0	5 12	1.0090 =	1	0 2	.8562 =	0	6 0	.9344 =	0	6 13
32	.7912 =	0	5 13	1.0677 =	1	0 11	.8812 =	0	6 4	.9782 =	0	6 20
33	.7919 =	0	5 13	1.1129 =	1	0 19	.9100 =	0	6 9	1.0186 =	1	0 3
34	.7920 =	0	5 13	1.1448 =	1	1 0	.9428 =	0	6 14	1.0557 =	1	0 9
35	.7914 =	0	5 13	1.1634 =	1	1 4	.9796 =	0	6 20	1.0895 =	1	0 15
36	.7902 =	0	5 13	1.1685 =	1	1 4	1.0202 =	1	0 3	1.1198 =	1	0 20
37	.8012 =	0	5 17	1.1893 =	1	1 8	1.0561 =	1	0 9	1.1454 =	1	1 0
38	.8245 =	0	5 19	1.2256 =	1	1 14	1.0873 =	1	0 15	1.1660 =	1	1 4
39	.8601 =	0	6 0	1.2776 =	1	1 23	1.1138 =	1	0 19	1.1818 =	1	1 6
40	.9080 =	0	6 9	1.3452 =	1	2 10	1.1355 =	1	0 23	1.1928 =	1	1 8
41	.9681 =	0	6 19	1.4283 =	1	3 0	1.1524 =	1	1 2	1.1988 =	1	1 9
42	1.0298 =	1	0 5	1.4972 =	1	3 12	1.1666 =	1	1 4	1.2180 =	1	1 13
43	1.0930 =	1	0 16	1.5520 =	1	3 21	1.1780 =	1	1 6	1.2504 =	1	1 18
44	1.1577 =	1	1 3	1.5925 =	1	4 4	1.1866 =	1	1 7	1.2958 =	1	2 2
45	1.2239 =	1	1 14	1.6189 =	1	4 8	1.1925 =	1	1 8	1.3544 =	1	2 11
46	1.2915 =	1	2 1	1.6310 =	1	4 10	1.1955 =	1	1 9	1.4261 =	1	3 0
47	1.3656 =	1	2 13	1.7232 =	1	5 1	1.2238 =	1	1 14	1.5264 =	1	3 16
48	1.4463 =	1	3 3	1.8955 =	1	6 6	1.2772 =	1	1 23	1.6552 =	1	4 14
49	1.5336 =	1	3 18	2.1478 =	2	1 1	1.3557 =	1	2 12	1.8125 =	1	5 16
50	1.6275 =	1	4 10	2.4802 =	2	3 9	1.4595 =	1	3 5	1.9984 =	1	6 23
51	1.7279 =	1	5 2	2.8926 =	2	6 6	1.5883 =	1	4 3	2.2127 =	2	1 12
52	1.8481 =	1	5 23	3.2658 =	3	1 21	1.7058 =	1	4 22	2.4452 =	2	3 3
53	1.9881 =	1	6 22	3.5998 =	3	4 5	1.8121 =	1	5 17	2.6958 =	2	4 21
54	2.1478 =	2	1 1	3.8944 =	3	6 6	1.9072 =	1	6 8	2.9645 =	2	6 18
55	2.3274 =	2	2 7	4.1499 =	4	1 1	1.9911 =	1	6 22	3.2514 =	3	1 18
56	2.5267 =	2	3 17	4.3660 =	4	2 13	2.0637 =	2	0 11	3.5563 =	3	3 21
57	2.6731 =	2	4 17	4.6942 =	4	4 21	2.1958 =	2	1 9	3.8357 =	3	5 20
58	2.7665 =	2	5 9	5.1346 =	5	0 23	2.3874 =	2	2 17	4.0895 =	4	0 15
59	2.8071 =	2	5 16	5.6872 =	5	4 20	2.6384 =	2	4 10	4.3178 =	4	2 5
60	2.7947 =	2	5 13	6.3520 =	6	2 11	2.9489 =	2	6 15	4.5206 =	4	3 15
61	2.7295 =	2	5 3	7.1289 =	7	0 22	3.3188 =	3	2 6	4.6979 =	4	4 21
62	2.7780 =	2	5 11	7.6746 =	7	4 17	3.6439 =	3	4 12	4.8113 =	4	5 16
63	2.9402 =	2	6 14	7.9891 =	7	6 22	3.9240 =	3	6 11	4.8608 =	4	6 0
64	3.2160 =	3	1 13	8.0722 =	8	0 12	4.1593 =	4	1 3	4.8462 =	4	5 22
65	3.6059 =	3	4 6	7.9241 =	7	6 11	4.3496 =	4	2 11	4.7678 =	4	5 9
66	4.1093 =	4	0 18	7.5446 =	7	3 20	4.4949 =	4	3 11	4.6252 =	4	4 9
67	4.4354 =	4	3 1	7.0400 =	7	0 7	4.6284 =	4	4 10	4.7216 =	4	5 1
68	4.5841 =	4	4 2	6.4104 =	6	2 21	4.7441 =	4	5 5	5.0570 =	5	0 10
69	4.5555 =	4	3 21	5.6557 =	5	4 14	4.8479 =	4	5 22	5.6314 =	5	4 10
70	4.3496 =	4	2 11	4.7760 =	4	5 10	4.9380 =	4	6 14	6.4469 =	6	3 3
	91.5305			153.5294			95.4192			119.4900		

TABLE LXXII.—TRADES' SICKNESS.

Age.	WHEELWRIGHTS.		WOOLCOMBERS.		Age.	WHEELWRIGHTS.		WOOLCOMBERS.	
	Weeks.	W. D. H.	Weeks.	W. D. H.		Weeks.	W. D. H.	Weeks.	W. D. H.
18	.3206 =	0 2 5	1.1659 =	1 1 4	45	.8178 =	0 5 17	1 6761 =	1 4 18
19	.3854 =	0 2 16	1.1669 =	1 1 4	46	.7713 =	0 5 10	1.7159 =	1 5 0
20	.4503 =	0 3 3	1.1680 =	1 1 4	47	.7383 =	0 5 4	1.7700 =	1 5 9
21	.5800 =	0 4 1	1.1700 =	1 1 4	48	.7190 =	0 5 1	1.8985 =	1 6 7
22	.6859 =	0 4 19	1.1581 =	1 1 3	49	.7132 =	0 5 0	1.9214 =	1 6 11
23	.7679 =	0 5 9	1.1450 =	1 1 0	50	.7211 =	0 5 1	2.0187 =	2 0 3
24	.8260 =	0 5 19	1.1308 =	1 0 22	51	.7425 =	0 5 5	2.1303 =	2 0 22
25	.8603 =	0 6 0	1.1026 =	1 0 17	52	.7768 =	0 5 10	2.2875 =	2 2 0
26	.8706 =	0 6 2	1.0669 =	1 0 11	53	.8240 =	0 5 18	2.4902 =	2 3 10
27	.8877 =	0 6 5	1.0605 =	1 0 10	54	.8841 =	0 6 5	2.7384 =	2 5 4
28	.9113 =	0 6 9	1.0834 =	1 0 14	55	.9570 =	0 6 17	3.0321 =	3 0 5
29	9416 =	0 6 14	1.1356 =	1 0 23	56	1.0427 =	1 0 7	3.3713 =	3 2 14
30	.9786 =	0 6 20	1.2171 =	1 1 12	57	1.1141 =	1 0 19	3.8531 =	3 5 23
31	1.0221 =	1 0 4	1.3279 =	1 2 7	58	1.1712 =	1 1 5	4.4778 =	4 3 8
32	1.0609 =	1 0 11	1.4152 =	1 2 22	59	1.2141 =	1 1 12	5.2469 =	5 1 17
33	1.0409 =	1 0 7	1.4789 =	1 3 8	60	1.2427 =	1 1 17	6.1553 =	6 1 2
34	1.0163 =	1 0 3	1.5191 =	1 3 15	61	1.2570 =	1 1 19	7.2081 =	7 1 11
35	.9689 =	0 6 18	1.5357 =	1 3 18	62	1.3770 =	1 2 15	8.0169 =	8 0 3
36	.8988 =	0 6 7	1.5286 =	1 3 17	63	1.6027 =	1 4 5	8.5816 =	8 4 3
37	.8488 =	0 5 22	1.3263 =	1 2 7	64	1.9341 =	1 6 13	8.7022 =	8 4 22
38	.8189 =	0 5 17	1.5286 =	1 3 17	65	2.3713 =	2 2 14	8.9788 =	8 6 20
39	.8091 =	0 5 16	1.5356 =	1 3 18	66	2.9142 =	2 6 10	8.8112 =	8 5 16
40	.8194 =	0 5 17	1.5473 =	1 3 20	67	3.4021 =	‾3 2 20	8.6637 =	8 4 15
41	.8498 =	0 5 22	1.5637 =	1 3 23	68	3.8352 =	3 5 20	8.5365 =	8 3 18
42	.8649 =	0 6 1	1.5847 =	1 4 2	69	4.2133 =	4 1 12	8.4294 =	8 3 0
43	.8646 =	0 6 1	1.6105 =	1 4 6	70	4.5366 =	4 3 18	8.3426 =	8 2 9
44	.8489 =	0 5 22	1.6409 =	1 4 12					
						64.0919		166.9683	

SECTION V.

————

MORTALITY AND SICKNESS EXPERIENCED IN VARIOUS LOCALITIES.

————

In a former portion of the work, it is stated that in analysing the Returns, the various localities were kept separate and distinct; it is now intended to direct attention to the Rate of Mortality and Average Sickness experienced in some of the Towns and Cities, the Town and Rural Districts of Lancashire and Yorkshire, and the Rural Districts of other counties. The following tables give the number of persons, deaths, and amount of sickness in periods of years, and the mean rate of mortality, and average amount of sickness for the mean period opposite to which the same is placed.

The experience of the large towns and cities includes those lodges only which are held in the towns and cities named; the counties of Gloucester, Northampton, rural parts of Lancashire and Yorkshire, include lodges held in the rural parts of those counties; the town districts of Lancashire and Yorkshire include all lodges in the town districts; the city district of Lancashire includes all those towns named at the head of Table LXXVI., Liverpool having been purposely excluded; and Scotland and Wales include all lodges wherever held in those places, whether in the rural, town, or city districts.

As these tables comprise a less amount of experience than the general results, it must be expected that the rate of mortality and average sickness will be more fluctuating than in a larger body; and it is surprising that the increase in the rate of mortality, and average sickness, more especially in the latter, should be so regular and uniform, with the small number of lives.

It is well known, by those who pay attention to the various returns published from time to time, how many persons are comprised in the various districts, and as a difference appears between those returns, and these now presented, it may be as well to explain that the returns here given embrace the whole of the members for three years, of the respective periods of life, but for one portion of the district only; as, for instance, all the members belonging to lodges which are held in the town of Birmingham, and whose returns were received, are included therein, and the same applies to any other city or town.

Q

TABLE LXXIII.

BIRMINGHAM —CITY DISTRICT.

Age.			No. of Persons.	DEATHS.		SICKNESS.	
				In Periods.	Per Cent.	In Periods.	Per Annum.
18	to	20	63	..	.0000	44.427	.7051
20	"	25	658	6	.9118	442.569	.6725
25	"	30	1628	19	1.1670	1208.140	.7421
30	"	35	1816	16	.8810	1398.141	.7699
35	"	40	1659	16	.9756	1672.426	1.0197
40	"	45	996	14	1.4056	1433.427	1.4391
45	"	50	431	8	1.8561	833.713	1.9343
50	"	55	68	3	4.4147	72.998	1.0715
55	"	60	8	..	0.0000	0.000	0.0000
60	"	65	1	..	0.0000	0.000	0.0000
			7328	82	1.1189	7105.841	.9696

BOLTON.—CITY DISTRICT.

Age.			No. of Persons.	DEATHS.		SICKNESS.	
				In Periods.	Per Cent.	In Periods.	Per Annum.
18	to	20	88	..	.0000	52.857	.6006
20	"	25	893	9	1.0078	495.569	.5549
25	"	30	1294	11	.8500	907.713	.7014
30	"	35	1175	7	.5957	816.141	.6945
35	"	40	1080	9	.8333	612.427	.5670
40	"	45	735	8	1.0884	1087.285	1.4792
45	"	50	517	6	1.1605	1386.570	2.6819
50	"	55	242	8	3.3057	594.570	2.4569
55	"	60	97	3	3.0927	418.712	4.3166
60	"	65	39	1	2.5641	307.427	7.8826
65	"	70	9	1	11.1111	103.000	11.4444
70	"	75	3	..	0.0000	1.000	.3333
			6172	63	1.0207	6783.271	1.0990

BRADFORD.—CITY DISTRICT.

Age.			No. of Persons.	DEATHS.		SICKNESS.	
				In Periods.	Per Cent.	In Periods.	Per Annum.
18	to	20	94	..	.0000	14.999	.1592
20	"	25	800	2	.2500	702.855	.8785
25	"	30	1484	11	.7078	1295.712	.8731
30	"	35	1553	12	.7726	1553.570	1.0003
35	"	40	1248	9	.7211	1128.427	.9041
40	"	45	859	10	1.1641	1302.999	1.5178
45	"	50	590	8	1.3590	950.998	1.6118
50	"	55	237	5	2.1096	573.426	2.3773
55	"	60	64	3	4.6875	144.569	2.2587
60	"	65	23	..	0.0000	306.284	13.3165
65	"	70	...	..	0.0000	0.000	0.0000
70	"	75	2	1	50.0000	42.714	21.3570
			6954	61	.8771	8016.553	1.1527

TABLE LXXIV.

BRISTOL.—CITY DISTRICT.

Age.			No. of Persons.	DEATHS.		SICKNESS.	
				In Periods.	Per Cent.	In Periods.	Per Annum.
18	to	20	24		.0000	15.000	.6250
20	"	25	573	4	.6980	381.998	.6666
25	"	30	1501	21	1.3990	1545.711	1.0297
30	"	35	1350	11	.8148	1106.140	.8193
35	"	40	925	4	.4324	1250.855	1.3522
40	"	45	173	..	.0000	327.142	1.8909
45	"	50	41	..	.0000	108.283	2.6409
50	"	55	2	..	.0000	8.142	4.0710
			4589	40	.8716	4743.271	1.0336

BURY.—CITY DISTRICT.

Age.			No. of Persons.	DEATHS.		SICKNESS.	
				In Periods.	Per Cent.	In Periods.	Per Annum.
18	to	20	49	1	2.0408	18.000	.3673
20	"	25	670	6	.8955	403.569	.6023
25	"	30	978	12	1.2269	745.140	.7619
30	"	35	981	10	1.0193	1134.997	1.1569
35	"	40	834	5	.5995	815.712	.9780
40	"	45	536	6	1.1194	843.855	1.5743
45	"	50	377	4	1.0610	819.999	2.1750
50	"	55	236	8	3.3898	686.284	2.9079
55	"	60	66	1	1.5151	228.855	3.4629
60	"	65	34	..	0.0000	126.284	3.7141
65	"	70	7	..	0.0000	13.714	1.9591
70	"	75	1	..	0.0000	1.000	1.0000
			4769	53	1.0131	5837.409	1.1159

GLASGOW—CITY DISTRICT3.

Age.			No. of Persons.	DEATHS.		SICKNESS.	
				In Periods.	Per Cent.	In Periods.	Per Annum.
18	to	20	70	..	.0000	19.427	.2775
20	"	25	652	8	1.2269	533.141	.8176
25	"	30	1417	23	1.6250	1659.998	1.1714
30	"	35	1461	29	1.9849	1988.283	1.3609
35	"	40	1116	24	2.1505	1708.999	1.5313
40	"	45	418	13	3.1100	833.283	1.9934
45	"	50	95	3	3.1578	283.570	2.9849
50	"	55	2	..	0.0000	....	0.0000
			5231	100	1.9116	7026.701	1.3432

TABLE LXXV.

GLOUCESTERSHIRE.—RURAL DISTRICTS.

AGE.			No. of Persons.	DEATHS.		SICKNESS.	
				In Periods.	Per Cent.	In Periods.	Per Annum.
18	to	20	114	..	.0000	47.999	.4210
20	"	25	983	7	.7121	599.141	.6095
25	"	30	1505	16	1.0631	1136.141	.7548
30	"	35	1313	13	.9901	1098.996	.8369
35	"	40	1001	7	.6993	693.713	.6930
40	"	45	264	1	.3787	230.712	.8739
45	"	50	48	1	2.0833	208.140	.4336
50	"	55	16	..	0.0000	24.570	1.5356
55	"	60	2	..	0.0000	0.000	0.0000
			5246	45	.8577	4039.412	.7664

LANCASHIRE.—RURAL DISTRICTS.

AGE.			No. of Persons.	DEATHS.		SICKNESS.	
				In Periods.	Per Cent.	In Periods.	Per Annum.
18	to	20	771	2	.2594	315.713	.4094
20	"	25	4441	39	.8781	3484.141	.7845
25	"	30	6272	57	.9088	4844.140	.7723
30	"	35	5399	49	.9075	4945.711	.9160
35	"	40	4368	31	.7097	4798.711	1.0984
40	"	45	3005	40	1.3311	3374.141	1.1227
45	"	50	2088	31	1.4846	3214.142	1.5393
50	"	55	866	20	2.3094	1942.284	2.2428
55	"	60	376	8	3.1277	1055.998	2.8085
60	"	65	155	5	2.2257	858.140	5.5363
65	"	70	65	2	3.0769	492.570	7.5780
70	"	75	20	..	0.0000	169.000	8.4500
75	"	80	5	..	0.0000	5.000	1.0000
80	"	85	1	1	100.0000	20.428	20.4280
			27832	285	1.0247	29520.119	1.0614

LANCASHIRE.—TOWN DISTRICTS.

AGE.			No. of Persons.	DEATHS.		SICKNESS.	
				In Periods.	Per Cent.	In Periods.	Per Annum.
18	to	20	1252	12	.9584	826.141	.6598
20	"	25	8160	68	.8333	6086.712	.7459
25	"	30	11603	106	.9135	9502.713	.8189
30	"	35	10467	92	.8789	9471.426	.9048
35	"	40	8996	95	1.0560	8699.854	.9670
40	"	45	6330	60	.9478	7849.283	1.2400
45	"	50	4556	64	1.3923	7027.569	1.5531
50	"	55	2390	52	2.1757	4592.283	1.9214
55	"	60	1330	41	3.0827	3990.712	3.0005
60	"	65	492	24	4.7880	2192.426	4.4561
65	"	70	156	10	6.4102	993.854	6.3708
70	"	75	47	...	0.0000	596.571	12.7930
75	"	80	16	1	6.2500	430.856	26.8750
80	"	85	7	1	14.2857	117.000	16.7142
			55802	626	1.1218	62377.400	1.1178

TABLE LXXVI.

LANCASHIRE.—CITY DISTRICTS.

ASHTON-UNDER-LYNE, BLACKBURN, BOLTON, BURY, MANCHESTER, OLDHAM, PRESTON, ROCHDALE,

SALFORD, WIGAN.

Age.			No. of Persons.	DEATHS.		SICKNESS.	
				In Periods.	Per Cent.	In Periods.	Per Annum.
18	to	20	650	3	.2812	290.570	.4470
20	,,	25	5580	44	.7885	3346.713	.5997
25	,,	30	8589	80	.9314	5892.569	.6860
30	,,	35	8012	72	.8986	6167.426	.7697
35	,,	40	6957	68	.9774	6419.428	.9227
40	,,	45	4622	73	1.5794	6174.427	1.3358
45	,,	50	3187	50	1.5688	5855.713	1.8373
50	,,	55	1638	51	3.1135	4326.854	2.6415
55	,,	60	776	18	2.3195	3078.426	3.9670
60	,,	65	324	12	3.7037	1979.426	6.1085
65	,,	70	113	10	8.8495	879.854	7.7862
70	,,	75	29	...	0.0000	373.713	12.8865
75	,,	80	11	1	9.9999	189.426	17.2205
80	,,	85	6	...	0.0000	119.000	19.8333
85	,,	90	1	...	0.0000	....	0.0000
			40495	482	1.1902	45093.545	1.1135

LEEDS.—CITY DISTRICT.

Age.			No. of Persons.	DEATHS.		SICKNESS.	
				In Periods.	Per Cent.	In Periods.	Per Annum.
18	to	20	61	...	.0000	19.570	.3223
20	,,	25	700	5	.7142	366.141	.5230
25	,,	30	1368	8	.5846	938.855	.6862
30	,,	35	1588	11	.6926	1209.977	.7619
35	,,	40	1280	7	.5468	1477.856	1.1545
40	,,	45	1076	15	1.3940	1662.856	1.5453
45	,,	50	857	18	2.1003	1697.141	1.9802
50	,,	55	416	14	3.3653	944.713	2.2709
55	,,	60	118	2	1.6949	514.283	4.3583
60	,,	65	21	...	0.0000	126.426	6.0200
65	,,	70	8	...	0.0000	58.571	7.3213
70	,,	75	2	...	0.0000	52.142	26.0710
75	,,	80	4	1	25.0000	82.713	20.6782
			7499	81	1.0801	9151.264	1.2203

TABLE LXXVII.

LIVERPOOL.—CITY DISTRICT.

Age.	No. of Persons.	DEATHS.		SICKNESS.	
		In Periods.	Per Cent.	In Periods.	Per Annum.
18 to 20	47	..	.0000	23.142	.4923
20 " 25	669	10	1.4947	529.712	.7917
25 " 30	2200	29	1.3181	2181.998	.9917
30 " 35	3086	41	1.3285	3101.140	1.0055
35 " 40	2662	59	2.2153	3453.855	1.2974
40 " 45	1574	41	2.6048	2504.998	1.5914
45 " 50	647	21	3.2457	1596.712	2.4678
50 " 55	69	3	4.3478	136.426	1.9680
55 " 60	6	..	0.0000	5.285	.8808
	10960	204	1.8613	13533.268	1.2346

SOUTH LONDON.—CITY DISTRICT.

Age.	No. of Persons.	DEATHS.		SICKNESS.	
		In Periods.	Per Cent.	In Periods.	Per Annum.
18 to 20	117	..	.0000	41.427	.3540
20 " 25	1502	12	.7989	1069.284	.7102
25 " 30	3081	29	.9412	2485.997	.8068
30 " 35	2775	25	.9009	2164.712	.7800
35 " 40	1604	20	1.2469	1652.569	1.0302
40 " 45	421	10	2.3753	611.283	1.4519
45 " 50	89	3	3.3707	99.854	1.1219
50 " 55	11	2	18.1818	9.998	.9890
55 " 60	7	..	0.0000	4.000	.5714
60 " 65	2	..	0.0000	0.000	.0000
65 " 70	2	..	0.0000	0.000	.0000
70 " 75	1	1	100.0000	4.571	4.5714
	9612	102	1.0611	8143.695	.8472

NORTH LONDON.—CITY DISTRICT.

Age.	No. of Persons.	DEATHS.		SICKNESS.	
		In Periods.	Per Cent.	In Periods.	Per Annum.
18 to 20	216	..	.0000	105.428	.4880
20 " 25	2321	12	.5170	1417.284	.6106
25 " 30	4793	34	.7093	3583.141	.7475
30 " 35	4097	33	.8054	3144.712	.7675
35 " 40	2298	23	1.0008	2435.426	1.0597
40 " 45	548	10	1.8248	897.856	1.6384
45 " 50	146	4	2.7397	234.570	1.6066
50 " 55	22	1	4.5454	66.426	3.1936
55 " 60	11	..	0.0000	35.713	3.2466
60 " 65	2	..	0.0000	27.857	13.9285
	14451	117	.8094	11948.413	.8266

TABLE LXXVIII.

NORTHAMPTON COUNTY.—RURAL DISTRICTS.

Age.			No. of Persons.	DEATHS.		SICKNESS.	
				In Periods.	Per Cent.	In Periods.	Per Annum.
18	to	20	269	2	.7434	183.569	.6823
20	"	25	1941	9	.4636	1285.141	.6620
25	"	30	2356	15	.6366	1628.567	.6911
30	"	35	1741	10	.5743	1245.855	.7155
35	"	40	1261	15	1.1895	1023.285	.8114
40	"	45	362	4	1.1049	444.141	1.1189
45	"	50	96	1	1.0416	89.282	.9300
50	"	55	7	..	0.0000	13.713	1.9590
			8033	56	.6936	5913.553	.7361

OLDHAM.—CITY DISTRICT.

Age.			No. of Persons.	DEATHS.		SICKNESS.	
				In Periods.	Per Cent.	In Periods.	Per Annum.
18	to	20	107	..	.0000	65.714	.6141
20	"	25	740	5	.6756	474.283	.6409
25	"	30	989	10	1.0111	719.142	.7271
30	"	35	1059	12	1.1331	709.999	.6704
35	"	40	1039	15	1.4435	782.714	.7532
40	"	45	895	12	1.3407	1195.712	1.3359
45	"	50	662	13	1.9637	1037.855	1.9427
50	"	55	425	14	3.2941	1286.142	3.0887
55	"	60	257	5	1.9455	1312.713	5.1077
60	"	65	151	7	4.6357	781.571	5.1759
65	"	70	44	2	4.5454	221.428	5.0322
70	"	75	11	..	0.0000	186.142	16.9220
75	"	80	7	1	14.2857	133.284	19.0405
80	"	85	3	..	0.0000	11.000	3.6666
85	"	90	1	..	0.0000	0.000	0.0000
			6390	96	1.5023	8917.699	1.3955

ROCHDALE.—CITY DISTRICT.

Age.			No. of Persons.	DEATHS.		SICKNESS.	
				In Periods.	Per Cent.	In Periods.	Per Annum.
18	to	20	130	..	.0000	67.142	.5164
20	"	25	844	7	.8293	599.856	.7107
25	"	30	1088	9	.8272	599.285	.5508
30	"	35	968	7	.9103	1080.140	1.1158
35	"	40	750	9	1.2000	859.998	1.1465
40	"	45	495	6	1.2120	728.427	1.4715
45	"	50	431	9	2.0881	488.713	1.1338
50	"	55	225	6	2.6666	514.713	2.2876
55	"	60	110	1	.8986	342.998	3.1181
60	"	65	27	3	11.1111	217.142	8.0421
65	"	70	14	4	28.5713	282.284	20.1620
70	"	75	2	..	0.0000	7.000	3.5000
			5084	61	1.1998	5787.698	1.1383

TABLE LXXIX.

SCOTLAND.—RURAL, TOWN, AND CITY DISTRICTS.

Age.	No. of Persons.	DEATHS.		SICKNESS.	
		In Periods.	Per Cent.	In Periods.	Per Annum.
18 to 20	414	1	2415	202.713	.4896
20 ,, 25	3982	48	1.2054	3617.854	.9085
25 ,, 30	6568	64	.9744	6006.570	.9145
80 ,, 35	5956	73	1.2256	5694.712	.9561
35 ,, 40	4176	55	1.3170	4528.712	1.0844
40 ,, 45	1362	23	1.6885	1812.998	1.3311
45 ,, 50	286	5	1.7482	533.142	1.8641
50 ,, 55	9	...	0.0000	1.428	0.1586
	22753	269	1.1822	22398.129	.9842 ·

SHEFFIELD.—CITY DISTRICT.

Age.	No. of Persons.	DEATHS.		SICKNESS.	
18 to 20	41	...	.0000	7.000	.1707
20 ,, 25	445	3	.6741	506.425	1.1381
25 ,, 30	1007	9	.8937	956.141	.8922
30 ,, 35	1122	11	.9803	1120.283	.9984
35 ,, 40	1002	16	1.5968	953.283	.9513
40 ,, 45	787	13	1.6518	1449.570	1.8418
45 ,, 50	544	18	3.3088	1433.140	3.1036
50 ,, 55	174	6	3.4482	577.570	3.3193
55 ,, 60	59	2	3.3898	383.998	6.5083
60 ,, 65	4	...	0.0000	104.284	26.0710
65 ,, 70	6	2	33.3333	135.856	22.6426
70 ,, 75	1	1	100.0000	1.285	1.2850
75 ,, 80	1	...	0.0000	52.142	52.1420
80 ,, 85	2	1	50.0000	84.142	42.0710
	5195	82	1.5784	7765.119	1.4947

STOCKPORT.—CITY DISTRICT.

Age.	No. of Persons.	DEATHS.		SICKNESS.	
18 to 20	38	...	.0000	6.000	.1578
20 ,, 25	478	3	.6276	271.712	.5684
25 ,, 30	809	8	.9888	614.569	.7596
30 ,, 35	885	5	.5649	969.856	1.0958
35 ,, 40	863	9	1.2178	870.569	1.1780
40 ,, 45	739	12	1.6238	985.141	1.3330
45 ,, 50	479	8	1.6701	695.140	1.4512
50 ,, .55	235	9	3.8297	712.569	3.0321
55 ,, 60	72	3	4.1666	696.998	9.6804
60 ,, 65	19	...	0.0000	137.000	7.2105
65 ,, 70	2	1	50.0000	30.428	15.2140
70 ,, 75	1	...	0.0000	0.000	0.0000
75 ,, 80	2	...	0.0000	58.142	29.0710
	4622	58	1.2548	6048.124	1.3085

WALES.—RURAL, TOWN, AND CITY DISTRICTS.

AGE.			No. of Persons.	DEATHS.		SICKNESS.	
				In Periods.	Per Cent.	In Periods.	Per Annum.
18	to	20	840	6	.7143	404.284	.4812
20	"	25	3867	43	1.1119	3111.998	.8047
25	"	30	6885	65	.9440	5683.569	.8109
30	"	35	6493	39	.6066	6006.426	.9250
35	"	40	5654	49	.8666	5216.998	.9223
40	"	45	3035	38	1.2191	3941.998	1.2988
45	"	50	1980	37	1.8686	3260.426	1.6466
50	"	55	444	7	1.5765	996.425	2.2441
55	"	60	145	2	1.3793	331.141	2.2973
60	"	65	27	3	11.1111	223.140	8.2597
65	"	70	6	1	16.6666	45.428	7.5713
70	"	75	1	..	0.0000	8.000	8.0000
75	"	80	1	..	0.0000	0.000	0.0000
			29378	290	.9883	29231.833	.9950

YORKSHIRE.—RURAL DISTRICTS.

AGE.			No. of Persons.	DEATHS.		SICKNESS.	
				In Periods.	Per Cent.	In Periods.	Per Annum.
18	to	20	910	10	1.0989	510.713	.5612
20	"	25	6928	46	.6639	5265.711	.7600
25	"	30	10722	65	.6062	7361.141	.6865
30	"	35	9544	69	.7229	8086.141	.8472
35	"	40	7995	47	.5878	7746.426	.9689
40	"	45	5296	56	1.0333	5407.284	1.0209
45	"	50	3753	46	1.2256	4931.427	1.3139
50	"	55	1140	24	2.1052	2176.569	1.9092
55	"	60	368	13	3.5326	1111.569	3.0203
60	"	65	126	3	2.3809	725.571	5.7584
65	"	70	48	1	2.0833	158.713	3.3064
70	"	75	16	1	6.2500	172.569	10.7850
75	"	80	3	..	0.0000	....	0.0000
80	"	85	2	..	0.0000	104.284	52.1420
			46851	381	.8132	43758.117	·9339

YORKSHIRE.—TOWN DISTRICTS.

AGE.			No. of Persons.	DEATHS.		SICKNESS.	
				In Periods.	Per Cent.	In Periods.	Per Annum.
18	to	20	641	3	.4680	263.713	.4114
20	"	25	4800	32	.6666	3066.854	.6389
25	"	30	7744	54	.6973	5827.140	.7524
30	"	35	7422	64	.8623	6423.141	.8654
35	"	40	6380	51	.7993	6672.428	1.0458
40	"	45	4490	50	1.1135	4944.569	1.1012
45	"	50	3114	45	1.4450	4853.284	1.5585
50	"	55	1403	21	1.4967	2750.854	1.9606
55	"	60	596	18	3.0340	1901.570	3.1838
60	"	65	183	7	3.8251	836.997	4.5736
65	"	70	66	2	3.0303	241.570	3.6517
70	"	75	11	1	9.0909	99.142	9.0129
75	"	80	5	1	20.0000	32.000	6.4000
80	"	85	2	..	0.0000	0.000	0.0000
			36857	349	.9469	37913.262	1.0286

R

Table LXXXI. shows the specific intensity at the ages given therein, and from what has been previously observed, some irregularity will be expected, indeed, it is surprising to find that no greater deviation presents itself, for an additional death or two at any of the periods of life, those periods containing so few persons, would very seriously affect the results for that period, and increase or decrease the intensity accordingly.

The Mortality Tables for all the localities have been commenced with 100,000 persons at age 18, corresponding with the previous Mortality Tables, and the last column in the table shows the age at which one-half of the lives are cut off.

Glasgow and Liverpool show the least vitality of any place given, half the lives in the former dying off at age 50-1, and in the latter 52-3, showing in the former instance an inferior vitality of four years, and in the latter an inferior vitality of two years to that of clerks, the least valuable lives in all the trades, and an inferior vitality of 11 and 9 years to that of the whole city districts, of which they form a portion.

Mr. Neison gives the decrements of life from the experience of friendly societies in Liverpool, and in his table, 96474 persons are living at age 18, and one-half of those lives are cut off at age 59-60, showing in that experience a superior vitality of seven years. In the same work is given a table of the decrements of life, calculated from the mortality bills for the City of Glasgow for the years 1832-41, and the population as enumerated in 1831 and 1841; this table gives 92,142 persons living at age 18, and one-half of that number die off before age 50-1, showing an equal vitality existing amongst the whole population of that City, as appears by this experience.

The Registrar General in his fifth Report gives the expectation of life for the whole population of Liverpool; Mr. Neison gives the expectation from the experience of friendly societies for that town; he also gives the expectation for the whole population of the city of Glasgow, and for friendly societies of the city districts of Scotland. They are here inserted as well as the expectation from this experience, for Glasgow and Liverpool.

Age.	Expectation of whole population of Liverpool. Registrar General.	Expectation of Friendly Societies. Mr. Neison.	Expectation of Liverpool from this Experience.	Expectation. City of Glasgow, whole population.	Expectation. City Districts of Scotland. Friendly Societies. Mr. Neison.	Expectation. City of Glasgow, this Experience.
20	33.000	37.9553	32.32	32.2656	34.5860	30.28
25	30.000	33.9067	29.23	27.8512	31.6603	26.90
30	27.000	30.1437	26.14	24.8998	28.6354	23.87
35	23.000	26.5260	22.86	22.1102	25.5674	21.01
40	21.000	23.1524	19.96	18.9409	22.6474	18.17
45	18.000	19.9908	17.42	16.9336	19.7948	15.59
50	16.000	17.0946	14.98	14.5350	17.3861	12.93

If the expectation for the whole population of each place be made the standard of comparison, a very superior expectation presents itself in the experience given by Mr. Neison, and an inferior expectation in this experience.

South London shows the next lowest vitality, half the lives being cut off at age 55-6; Sheffield follows, half dying off at age 57-8; North London occurs next in the scale, half the lives dying away at age 58-9. In the whole of these last named places, the rate of mortality appears similar to the city districts up to the middle ages, an increased rate then appears to such an extent as to decrease the vitality, and cause half the lives to die off at the ages named.

Scotland exhibits the next lowest vitality, and one cause of this must be very apparent,— the rate of mortality existing in Glasgow (this city being included therein, and forming 22 per cent. of the persons in Scotland whose experience has been obtained), which must materially affect the whole.   Half the lives die off at age 59-60, and from the experience of societies in the rural, town, and city districts of Scotland given by Mr. Neison, half the lives living at age 18 die off at age 65-6, showing a superior vitality of six years to the latter named class of lives.

Birmingham shows a vitality equal to Scotland, and one year inferior to the city districts, half the lives dying off at age 59-60.   Oldham shows a vitality equal to the city districts ; Rochdale, Bradford, Wales, and the city and town districts of Lancashire, present a superior vitality of one year, half the lives dying off at age 62-8.   The town districts of Lancashire exhibit a less vitality than the town districts of the general class of experience; Bolton, Leeds, and the rural parts of Yorkshire, show a superior vitality of two years in comparison with the city districts, half the lives being cut off at age 63-4 ; and if the rural district of Yorkshire be compared with the general rural district, embracing all the experience of that district, there appears an inferior vitality of two years ; the increased rate of mortality for the rural parts of Yorkshire appears most conspicuous at the early age, and again after the age 50.

The town districts of Yorkshire and the rural districts of Lancashire show an equal vitality to that of the whole rural districts, and an inferior vitality of two years in comparison with the general town districts, half the lives dying off at age 65-6.   The rural district of Yorkshire exhibits an inferior vitality of two years to that of the town districts of the same place, the increased rate of mortality being at the periods previously stated.

The rural districts of the county of Northampton present the least vitality of any of the places given, half the lives dying off at age 66-7 — being one year inferior to that of agricultural labourers, and one year superior to the whole of the rural districts combined.

The lowest age at which half the lives die off is 50-1, for the city of Glasgow, and the highest age 66-7 for the rural districts of the county of Northampton.   A difference in vitality equal to 16 years thus appears in localities widely apart.   In trades, the lowest ascertained vitality was that of clerks, half dying of at age 54-5, and the highest that of carpenters, half dying off at age 69-70, showing a difference of 15 years.   Whether locality or employment be most destructive to human life, appears a question not yet solved, that both assist in that destruction must be evident from the results here given for the various localities, and from the facts previously presented in reference to the various employments.

Table LXXXII. gives the average sickness experienced at each quinquennial period of life, for the town, rural, and city districts, and those combined, and for the other places named therein.   At the first period, age 20, in many of the towns and cities, less average sickness is experienced than by the general class of lives, and in a few cities only does there appear an excess; at the other periods persons resident in the large cities generally experience more than the average sickness, but not invariably so.   Glasgow, Liverpool, Bristol, and Sheffield, show an excess at every period ; some places show an excess at one period, and others at another. Reference, however, to Table LXXXIII. will supply detailed results as to the amount of sickness experienced in each town and place for different periods of years, and for each respective town, city, or locality.

At the first period, age 20-30, persons resident in the towns of * Leeds, Stockport, city and town districts of Lancashire, Bolton, Rochdale, Bury, North London, and Oldham, experience less, and in the towns of South London, Birmingham, Bradford, Bristol, Liverpool, Glasgow, and Sheffield, greater aggregate sickness than the general class of city districts.   In the next period, 30-40, Bolton, Oldham, city districts of Lancashire, South London, North

---

* The towns are placed according to the aggregate sickness experienced for the period.

London, and Leeds, experience less,· and Bradford, Sheffield, Bury, Rochdale, Bristol, Stockport, Liverpool, and Glasgow, more aggregate sickness; in the period 40-50, Rochdale, Stockport, city districts of Lancashire, Bradford, Oldham, South London, and North London, experience less, and Leeds, Bury, Bolton, Liverpool, Bristol, Sheffield, and Glasgow, more aggregate sickness; for the period 50-60, Rochdale, Bradford, Bury, Leeds, and city districts of Lancashire, experience less, and Bolton, North London, Oldham, Sheffield, and Stockport, more aggregate sickness. Those places not named in the last period have not sufficient experience for that period from which to ascertain the aggregate sickness.

If reference be made to the aggregate sickness for periods 20-50, it will be seen that Oldham, the city districts of Lancashire, Rochdale, Stockport, Bolton, South London, Birmingham, Leeds, North London, and Bradford, experience less, and Bury, Liverpool, Bristol, Sheffield, and Glasgow, more aggregate sickness; for the period 20-60, Rochdale, Bradford, city districts of Lancashire, Leeds, Bury, and Bolton, experience less, North London, an equal, and Oldham, Stockport, and Sheffield, greater aggregate sickness than that of the general class of city districts.

If the aggregate sickness for period 20-50 or 20-60 be noticed, locality does not seem to exercise that influence which appears so conspicuous from a comparison of sickness experienced by persons following different occupations. The greatest difference of aggregate sickness experienced is 25.5528 = 25 weeks, 3 days, 20 hours; the rural districts of Gloucester showing an aggregate sickness for period 20-50 of 21.3443 = 21 weeks, 2 days, 10 hours, and the city of Glasgow an aggregate of 46.8971 = 46 weeks, 6 days, 6 hours; and the difference of aggregate sickness between clerks and miners for the same period is 30.6215 = 30 weeks, 4 days, 8 hours. In numerous instances also the difference of aggregate sickness experienced by persons following one employment and another far exceeds the difference appearing between one locality and another.

The rural districts of the counties of Gloucester and Northampton show a less aggregate sickness for the period 20-50 than the rural districts of the general class; in the former by 28, and in the latter by 20 per cent. The rural districts of Lancashire show about three per cent., and the rural districts of Yorkshire 17 per cent. less than the general class of the rural districts. For the period 20-70 the rural districts of Lancashire show an equal, and the rural districts of Yorkshire 10 per cent. less aggregate sickness than the same districts of the general class.

The rural, town, and city districts of Wales experience an average sickness of seven per cent. more than the general class of all districts combined, for the period 20-70 years. In the combination of trades, a larger number of persons following dangerous and unhealthful occupations, enter into the rural, town, and city districts of Wales (in comparison with the total numbers of each), than are comprised in the same districts of the general class; and this at once accounts for the increased sickness apparent in this class.

Mr. Neison gives the average sickness experienced by friendly societies in Scotland to be— Age 20 .8570 = 0 6 0; age 30 .8376 = 0 5 20; age 40 .9767 = 0 6 20; age 50 1.8548 = 1 5 23. On reference to the average sickness experienced from the lives under consideration, at age 20 and 50 it will be seen that these lives present a less, and at the other periods a greater, average sickness. The aggregate sickness experienced by the friendly societies of Scotland, by Mr. Neison's tables, for period 20-50, is 29.8780 = 29 weeks, 6 days, 1 hour, and the aggregate of this experience, for the same period, is 32.7206 = 32 weeks, 5 days, 1 hour, showing an excess of 9.5 per cent. over and above the rural, town, and city districts of Scotland, as given by Mr. Neison.

TABLE LXXXI.

SPECIFIC INTENSITY AT EACH QUINQUENNIAL PERIOD OF LIFE, AND AGE AT WHICH HALF THE NUMBER OF PERSONS LIVING AT AGE 18, WILL DIE OFF.

TOWNS.	20	25	30	35	40	45	50	55	60	Half Lives Dying off.
Rural Districts	148.45	132.67	131.40	128.71	118.10	86.85	68.71	48.62	30.44	65·6
Town ditto	127.97	145.56	137.09	105.66	97.34	82.71	62.41	42.62	25.98	63·4
City ditto	261.86	117.56	102.44	96.31	74.99	57.47	42.06	33.88	34.68	61·2
Rural, Town, and City ditto	165.72	128.89	119.93	111.01	95.17	75.28	56.72	40.94	28.33	62·3
Birmingham	235.57	98.63	95.00	108.83	80.16	63.05	37.14	25.94	26.56	59·60
Bolton	187.79	105.84	133.61	144.78	106.91	89.50	49.54	31.05	34.70	63·4
Bradford	436.11	230.94	136.81	132.97	111.34	80.48	37.17	25.84	34.68	62·3
Bristol	244.79	102.21	85.96	107.57	75.05	57.37	41.90	33.79	34.56	61·2
Bury	110.21	97.26	87.88	117.43	123.83	91.45	50.19	33.22	35.04	62·3
Glasgow	117.33	72.14	56.53	48.75	39.45	31.95	27.78	18.15	12.48	50·1
Gloucester Rural, ...	154.91	117.30	96.72	114.42	175.10	94.29	51.96	48.73	30.65	64·5
Lancashire, Rural ...	197.31	87.45	110.09	117.99	104.35	71.81	55.11	44.70	38.95	65·6
Ditto, Town ...	109.99	118.25	111.39	105.29	98.73	88.84	58.63	39.39	26.56	62·3
Ditto, City ...	232.55	118.25	108.88	107.52	82.08	63.48	45.73	36.02	34.80	62·3
Leeds	228.99	150.96	159.28	157.73	112.91	59.65	38.36	37.07	34.23	63·4
Liverpool	101.89	70.22	75.62	59.42	42.17	34.95	28.19	23.10	19.85	52·3
South London ...	212.72	116.86	108.12	96.23	58.75	36.00	27.57	26.68	27.30	55·6
North London ...	279.48	168.47	133.74	113.70	75.16	45.64	28.88	26.17	33.61	58·9
Northampton, Rural ...	158.32	187.68	163.45	122.18	86.53	111.35	78.70	50.85	31.93	66·7
Oldham	237.36	123.48	94.56	79.53	71.30	64.52	40.06	36.30	33.09	61·2
Rochdale	207.16	120.70	116.22	97.90	83.00	64.00	43.11	36.67	32.51	62·3
Scotland	159.35	89.84	93.04	79.23	68.23	58.40	49.68	32.07	22.07	59·60
Sheffield	237.69	131.25	107.72	81.50	61.77	43.20	29.72	29.19	26.27	57·8
Stockport	248.75	129.53	122.07	121.06	72.45	60.89	37.68	25.22	24.28	59·60
Wales	114.50	97.56	124.59	141.43	99.24	67.61	57.08	41.18	23.99	62·3
Yorkshire, Rural... ...	108.11	156.03	153.18	149.49	130.54	88.69	63.39	37.42	25.82	63·4
Ditto, Town ...	182.08	147.31	131.01	120.03	108.11	80.25	68.23	47.35	30.54	65·6

TABLE LXXXII.

AVERAGE SICKNESS PER ANNUM TO EACH PERSON, EXPRESSED IN WEEKS.

LOCALITY.	AGE 20.				AGE 30.				AGE 40.				AGE 50.				AGE 60.			
	Weeks.	W.	D.	H.	Weeks.	W.	D.	H.	Weeks.	W.	D.	H.	Weeks.	W.	D.	H.	Weeks.	W.	D.	H.
Rural Districts	.6012	0	4	5	.7785	0	5	11	.9730	0	6	19	1.7038	1	4	22	4.2157	4	1	12
Town ditto	.5703	0	4	0	.8166	0	5	17	1.0644	1	0	11	1.7499	1	5	6	3.9371	3	6	13
City ditto	.5181	0	3	15	.8298	0	5	19	1.2379	1	1	16	2.1967	2	1	9	5.3237	5	2	6
Rural, Town, and City ditto	.5848	0	4	2	.8034	0	5	15	1.0779	1	0	13	1.8533	1	5	23	4.3985	4	2	19
Birmingham	.6920	0	4	20	.7535	0	5	7	1.1874	1	1	7	1.5922	1	4	3				
Bolton	.5822	0	4	2	.6984	0	4	21	.9314	0	6	12	2.5919	2	4	3	5.7430	5	5	5
Bradford	.5610	0	3	22	.9239	0	6	11	1.1490	1	1	1	1.9180	1	6	10	6.6821	6	4	18
Bristol	.6416	0	4	12	.9455	0	6	15	1.5676	1	3	23	3.0129	3	0	2				
Bury	.4613	0	3	6	.9183	0	6	10	1.2164	1	1	12	2.4682	2	3	7	3.5633	3	3	22
Glasgow	.4935	0	3	11	1.2472	1	1	17	1.7161	1	5	0	3.3596	3	2	12				
Gloucester, Rural	.4964	0	3	11	.7877	0	5	12	.7653	0	5	9	.8544	0	5	23				
Lancashire, Rural	.5594	0	3	22	.8297	0	5	19	1.1080	1	0	18	1.8207	1	5	18	3.8995	3	6	7
Ditto, Town	.6942	0	4	21	.8532	0	5	23	1.0742	1	0	12	1.7003	1	4	21	3.5827	3	4	2
Ditto, City	.5080	0	3	11	.7194	0	5	1	1.0879	1	0	15	2.1594	2	1	3	4.8234	4	5	18
Leeds	.4045	0	2	20	.7164	0	5	0	1.3047	1	2	3	2.0964	2	0	16	5.0229	5	0	4
Liverpool	.6120	0	4	7	.9972	0	6	23	1.4150	1	2	22	2.2679	2	1	21				
South London	.4964	0	3	11	.7962	0	5	14	1.1961	1	1	9	1.0687	1	0	11				
North London	.5370	0	3	18	.7555	0	5	7	1.2911	1	1	21	2.2414	2	1	16	7.5194	7	3	15
Northampton, Rural	.6743	0	4	17	.7008	0	4	22	.9344	0	6	13	1.3417	1	2	9				
Oldham	.6248	0	4	9	.7045	0	4	22	.9862	0	6	22	2.4011	2	2	20	5.1335	5	0	22
Rochdale	.5941	0	4	4	.7768	0	5	10	1.2765	1	1	22	1.5952	1	4	4	5.0877	5	0	14
Scotland	.5081	0	3	14	.9311	0	6	12	1.1830	1	1	7	1.1819	1	1	6				
Sheffield	.5575	0	3	22	.9346	0	6	13	1.3075	1	2	4	3.1898	3	1	8				
Stockport	.3220	0	2	6	.8940	0	6	0	1.2400	1	1	16	2.1230	2	1	20	14.3834	14	2	8
Wales	.6106	0	4	6	.8605	0	6	0	1.0669	1	0	11	1.8856	1	6	5	8.6924	8	4	20
Yorkshire, Rural	.6406	0	4	12	.7507	0	5	6	.9897	0	6	22	1.5519	1	3	20	4.6823	4	4	18
Ditto, Town	.5024	0	3	18	.7976	0	5	14	1.0677	1	0	11	1.7193	1	5	1	4.1155	4	0	19
																	3.7396	3	5	4

TABLE LXXXIII.

COMPARATIVE AMOUNT OF SICKNESS EXPERIENCED IN DIFFERENT PERIODS OF YEARS.

Age.	Rural District.		Town District.		City District.		Birmingham.		Bolton.	
	Weeks.	W. D. H.	Weeks.	W. D. H.	Weeks.	W. D. H.	Weeks.	W. D. H.	Weeks.	W. D. H.
20 to 30	7.0917	= 7 0 15	7.0251	= 7 0 4	6.9520	= 6 6 16	7.0599	= 7 0 10	6.1953	= 6 1 9
30 ,, 40	8.4861	= 8 3 9	9.2770	= 9 1 22	9.6095	= 9 4 6	8.8274	= 8 5 19	6.8103	= 6 5 16
40 ,, 50	12.3664	= 12 2 13	13.0873	= 13 0 14	16.4323	= 16 3 0	15.4577	= 15 3 4	18.2331	= 18 1 15
50 ,, 60	24.3749	= 24 2 15	25.5245	= 25 3 16	32.7484	= 32 5 5			33.7491	= 33 5 6
20 ,, 50	27.9442	= 27 6 14	29.3894	= 29 2 17	32.9938	= 32 6 22	31.3450	= 31 2 10	31.2387	= 31 1 16
20 ,, 60	52.3191	= 52 2 5	54.9139	= 54 6 9	65.7422	= 65 5 4			64.9878	= 64 6 21

Age.	Bradford.		Bristol.		Bury.		Glasgow.		Gloucester Rural.	
	Weeks.	W. D. H.	Weeks.	W. D. H.	Weeks.	W. D. H.	Weeks.	W. D. H.	Weeks.	W. D. H.
20 to 30	7.9265	= 7 6 11	8.0554	= 8 0 9	6.4885	= 6 3 10	8.9107	= 8 6 9	6.4444	= 6 3 2
30 ,, 40	9.6844	= 9 4 19	10.8339	= 10 5 20	10.5326	= 10 3 17	14.3855	= 14 2 16	7.7505	= 7 5 6
40 ,, 50	15.1796	= 15 1 6	21.7264	= 21 5 2	17.6028	= 17 4 5	23.6009	= 23 4 4	7.1494	= 7 1 1
50 ,, 60	26.6497	= 26 4 13			30.3732	= 30 2 15				
20 ,, 50	32.7905	= 32 5 12	40.6157	= 40 4 7	34.6239	= 34 4 8	46.8971	= 46 6 6	21.3443	= 21 2 9
20 ,, 60	59.4402	= 59 3 2			64.9971	= 64 6 23				

TABLE LXXXIII.—CONTINUED.

Age.	Lancashire, Rural.		Lancashire, Town.		Lancashire, City.		Leeds.		Liverpool.	
	Weeks.	W. D. H.	Weeks.	W. D. H.	Weeks.	W. D. H.	Weeks.	W. D. H.	Weeks.	W. D. H.
20 to 30	7.3337	7 2 8	7.6648	7 4 15	6.1606	6 1 3	5.6331	5 4 10	8.3030	8 2 13
30 " 40	9.6976	9 4 21	9.6850	9 4 19	8.3575	8 2 12	9.2328	9 1 15	11.3204	11 2 5
40 " 50	13.3198	13 2 5	13.4150	13 2 22	15.1075	15 0 18	16.7370	16 5 3	18.8078	18 5 15
50 " 60	24.7961	24 5 18	23.5983	23 4 4	31.4490	31 3 3	31.3153	31 2 5		
20 " 50	30.3511	30 2 11	30.7648	30 5 8	29.6256	29 4 9	31.6029	31 4 5		
20 " 60	55.1472	55 1 0	54.3631	54 2 13	61.0746	61 0 12	62.9182	62 6 10	38.4312	38 3 0

Age.	South London.		North London.		Northampton, Rural.		Oldham.		Rochdale.	
	Weeks.	W. D. H.	Weeks.	W. D. H.	Weeks.	W. D. H.	Weeks.	W. D. H.	Weeks.	W. D. H.
20 to 30	6.9783	6 6 20	6.4894	6 3 10	6.7920	6 5 13	6.6925	6 4 20	6.4210	6 2 22
30 " 40	8.9444	8 6 14	9.0441	9 0 7	7.6068	7 4 5	7.3477	7 2 10	10.6191	10 4 8
40 " 50	15.5436	15 3 19	16.0814	16 0 13	10.4344	10 3 1	15.4277	15 2 23	13.3708	13 2 14
50 " 60			34.1687	34 1 4			37.3842	37 2 16	26.5516	26 3 20
20 " 50	31.4663	31 3 6	31.6149	31 4 7	24.8832	24 5 20	29.4679	29 3 6	30.4109	30 2 21
20 " 60			65.7836	65 5 11			66.8521	66 5 23	56.9626	56 6 17

TABLE LXXXIII.—CONTINUED.

Age.	Scotland.		Sheffield.		Stockport.		Wales.		Yorkshire, Rural.		Yorkshire, Town.	
	Weeks.	W. D. H.	Weeks.	W. D. H.	Weeks.	W. D. H.	Weeks.	W. D. H.	Weeks.	W. D. H.	Weeks.	W. D. H.
20 to 30	8.1919 =	8 1 8	9.0848 =	9 0 14	6.1074 =	6 0 18	7.6679 =	7 4 16	7.0910 =	7 0 15	6.5694 =	6 3 23
30 to 40	10.1139 =	10 0 19	10.0226 =	10 0 3	10.8771 =	10 6 3	9.2459 =	9 1 17	8.7536 =	8 5 6	9.2189 =	9 1 12
40 to 50	14.4148 =	14 2 21	22.3778 =	22 2 15	14.2175 =	14 1 12	14.0841 =	14 0 14	11.5418 =	11 3 19	12.9091 =	12 6 8
50 to 60			53.4712 =	53 3 7	53.7498 =	53 5 6	25.1016 =	25 0 17	23.7982 =	23 5 14	24.6908 =	24 4 20
20 to 50	32.7206 =	32 5 1	41.4852 =	41 3 9	31.2026 =	31 1 10	30.9979 =	30 6 23	27.3864 =	27 2 17	28.6974 =	28 4 21
20 to 60			94.9564 =	94 6 16	84.9518 =	84 6 15	56.0995 =	56 0 16	51.1846 =	51 1 7	53.3882 =	53 2 17

SECTION VI.

ANNUITY, &c., TABLES.

HAVING obtained the results already given, it was deemed advisable that tables, showing the value of annuities, sick-gift, temporary annuity, and assurance at death, for the various districts, should be calculated from the returns, for the purpose of comparing the values with each district, and with other tables of a similar nature.

This portion of the work being intended mainly for the use of members of the Manchester Unity, and other benefit societies, it is believed that a plain and simple explanation of the .nature of the various payments requisite to be made, and of the mode of adjusting and determining their amounts, will be more acceptable, and more conducive to the establishment on a permanent basis of similar institutions, than any elaborate or scientific disquisition.

Attention must first be directed to the Annuity Table No. LXXXIV., for the districts separate and combined; this table gives the value of an annuity of £1 per annum, according to the mortality existing in those districts, and for the ages given in that table. Supposing, for example, a person 20 years of age, residing in the rural districts, wished to secure an annuity of £1 per annum during his life, on referring to the table named, under the head Rural District, and opposite age 20, will be found £22.6698 = £22 : 13 : 5, being the amount which ought to be paid for the required annuity; and every other annuity bears the same proportion.

An annual contribution may be termed an annuity, and supposing a person desired to possess a property, and had not immediate means, but instead of making one present payment, proposed to pay a certain annual amount during life, it is by reversing the former position, viz., by dividing the value of such purchase by the value of an annuity for the age of the person, that the amount of such an annual contribution as would be equal to a present payment is obtained; that is, supposing the annual payment to be made at the end of every year; if made at the commencement of each year, unity must be added to the value of the annuity, before dividing the present value by the value of the annuity. This will be more fully explained in treating of contributions.

The value of annuities depends upon the probability of life, and upon the rate of discount in money, and it may be advisable that a brief explanation be given of these terms.

In a numerical point of view, the probability of any future event occurring is the result of dividing the number of cases by which such event can happen, by the number of cases favourable and against the same. At Table XI., age 18, for example, it is seen that 100,000 persons are alive, and that in passing through that year 552 cases of death occur, leaving 99,448 persons who enter on the nineteenth year; there are therefore 552 cases in favour, and 99,448 cases against, the occurrence of the event; if the cases that happen, 552, be divided by all the cases (552 + 99,448 = 100,000) it will give the probability of dying, before entering on the next year of life, and if the cases against the happening of the event, 99,448, be divided by the whole number of cases for and against, it will give the probability of living, and entering on the nineteenth year. To ascertain the probability of living to age 20, and of dying before that year, we must observe, in the same table, at age 20, that 98,874 persons are alive, and that in passing from 18 to 20, 1,126 persons have died; the probability of living from age 18 to 20, is the number living and entering on the twentieth year, divided by the numbers living at age 20, and the number that have died in passing from 18 to 20: $\frac{98874}{1126+98874} = 98,874$, the probability of living. And the probability of dying is the cases of death that occur in passing from age 18 to 20, divided by the whole number of cases in favour or against the happening of the event $\frac{1126}{1126+98874} = 1126$, the probability of dying before entering on the twentieth year. In the same manner the probability, at age 18, of dying before attaining age 70, is the number of deaths that occur up to that time, 66,455, divided by the whole number of cases in favour and against the happening of the event: $\frac{66455}{33545+66455} = 66,455$, the probability of dying before entering on the seventieth year. And the probability of living at age 18, to enter on that year of life, is the number of cases living at age 70, divided by the number of cases living and dying: $\frac{33545}{33545+66455} = 33,545$, the probability of living at 18 to 70 years of age.

Let it be supposed that the 100,000 persons at age 18 enter into an agreement that all the persons living and entering on their seventieth year should receive the sum of £1 each; it is very evident that each of the 100,000 persons would have to pay at once a sum of money equal to the probability of the event, .33545 = £0 : 6 : 8½, and this amount, being paid by all at age 18, would pay to each person living and entering on the seventieth year the sum of £1; or, suppose that these 100,000 persons enter into another arrangement, to make a present payment of such a sum as would give £1 each to every person who might die before attaining age 70; it has been shown that the probability of dying before attaining that age is .66455, those persons would therefore have to pay each the amount of the probability, £.66455 = £0 : 13 : 3½, and this amount being paid by all the persons would realise £66,455, the amount requisite to pay the friends of each person the sum of £1 when death occurred.

It will have been observed that what has been hitherto advanced has had reference to probability only, without regard to interest of money, and it was stated that if 100,000 persons were to pay each the sum of £.33545 = £0 : 6 : 8½, it would yield to each person living and entering on the seventieth year the sum of £1; and as this amount would not be required for 52 years, each person should pay such a sum of money as would, at compound interest, realise the amount of £0 : 6 : 8½; now, to find the present payment, that amount must be discounted * for 52 years; that is, such a sum of money must be paid as would, at interest, by the time it was required, realise the amount named, and if the sum of £.072126 = £0 : 1 : 5 be invested at three per cent. per annum, compound interest, by each person at 18 years of age, this amount would accumulate to the sum of £.33545 = £0 : 6 : 8½, and for 100,000 persons would yield an amount of £33545, which would allow to each person on entering the seventieth year the sum of £1.

From the probability of living, and the discounting of money, a table of the value of annuities can be calculated, and throughout the whole of the following tables the sum of £1 has been made the subject of calculation, as the values of that sum having been obtained, any other amount will bear a relative proportion to it.

---

* Most of the works which treat on annuities and reversions give tables of the present value of £1 to be discounted for any number of years under 100, at various per centages; if reference be made to one of these tables, and it is wished to discount £1 for 52 years at three per cent., it will be seen that the present value of £1 discounted 52 years, is £.215013, or, in other words, this amount, improved at three per cent. compound interest for 52 years, will yield £1, and if any other sum, would be in proportion.

On reference to the same Table it will be seen that 100,000 persons are alive at age 18, and were they to provide for an annuity of £1 to every person who might be living at the end of the year, it is evident they must pay such an amount as would yield to 99,448 persons the sum of £1 each; the amount, then, divided by 100,000 $\frac{99448}{100000}$ = £.99448, the value of the annuity for that year. At age 19, 98,874 live to the end of the year, and enter on the 20th year, these persons, for that year, would consequently receive the annuity, and the amount, 98,874, divided by the 100,000 living at age 18, $\frac{98874}{100000}$ = £.98874, would be the value of the annuity for that year. In passing through the next year, age 20, 596 persons die, leaving 98,278 persons who live to receive the annuity, and who enter on the 21st year of life, and which value would be $\frac{98278}{100000}$ = £.98278. In the following year, age 21, 642 persons die, leaving 97,636 persons alive at the end of the year, and who would become entitled to the annuity, and the value of which would be $\frac{97636}{100000}$ = £.97636; and if each age in the table were taken in the same manner, the sum total of these amounts would be the value of the annuity, at age 18, calculated on the probability of life.

It will be observed that these respective amounts are paid *immediate*, and as the annuity for the first year would only have to be paid at the end of the year, such an amount only need be *immediately* paid, as would, with its interest, increase to the actual money value at the end of that year; therefore, if the value of the first year's annuity be discounted for one year, the value of the annuity calculated upon the probability of life and interest of money, would be obtained for the first year; the second year's annuity would only require to be paid at the end of the second year, the third year's annuity at the end of the third year; therefore the amount required for payment of that annuity would be required to be discounted for two, three, &c. years, so that it would ultimately stand as follows :—

	Annuity.	Probability.	Discount.	Value each year.
Age 18	£1 ×	$\frac{99448}{100000}$	× .970874	= .96542
„ 19	£1 ×	$\frac{98874}{100000}$	× .942596	= .93198
„ 20	£1 ×	$\frac{98278}{100000}$	× .915142	= .89938
„ 21	£1 ×	$\frac{97636}{100000}$	× .888487	= .86748
„ 22	£1 ×	$\frac{96936}{100000}$	× .862609	= .83604

$$4.50030$$

So that, at age 18, for an annuity of £1 per annum for five years, should the person live so long, he ought to pay £4.50030 = £4 10s. 0d. for the same, interest of money being calculated at three per cent. per annum; and if this course were continued for every age in the table, the sum total would give the value of an annuity of £1 per annum for life to a person of 18 years of age, and if a similar course were pursued for every age in the table, the value of an annuity for each age would be obtained. Those persons requiring further information on the practicability of constructing a table of life annuities are referred to Dr. Price's Observations on Reversionary Payments.

Table LXXXIV. gives the value of annuities for the rural, town, and city districts, and for the three districts combined, and the following extracts from those tables are inserted to give a general idea of the relative value in the different districts.

VALUE OF ANNUITIES.

Age.	Rural.	Town.	City.	Rural, Town, and City.
20	22.3304	21.8354	21.0815	21.6287
30	20.4327	19.6058	18.6639	19.4738
40	17.8174	16.9020	15.8062	16.6688
50	14.5655	13.4596	12.6709	13.2924
60	11.1577	9.8730	9.3910	9.8008
70	8.5435	7.7379	6.0344	7.0833

EXPLANATION.—*If it be required to know the present value of a contribution to be paid annually at the termination of the year if the person lives, as suppose at age 20, rural, town, and city, multiply the contribution by the value here given, and 21.6287 will give the present value, or such a sum of money which any person of that age ought to pay in place of an annual contribution for life; but if the contribution is to be paid annually at the commencement of the year, the amount must be multiplied by* $21.6287 + 1 = 22.6287$, *for the reasons before stated.*

VALUE OF SICK ALLOWANCE.

In ascertaining the value of a sick allowance three elements enter into the calculation, probability of life, interest of money, and amount of sickness. On reference to Table XIII., rural, town, and city districts, it will be observed, that at age 18 each person experiences .5449 weeks average sickness, and, as previously stated, the sick allowance of £1 per week will form the basis of calculation; the value of that person's sickness for that year will be £.5449, and as the average sickness will be spread over the year, some persons experiencing sickness the first day in the year, some the second, and so on, it has been demonstrated that the probability of being sick any day during the year, is within a fraction equal to the discounting of the value of the year's sick allowance for six months; therefore the above amount, £.5449, will have to be discounted for half a year, and this would be the value of the first year's sick allowance.

During the next year, age 19, each person experiences .5648 weeks of average sickness, the value of which is £5648; this amount requires discounting half a year, as before, and as previously stated, as only 99,448 persons out of the 100,000 persons living at age 18 enter on their 19th year, the amount of sick allowance would be reduced by the probability of living to receive it, and which is $\frac{99448}{100000} = .99448$; and again, the amount, if paid at age 18, could, in the mean time, be invested on interest; therefore this amount would require to be discounted for one year, and this would give the value of the second year's sick gift. The next year in the table, age 20, shows an average sickness experienced of .5648 week's sickness, the value of which is £.5849; this, being discounted half a year, as before, multiplied by the probability of living from age 18 to this year of life, $\frac{98874}{100000} = .98874$, and this amount, discounted for two years, gives the present value of an allowance for sickness for the third year; and if this course be pursued up to age 70, the present value of a sick allowance of £1 per week, for a person of 18 years of age, for each year of life, will be obtained, and the sum total of all these values will give the present value of a sick allowance for the whole period from 18 to 70 years of age.

The following table shows the value of a sick-gift to a person 65 years of age, for each year of life up to 70; the second column gives the value in sickness at each age; the third, discount for half a year; the fourth, the probability of living from 65 to the age opposite that probability; the fifth, the discount of £1 for the number of years; and the last column gives the value of the sick allowance for that year only; and the sum total the value of an allowance of £1 per week during sickness, from 65 to 70 years of age.

VALUE OF SICK GIFT OF £1 PER WEEK FOR EACH YEAR FROM 65 to 70.

Age.	Amount of Sickness.		Discount Half a Year.		Probability of Living.		Discounted for No. of Years.		Value.
65	£6.2299	×	.985221	×				=	6.1378
66	6.4621	×	.985221	×	.94506	×	.970874	=	5.8416
67	6.9126	×	.985221	×	.88886	×	.942596	=	5.7060
68	7.5615	×	.985221	×	.83282	×	.915142	=	5.6928
69	8.4688	×	.985221	×	.77806	×	.888487	=	5.7680
	35.6549								29.1462

It is seen that a person living experiences, in passing from 65 to 70 years of age, 35.6549 = 35 weeks, 4 days, 14 hours' sickness, the value of which is £35.6549 = £35 : 13 : 1; but from the probability of living, and discounting of money, the value, at age 65, for an allowance of £1 per week during sickness, up to age 70, is £29.1462 = £29 : 2 : 10; and this amount ought to be paid, to effect an equitable assurance of £1 per week during sickness, for that period.

The following abstract from Table LXXXV. shows the present value, at any of the given ages, for an allowance of £1 per week during sickness; and for other ages reference is made to that table.

PRESENT VALUE OF AN ALLOWANCE OF £1 PER WEEK DURING SICKNESS.

Age.	Rural.				Town.				City.				Rural, Town, and City.			
	£	£	s.	d.	£	£	s.	d.	£	£	s.	d.	£	£	s.	d.
20	30.0384 = 30	0	9		28.7868 = 28	15	9		32.7033 = 32	14	1		29.6897 = 29	13	9	
30	34.9219 = 34	18	5		33.1160 = 33	2	4		39.2419 = 39	4	10		35.2097 = 35	4	2	
40	40.6347 = 40	12	8		37.0724 = 37	1	5		47.0024 = 47	0	1		40.8040 = 40	16	0	
50	45.9933 = 45	19	10		40.1698 = 40	3	5		53.9705 = 53	19	5		45.4933 = 45	9	10	
60	44.8617 = 44	17	3		35.1881 = 35	3	9		53.0085 = 53	0	2		42.5792 = 42	11	7	

An inspection of the above shows the least value of the sick allowance to be in the town districts; this arises from two causes — the increased average sickness experienced in the rural districts from age 60 to 70, and the higher value of life in that district, more persons living to claim the sick allowance for that period : out of 100,000 persons, in each district, at 18 years of age, in the rural, 61,371, and in the town only 58,325, persons live to the sixtieth year of age, when the average sickness increases so much.

Table LXXXVI. gives the value in one single payment — an annual payment during life — and an annual payment until attaining age 70. For an allowance of £1 per week during sickness, a comparison of the present value, at age 20, with rural, town, and city districts, Table LXXXV will show that the value of a sick allowance during life is worth 31 per cent. more than the same allowance up to age 70, and that the per centage of increased value increases at every period in the table.

Mr. Neison, in an appendix to his "Vital Statistics," gives the value of a sick allowance during life, which considerably exceeds the value given at Table LXXXVI.: at age 30 the excess is more than 36 per cent., and after that period it increases more in value than the results here given; and at age 69 it shows an excess of above 50 per cent., arising from the higher average sickness and the higher value of life, as shown by the experience obtained by him. If reference be made to that table, it must be recollected that the annual premiums given at Table LXXXVI. are calculated for monthly payments, and the table of premiums by Mr. Neison for annual payments, to be made at the commencement of the assurance, and would consequently be certain of being received; in monthly payments they would be paid at the commencement of the month; there is therefore a probability that all the monthly payments for the year would not be made, as death might take place before the expiration of the year; this increases the annual premium, and to a considerable extent, at an advanced period of life.

DEFERRED ANNUITIES.

The average sickness experienced increases to such an extent after 70 years of age, as will be seen on reference to the value of a sick allowance for life, Table LXXXVI., that persons after that period become nearly permanent claimants, for if not incapacitated by sickness, they become incapable of following any regular employment. In many societies the principle of deferred annuities has been established for the purpose of making provision for members at an advanced age; and if contributions for such purpose be commenced in the early period of life, the annual payment required is very inconsiderable in comparison with the benefits that arise from making such a provision. The value of an annuity of £1 per annum has been already shown, and if 70 years of age be taken as the period at which the payment of annuities is to commence, it will be seen on reference to Table LXXXIV. rural, town, and city districts, that the value of an annuity of £1 per annum at age 70 is £7.0833 = £7 1s. 8d.; therefore that sum ought to be paid by any person for that annuity, to receive the same so long as he lived; but if this value of an annuity, to be received on arriving at age 70, were paid for at an early period of life, the value would be reduced by the probability of living to that age, and if reference be made to Table XI., it will be seen that out of 100,000 persons living at age 18, 33,545 enter on their 70th year; if this annuity were purchased for these 33,545 persons at age 18 the amount would be paid by the 100,000 persons, so that it would then be impossible to predict who would live to receive it; this is the probability of living to age 70 : $\frac{33545}{100000} = .33545$; and as the amount would be paid immediately, such an amount would only require to be paid, as would realise that sum at compound interest by the time it was required. If the amount, therefore, be discounted for 52 years, it will give the present value at age 18.   Therefore the value of an annuity of £1 per annum at age 70 — the probability of living to that age — and £1 discounted for the number of years, are required to ascertain the value of an annuity after 70 years of age, the value thereof to be paid at age 18.

Value of annuity of £1 per annum at age 70 = 7.0833.

Probability of living to that age $\frac{33545}{100000}$ = .33545.

£1 discounted, intervening term, 52 years   .215008.

Then 7.0833 × .33545 × .215008 = .5180 = £0 10s. 4d., present value of an annuity at age 18; such annuity to commence on attaining 70 years of age.   It will be observed, that the value here given, and the value given in Table LXXXVII. for the same annuity, vary, the one annuity being paid monthly, and the other annually, which will be hereafter more fully explained.

To revert to the deferred annuity: it has been shown that a payment of £0 10s. 4d., at age 18, will purchase an annuity of £1 per annum, to be received after attaining 70 years of age; it will be observed that 100,000 persons pay the sum, and the amount paid, being invested at compound interest, will have accumulated, when the lives have arrived at 70 years of age, to such an amount as will precisely pay the sum of £7 1s. 8d. for each of the 33,545 persons then living.

The following abstract shows the value of an annuity to be received after 70 years of age, and will give an idea of the variation in amount for the various districts.

VALUE OF AN ANNUITY AFTER 70 YEARS OF AGE, AT THE AGES GIVEN.

Age.	Rural.	Town.	City.	Rural, Town, and City.
	£ £ s. d.	£ £ s. d.	£ £ s. d.	£ £ s. d.
20	.8407 = 0 16 10	.6288 = 0 12 7	.4418 = 0 8 10	.5836 = 0 11 8
30	1.2136 = 1 4 3	.9073 = 0 18 2	.6416 = 0 12 10	.8452 = 0 16 10
40	1.7705 = 1 15 5	1.3355 = 1 6 9	.9590 = 0 19 2	1.2435 = 1 4 10
50	2.6625 = 2 13 3	2.0284 = 2 0 7	1.5323 = 1 10 8	1.9121 = 1 18 3
60	4.4107 = 4 8 3	3.4616 = 3 9 3	2.7279 = 2 14 7	3.2726 = 3 5 5

It will be observed that the present value of an annuity, in the rural districts, varies from 61 to 90 per cent. more than in the city districts; in the latter many would not live to claim the annuity, in comparison with the rural districts; for out of 100,000 persons living at age 18, 40,413 persons would live to 70 years of age in the rural, and only 29,653 in the city, so that in the former instance provision would have to be made for the 40,413 persons receiving the first, and every other annuity so long as they lived; in the latter instance provision would only have to be made for 29,653 persons receiving the annuity annually.

ASSURANCE AT DEATH.

Table XI. shows that at age 18, 100,000 persons are living, and that during that year 552 persons have died, leaving 99,448 persons who live to enter on the 19th year; during the next year, age 19, 574 persons die, leaving 98,874 persons, who live to enter on the 20th year; in the following year, age 20, 596 persons die, and 98,278 persons live, and enter on the 21st year of age; to provide an assurance of £1 each to every person at death, to be paid by the 100,000 persons living, it is evident that by dividing the number of deaths each year by the 100,000 persons living, the amount that should be paid by these persons would be found; and the number of deaths occurring, each year, divided by the number of living at age 18, gives the probability of dying during each successive year, and equal to the value of the assurance for the year.

$$\text{At age } 18 \text{ the probability of dying is } \tfrac{552}{100000} = .00552$$
$$\text{,, } 19 \text{ ,, ,, } \tfrac{574}{100000} = .00574$$
$$\text{,, } 20 \text{ ,, ,, } \tfrac{596}{100000} = .00596$$
$$\text{,, } 21 \text{ ,, ,, } \tfrac{642}{100000} = .00642$$

And if every age in the table were treated in a similar manner, the amount which ought to be paid by every person of the 100,000 for each year of life would be obtained, and the sum total, would give the total amount to be paid by every person to assure the sum of £1 at death, calculated on the probability of dying during the year; but if this amount were paid at age 18, it is obvious that it would be accumulating at interest, and as the amount for the first year would only be paid at the termination of the year, if such a sum of money were paid as would, at interest, at the time it was required, realise the amount, it would be quite sufficient; if the first year's amount be then discounted for one year, the second year's amount discounted for two years, the third year's amount discounted for three years, and the same course adopted for every year in the table, the present value of £1 for an assurance of £1 at death would be obtained for every age of life, and the sum total would give the present value for the sum of £1 at death, whenever that might occur. The following table more clearly expresses the mode of such value.

PRESENT VALUE OF AN ASSURANCE OF £1 AT DEATH, FOR 6 YEARS.

Age.	Assu-rance.	Probability of Dying.	£1 Discounted. No. of Years.		Value of Assurance for £1 for one year	Value of Assurance for one year for £10.	Value of Assurance for one year for £10.		
18	1 ×	.00552	× .970874	=	.00535	.0535	= 0	1	0¾
19	1 ×	.00574	× .942596	=	.00541	.0541	= 0	1	1
20	1 ×	.00596	× .915142	=	.00545	.0545	= 0	1	1¼
21	1 ×	.00642	× .888487	=	.00570	.0570	= 0	1	1½
22	1 ×	.00700	× .862609	=	.00603	.0603	= 0	1	2¼
23	1 ×	.00709	× .837484	—	.00587	.0587	= 0	1	2
					.03381	.3381	= 0	6	9

The second column gives the amount of assurance, the third column the probability of dying during the year, the fourth column the value of £1 discounted number of years, the fifth column gives the value of an assurance of £1 at death for each of those years, and the total the value of an assurance of £1 at death, for the six years. This last column being small in value, it was thought advisable to attach two other columns, giving the value of an assurance for the sum of £10 at deaths for each of the years, and the total gives the value of an assurance of £10 at death for the six years there given.

T

The following values, abstracted from Table LXXXVIII., will show the relative amounts to be paid in one sum at the ages given, for an assurance of £1 at death, whenever the same may occur.

PRESENT VALUE FOR THE ASSURANCE OF £1 AT DEATH.

Age.	Rural.				Town.				City.				Rural, Town, and City.			
	£	£	s.	d.	£	£	s.	d.	£	£	s.	d.	£	£	s.	d.
20	.3204	= 0	6	5	.3348	= 0	6	8½	.3568	= 0	7	1½	.3409	= 0	6	10
30	.3757	= 0	7	6	.3998	= 0	8	0	.4272	= 0	8	6½	.4046	= 0	8	1
40	.4519	= 0	9	0½	.4785	= 0	9	7	.5104	= 0	10	2½	.4853	= 0	9	8
50	.5466	= 0	10	11	.5788	= 0	11	7	.6018	= 0	12	0½	.5827	= 0	11	7¾
60	.6458	= 0	12	11	.6833	= 0	13	8	.6973	= 0	13	11½	.6869	= 0	13	8¾

For the practical method of obtaining the values of life assurances, reference is made to Dr. Price's Observations on Reversionary Payments.

ANNUITIES PAYABLE MORE FREQUENTLY THAN ONCE IN A YEAR.

"The values of annuities already treated of, suppose such annuities to be payable but once in the year. If an annuity be payable more frequently its value will be increased. A person who receives an annuity, by equal instalments, half-yearly, will, for two reasons, be placed under more favourable circumstances than he who receives an annuity yearly. In the first place he receives the half of his annuity six months earlier, and so gains one-half year's interest on every moiety; and, further, he may live to receive a half-year's annuity more than the person who receives an annuity only once in, and at the end of, each year. An annuity payable half-yearly will therefore be of greater present value than one which is payable yearly. For similar reasons, an annuity payable quarterly will be of greater value than that which is payable half-yearly; and as the number of times at which an annuity may be payable in a year increases, so will its present value increase. The investigations requisite to determine, precisely and with explicitness, the differences in these values, would occupy some space, and, as they are to be found in most works written expressly on the subject of life annuities, it is not deemed necessary to enter into them here. * It is thought sufficient to note that the excess in value of an annuity, payable in m equal instalments, at m equal intervals of a year, over the value of the same annuity payable yearly, will be $\frac{m-1}{2m}$ of a year's purchase, within a very insignificant fraction. This supposes that the first payment of the mth part of the annuity will be made at the end of the mth part of a year from its commencement. When, therefore, the annuity is payable twice in each year, such excess of value is

$$\frac{2-1}{2\times2} \text{ or } \tfrac{1}{4} \text{ of a year's purchase :}$$

When the annuity is payable } $\frac{4-1}{2\times4} = \tfrac{3}{8}$ of a year's purchase :
four times in the year, it is }

---

* See particularly Mr. J. Milne's Treatise on Annuities and Assurances, v. i., page 251, et seq.

When monthly ... ... $\frac{12-1}{2\times 12} = \frac{11}{24}$ of a year's purchase :

When weekly ... ... $\frac{52-1}{2\times 52} = \frac{51}{104}$ of a year's purchase :

When payable daily ... ... $\frac{365-1}{2\times 365} = \frac{182}{365}$ of a year's purchase :

And when it is payable *momently*, or an infinite number of times in a year, $\frac{m-1}{2m}$ is equal to half, which is the limit of the increase in value to a yearly annuity that can arise in consideration of the annuity being payable more frequently than once in a year. So that, if we have found the value of an annuity on a given life *payable yearly*, the following additions should be made to such value, in order to obtain the value of an annuity on the same life, payable half-yearly, quarterly, monthly, weekly, daily, or momently.

		The Additions to the value of the Yearly Annuity should be
If an annuity be payable half-yearly		.2500
,,	quarterly	.3750
,,	monthly	.4583
,,	weekly	.4904
,,	daily	.4986
,,	momently	.5000

And in determining the present value of a temporary or of a deferred annuity payable oftener than once in each year, we must for A and $A[t]$* payable yearly, substitute the values of annuities on the same lives increased by the above mentioned quantities, as the cases may apply.

The foregoing values are those of annuities of £1, but it will be readily perceived that an annuity of £2 must be of double the value of an annuity of £1, or that $1 : 2 :: A : 2A$; and if the annuity be of any other amount, as £a, the value will be proportionately increased, so that as $1 : a :: A : aA$. If, therefore, we know the value of (A), an annuity of £1 : and we require the value of an annuity of £a, we must multiply by £a, the value of (A), an annuity of £1 : and the same would evidently be true, if for A we substitute $A[t]$ or $A[t]$. † "

Table LXXXIV gives the value of an annuity of £1 per annum at age 18 to be 22.0549 ; if the annuity were to be paid at more times in the year the value would be

If paid half-yearly, .2500 + 22.0549 = 22.3049

If paid quarterly its value would be .3750 + 22.0549 = 22.4299

,, monthly ,, .4583 + 22.0549 = 22.5132

,, weekly ,, .4904 + 22.0549 = 22.5453

,, daily ,, .4986 + 22.0549 = 22.5535

,, momently ,, .5000 + 22.0549 = 22.5549

ANNUAL CONTRIBUTIONS FOR SICK GIFTS, ANNUITIES, AND SUM AT DEATH.

When persons assure for any of the above benefits, they do not generally pay down at once the total present value of such sums, but engage to pay at stated periods such an annuity, called an annual premium, as may be equal, in present value, to that of the benefit to be received. The "present value" of an annuity is the present worth of a given payment to be

---

* A value of an annuity ; $A[t]$ value of an annuity to be entered on in [t] years.
Treatise on Friendly Societies by C. Ansell, Esq., F. R. S.

made at the end of every year; but in paying, by annual premiums, the consideration for an assurance of any of these benefits, it is customary to pay one of such annual premiums at the commencement of the year in which the assurance may be made; so that if the annual premium were £1, the present worth of it, on the life of a person age 18 (rural, town, and city districts), would be $1 + 22.0549 = 23.0549$; that is, it would be the value of an annuity on such life *increased by unity;* because the present value of the payment of £1, at the end of every year, has been previously calculated upon, and as the £1 to be paid, at the beginning of the first year, would certainly be received, and would be unaffected by discount or probability, its value would of course be precisely £1; — thus making the total value of an annual premium of £1 to be £1 + £22.0549 = £23.0549, as previously stated.

If it be intended that the premiums should be payable m times in each year, we must, for the above value, substitute the value of an annuity, on the same life, payable m times in each year (which has just been shown), increased by the mth part of a year's purchase; because, as the value of an annuity payable m times in each year supposes the payment of the mth part of the annuity to be made at the end of the mth part of a year from its commencement, while the mth part of the year's premium would be paid at the commencement of the assurance, the real value of the annuity or premium that the person assuring would contract to pay, would be $\frac{1}{m}$ + the annuity payable m times in the year. The quantity, $\frac{1}{m}$, would, if the annuity were

$$
\begin{array}{lll}
& \text{Payable half-yearly, be} & = .5000 \\
\text{If payable} & \text{quarterly, it would be} & = .2500 \\
& \text{monthly,} \quad ,, & = .0833 \\
& \text{weekly} \quad ,, & = .0192 \\
& \text{daily} \quad ,, & = .0027 \\
& \text{momently} \quad ,, & = .0000 \\
\end{array}
$$

The present values for a sick allowance of £1 per week during sickness, an annuity of £1 per annum after age 70, and an assurance of £1 at death, have already been treated of; if the present values of any of those benefits, at any of the ages, be divided by the value of an annuity of that age, it will give the annual premium requisite to be paid at the end of each year. As just observed, it is usual to pay the assurance at the commencement of the year, therefore, to find the annual premium payable at the commencement of the year, the present value must be divided by the annuity + 1; and if it were required to find the annual premium to be paid by monthly instalments at the commencement of the assurance, the present value of the benefit must be divided by the value of an annuity payable monthly, increased by one-twelfth of a year's purchase, .0833. The value of an annuity at age 18, payable monthly, as shown at page 147, and .0833 added thereto, would give 22.5965; and the present value of a sick allowance, or any other benefit, at the same age, divided by this sum, would give the annual premium payable monthly in advance during life, which ought to be paid for that benefit.

Table LXXXV. shows the present value of a sick allowance, at age 18, rural, town, and city districts, to be 29.200; and it has been shown that the value of a contribution of any amount per annum is worth 22.0549 year's purchase = the value of an annuity at the age; if the present value of the sick allowance were divided by that number of years' purchase, it would give the amount of contribution to be paid annually so long as life continued; but it might be very probable that the person, not having any claim on the sick gift after 70 years of age, might cease to contribute; it therefore becomes requisite to make provision for the payment in the same period of time that he is entitled to the sick allowance, say up to 70 years of age. The value of the sick allowance must therefore be divided by the value of an annuity for the time he is entitled to the said allowance, and to obtain the value of an annuity for that period of time, the value of an annuity after 70 years of age must be deducted from the value of an annuity for life, and the remainder would be the value of an annuity up to 70 years of age. It will be observed that the annuity being paid monthly, the value thereof will be increased by the amount previously stated to be added to the value of annuities payable annually.

The value, by Table LXXXIV., rural, town, and city districts, of an annuity of £1 per annum, at 70 years of age, is 7.0833 ; and if .4583, on account of the same being paid monthly, be added thereto, it makes the value of an annuity of £1 per annum, at 70 years of age, payable monthly, to be 7.5416 ; and if this value of the annuity at 70 years of age be required for a person 18 years of age, it is evident that if such a sum were paid at the latter age as would realise, at compound interest, the value of the annuity at age 70, it would be quite sufficient ; and if 7.5416 be discounted for 52 years, the difference in years between 18 and 70, such a sum would be obtained as would be the value of an annuity of £1 per annum, to commence at age 70 and to be paid for at 18 years of age. This amount is £1.6215 = £1 : 12 : 5, or the sum of £1 : 12 : 5 invested at three per cent., compound interest, when 18 years of age, would, by the time a person arrived at 70 years of age, realise the sum of £7.5416 = £7 : 10 : 10. On reference to Table XI. it will be seen that, out of 100,000 persons living at age 18, only 33,545 persons live to enter on the 70th year of age, the remainder having died in passing through those years ; therefore the amount is farther reduced, such a sum being required to be paid by each of the 100,000 persons as will provide £1.6215 = £1 : 12 : 5 for each of the 33,545 who may live to 70 years of age. The value of the annuity, after being discounted, being multiplied by the probability of living to 70 years of age, $\frac{33545}{100000} = .33545$, would give the present value, £.5439 = £0 : 10 : 11, of an annuity of £1 per annum after 70 years of age, calculated from the discounting of money and probability of living ; and that amount being deducted from 22.5132 (the value of an annuity payable monthly for life), would give the value of an annuity of £1 per annum up to age 70. And this amount, being increased by one-twelfth of a year's purchase, would give the value of an annuity, payable monthly, up to age 70, £22.0526 ; and the present value of the sick allowance, being divided by this sum, would give the annual contribution, payable monthly, for a sick-gift of £1 per week up to 70 years of age.

Value of annuity at age 70, Table LXXXIV.	7.0833
Payable monthly	.4583
	7.5416
Probability of living at age 18 to age 70, $\frac{33545}{100000}$ = ...	.33545
Unity, discounted number of years (52)	.215008

Then 7.0833 × .33545 × .215008 = .5339, value of an annuity after 70 years of age.

Value of an annuity at age 18, Table LXXXIV.	22.0549
Payable monthly	.4583
	22.5132
Value of annuity after 70 years of age	·5439
	21.9693
One-twelfth of a year's purchase ... ...;	.0833
Value of annuity from 18 to 70 years of age, payable monthly	22.0526
Value of sick allowance at age 18, Table LXXXV.	29,2000

Then $\frac{29.2000}{22.0526} = 1.324 = £1 : 6 : 6$, annual contribution payable at age 18, by twelve monthly instalments, for an allowance of £1 per week during sickness, up to 70 years of age.

The rate of contributions given at Table LXXXIX., for each of the districts, and the same combined, have been calculated for twelve monthly payments in the year, and those payments to cease on arriving at 70 years of age ; if it were desired to ascertain the contribution payable for life, the value of the sick-gift for the respective age, divided by the value of an annuity for life, payable monthly, and one-twelfth of a year's purchase, would give the annual contribution payable monthly during life for the sick-gift.

Value of annuity payable monthly, age 18 ... ...   22.5132

One-twelfth of a year's purchase 0833

                                                            22.5965

Value of sick allowance, age 18, Table LXXXV. 29.2000

Then $\frac{29.2000}{22.5965} = 1.2992 = £1 : 5 : 10$, annual contribution payable for life at age 18, for an allowance of £1 per week during sickness, up to age 70.

Table LXXXIX. gives the amount of annual payments, by monthly instalments, up to age 70, for an allowance of £1 per week during sickness, up to that age.

The attention of persons forming benefit societies cannot be drawn too frequently to the necessity of making provision for an annuity after a certain age ; and the amount of payment, when commenced at an early period of life, is so inconsiderable, when taken into consideration with the amount of benefits conferred, that it is presumed the question requires only to be more generally understood, to be more widely reduced to practice ; and in the adoption of such a principle the utmost caution is necessary, that it be placed upon a firm basis, for the purpose of giving security to societies granting deferred annuities. At the time this work is passing through the press, the Friendly Societies' Bill, now before Parliament, contains a very judicious clause, preventing the legalisation of any society granting deferred annuities, until the rates of payment have been sanctioned by an actuary of sufficient standing ; for if the rate of payment for the securing of deferred annuities were left to be fixed by incompetent parties, and an amount charged not sufficient to secure those annuities at the time they were required, greater injustice would be committed upon the annuitants, than allowing them to remain in their original position of not having made any provision of the kind.

The present value, at age 18, of an annuity payable monthly, after 70 years of age, has been shown at page 149 to be £.5439 = £0 : 10 : 11, and the value of an annuity payable monthly, to age 70, is 22.0526, same page ; the value of the annuity, .5439, being divided by the value of an annuity payable to age 70, will give the amount of annual premium payable by twelve monthly instalments up to age 70, for an annuity of £1 per annum after that age, should the life so long continue ; and if it be required that the annual premium should be paid for life, the value of the annuity at age 70, being divided by the value of an annuity payable monthly for life, as shown above, will give the annual contribution payable for life, for an annuity after 70 years of age.

Table XC. gives the amount of annual contributions requisite to be paid at each age for an annuity of £1 after 70 years of age.

Table LXXXVIII. gives the present value, at the ages stated, for an assurance of £1 at death, and at page 145 is explained the principle of obtaining that present value ; and it being customary, as before stated, for members of friendly societies to pay an equivalent to such present value by instalments, it becomes requisite to ascertain the premium to be paid in place of that present value. At age 18, Table LXXXVIII., rural, town, and city districts, the present value, in one single payment, is £.3284 = £0 : 6 : 7.

Table LXXXIV., rural, town, and city districts, age 18, gives the value of an annuity payable annually for life to be 22.0549 ; and as the premiums hereafter given are for monthly payments, .4583 added thereto, and one-twelfth of a year's purchase, .0833, gives the value of an annuity payable monthly during life to be 22.5965; and if the present value be divided by the value of the annuity payable monthly during life, the annual premium payable by monthly instalments for the assurance of £1 at death will be obtained. Any other assurance will bear a relative proportion; if it were required, for example, to ascertain the annual premium payable for an assurance of £100 at death: the present value of £1 at death, .3284, multiplied by the assurance £100, would give 32.84, and this amount, being divided by the value of the annuity just given, would give an annual premium of £1 : 9 : 7 to be paid by monthly instalments for the assurance of £100 at death.

Table XCI. shows the amount of contributions requisite for an assurance of £1 at death, and Table LXXXIX. gives the amount of contributions requisite to be paid for the assurance of a sick gift of £1 per week during sickness up to age 70, the payment of contributions then to cease; Table XC. gives the amount of contributions requisite to be paid up to age 70 for an annuity of £1 per annum after that age; and if it were required to find the contribution requisite for any other benefit, it will be a proportional part; if for an assurance of £10 at death, the contribution must be ten times the amount given in the table; if for an assurance of 10 shillings per week in sickness $\frac{10}{20}$ = .5 of the amount; and if for an annuity of £6 : 10 : 0 per annum, six and a half times the amount of contribution required for £1.

At page 152 are given extracts from the various tables of rural, town, and city districts, and for the three districts combined, but calculated according to the benefits, showing the amount requisite to be paid annually, in equal monthly instalments, up to age 70, for a sick gift of 10 shillings per week, during sickness, up to that age, both the sick gift and contribution then to cease, — amount of contribution for an annuity of £6 : 10 : 0 per annum after 70 years of age, the contribution to cease at the commencement of the annuity, — and the annual contribution requisite, by monthly instalments, to be paid during life, for an assurance of £10 at death.

It will be observed that the contribution for a sick allowance is highest in the city districts, in consequence of the amount of sickness experienced by persons in these districts presenting a greater average than is experienced by the rural or town districts, and that the contribution necessary to be paid for a sick allowance, is less in the town than in the rural districts, as far more persons in the rural districts live to an advanced period of life, when the sickness so much increases.

The contribution necessary for an annuity after 70 years of age is least in the city districts, and highest in the rural districts; in comparison with the rural districts few live to 70 years of age in the city districts to claim the annuity, and less in the town districts than in the rural districts, consequently a less contribution is requisite than in the rural districts.

The amount of contribution to be paid for assurance at death is lowest in the rural, and highest in the city districts; this must at once be apparent, from the higher value of life in the one than in the other; the persons in the rural districts, living a longer period of years, have longer time to contribute for the assurance at death.

The general contribution for the whole of the benefits, it is seen, is least in the town districts, and for the rural and city districts approaches very near at every period in the table, with a less contribution for sickness and assurance at death appears a higher contribution for annuity, and by this means nearly equalises the payments, in each district of rural and city.

It is very apparent, that the utmost caution is necessary in adopting any scale of payments, so much variation exists in regard to locality, and a combination of the various trades; the amount of contribution which would be sufficient to assure the benefits in one locality, or amongst one class of trades, would be found quite insufficient if adopted by persons in another

AMOUNT OF CONTRIBUTION TO BE PAID, UP TO 70 YEARS OF AGE, FOR A SICK ALLOWANCE OF TEN SHILLINGS PER WEEK, UP TO THAT AGE,—CONTRIBUTION TO BE PAID, UP TO 70 YEARS OF AGE, FOR AN ANNUITY OF £6 : 10 : 0 PER ANNUM AFTER THAT AGE,—AND CONTRIBUTION PAYABLE FOR LIFE TO ASSURE £10 AT DEATH, TO BE PAID IN TWELVE MONTHLY INSTALMENTS.

	Rural DISTRICTS.				TOWN DISTRICTS.			
Age.	Sick Gift.	Annuity.	Assurance at Death.	Total.	Sick Gift.	Annuity.	Assurance at Death.	Total.
	£ s. d.	£ s. d.	£ s. d.	£ s. d.	£ s. d.	£ s. d.	£ s. d.	£ s. d.
20	0 13 7½	0 4 11	0 2 9½	1 1 4	0 13 3	0 3 1½	0 2 11	0 19 3½
25	0 15 5½	0 6 3	0 3 1½	1 4 10	0 15 0½	0 4 9	0 3 3½	1 3 1
30	0 17 8	0 7 9½	0 3 6½	1 9 0	0 17 1	0 6 1	0 3 10½	1 7 10½
35	1 0 7	0 10 4½	0 4 1½	1 15 1	0 19 10½	0 8 0	0 4 6½	1 12 5
40	1 4 6	0 13 10	0 4 11	2 3 3	1 3 0	0 10 9	0 5 4	1 19 1
45	1 9 10	0 19 2	0 5 11	2 14 11	1 7 6½	0 15 0	0 6 6	2 9 0½
50	1 16 11½	1 7 9½	0 7 2½	3 11 11½	1 13 6½	1 2 0	0 8 0½	3 3 7

	CITY DISTRICTS.				RURAL TOWN AND CITY DISTRICTS.			
Age.	Sick Gift.	Annuity.	Assurance at Death.	Total.	Sick Gift.	Annuity.	Assurance at Death.	Total.
20	0 15 5½	0 2 8½	0 3 3½	1 1 5½	0 13 11½	0 3 6½	0 3 1½	1 0 7½
25	0 18 0½	0 3 5½	0 3 10	1 5 4	0 16 0	0 4 4	0 3 6½	1 3 10½
30	1 1 1½	0 4 5½	0 4 5	1 10 0	0 18 4½	0 5 8½	0 3 11½	1 8 0½
35	1 5 2½	0 5 11½	0 5 2½	1 16 4½	1 1 5½	0 7 7	0 4 9½	1 13 10
40	1 10 6½	0 7 10½	0 6 2½	2 4 7½	1 5 7	0 10 0	0 5 7½	2 1 2½
45	1 17 4	0 11 5	0 7 5½	2 16 2½	1 10 11½	0 14 1	0 6 10½	2 11 11
50	2 6 4	0 17 0½	0 9 0½	3 12 5	1 18 2	1 0 10½	0 8 4	3 7 4½

locality, or by societies of a different composition of trades, subject to a higher average sickness, and a different rate of mortality. The tables have been given more to show the mode of calculation, and the general contribution which would be required if the experience before given were to be acted upon as a whole; but as the sickness experienced in various branches does vary on account of locality, and being affected by employment, the result before given cannot be supposed to be that experienced by each separate branch, but by every branch, and as the whole general experience.

If any branch or society should deem it advisable to adopt the scale of payments here given, it is very prudent, at the same time, that they ascertain the valuation of their assets and liabilities at certain periods, even whatever scale of payments they may adopt; it is very necessary that a quinquennial valuation should take place, and that the position of the society should be placed before its own members. As such valuation can be made by parties who may be fairly acquainted with the common rules of arithmetic, the mode of ascertaining the valuation of the assets and liabilities of a society are hereafter given.

TABLE LXXXIV.

VALUE OF ANNUITIES.—INTEREST THREE PER CENT.

Age.	RURAL.			TOWN.			CITY.			RURAL, TOWN, & CITY.		
	£	£ s.	d.	£	£ s.	d.	£	£ s.	d.	£	£ s.	d.
18	22.6698 = 22	13	5	22.1486 = 22	3	0	21.6584 = 21	13	2	22.0549 = 22	1	1
19	22.5015 = 22	10	0	21.9957 = 21	19	11	21.3562 = 21	7	1	21.8448 = 21	16	11
20	22.3304 = 22	6	7	21.8354 = 21	16	8	21.0815 = 21	1	7	21.6287 = 21	12	7
21	22.1561 = 22	3	1	21.6630 = 21	13	3	20.8094 = 20	16	2	21.4127 = 21	8	3
22	21.9819 = 21	19	8	21.4856 = 21	9	9	20.5520 = 20	11	0	21.2001 = 21	4	0
23	21.8068 = 21	16	2	21.2979 = 21	5	11	20.3063 = 20	6	1	20.9938 = 20	19	11
24	21.6282 = 21	12	7	21.0991 = 21	2	0	20.0691 = 20	1	4	20.7830 = 20	15	8
25	21.4453 = 21	8	11	20.8877 = 20	17	9	19.8371 = 19	16	8	20.5699 = 20	11	5
26	21.2567 = 21	5	2	20.6631 = 20	13	3	19.6075 = 19	12	1	20.3527 = 20	7	1
27	21.0602 = 21	1	2	20.3748 = 20	7	6	19.3770 = 19	7	6	20.1297 = 20	2	7
28	20.8622 = 20	17	3	20.1277 = 20	2	7	19.1440 = 19	2	10	19.9487 = 19	19	0
29	20.6512 = 20	13	0	19.8688 = 19	17	5	18.9069 = 18	18	1	19.7144 = 19	14	3
30	20.4327 = 20	8	8	19.6058 = 19	12	1	18.6639 = 18	13	3	19.4738 = 19	9	6
31	20.2069 = 20	4	2	19.3423 = 19	6	10	18.4134 = 18	4	3	19.2289 = 19	4	7
32	19.9740 = 19	19	6	19.0817 = 19	1	8	18.1531 = 18	3	0	18.9751 = 18	19	6
33	19.7333 = 19	14	8	18.8213 = 18	16	5	17.8843 = 17	17	8	18.7120 = 18	14	3
34	19.4822 = 19	9	8	18.5605 = 18	11	3	17.6069 = 17	12	1	18.4436 = 18	8	10
35	19.2239 = 19	4	7	18.2963 = 18	5	11	17.3215 = 17	6	5	18.1673 = 18	3	4
36	18.9556 = 18	19	1	18.0240 = 18	0	6	17.0283 = 17	0	6	17.8867 = 17	17	4
37	18.6767 = 18	13	6	17.7447 = 17	14	11	16.7277 = 16	14	6	17.5924 = 17	11	10
38	18.3891 = 18	7	9	17.4996 = 17	1	0	16.4221 = 16	8	5	17.2906 = 17	5	10
39	18.0946 = 18	1	11	17.2052 = 17	4	1	16.1142 = 16	2	3	16.9823 = 16	19	8
40	17.8174 = 17	16	4	16.9020 = 16	18	0	15.8062 = 15	16	1	16.6688 = 16	13	5
41	17.4915 = 17	9	10	16.5896 = 16	11	10	15.5003 = 15	10	0	16.3511 = 16	7	0
42	17.1551 = 17	3	1	16.2678 = 16	5	4	15.1984 = 15	3	11	16.0304 = 16	0	7
43	16.8470 = 16	16	11	15.9377 = 15	18	9	14.8987 = 14	17	11	15.7061 = 15	14	1
44	16.5362 = 16	10	9	15.6001 = 15	12	0	14.5984 = 14	11	11	15.3774 = 15	7	7
45	16.2219 = 16	4	5	15.2555 = 15	5	1	14.2944 = 14	5	10	15.0433 = 15	0	10
46	15.9032 = 15	18	1	14.9054 = 14	18	1	13.9838 = 13	19	8	14.7030 = 14	14	1
47	15.5798 = 15	11	7	14.5502 = 14	11	0	13.6642 = 13	13	3	14.3554 = 14	7	1
48	15.2361 = 15	4	9	14.1905 = 14	3	10	13.3083 = 13	6	2	14.0034 = 14	0	1
49	14.9031 = 14	18	1	13.8268 = 13	16	6	12.9858 = 12	19	8	13.6485 = 13	13	0
50	14.5655 = 14	11	4	13.4596 = 13	9	2	12.6709 = 12	13	5	13.2924 = 13	5	9
51	14.1891 = 14	3	9	13.0889 = 13	1	9	12.3689 = 12	7	4	12.9368 = 12	18	9
52	13.8080 = 13	16	2	12.7154 = 12	14	4	12.0849 = 12	1	8	12.6096 = 12	12	2
53	13.4580 = 13	9	2	12.3411 = 12	6	10	11.8092 = 11	16	2	12.2586 = 12	5	2
54	13.1080 = 13	2	2	11.9681 = 11	19	4	11.5317 = 11	10	7	11.9069 = 11	18	1
55	12.7627 = 12	15	3	11.5983 = 11	12	0	11.2426 = 11	4	10	11.5542 = 11	11	1
56	12.4216 = 12	8	5	11.2329 = 11	4	8	10.9319 = 10	18	7	11.1988 = 11	4	0
57	12.0876 = 12	1	9	10.8742 = 10	17	6	10.5899 = 10	11	9	10.8392 = 10	16	9
58	11.7636 = 11	15	3	10.5257 = 10	10	6	10.2180 = 10	4	4	10.4792 = 10	9	7
59	11.4527 = 11	9	1	10.1832 = 10	3	8	9.8254 = 9	16	6	10.1485 = 10	3	0
60	11.1577 = 11	3	1	9.8730 = 9	7	9	9.3910 = 9	7	9	9.8008 = 9	16	0
61	10.8824 = 10	17	8	9.5761 = 9	11	6	8.9599 = 8	19	2	9.4642 = 9	9	3
62	10.6286 = 10	12	7	9.3049 = 9	6	1	8.5145 = 8	10	3	9.1417 = 9	2	10
63	10.3886 = 10	7	8	9.0552 = 9	1	1	8.0897 = 8	1	9	8.8342 = 8	16	8
64	10.1552 = 10	3	1	8.8295 = 8	16	7	7.6641 = 7	13	3	8.5425 = 8	10	10
65	9.9228 = 9	18	5	8.6220 = 8	12	5	7.2689 = 7	5	4	8.2670 = 8	5	4
66	9.6794 = 9	13	7	8.4395 = 8	8	9	6.9170 = 6	18	4	8.0107 = 8	0	3
67	9.4189 = 9	8	15	8.2819 = 8	5	8	6.6223 = 6	12	5	7.7727 = 7	15	5

TABLE LXXXIV.—Continued.

Age.	RURAL.				TOWN.				CITY.				RURAL, TOWN, & CITY.			
	£	£	s.	d.	£	£	s.	d.	£	£	s.	d.	£	£	s.	d.
68	9.1447 =	9	2	10	8.1267 =	8	2	6	6.3790 =	6	7	6	7.5447 =	7	10	11
69	8.8522 =	8	17	0	7.9529 =	7	19	0	6.1838 =	6	3	8	7.3181 =	7	6	4
70	8.5435 =	8	10	10	7.7379 =	7	14	9	6.0344 =	6	0	8	7.0833 =	7	1	8
71	8.2187 =	8	4	4	7.4589 =	7	9	2	5.9463 =	5	18	11	6.8309 =	6	16	7
72	7.8772 =	7	17	6	7.0946 =	7	1	10	5.8912 =	5	17	10	6.5507 =	6	11	0
73	7.5268 =	7	10	6	6.6838 =	6	13	8	5.8633 =	5	17	3	6 2488 =	6	5	0
74	7.1744 =	7	3	5	6.2628 =	6	5	3	5.8496 =	5	17	0	5.9303 =	5	18	7
75	6.8260 =	6	16	6	5.8643 =	5	17	8	5.8293 =	5	16	7	5.6001 =	5	12	0
76	6.4878 =	6	9	9	5.5188 =	5	10	4	5.7789 =	5	15	6	5.2619 =	5	5	3
77	6.1650 =	6	3	3	5.2577 =	5	5	1	5.6724 =	5	13	5	4.9187 =	4	18	4
78	5.8576 =	5	17	1	5.0596 =	5	1	2	5.5058 =	5	10	1	4.5780 =	4	11	7
79	5.5649 =	5	11	3	4.9061 =	4	18	1	5.3194 =	5	6	4	4.2462 =	4	4	11
80	5.2871 =	5	5	8	4.7769 =	4	15	6	5.1122 =	5	2	2	3.9288 =	3	18	7
81	5.0241 =	5	0	5	4.6493 =	4	12	11	4.8975 =	4	17	11	3.6305 =	3	12	7
82	4.7753 =	4	15	6	4.5076 =	4	10	1	4.6780 =	4	13	11	3.3560 =	3	7	1
83	4.5327 =	4	10	7	4.3441 =	4	6	10	4.4745 =	4	9	5	3.1024 =	3	2	1
84	4.2883 =	4	5	9	4.1557 =	4	3	1	4.2542 =	4	5	1	2.8765 =	2	17	6
85	4.0320 =	4	0	7	3.9363 =	3	18	8	4.0162 =	4	0	3	2.7016 =	2	14	0
86	3.7542 =	3	15	1	3.6807 =	3	13	7	3.7514 =	3	15	0	2.5128 =	2	10	3
87	3.4434 =	3	8	10	3.3808 =	3	7	7	3.4416 =	3	8	10	2.3416 =	2	6	10
88	3.1177 =	3	2	4	3.0569 =	3	1	1	3.1214 =	3	2	5	2.1856 =	2	3	8
89	2.7932 =	2	15	10	2.7428 =	2	14	10	2.7914 =	2	15	9	2.0424 =	2	0	10
90	2.4821 =	2	9	7	2.4216 =	2	8	5	2.4806 =	2	9	7	1.9082 =	1	18	2
91	2.1959 =	2	3	11	2.1905 =	2	3	9	2.1935 =	2	3	10	1.7783 =	1	15	7
92	1.9448 =	1	18	10	1.9372 =	1	18	8	1.9402 =	1	18	9	1.6489 =	1	13	0
93	1.7215 =	1	14	5	1.7114 =	1	14	2	1.7149 =	1	14	3	1.5198 =	1	10	5
94	1.5191 =	1	10	4	1.5038 =	1	10	0	1.5083 =	1	10	2	1.3873 =	1	7	9
95	1.3103 =	1	6	2	1.3056 =	1	6	1	1.3126 =	1	6	3	1.2527 =	1	5	1
96	1.1020 =	1	2	0	1.1054 =	1	2	1	1.1134 =	1	2	3	1.0955 =	1	1	11
97	.8716 =	0	17	5	.8779 =	0	17	6	.8850 =	0	17	6	.9061 =	0	18	1
98	.6225 =	0	12	5	.6375 =	0	12	9	.6480 =	0	12	11	.7267 =	0	14	6
99	.3883 =	0	7	9	.3883 =	0	7	9	.3883 =	0	7	9	.5758 =	0	11	6

TABLE LXXXV.

VALUE OF SICK GIFT OF £1 PER WEEK, TO BE RECEIVED UNTIL 70 YEARS OF AGE.—INTEREST THREE PER CENT.

Age.	RURAL. £	£ s. d.	TOWN. £	£ s. d.	CITY. £	£ s. d.	RURAL, TOWN, & CITY. £	£ s. d.
18	28.7783=28	17 9	27.7431=27	14 10	31.5769=34	11 5	29.2000=29	4 0
19	29.5566=29	11 1	28.2675=28	5 4	32.1157=32	2 3	29.6897=29	13 10
20	30.0384=30	0 9	28.7868=28	15 8	32.7033=32	14 0	30.1767=30	3 6
21	30.5349=30	10 8	29.2946=29	5 10	33.3045=33	6 0	30.6735=30	13 6
22	31.0109=31	0 2	29.7767=29	15 6	33.9148=33	18 3	31.1739=31	3 6
23	31.4822=31	9 7	30.2325=30	4 7	34.5359=34	10 8	31.6573=31	13 2
24	31.9499=31	18 11	30.6675=30	13 4	35.1688=35	3 4	32.1435=32	2 10
25	32.4209=32	8 5	31.0866=31	1 8	35.8132=35	16 3	32.6335=32	12 8
26	32.8979=32	17 11	31.4956=31	9 10	36.4720=36	9 5	33.1301=33	2 7
27	33.3835=33	7 8	31.9003=31	18 0	37.1443=37	2 10	33.6378=33	12 9
28	33.8963=33	17 11	32.3095=32	6 2	37.8302=37	16 7	34.1536=34	3 1
29	34.4042=34	8 1	32.7118=32	14 2	38.5295=38	10 7	34.6776=34	13 7
30	34.9219=34	18 5	32.1166=33	2 4	39.2419=39	4 10	35.2097=35	4 2
31	35.4492=35	8 11	33.5259=33	10 6	39.9674=39	19 4	35.7528=35	15 1
32	35.9861=35	19 8	33.9433=33	18 10	40.7046=40	14 1	36.2984=36	6 0
33	36.5215=36	10 5	34.3669=34	7 4	41.5484=41	10 11	36.8459=36	16 11
34	37.0743=37	1 5	34.7981=34	15 11	42.3097=42	6 2	37.4062=37	8 1
35	37.6335=37	12 8	35.2357=35	4 8	43.0796=43	1 7	37.9674=37	19 4
36	38.1973=28	3 11	35.6730=35	13 5	43.8564=43	17 1	38.5323=38	10 8
37	38.7635=38	15 3	36.1149=36	2 3	44.6395=44	12 9	39.0990=39	2 0
38	39.4237=39	8 5	36.5572=36	11 1	45.4264=45	8 6	39.6674=39	13 4
39	40.0016=40	0 0	36.6590=36	13 2	46.2177=46	4 4	40.2357=40	4 9
40	40.6347=40	12 8	37.0724=37	1 5	47.0024=47	0 0	40.8040=40	16 1
41	41.1772=41	3 6	37.4893=37	9 9	47.7932=47	15 10	41.3688=41	7 5
42	41.7977=41	15 11	37.8980=37	17 11	48.5812=48	11 7	41.9294=41	18 7
43	42.4075=42	8 1	38.2929=38	5 10	49.3635=49	7 8	42.4534=42	9 1
44	43.0112=43	0 2	38.6678=38	13 4	50.1316=50	2 7	42.9877=42	17 9
45	43.5985=43	11 11	39.0177=39	0 4	50.6453=50	12 10	43.5000=43	10 0
46	44.1583=44	3 2	39.3344=39	6 8	51.3529=51	7 0	43.9786=43	19 7
47	44.6807=44	13 7	39.6121=39	12 2	52.0240=52	0 5	44.4267=44	8 6
48	45.1751=45	3 6	39.8466=39	16 11	52.6713=52	13 5	44.8334=44	16 8
49	45.6086=45	12 2	40.0328=40	0 7	53.3141=53	6 3	45.1631=45	3 3
50	45.9933=45	19 10	40.1698=40	3 4	53.9705=53	19 4	45.4933=45	9 10
51	46.3183=46	6 4	40.2437=40	4 10	54.6601=54	13 2	45.7844=45	15 11
52	46.5817=46	11 7	40.2526=40	5 0	55.4047=55	8 1	46.1252=46	2 5
53	46.7779=46	15 6	40.1502=40	3 0	56.1251=56	2 6	46.3130=46	6 3
54	46.9439=46	8 10	39.9590=39	19 2	56.7337=56	14 8	46.3952=46	7 11
55	46.9881=46	19 9	39.6302=39	12 7	57.1441=57	2 10	46.3389=46	6 9
56	46.9442=46	18 10	39.1342=39	2 8	57.2399=57	4 9	46.1039=46	2 1
57	46.8043=46	16 1	38.5457=38	10 10	56.9215=56	18 5	45.6482=45	13 0
58	46.4769=46	9 6	37.6483=37	12 11	56.1418=56	2 10	44.9359=44	18 9
59	45.8651=45	17 3	36.4980=36	9 11	54.8929=54	17 10	43.9280=43	18 7
60	44.8617=44	17 2	35.1881=35	3 9	53.0085=53	0 2	42.5792=42	11 7
61	43.3524=43	7 0	33.5389=33	10 9	50.6570=50	13 1	40.8343=40	16 8
62	41.2004=41	4 0	31.5784=31	11 6	47.6830=47	13 7	38.6315=38	12 8
63	38.4064=38	8 1	29.2989=29	5 11	44.2518=44	5 0	35.9818=35	19 8
64	34.9732=34	17 5	26.6875=26	13 9	40.2408=40	4 9	32.8719=32	17 5
65	30.9103=30	18 2	23.7279=23	14 6	35.7612=35	15 2	29.2978=29	5 7
66	26.2152=26	4 3	20.3940=20	7 10	30.8029=30	16 0	25.2416=25	4 10
67	21.9111=21	18 2	16.6643=16	13 3	25.3075=25	6 0	20.6704=20	13 5
68	15.8310=15	16 7	12.2293=12	4 7	18.7619=18	15 2	15.2365=15	4 9
69	8.6255= 8	12 6	6.7651= 6	15 3	10.5662=10	11 3	8.3436= 8	6 10

TABLE LXXXVI.

SINGLE AND PRESENT VALUE OF A SICK ALLOWANCE OF £1 PER WEEK FOR LIFE, AND ANNUAL PREMIUM PAYABLE FOR LIFE, AND UP TO AGE 70, THE SAME TO BE PAID MONTHLY.—RURAL, TOWN, AND CITY DISTRICTS.—INTEREST THREE PER CENT.

Age.	SINGLE PREMIUM.				ANNUAL PREMIUM PAYABLE DURING LIFE.				ANNUAL PREMIUM PAYABLE TO 70.			
	£	£	s.	d.	£	£	s.	d.	£	£	s.	d.
18	38.0943 =	38	1	11	1.7251 =	1	14	6	1.7274 =	1	14	7
19	38.9061 =	38	18	1	1.7379 =	1	14	9	1.7825 =	1	15	8
20	39.7259 =	39	14	6	1.7918 =	1	15	10	1.8445 =	1	16	11
21	40.5689 =	40	11	5	1.8391 =	1	16	9	1.8913 =	1	17	10
22	41.4228 =	41	8	5	1.9052 =	1	18	1	1.9618 =	1	19	3
23	42.2899 =	42	5	10	1.9637 =	1	19	3	2.0248 =	2	0	6
24	43.1765 =	43	3	6	2.0247 =	2	0	6	2.0909 =	2	1	10
25	44.0843 =	44	1	8	2.0881 =	2	1	9	2.1598 =	2	3	2
26	45.0166 =	45	0	4	2.1555 =	2	3	1	2.2327 =	2	4	8
27	45.9776 =	45	19	7	2.2242 =	2	4	6	2.3085 =	2	6	2
28	46.9657 =	46	19	4	2.2920 =	2	5	10	2.3844 =	2	7	8
29	47.9815 =	47	19	8	2.3687 =	2	7	4	2.4679 =	2	9	4
30	49.0261 =	49	0	6	2.4494 =	2	9	0	2.5574 =	2	11	2
31	50.1049 =	50	2	1	2.5343 =	2	10	8	2.6521 =	2	13	1
32	51.2075 =	51	4	2	2.6237 =	2	12	6	2.7524 =	2	15	1
33	52.3327 =	52	6	8	2.7180 =	2	14	4	2.8587 =	2	17	2
34	53.4950 =	53	9	11	2.8177 =	2	16	4	2.9718 =	2	19	5
35	54.6873 =	54	13	9	2.9230 =	2	18	6	3.0921 =	3	1	10
36	55.9102 =	55	18	2	3.0339 =	3	0	8	3.2197 =	3	4	5
37	57.1625 =	57	3	3	3.1522 =	3	3	1	3.3568 =	3	7	2
38	58.4479 =	58	8	11	3.2776 =	3	5	7	3.5034 =	3	10	1
39	59.7677 =	59	15	4	3.4137 =	3	8	3	3.6602 =	3	13	2
40	61.1245 =	61	2	6	3.5516 =	3	11	0	3.8306 =	3	16	7
41	62.5209 =	62	10	5	3.7010 =	3	14	0	4.0074 =	4	0	2
42	63.9591 =	63	19	2	3.8594 =	3	17	2	4.2012 =	4	4	0
43	65.4116 =	65	8	3	4.0258 =	4	0	6	4.4169 =	4	8	2
44	66.6203 =	66	12	5	4.1849 =	4	3	8	4.6091 =	4	12	0
45	68.1560 =	68	3	1	4.3732 =	4	7	6	4.8487 =	4	17	0
46	69.7159 =	69	14	4	4.5731 =	4	11	6	5.1049 =	5	2	1
47	71.3090 =	71	6	2	4.7978 =	4	15	11	5.3897 =	5	7	10
48	72.9293 =	72	18	7	5.0140 =	5	0	3	5.6960 =	5	13	9
49	74.5532 =	74	11	1	5.2538 =	5	5	1	6.0277 =	6	0	7
50	76.2687 =	76	5	4	5.5131 =	5	10	3	6.3973 =	6	7	11
51	78.0517 =	78	1	0	5.7906 =	5	15	10	6.8051 =	6	16	1
52	79.8876 =	79	17	9	6.0745 =	6	1	6	7.2284 =	7	4	7
53	81.8130 =	81	16	3	6.3915 =	6	7	5	7.7235 =	7	14	6
54	83.7724 =	83	15	5	6.7450 =	6	14	11	8.2745 =	8	5	6
55	85.7480 =	85	15	0	7.0890 =	7	1	9	8.8904 =	8	17	10
56	87.7103 =	87	14	2	7.4708 =	7	9	5	9.5828 =	9	11	8
57	89.6338 =	89	12	8	7.8758 =	7	17	6	10.3674 =	10	7	3
58	91.5184 =	91	10	4	8.3040 =	8	6	1	11.2654 =	11	5	4
59	93.3715 =	93	7	5	8.7343 =	8	14	8	12.3783 =	12	7	7
60	95.2013 =	95	4	0	9.2051 =	9	4	1	13.4659 =	13	9	4
61	97.0279 =	97	0	7	9.6961 =	9	13	11	14.6736 =	14	13	3
62	98.8364 =	98	16	9	10.2068 = 10	4	2		16.6416 =	16	12	10
63	100.7485 = 100	15	0		10.7455 = 10	14	11		18.8385 =	18	16	9
64	102.8310 = 102	16	7		11.3195 = 11	6	5		21.7246 =	21	14	6
65	105.1937 = 105	3	10		11.9413 = 11	18	10		25.7216 =	25	14	5
66	107.9621 = 107	19	3		12.6237 = 12	12	6		31.6771 =	31	13	7
67	111.2586 = 111	5	2		13.3813 = 13	7	8		41.5021 =	41	10	1
68	114.8210 = 114	16	5		14.1994 = 14	4	0		60.6427 =	60	12	10
69	118.2344 = 118	2	8		15.0303 = 15	0	7		114.4713 = 114	9	5	

TABLE LXXXVII.

SHEWING THE PRESENT VALUE, AT THE GIVEN AGES, FOR AN ANNUITY OF £1 PER ANNUM, AFTER 70 YEARS OF AGE.—INTEREST THREE PER CENT.

Age.	RURAL.				TOWN.				CITY.				RURAL, TOWN, & CITY.			
	£	£	s.	d.	£	£	s.	d.	£	£	s.	d.	£	£	s.	d.
18	.7821=	0	15	7½	.5834=	0	11	8	.4139=	0	8	3	.5439=	0	10	11
19	.8108=	0	16	2½	.6057=	0	12	1	.4274=	0	8	6½	.5634=	0	11	3
20	.8407=	0	16	9½	.6288=	0	12	6½	.4418=	0	8	10	.5836=	0	11	8
21	.8719=	0	17	5	.6526=	0	13	0½	.4570=	0	9	1½	.6047=	0	12	1
22	.9043=	0	18	1	.6774=	0	13	6½	.4733=	0	9	5½	.6270=	0	12	6
23	.9382=	0	18	9	.7030=	0	14	0½	.4907=	0	9	10	.6505=	0	13	0
24	.9735=	0	19	5½	.7295=	0	14	7	.5091=	0	10	2	.6749=	0	13	6
25	1.0108=	1	0	2½	.7567=	0	15	1½	.5286=	0	10	6½	.7005=	0	14	0
26	1.0485=	1	0	10	.7848=	0	15	8	.5491=	0	10	11½	.7271=	0	14	7
27	1.0882=	1	1	9	.8137=	0	16	3	.5707=	0	11	5	.7549=	0	15	1
28	1.1293=	1	2	7	.8438=	0	16	10½	.5945=	0	11	11	.7838=	0	15	8
29	1.1720=	1	3	5	.8749=	0	17	6	.6169=	0	12	4	.8139=	0	16	3
30	1.2136=	1	4	3	.9073=	0	18	1½	.6416=	0	12	10	.8452=	0	16	11
31	1.2624=	1	5	3	.9414=	0	18	10	.6674=	0	13	6½	.8780=	0	17	7
32	1.3104=	1	6	2½	.9774=	0	19	6½	.6942=	0	13	11	.9121=	0	18	3
33	1.3602=	1	7	2½	1.0153=	1	0	3½	.7222=	0	14	5½	.9475=	0	18	11
34	1.4119=	1	8	2½	1.0551=	1	1	1	.7514=	0	15	0	.9845=	0	19	8
35	1.4657=	1	9	3½	1.0968=	1	1	11	.7819=	0	15	7½	1.0232=	1	0	6
36	1.5215=	1	10	5	1.1406=	1	2	9½	.8138=	0	16	3	1.0634=	1	1	3
37	1.5794=	1	11	7	1.1862=	1	3	8½	.8472=	0	16	11½	1.1054=	1	2	1
38	1.6396=	1	12	9½	1.2338=	1	4	8	.8823=	0	17	7½	1.1493=	1	3	0
39	1.7025=	1	14	0½	1.2835=	1	5	8	.9195=	0	18	4½	1.1952=	1	3	11
40	1.7705=	1	15	7	1.3355=	1	6	8½	.9590=	0	19	2	1.2435=	1	4	10
41	1.8375=	1	16	9	1.3899=	1	7	9½	1,0001=	1	0	0	1.2915=	1	5	10
42	1.9112=	1	18	2½	1.4467=	1	8	11	1.0462=	1	0	11	1.3482=	1	7	0
43	1.9883=	1	19	9	1.5063=	1	10	1½	1.0944=	1	1	8	1.4050=	1	8	1
44	2.0696=	2	1	4½	1.5689=	1	11	4½	1.1458=	1	2	11	1.4651=	1	9	4
45	2.1554=	2	3	1	1.6348=	1	12	8	1.2005=	1	4	0	1.5285=	1	10	7
46	2.2460=	2	4	11	1.7044=	1	14	1	1.2555=	1	5	1	1.5882=	1	11	9
47	2.3415=	2	6	10	1.7782=	1	15	4½	1.3196=	1	6	6	1.6666=	1	13	4
48	2.4424=	2	8	10	1.8564=	1	17	1½	1.3850=	1	7	8½	1.7416=	1	14	10
49	2.5493=	2	11	0	1.9397=	1	18	9½	1.4555=	1	9	1	1.8218=	1	16	5
50	2.6625=	2	13	3	2.0284=	2	0	6½	1.5323=	1	10	7½	1.9121=	1	18	3
51	2.7829=	2	15	7½	2.1233=	2	2	5½	1.6167=	1	12	4	2.0095=	2	0	2
52	2.9110=	2	18	2½	2.2249=	2	4	5½	1.7102=	1	14	2½	2.0994=	2	2	0
53	3.0480=	3	0	11½	2.3344=	2	6	8	1.8127=	1	16	3	2.2075=	2	4	2
54	3.1954=	3	3	11	2.4529=	2	9	0½	1.9236=	1	18	5½	2.3244=	2	6	6
55	3.3548=	3	7	1	2.5821=	2	11	7½	2.0422=	2	0	10½	2.4508=	2	9	0
56	3.5280=	3	10	6½	2.7234=	2	14	5½	2.1674=	2	3	4	2.5875=	2	11	4
57	3.6325=	3	12	7½	2.8134=	2	16	3	2.2456=	2	4	11	2.7355=	2	14	9
58	3.9250=	3	18	6	3.0514=	3	1	0	2.4347=	2	8	8	2.8970=	2	17	11
59	4.1549=	4	3	1	3.2494=	3	4	11½	2.5794=	2	11	7	3.1469=	3	2	11
60	4.4107=	4	8	2½	3.4616=	3	9	2½	2.7279=	2	14	6½	3.2726=	3	5	5
61	4.6972=	4	13	11	3.7081=	3	14	2	2.8932=	2	17	10½	3.4941=	3	9	11
62	5.0191=	5	0	4½	3.9991=	3	19	11½	3.0722=	3	1	0½	3.7442=	3	14	11
63	5.3780=	5	7	9	4.3121=	4	6	3	3.2798=	3	5	7	4.0278=	4	0	7
64	5.7748=	5	15	6	4.6808=	4	13	7	3.5126=	3	10	3	4.3507=	4	7	0
65	6.2113=	6	2	2½	5.1029=	5	2	0½	3.7898=	3	15	9½	4.7195=	4	14	5
66	6.6850=	6	13	8½	5.5871=	5	11	9	4.1277=	4	2	6½	5.1441=	5	2	11
67	7.1957=	7	3	11	6.1447=	6	2	11	4.5486=	4	10	11½	5.6335=	5	12	8
68	7.7501=	7	15	0	6.7714=	6	15	5	5.0683=	5	1	4½	6.1929=	6	3	10
69	8.3496=	8	7	0	7.4599=	7	9	2	5.7076=	5	14	1½	6.8277=	6	16	7

TABLE LXXXVIII.

SHEWING THE AMOUNT TO BE PAID IN ONE SUM, AT ANY OF THE AGES GIVEN TO ASSURE £1 AT DEATH.—INTEREST THREE PER CENT.

Age.	RURAL. £	= £	s.	d.	TOWN. £	= £	s.	d.	CITY. £	= £	s.	d.	RURAL, TOWN, & CITY. £	= £	s.	d.
18	.3105	0	6	2½	.3257	0	6	6	.3400	0	6	9½	.3284	0	6	7
19	.3154	0	6	3½	.3302	0	6	7	.3488	0	6	11½	.3346	0	6	8
20	.3204	0	6	5	.3348	0	6	8½	.3568	0	7	1½	.3409	0	6	9½
21	.3255	0	6	6	.3399	0	6	9½	.3647	0	7	3½	.3471	0	6	11
22	.3306	0	6	7½	.3450	0	6	11	.3722	0	7	5½	.3533	0	7	0½
23	.3357	0	6	8½	.3505	0	7	0	.3794	0	7	7	.3594	0	7	2
24	.3418	0	6	10	.3563	0	7	1½	.3863	0	7	8½	.3651	0	7	3½
25	.3462	0	6	11	.3624	0	7	3	.3930	0	7	10½	.3734	0	7	5½
26	.3517	0	7	0	.3690	0	7	4½	.3997	0	8	0	.3780	0	7	6½
27	.3574	0	7	2	.3774	0	7	6½	.4074	0	8	2	.3826	0	7	7½
28	.3632	0	7	3	.3846	0	7	8½	.4132	0	8	3½	.3898	0	7	9½
29	.3693	0	7	4½	.3921	0	7	10	.4201	0	8	5	.3966	0	7	11
30	.3757	0	7	6	.3998	0	8	0	.4272	0	8	6½	.4046	0	8	1
31	.3823	0	7	8	.4075	0	8	2	.4335	0	8	8	.4108	0	8	2½
32	.3899	0	7	9½	.4150	0	8	3½	.4421	0	8	10	.4182	0	8	4
33	.3961	0	7	11	.4226	0	8	5½	.4499	0	9	0	.4257	0	8	6
34	.4034	0	8	1	.4309	0	8	7½	.4580	0	9	2	.4336	0	8	8
35	.4109	0	8	2½	.4379	0	8	9	.4663	0	9	4	.4409	0	8	9½
36	.4186	0	8	4½	.4459	0	8	11	.4749	0	9	6	.4509	0	9	0
37	.4268	0	8	6½	.4540	0	9	1	.4836	0	9	8	.4584	0	9	2
38	.4382	0	8	9	.4611	0	9	2½	.4925	0	9	10	.4672	0	9	4
39	.4438	0	8	10½	.4697	0	9	4½	.5015	0	10	0½	.4760	0	9	6
40	.4519	0	9	0½	.4785	0	9	7	.5104	0	10	2½	.4853	0	9	8½
41	.4614	0	9	2½	.4876	0	9	9	.5194	0	10	4½	.4946	0	9	10½
42	.4712	0	9	3	.4962	0	9	11	.5282	0	10	7	.5039	0	10	1
43	.4801	0	9	7	.5066	0	10	1½	.5369	0	10	9	.5134	0	10	3
44	.4892	0	9	9½	.5165	0	10	4	.5456	0	10	11	.5229	0	10	5½
45	.4983	0	9	11½	.5265	0	10	6½	.5545	0	11	1	.5327	0	10	8
46	.5076	0	10	2	.5367	0	10	9	.5635	0	11	3½	.5426	0	10	10
47	.5170	0	10	4	.5470	0	10	11½	.5728	0	11	5½	.5527	0	11	1
48	.5271	0	10	6½	.5575	0	11	2	.5832	0	11	8	.5631	0	11	3
49	.5368	0	10	9	.5681	0	11	4½	.5926	0	11	10	.5733	0	11	5½
50	.5466	0	10	11	.5788	0	11	7	.6018	0	12	0½	.5827	0	11	7½
51	.5575	0	11	2	.5896	0	11	9½	.6106	0	12	2½	.5940	0	11	10½
52	.5686	0	11	4½	.6005	0	12	0	.6188	0	12	4½	.6036	0	12	1
53	.5788	0	11	7	.6114	0	12	3	.6259	0	12	6	.6138	0	12	3
54	.5890	0	11	9½	.6222	0	12	5½	.6349	0	12	8½	.6240	0	12	5½
55	.5991	0	12	0	.6330	0	12	8	.6433	0	12	10½	.6343	0	12	8
56	.6090	0	12	2	.6437	0	12	10½	.6524	0	13	0½	.6446	0	12	10½
57	.6188	0	12	4½	.6541	0	13	1	.6624	0	13	3	.6551	0	13	1
58	.6282	0	12	7	.6643	0	13	3½	.6732	0	13	5½	.6656	0	13	3½
59	.6373	0	12	9	.6742	0	13	6	.6847	0	13	8½	.6752	0	13	6
60	.6458	0	12	11	.6833	0	13	8	.6973	0	13	11½	.6869	0	13	9
61	.6539	0	13	1	.6919	0	13	10	.7099	0	14	2½	.6952	0	13	11
62	.6613	0	13	2½	.6998	0	13	0	.7228	0	14	5½	.7046	0	14	1
63	.6682	0	13	4½	.7071	0	14	1½	.7352	0	14	8½	.7130	0	14	3
64	.6750	0	13	6	.7175	0	14	4	.7476	0	14	11½	.7220	0	14	5
65	.6818	0	13	7½	.7197	0	14	5	.7591	0	15	2	.7292	0	14	7
66	.6889	0	13	9½	.7250	0	14	6	.7694	0	15	4½	.7375	0	14	9
67	.6965	0	13	11	.7296	0	14	7	.7779	0	15	6½	.7444	0	14	10½
68	.7064	0	14	1½	.7341	0	14	8	.7850	0	15	8½	.7511	0	15	0
69	.7130	0	14	3	.7392	0	14	9	.7907	0	15	10	.7577	0	15	1½

TABLE LXXXIX.

SHEWING THE ANNUAL CONTRIBUTION PAYABLE MONTHLY FOR A SICK GIFT OF £1 PER WEEK UP TO AGE 70, BOTH THE CONTRIBUTION AND SICK GIFT THEN TO CEASE.

Age.	RURAL.				TOWN.				CITY.				RURAL, TOWN, & CITY.			
	£	£	s.	d.	£	£	s.	d.	£	£	s.	d.	£	£	s.	d.
18	1.2836 = 1		5	8	1.2406 = 1		4	10	1.4493 = 1		9	0	1.3241 = 1		6	6
19	1.3293 = 1		6	7	1.2888 = 1		5	9	1.4958 = 1		9	11	1.3604 = 1		7	3
20	1.3634 = 1		7	3	1.3236 = 1		6	6	1.5439 = 1		10	11	1.3979 = 1		7	11
21	1.3990 = 1		8	0	1.3549 = 1		7	1	1.5944 = 1		11	11	1.4300 = 1		8	7
22	1.4344 = 1		8	8	1.3947 = 1		7	11	1.6447 = 1		12	11	1.4764 = 1		9	6
23	1.4704 = 1		9	5	1.4300 = 1		8	7	1.6964 = 1		13	11	1.5157 = 1		10	4
24	1.5073 = 1		10	5	1.4665 = 1		9	4	1.7495 = 1		15	0	1.5566 = 1		11	2
25	1.5456 = 1		10	11	1.5037 = 1		10	1	1.8042 = 1		16	1	1.5988 = 1		12	0
26	1.5854 = 1		11	8	1.5423 = 1		10	10	1.8608 = 1		17	3	1.6436 = 1		12	10
27	1.6273 = 1		12	7	1.5870 = 1		11	9	1.9198 = 1		18	5	1.6889 = 1		13	9
28	1.6680 = 1		13	9	1.6296 = 1		12	7	1.9815 = 1		19	8	1.7339 = 1		14	8
29	1.7184 = 1		14	4	1.6744 = 1		13	6	2.0460 = 2		0	11	1.7836 = 1		15	8
30	1.7672 = 1		15	4	1.7093 = 1		14	2	2.1138 = 2		2	3	1.8366 = 1		16	9
31	1.8192 = 1		16	5	1.7698 = 1		15	5	2.1854 = 2		3	9	1.8924 = 1		17	10
32	1.8737 = 1		17	6	1.8200 = 1		16	5	2.2613 = 2		5	3	1.9510 = 1		19	0
33	1.9308 = 1		18	7	1.8731 = 1		17	6	2.3468 = 2		6	11	2.0127 = 2		0	3
34	1.9919 = 1		19	10	1.9281 = 1		18	7	2.4319 = 2		8	8	2.0780 = 2		1	7
35	2.0564 = 2		1	2	1.9861 = 1		19	9	2.5220 = 2		10	5	2.1467 = 2		2	11
36	2.1249 = 2		2	6	2.0472 = 2		1	0	2.6173 = 2		12	4	2.2189 = 2		4	5
37	2.1976 = 2		4	0	2.0936 = 2		1	10	2.7182 = 2		14	4	2.2960 = 2		5	11
38	2.2800 = 2		5	7	2.1859 = 2		3	9	2.8244 = 2		16	6	2.3777 = 2		7	7
39	2.3622 = 2		7	3	2.2587 = 2		5	2	2.9369 = 2		18	9	2.4641 = 2		9	3
40	2.4495 = 2		9	0	2.3014 = 2		6	0	3.0535 = 3		1	1	2.5570 = 2		11	2
41	2.5424 = 2		10	10	2.3813 = 2		7	8	3.1773 = 3		3	7	2.6516 = 2		13	0
42	2.6478 = 2		13	0	2.4668 = 2		9	4	3.3062 = 3		6	2	2.7541 = 2		15	1
43	2.7473 = 2		15	0	2.5574 = 2		11	2	3.4407 = 3		8	10	2.8602 = 2		17	2
44	2.8658 = 2		17	4	2.6533 = 2		13	1	3.5823 = 3		11	8	2.9741 = 2		19	6
45	2.9845 = 2		19	8	2.7550 = 2		15	1	3.7313 = 3		14	8	3.0946 = 3		1	11
46	3.1100 = 3		2	2	2.8622 = 2		17	3	3.8698 = 3		17	5	3.2203 = 3		4	5
47	3.2471 = 3		5	0	2.9753 = 2		19	6	4.0372 = 4		0	9	3.3579 = 3		7	2
48	3.3875 = 3		7	7	3.0948 = 3		1	11	4.2257 = 4		4	6	3.5016 = 3		10	0
49	3.5368 = 3		10	9	3.2471 = 3		5	0	4.4163 = 4		8	4	3.6515 = 3		13	0
50	3.6958 = 3		13	11	3.3550 = 3		7	1	4.6313 = 4		12	8	3.8159 = 3		16	4
51	3.9339 = 3		18	8	3.4972 = 3		10	0	4.8401 = 4		16	10	3.9918 = 3		19	10
52	4.0732 = 4		1	6	3.6486 = 3		13	0	5.0871 = 5		1	9	4.1735 = 4		3	10
53	4.2713 = 4		5	5	3.8427 = 3		16	10	5.3259 = 5		6	6	4.3721 = 4		7	5
54	4.4900 = 4		9	10	3.9733 = 3		19	6	5.5896 = 5		11	9	4.5826 = 4		11	8
55	4.7226 = 4		14	5	4.1463 = 4		2	11	5.7322 = 5		14	8	4.8044 = 4		16	1
56	4.9754 = 4		19	6	4.3237 = 4		6	6	6.1507 = 6		3	0	5.0370 = 5		0	9
57	5.2143 = 5		4	3	4.4808 = 4		9	7	6.4058 = 6		8	1	5.2798 = 5		5	7
58	5.5460 = 5		10	11	4.6967 = 4		13	11	6.7442 = 6		14	11	5.5313 = 5		10	8
59	5.8505 = 5		17	0	4.8834 = 4		17	8	7.0489 = 7		1	0	5.8235 = 5		16	6
60	6.1550 = 6		3	1	5.0608 = 5		1	3	7.3574 = 7		7	2	6.0226 = 6		0	5

TABLE XC.

SHEWING THE ANNUAL CONTRIBUTION PAYABLE MONTHLY UNTIL AGE 70, FOR AN ANNUITY OF

£1 PER ANNUM AFTER THAT TIME, THE CONTRIBUTION THEN CEASING.

Age.	RURAL. £	£ s. d.	TOWN. £	£ s. d.	CITY. £	£ s. d.	RURAL, TOWN, & CITY. £	£ s. d.
18	.0348=0	0 8½	.0263=0	0 6½	.0190=0	0 4½	.0246=0	0 6
19	.0364=0	0 9	.0276=0	0 6½	.0199=0	0 5	.0258=0	0 6
20	.0381=0	0 9	.0289=0	0 7	.0208=0	0 5	.0270=0	0 6½
21	.0399=0	0 9½	.0301=0	0 7	.0218=0	0 5½	.0281=0	0 6½
22	.0418=0	0 10	.0317=0	0 7½	.0229=0	0 5½	.0290=0	0 7
23	.0438=0	0 10½	.0332=0	0 8	.0241=0	0 6	.0311=0	0 7
24	.0459=0	0 11	.0348=0	0 8½	.0253=0	0 6	.0326=0	0 7½
25	.0481=0	0 11½	.0366=0	0 9	.0266=0	0 6½	.0343=0	0 8
26	.0505=0	1 0	.0384=0	0 9	.0278=0	0 6½	.0360=0	0 8½
27	.0530=0	1 1	.0404=0	0 9½	.0294=0	0 7	.0379=0	0 9
28	.0555=0	1 1½	.0425=0	0 10	.0311=0	0 7½	.0397=0	0 9½
29	.0585=0	1 2	.0447=0	0 11	.0327=0	0 8	.0418=0	0 10
30	.0600=0	1 2½	.0471=0	0 11½	.0345=0	0 8½	.0440=0	0 10½
31	.0647=0	1 3½	.0497=0	1 0	.0364=0	0 8½	.0464=0	0 11½
32	.0682=0	1 4½	.0524=0	1 0½	.0385=0	0 9½	.0490=0	1 0
33	.0719=0	1 5½	.0553=0	1 1½	.0407=0	0 10	.0517=0	1 0½
34	.0758=0	1 6	.0584=0	1 2	.0435=0	0 10½	.0546=0	1 1
35	.0800=0	1 7	.0618=0	1 3	.0457=0	0 11	.0578=0	1 2
36	.0846=0	1 8½	.0654=0	1 3½	.0485=0	0 11½	.0612=0	1 3
37	.0895=0	1 9½	.0687=0	1 4½	.0515=0	1 0½	.0649=0	1 3½
38	.0948=0	1 11	.0737=0	1 5½	.0548=0	1 1	.0688=0	1 4½
39	.1005=0	2 0	.0783=0	1 7	.0584=0	1 2	.0731=0	1 5½
40	.1067=0	2 1½	.0829=0	1 8	.0623=0	1 3	.0779=0	1 6½
41	.1134=0	2 3	.0882=0	1 9	.0665=0	1 4	.0829=0	1 7½
42	.1213=0	2 5	.0941=0	1 10½	.0712=0	1 5	.0885=0	1 8
43	.1291=0	2 7	.1006=0	2 0	.0762=0	1 6½	.0946=0	1 10½
44	.1379=0	2 9	.1077=0	2 2	.0818=0	1 7½	.1013=0	2 0
45	.1475=0	2 11½	.1154=0	2 3½	.0880=0	1 9	.1087=0	2 2
46	.1581=0	3 2	.1240=0	2 6	.0984=0	1 11½	.1168=0	2 4
47	.1701=0	3 5	.1335=0	2 8	.1024=0	2 0½	.1259=0	2 6
48	.1831=0	3 8	.1442=0	2 11	.1111=0	2 3	.1360=0	2 8½
49	.1976=0	3 11½	.1573=0	3 2	.1205=0	2 5	.1472=0	2 11
50	.2139=0	4 3½	.1694=0	3 4½	.1311=0	2 7½	.1603=0	3 2½
51	.2363=0	4 8½	.1845=0	3 8½	.1431=0	2 10½	.1744=0	3 6
52	.2544=0	5 1	.2016=0	4 0	.1570=0	3 1½	.1899=0	3 9½
53	.2783=0	5 5½	.2234=0	4 5½	.1720=0	3 5½	.2084=0	4 2
54	.3056=0	6 1½	.2439=0	4 10½	.1895=0	3 9½	.2295=0	4 7
55	.3371=0	6 9	.2701=0	5 5	.2096=0	4 2½	.2541=0	5 1
56	.3654=0	7 6	.3009=0	6 0	.2329=0	4 8	.2827=0	5 7½
57	.4037=0	8 1	.3270=0	6 6½	.2527=0	5 0½	.3170=0	6 4
58	.4683=0	9 4½	.3806=0	7 7½	.2924=0	5 10	.3566=0	7 1½
59	.5300=0	10 7	.4336=0	8 8	.3312=0	6 7½	.4171=0	8 4
60	.6051=0	12 1	.4978=0	9 11½	.3778=0	7 6	.4629=0	9 3

x

TABLE XCI.

SHEWING THE ANNUAL CONTRIBUTION PAYABLE MONTHLY FOR LIFE, TO ASSURE THE SUM OF £1 AT DEATH.

Age.	RURAL.				TOWN.				CITY.				RURAL, TOWN, & CITY.			
	£	£	s.	d.	£	£	s.	d.	£	£	s.	d.	£	£	s.	d.
18	.0133	=0	0	3¼	.0141	=0	0	3½	.0153	=0	0	3¼	.0145	=0	0	3½
19	.0136	=0	0	3¼	.0144	=0	0	3½	.0159	=0	0	3¾	.0149	=0	0	3½
20	.0140	=0	0	3½	.0147	=0	0	3½	.0165	=0	0	4	.0153	=0	0	3¾
21	.0143	=0	0	3½	.0150	=0	0	3½	.0170	=0	0	4	.0157	=0	0	3¾
22	.0146	=0	0	3½	.0154	=0	0	3¾	.0176	=0	0	4¼	.0162	=0	0	4
23	.0150	=0	0	3¾	.0157	=0	0	3¾	.0182	=0	0	4¼	.0166	=0	0	4
24	.0154	=0	0	3¾	.0161	=0	0	3¾	.0187	=0	0	4½	.0171	=0	0	4
25	.0157	=0	0	3¾	.0166	=0	0	4	.0192	=0	0	4½	.0176	=0	0	4¼
26	.0161	=0	0	4	.0171	=0	0	4	.0198	=0	0	4¾	.0181	=0	0	4¼
27	.0165	=0	0	4	.0177	=0	0	4¼	.0204	=0	0	5	.0185	=0	0	4½
28	.0169	=0	0	4	.0182	=0	0	4¼	.0210	=0	0	5	.0190	=0	0	4½
29	.0174	=0	0	4¼	.0188	=0	0	4½	.0216	=0	0	5¼	.0195	=0	0	4¾
30	.0179	=0	0	4¼	.0194	=0	0	4¾	.0222	=0	0	5¼	.0201	=0	0	4¾
31	.0184	=0	0	4½	.0201	=0	0	5	.0229	=0	0	5½	.0207	=0	0	5
32	.0190	=0	0	4½	.0207	=0	0	5	.0236	=0	0	5¾	.0214	=0	0	5¼
33	.0195	=0	0	4¾	.0214	=0	0	5¼	.0244	=0	0	5¾	.0221	=0	0	5¼
34	.0201	=0	0	5	.0221	=0	0	5¼	.0252	=0	0	6	.0228	=0	0	5½
35	.0207	=0	0	5	.0227	=0	0	5½	.0261	=0	0	6¼	.0235	=0	0	5¾
36	.0214	=0	0	5¼	.0235	=0	0	5¾	.0270	=0	0	6½	.0244	=0	0	5¾
37	.0222	=0	0	5¼	.0243	=0	0	5¾	.0280	=0	0	6¾	.0252	=0	0	6
38	.0231	=0	0	5½	.0250	=0	0	6	.0291	=0	0	7	.0262	=0	0	6¼
39	.0238	=0	0	5¾	.0259	=0	0	6¼	.0302	=0	0	7¼	.0271	=0	0	6½
40	.0246	=0	0	6	.0268	=0	0	6½	.0312	=0	0	7½	.0282	=0	0	6¾
41	.0256	=0	0	6¼	.0278	=0	0	6¾	.0323	=0	0	7¾	.0292	=0	0	7
42	.0266	=0	0	6½	.0288	=0	0	7	.0335	=0	0	8	.0304	=0	0	7¼
43	.0276	=0	0	6¾	.0300	=0	0	7¼	.0347	=0	0	8¼	.0315	=0	0	7½
44	.0286	=0	0	6¾	.0312	=0	0	7½	.0360	=0	0	8¾	.0328	=0	0	7¾
45	.0297	=0	0	7	.0325	=0	0	7¾	.0373	=0	0	9	.0341	=0	0	8¼
46	.0308	=0	0	7½	.0339	=0	0	8¼	.0387	=0	0	9¼	.0355	=0	0	8½
47	.0320	=0	0	7¾	.0353	=0	0	8½	.0403	=0	0	9½	.0371	=0	0	9
48	.0334	=0	0	8	.0369	=0	0	9	.0421	=0	0	10	.0387	=0	0	9¼
49	.0347	=0	0	8¼	.0385	=0	0	9¼	.0438	=0	0	10½	.0404	=0	0	9¾
50	.0361	=0	0	8¾	.0402	=0	0	9¾	.0454	=0	0	11	.0421	=0	0	10
51	.0378	=0	0	9	.0421	=0	0	10	.0472	=0	0	11¼	.0440	=0	0	10½
52	.0396	=0	0	9½	.0440	=0	0	10½	.0490	=0	0	11¾	.0458	=0	0	11
53	.0414	=0	0	10	.0461	=0	0	11	.0506	=0	1	0	.0479	=0	0	11½
54	.0431	=0	0	10¼	.0482	=0	0	11½	.0525	=0	1	0½	.0502	=0	1	0
55	.0450	=0	0	10¾	.0505	=0	1	0	.0546	=0	1	1	.0524	=0	1	0½
56	.0469	=0	0	11¼	.0529	=0	1	0¾	.0568	=0	1	1¾	.0549	=0	1	1¼
57	.0489	=0	0	11¾	.0556	=0	1	1¼	.0595	=0	1	2¼	.0575	=0	1	1¾
58	.0511	=0	1	0¼	.0580	=0	1	2	.0625	=0	1	3	.0605	=0	1	2½
59	.0531	=0	1	0¾	.0607	=0	1	2½	.0660	=0	1	3¾	.0631	=0	1	3¼
60	.0552	=0	1	1¼	.0633	=0	1	3¼	.0702	=0	1	5	.0661	=0	1	4

All the previous tables have been calculated upon the supposition of three per cent. upon the Capital Stock of the Society being realized, and it is presumed that, looking forward for the period of time such calculations embrace, societies will not be able to realize a larger per centage; and it is very questionable whether, on the general average, they will be able to realize that amount; in a few instances, doubtless, a larger per centage is realized, and for the purpose of drawing the attention of societies to the necessity of the best investments of funds, the values of an annuity, sick allowance, annuity, and sum at death, have been given, and the contributions requisite to be paid as equivalent to those present values, or the probability of living, as experienced in the rural, town, and city districts; interest of money being taken at four per cent. per annum.

TABLE XCII.

VALUE OF ANNUITY.—RURAL, TOWN, AND CITY.

INTEREST FOUR PER CENT. PER ANNUM.

Age.	VALUE OF ANNUITY.				Age.	VALUE OF ANNUITY.				Age.	VALUE OF ANNUITY.			
	£	£	s.	d.		£	£	s.	d.		£	£	s.	d.
18	18.6615 = 18	13	3		45	13.4643 = 13	9	8		72	6.2025 = 6	4	1	
19	18.5175 = 18	10	4		46	13.1913 = 13	3	10		73	5.9202 = 5	18	7	
20	18.3683 = 18	7	4		47	12.9104 = 12	18	2		74	5.6408 = 5	12	10	
21	18.2198 = 18	4	5		48	12.6242 = 12	12	6		75	5.3389 = 5	6	9	
22	18.0732 = 18	1	6		49	12.3343 = 12	6	8		76	5.0278 = 5	0	7	
23	17.9319 = 17	18	8		50	12.0416 = 12	0	10		77	4.7103 = 4	14	2	
24	17.7866 = 17	15	8		51	11.7480 = 11	15	0		78	4.3936 = 4	7	10	
25	17.6393 = 17	12	8		52	11.4503 = 11	9	0		79	4.0837 = 4	1	8	
26	17.4884 = 17	9	8		53	11.1566 = 11	3	1		80	3.7862 = 3	15	9	
27	17.3323 = 17	6	8		54	10.8771 = 10	17	7		81	3.5058 = 3	10	1	
28	17.1704 = 17	3	5		55	10.5798 = 10	11	7		82	3.2472 = 3	4	11	
29	17.0026 = 17	0	1		56	10.2785 = 10	5	7		83	3.0079 = 3	0	2	
30	16.8290 = 16	16	7		57	9.9718 = 9	19	5		84	2.7862 = 2	15	9	
31	16.6513 = 16	13	0		58	9.6691 = 9	13	3		85	2.6202 = 2	12	5	
32	16.4654 = 16	9	4		59	9.3563 = 9	7	2		86	2.4400 = 2	8	10	
33	16.2710 = 16	5	5		60	9.0546 = 9	1	1		87	2.2763 = 2	5	6	
34	16.0722 = 16	1	5		61	8.7613 = 8	15	3		88	2.1268 = 2	2	6	
35	15.8648 = 15	17	4		62	8.4796 = 8	9	7		89	1.9893 = 1	19	9	
36	15.6493 = 15	13	0		63	8.2104 = 8	4	2		90	1.8602 = 1	17	2	
37	15.4247 = 15	8	6		64	7.9548 = 7	19	1		91	1.7348 = 1	14	8	
38	15.1926 = 15	3	10		65	7.7138 = 7	14	3		92	1.6091 = 1	12	1	
39	14.9575 = 14	19	2		66	7.4888 = 7	9	9		93	1.4828 = 1	9	8	
40	14.7132 = 14	14	3		67	7.2808 = 7	5	7		94	1.3518 = 1	7	0	
41	14.4641 = 14	9	3		68	7.0816 = 7	1	8		95	1.2163 = 1	4	4	
42	14.2463 = 14	4	11		69	6.8833 = 6	17	8		96	1.0544 = 1	1	1	
43	13.9910 = 13	19	10		70	6.6768 = 6	13	6		97	.8524 = 0	17	1	
44	13.7306 = 13	14	7		71	6.4532 = 6	9	1		98	.6401 = 0	12	10	

TABLE XCIII.

PRESENT VALUE OF A SICK ALLOWANCE OF £1 PER WEEK UP TO AGE 70, VALUE OF AN ANNUITY
OF £1 PER ANNU° AFTER THAT AGE, AND PRESENT VALUE OF £1 AT DEATH.—RURAL, TOWN,
AND CITY DISTRICTS.—INTEREST FOUR PER CENT.

Age.	SICK ALLOWANCE.				VALUE OF ANNUITY.				VALUE OF £1 AT DEATH.			
	£	£	s.	d.	£	£	s.	d.	£	£	s.	d.
18	22.5625	= 22	11	3	.3106	= 0	6	3	.2437	= 0	4	10
19	23.0388	= 23	0	9	.3256	= 0	6	6	.2493	= 0	5	0
20	23.5181	= 23	10	4	.3406	= 0	6	10	.2554	= 0	5	1
21	24.0074	= 24	0	2	.3564	= 0	7	2	.2607	= 0	5	3
22	24.4907	= 24	9	10	.3730	= 0	7	6	.2664	= 0	5	4
23	24.9675	= 24	19	4	.3908	= 0	7	10	.2718	= 0	5	5
24	25.4511	= 25	9	0	.4094	= 0	8	2	.2774	= 0	5	7
25	26.0038	= 26	0	1	.4290	= 0	8	7	.2830	= 0	5	8
26	26.5066	= 26	10	2	.4497	= 0	9	0	.2889	= 0	5	9
27	27.0241	= 27	0	6	.4714	= 0	9	5	.2949	= 0	5	11
28	27.5555	= 27	11	1	.4942	= 0	9	11	.3011	= 0	6	0
29	28.1003	= 28	2	0	.5181	= 0	10	4	.3075	= 0	6	2
30	28.6589	= 28	13	2	.5433	= 0	10	10	.3142	= 0	6	3
31	29.2331	= 29	4	8	.5698	= 0	11	5	.3211	= 0	6	5
32	29.8174	= 29	16	4	.5977	= 0	11	11	.3282	= 0	6	7
33	30.4099	= 30	8	2	.6270	= 0	12	6	.3357	= 0	6	9
34	31.0177	= 31	0	4	.6578	= 0	13	2	.3433	= 0	6	10
35	31.6370	= 31	12	9	.6902	= 0	13	10	.3513	= 0	7	0
36	32.2675	= 32	5	4	.7244	= 0	14	6	.3596	= 0	7	2
37	32.9076	= 32	18	2	.7603	= 0	15	2	3682	= 0	7	4
38	33.5579	= 33	11	2	.7981	= 0	16	0	.3772	= 0	7	7
39	34.2155	= 34	4	4	.8381	= 0	16	9	.3862	= 0	7	8
40	34.8800	= 34	17	7	.8805	= 0	17	7	.3956	= 0	7	11
41	35.5496	= 35	11	0	.9254	= 0	18	6	.4052	= 0	8	1
42	36.2214	= 36	4	5	.9710	= 0	19	5	.4136	= 0	8	3
43	36.8949	= 36	17	11	1.0241	= 1	0	6	.4234	= 0	8	6
44	37.5600	= 37	11	2	1.0782	= 1	1	7	.4334	= 0	8	8
45	38.2113	= 38	4	3	1.1358	= 1	2	9	.4436	= 0	8	10
46	38.8384	= 38	16	9	1.1971	= 1	3	11	.4541	= 0	9	1
47	39.5395	= 39	10	9	1.2625	= 1	5	3	.4649	= 0	9	4
48	40.1195	= 40	2	5	1.3322	= 1	6	8	.4759	= 0	9	6
49	40.6709	= 40	13	5	1.4070	= 1	8	2	.4871	= 0	9	9
50	41.1931	= 41	3	10	1.4912	= 1	9	10	.4984	= 0	10	0
51	41.6860	= 41	13	9	1.5750	= 1	11	6	.5103	= 0	10	2
52	42.1337	= 42	2	8	1.6692	= 1	13	5	.5211	= 0	10	5
53	42.5354	= 42	10	8	1.7721	= 1	15	5	.5332	= 0	10	8
54	42.8414	= 42	16	10	1.8841	= 1	17	8	.5420	= 0	10	10
55	43.0183	= 43	0	4	2.0058	= 2	0	1	.5548	= 0	11	1
56	43.0256	= 43	0	6	2.1383	= 2	2	9	.5662	= 0	11	4
57	42.8209	= 42	16	5	2·2825	= 2	5	8	.5780	= 0	11	7
58	42.3646	= 42	7	4	2.4400	= 2	8	10	.5898	= 0	11	10
59	41.6175	= 41	12	4	2.6158	= 2	12	4	.5987	= 0	12	0
60	40.5303	= 40	10	7	2.8110	= 2	16	3	.6132	= 0	12	3
61	39.0449	= 39	0	11	3.0304	= 4	0	7	.6245	= 0	12	6
62	37.0959	= 37	1	11	3.2789	= 3	5	7	.6354	= 0	12	8
63	34.6853	= 34	13	8	3 5615	= 3	11	3	.6457	= 0	12	11
64	31.8607	= 31	17	3	3.8844	= 3	17	8	.6555	= 0	13	1
65	28.4402	= 28	8	11	4.2546	= 4	5	1	.6648	= 0	13	4
66	24.5820	= 24	11	8	4.6823	= 4	13	8	.6735	= 0	13	6
67	20.1769	= 20	3	6	5.1775	= 5	3	7	.6815	= 0	13	8
68	14.8843	= 14	17	8	5.7470	= 5	14	11	.6899	= 0	13	9
69	8.3027	= 8	6	1	6.3976	= 6	7	11	.6967	= 0	13	11

TABLE XCIV.

SHOWING THE ANNUAL CONTRIBUTION PAYABLE MONTHLY UP TO AGE 70 FOR £1 PER WEEK DURING SICKNESS UP TO THAT AGE, THE ANNUAL CONTRIBUTION PAYABLE MONTHLY UP TO AGE 70 FOR AN ANNUITY OF £1 PER ANNUM AFTER THAT AGE, AND THE ANNUAL CONTRIBUTION PAYABLE DURING LIFE FOR THE ASSURANCE OF £1 AT DEATH.—RURAL, TOWN, AND CITY DISTRICTS.—INTEREST FOUR PER CENT. PER ANNUM.

Age.	Annual Contribution for Sick Allowance.					Annual Contribution for Annuities.					Annual Contribution for £1 at Death.				
	£		£	s.	d.	£		£	s.	d.	£		£	s.	d.
18	1.1970	=	1	3	11	.0164	=	0	0	4	.0126	=	0	0	3
19	1.2298	=	1	4	7	.0173	=	0	0	4¼	.0130	=	0	0	3
20	1.2665	=	1	5	4	.0183	=	0	0	4½	.0135	=	0	0	3¼
21	1.3043	=	1	6	1	.0193	=	0	0	4¾	.0138	=	0	0	3¼
22	1.3425	=	1	6	10	.0204	=	0	0	5	.0143	=	0	0	3½
23	1.3807	=	1	7	7	.0216	=	0	0	5¼	.0147	=	0	0	3½
24	1.4203	=	1	8	5	.0228	=	0	0	5½	.0151	=	0	0	3½
25	1.4614	=	1	9	3	.0241	=	0	0	5¾	.0155	=	0	0	3¾
26	1.5077	=	1	10	2	.0255	=	0	0	6¼	.0160	=	0	0	3¾
27	1.5528	=	1	11	1	.0270	=	0	0	6½	.0164	=	0	0	4
28	1.5996	=	1	12	0	.0287	=	0	0	7	.0170	=	0	0	4
29	1.6504	=	1	13	0	.0304	=	0	0	7¼	.0175	=	0	0	4¼
30	1.7031	=	1	14	1	.0321	=	0	0	7¾	.0180	=	0	0	4¼
31	1.7585	=	1	15	2	.0342	=	0	0	8¼	.0186	=	0	0	4½
32	1.8170	=	1	16	4	.0364	=	0	0	8¾	.0193	=	0	0	4¾
33	1.8788	=	1	17	7	.0387	=	0	0	9¼	.0199	=	0	0	4¾
34	1.9439	=	1	18	11	.0412	=	0	0	10	.0206	=	0	0	5
35	2.0130	=	2	0	3	.0439	=	0	0	10½	.0215	=	0	0	5¼
36	2.0862	=	2	1	9	.0468	=	0	0	11¼	.0222	=	0	0	5¼
37	2.1641	=	2	3	3	.0500	=	0	1	0	.0230	=	0	0	5½
38	2.2467	=	2	4	11	.0534	=	0	1	0¾	.0239	=	0	0	5¾
39	2.3337	=	2	6	8	.0571	=	0	1	1¾	.0249	=	0	0	6
40	2.4237	=	2	8	6	.0612	=	0	1	2¾	.0259	=	0	0	6¼
41	2.5247	=	2	10	6	.0657	=	0	1	3¾	.0270	=	0	0	6½
42	2.6215	=	2	12	5	.0702	=	0	1	4¾	.0279	=	0	0	6¾
43	2.7312	=	2	14	7	.0758	=	0	1	6¼	.0291	=	0	0	7
44	2.8467	=	2	16	11	.0817	=	0	1	7½	.0303	=	0	0	7¼
45	2.9689	=	2	19	5	.0882	=	0	1	9¼	.0316	=	0	0	7½
46	3.0082	=	3	2	0	.0955	=	0	1	11	.0330	=	0	0	8
47	3.2362	=	3	4	9	.1035	=	0	2	0¾	.0345	=	0	0	8¼
48	3.3903	=	3	7	10	.1125	=	0	2	3	.0361	=	0	0	8¾
49	3.5461	=	3	10	11	.1226	=	0	2	5½	.0378	=	0	0	9
50	3.7137	=	3	14	3	.1344	=	0	2	8¼	.0396	=	0	0	9½
51	3.8905	=	3	17	10	.1470	=	0	2	11¼	.0415	=	0	0	10
52	4.0816	=	4	1	8	.1617	=	0	3	2¾	.0434	=	0	0	10½
53	4.2852	=	4	5	8	.1785	=	0	3	6¾	.0455	=	0	0	11
54	4.4932	=	4	9	10	.1976	=	0	3	11½	.0474	=	0	0	11½
55	4.7191	=	4	14	5	.2200	=	0	4	4¾	.0498	=	0	1	0
56	4.9558	=	4	19	1	.2463	=	0	4	11	.0523	=	0	1	0½
57	5.2024	=	5	4	1	.2773	=	0	5	6½	.0549	=	0	1	1¼
58	5.4567	=	5	9	2	.3143	=	0	6	3½	.0578	=	0	1	1¾
59	5.7150	=	5	14	4	.3592	=	0	7	2¼	.0604	=	0	1	2½
60	5.9733	=	5	19	6	.4142	=	0	8	3½	.0639	=	0	1	3¼

SECTION VII.

VALUATION OF ASSETS AND LIABILITIES.

Societies should, in the first onset, be based on sound principles, and at all times they should be able to ascertain their financial position, by a valuation of the assets and liabilities. They could, by a very simple process, so adjust their payments, as that no individual member would be a sufferer thereby, and they could, from period to period, so regulate their proceedings as always to maintain a solvent position. If these valuations were made at the end of every five years, it would enable societies to form an opinion, as to the sufficiency of the scale of payments adopted by them, and whether they were prepared to meet those liabilities that were from time to time ensuing; it would restore confidence in the management, and by the publication of such valuations would give the public confidence that the Society was properly managed.

The following table, No. XCV., only shows the mode of such calculation, and an equal contribution payable by each person is only supposed, for it must not be presumed that the writer would, for a moment, recommend an equal contribution to be paid by every member on entering into a society; from the tables previously given it must at once be very apparent that to charge the person at age 18 and the person at age 30 one rate of contribution, is so unjust in principle, that it ought at once to be rejected by every society; for those who have already made these engagements, to repudiate them would be more unjust, but not a moment ought to be delayed in making other provisions for the future.

Presuming that a society contained 86 members of the ages given in the table, on reference to Table LXXXIV., rural, town, and city districts, the value of an annuity payable annually is 22.0549, when the annuity is paid monthly it becomes of increased value, and $\frac{11}{24}$ = .4583, added thereto, gives the value of an annuity payable monthly. It is presumed, that the contributions will be paid in advance, and if they were paid one year in advance, an annuity payable yearly would have to be increased by unity; and as they are supposed to be paid one month in advance, $\frac{1}{12}$ of a year's purchase, .0833, must be added thereto; this gives the amount 22.5965, and the annual contribution multiplied by this sum, gives the present value

~of one member's contribution for life ; being further multiplied by the number of members of that age, 18, gives the total value of the contributions for all members of that age. The annuity at age 19 being then taken, .4583 and .0833 being added thereto, and multiplied by the number of members of this age, the value of those member's contributions for life would be obtained ; pursuing the same course for every age in the table, the sum total of these amounts would give the valuation of all the members' contributions, and the amount of cash on hand, arrears of contribution, and any other sums owing to the Society, added thereto, would give the total of the assets of the Society.

The amount of contributions, sick benefits, annuity, and sum at death, are stated at the head of the table ; it is not therefore thought advisable to repeat them ; but to proceed to ascertain the liabilities. Table LXXXV., rural, town, and city district, shows the value of a sick gift at age 18 of £1 per week, and to be paid during sickness up to age 70, £29.2000, a sick gift of 12 shillings per week will be a proportional part, and the present value is £17.52 = £17 : 10 : 4. Table LXXXVII., rural, town, and city district, age 18, shows the valuation of an annuity payable monthly of £1 per annum, after age 70, to be £.5439 ; and as the value of any other annuity payable after that time, and for that age, will be in proportion, the present value of an annuity of £6 : 10 : 0 per annum will be £3.2634 = £3 : 5 : 3. Table LXXXVIII., rural, town, and city districts, gives the present value, age 18, of £1 payable at death, to be £.3284 ; and, as in the other cases, any other sum at death will be of proportionate value ; £10 at death, for example, will be ten times the value £3.284 = £3 : 5 : 8.

The present value, therefore, for a sick gift of 12 shillings per week during sickness, up to 70 years, the present value of an annuity of £6 : 10 : 0 per annum, to commence, if the person should be living at that age, and the present value for an assurance at death, are respectively £17.5200 + £3.2634 + £3.2840 = £24.0674 = £24 : 1 : 5 ; and this amount shows the liability of the Society to the person at that age ; and if multiplied by the number of members of the age, it will give the liabilities of all those members for that respective age ; and if the same course be adopted, taking the values of sick gift, annuity, and assurance at death for each of the ages, and multiplying by the number of members of that age, the liabilities are obtained. The sum total of all these liabilities gives the total liabilities to the members, and if to this be added any amount owing by the Society it will give its total liabilities. Any deficiency in the assets to meet those liabilities shows the insolvency of the Society to that extent.

Many societies, and it is a very advisable course to adopt, keep a separate and distinct account for each benefit allowed to members ; when such is the case, the valuation of each fund can be ascertained in a similar manner, taking the valuation of the contribution to that fund only, the amount of cash arrears, or any amount owing in connection therewith as assets, and the liabilities of the member, together with any amount owing by that fund, only, as the liabilities of the Society, and any surplus or deficiency over or less than the liabilities, which shows the solvency or insolvency of that separate fund.

TABLE XCV.

FORM OF VALUATION OF A SOCIETY,

SUPPOSED TO CONSIST OF 86 MEMBERS AT THE AGES STATED, EACH MEMBER PAYING A CONTRIBUTION OF SIXPENCE PER WEEK, 12 PAYMENTS; SUCH PAYMENT TO BE MADE DURING LIFE, AND EACH MEMBER TO RECEIVE 12 SHILLINGS PER WEEK IN SICKNESS UP TO AGE 70; AFTER THAT AGE AN ANNUITY OF TWO SHILLINGS AND SIXPENCE PER WEEK, AND THE SUM OF £10 AT DEATH.

MORTALITY AND SICKNESS.—RURAL, TOWN, AND CITY DISTRICTS.

Age.	ASSETS.			LIABILITIES.					
	Value of Contributions at each age.	No. of Members	Value of Contributions for Total Members at each age.	Value of Sick Gift at each age.	Value of Annuity at each age.	Value of £10 at Death.	Total value for each Member at age.	No. of Members.	Total value for all Members at each age.
18	29 7 6	1	29 7 6	17 10 4	3 10 8	3 5 8	24 6 8	1	24 6 8
19	29 2 0	2	58 4 0	17 16 4	3 13 3	3 6 10	24 16 5	2	49 12 10
20	28 16 5	3	86 9 3	18 2 1	3 15 10	3 8 2	25 6 1	3	75 18 3
21	28 10 9	4	114 3 0	18 8 0	3 18 7	3 9 5	25 16 0	4	103 4 0
22	28 5 3	5	141 6 3	18 14 1	4 1 6	3 10 8	26 6 3	5	131 11 3
23	28 0 0	6	168 0 0	18 19 10	4 4 7	3 11 10	26 16 3	6	160 17 6
24	27 14 4	3	83 3 0	19 5 8	4 7 8	3 13 0	27 6 4	3	81 19 0
25	27 8 10	2	54 17 8	19 11 7	4 11 0	3 14 8	27 17 3	2	55 14 6
26	27 3 2	5	135 15 10	19 17 4	4 14 6	3 15 7	28 7 5	5	141 17 1
27	26 17 5	6	161 4 6	20 3 7	4 18 1	3 16 6	28 18 2	6	173 9 0
28	26 12 8	4	106 10 8	20 9 10	5 1 10	3 17 11	29 9 7	4	117 18 4
29	26 6 8	3	79 0 0	20 16 1	5 5 9	3 19 4	30 1 2	3	90 3 6
30	26 0 4	5	130 1 8	21 2 6	5 9 10	4 0 11	30 13 3	5	153 5 3
31	25 14 0	4	102 16 0	21 9 0	5 14 1	4 2 2	31 5 3	4	125 1 0
32	25 7 5	2	50 14 0	21 15 7	5 18 7	4 3 7	31 17 9	2	63 15 6
33	25 0 7	1	25 0 7	22 2 2	6 3 2	4 5 2	32 10 6	1	32 10 6
34	24 13 7	6	148 1 6	22 8 10	6 8 4	4 6 8	33 3 10	6	199 3 0
35	24 6 5	3	72 19 3	22 15 7	6 13 0	4 8 2	33 16 9	3	101 10 7
36	23 19 1	4	95 16 4	23 2 4	6 18 3	4 10 2	34 10 9	4	138 3 0
37	23 11 5	2	47 2 10	23 9 2	7 3 8	4 11 8	35 4 6	2	70 9 0
38	23 3 7	3	69 10 9	23 16 0	7 9 5	4 13 5	35 18 10	3	107 15 6
40	22 7 5	3	67 2 3	24 9 7	8 1 3	4 15 0	37 7 10	3	112 3 6
42	21 10 10	2	43 1 8	25 3 2	8 17 3	5 0 9	39 1 2	2	78 2 4
44	20 3 10	2	40 7 8	25 15 10	9 10 5	5 4 7	40 10 10	2	80 1 8
46	19 16 4	2	39 12 8	26 7 9	10 6 5	5 8 6	42 2 8	2	84 5 4
50	17 19 8	1	17 19 8	27 5 11	12 8 7	5 16 6	45 11 0	1	45 11 0
52	16 9 5	1	16 9 5	27 13 6	13 12 10	6 0 9	47 7 1	1	47 7 1
56	15 5 3	1	15 5 3	27 13 2	16 16 4	6 8 11	50 18 5	1	50 18 5

	86	£2200 3 2				Members...86	£2696 14 7
Arrears of Contributions...		8 10 0			Amount Owing by Society...		3 14 6
Balance.........		491 15 11					
		£2700 9 1					£2700 9 1